S0-DUD-722

American Notes & Queries

Supplement

Volume II

Dedicated To Our Mothers:

Dolly Griffin Hodgson
Charlotte Keehne Briscoe
Blanche Porter Rhodes

American Notes & Queries

Supplement

Volume II

First Person Female American:

A Selected and Annotated Bibliography of the Autobiographies

Of

American Women Living after 1950

Carolyn H. Rhodes
editor

Mary Louise Briscoe and Ernest L. Rhodes
associate editors

The Whitston Publishing Company
Troy, New York
1980

ACKNOWLEDGMENTS

We acknowledge indebtedness to the following persons, publishers, and libraries who have granted permission to use in this book copyrighted material:

America
from G. M. Costello's review (Sept. 5, 1930); Gordon C. Zahn's review (April 20, 1974) Copyright © 1930, 1974 by *America*, 106 W. 56th St., New York, N. Y. 10019.

The American Library Association
from review reprinted by permission of the American Library Association from *The Booklist* (Oct. 15, 1945) Copyright © 1945.

American Quarterly
from William C. Spengemann and L. R. Lundquist's "Autobiography and the American Myth" Copyright © 1965 Trustees of the University of Pennsylvania.

Arbor House
from *Herself*, by Hortense Calisher. © 1972 by Hortense Calisher. Used by permission of Arbor House Publishing Co., Inc.

The Atlantic Monthly
from reviews by Phoebe Adams (June 1971) (Nov. 1971) (Feb. 1976) by C. J. Rollo (June 1975) Copyright © 1971, 1975, 1976 by the Atlantic Monthly Company, Boston, Mass. Reprinted with permission.

Best Sellers
from review (Oct. 1, 1966); review by T. J. Bazzett (Nov. 1975) Copyright © 1966, 1975. Reprinted with permission *Best Sellers*, University of Scranton, Scranton, PA. 18510.

Bobbs-Merrill
from Beverly Sills's *Bubbles: A Self-Portrait.* Copyright © 1976.

Thomas Y. Crowell
 from *The Buried Life: A Nun's Journey* by Midge Turk, Copyright ©
1971, Thomas Y. Crowell.

Crown Publishers
 from *Yesterday is Tomorrow* by Malvina Hoffman. Copyright © 1965
by Malvina Hoffman. Used by permission of Crown Publishers, Inc.

Dallas *Times Herald*
 from article by Maurine Block in Dallas *Times* (March 12, 1939).
Copyright © 1939 by Dallas *Times Herald*. Used with permission of Dallas
Times Herald.

Dance Horizons
 from *An Unfinished Life: An Autobiography* by Ruth St. Dennis,
Copyright © 1964, Dance Horizons 1001 E. 26th St. Brooklyn, N. Y.
11229.

Delacorte Press
 from *The Collected Essays and Occasional Writings of Katherine Anne
Porter* by Katherine Anne Porter, Copyright © 1970 by Katherine Anne
Porter. Used by permission of Delacorte Press/Seymour Lawrence.

Dial Press
 from *Woman Surgeon: The Autobiography of Else K. La Roe, M.D.*
by Else Kienle La Rose, Copyright © 1957 by Else Kienle La Roe. Used by
permission of The Dial Press; from *Coming of Age in Mississippi* by Anne
Moody, Copyright © 1968 by Anne Moody. Used by permission of The
Dial Press; from *Confession from the Malaga Madhouse: A Christmas Diary*
by Charlotte Painter, Copyright © 1971 by Charlotte Painter. Used by permission of The Dial Press.

Doubleday
 from *His Eye is on the Sparrow* by Ethel Waters, Copyright © 1950,
1951 by Ethel Waters and Charles Samuels; from *A Portrait of Joan* by
Joan Crawford, Copyright © 1962 by Joan Crawford Steele; from *Miller's
High Life* by Ann Miller and Norma Lee Browning, Copyright © 1972 by
Ann Miller; from *Looking Back* by Joyce Maynard. Copyright © 1972,
1973 by Joyce Maynard; from *Detective Marie Cirile* by Marie Cirile, Copyright © 1975 by Marie Cirile. Used by permission of Doubleday & Company, Inc.

The Economist (London)
  from review (Nov. 2, 1970) Copyright © 1970 *The Economist,* London.

Farrar, Straus & Giroux
  from *A Circle of Quiet* by Madeleine L'Engle. Copyright © 1972 by Madeleine L'Engle Franklin; from *The Summer of the Great-Grandmother* by Madeleine L'Engle. Copyright © 1974 by Crosswicks, Ltd.; from *The Verdict* by Hildegard Knef. Translated from the German by David Anthony Palastagna. Translation Copyright © 1975 by Farrar, Straus & Giroux, Inc. Reprinted with the permission of Farrar, Straus & Giroux, Inc.

University of Florida Press
  from *Frontier Eden* by Gordon Bigelow, Gopyright © 1966, University of Florida Press.

Georgia Review
  from review by E. C. Bufkin (Summer 1971), Copyright © 1971, Georgia Review, University of Georgia, Athens, Georgia 30602.

Grosset & Dunlap
  from *A State of Heat* by Sheilah Graham, Copyright © 1972 Grosset & Dunlap, Inc.

Harcourt Brace Jovanovich
  from *A Touch of Innocence* by Katherine Dunham Copyright © 1959; from *The Notebooks of Martha Graham* by Martha Graham Copyright © 1973; from *The Diary of Anais Nin* by Anais Nin Copyright © 1966, 1967, 1969, 1971, 1975, 1976 Harcourt Brace Jovanovich, Inc.

Harper & Row
  from *Memories: An Autobiography* by Ethel Barrymore Copyright © 1955; from *These Strange Ashes* by Elisabeth Elliott Copyright © 1975; from *Gypsy: A Memoir* by Gypsy Rose Lee Copyright © 1957; from *Letters Home* by Sylvia Plath, Selected and Edited with Commentary by Aurelia Schober Plath, Copyright © 1975 by Aurelia Schober Plath; from *The Autobiography of Eleanor Roosevelt* Copyright © 1961; from *To Me It's Wonderful* by Ethel Waters Copyright © 1972; from *Invitation to Joy: A Personal Story* by Eleanor Searle Whitney Copyright © 1971; from *Fifth Chinese Daughter* and from *No Chinese Stranger* by Jade Snow Wong Copyright © 1950, 1975. Reprinted by permission of Harper & Row Publishers, Inc.

Harper's Magazine
   from Robert Kotlowitz's review (June 1969), from Ed Yoder's review
(March 1970), Copyright © 1969, 1970 by Harper's Magazine. All rights
reserved.

Hawthorne Books
   from *With a Feather on My Nose* by Billie Burke Copyright © 1949;
from *Movin' On Up* by Mahalia Jackson Copyright © 1966 Hawthorne
Books, Inc.

Horizon Press
   from *My Own Woman: The Diary of an Analysis* by Suzanne Mitchell,
Copyright © 1973, by permission of the publisher Horizon Press, New York.

Houghton Mifflin
   from *The Mortgaged Heart* by Carson McCullers, Edited by Margarita
G. Smith, Copyright © 1971, Houghton Mifflin Company.

Hudson Review
   from review by Hayden Carruth, Copyright © 1973, *Hudson Review;*
from review-essay "Free Women" by Patricia Meyer Spacks, Copyright ©
1971-72 by Patricia Meyer Spacks, first published in *The Hudson Review,*
Vol. XXIV, No. 4 (Winter) 1971-72.

Hutchinson
   from *Early Havoc* by June Havoc, Copyright © 1960, Hutchinson
Publishing Group Limited, London WI.

I.H.T. Corporation
   from reviews taken from the New York *Herald-Tribune.* Copyright
© 1938, 1940, 1948, 1950, 1953, 1954, 1957, 1959 by I.H.T. Corporation.
Reprinted by permission.

International Publishers
   from *Helen Keller, Her Socialist Years: Writings and Speeches,* Edited
by Philip S. Phroner, Copyright © 1967, International Publishers Co., New
York.

Elizabeth Janeway
   from "More Tragic than the Male" by Elizabeth Janeway, first published in *Harper's Magazine* (Nov. 1967) Copyright © 1967 by Harper's
Magazine.

1974); from review by Patricia Hempel (Aug. 1975); from review by Michele Slung (April 1976); Copyright © 1974, 1975, 1976 Ms. Magazine Corporation.

The Nation
   from review (Aug. 30, 1917); from review by H. E. Stears (Jan. 15, 1936); from review by Mina Curtiss (May 6, 1939); from review Harriet Zinnes (May 18, 1974); from review (Feb. 15, 1975); Copyright © 1917, 1936, 1939, 1974, 1975 The Nation, Inc.

The National Observer
   from review (Oct. 9, 1976), Copyright © 1976, *National Observer.*

The National Review
   from review by William F. Buckley (Jan. 29, 1977), Copyright © 1977, *National Review.*

New Directions
   from *The Poet in the World* by Denise Levertov, Copyright © 1973. Permission to quote granted by New Directions Publishing Corp.

New Hampshire State Library
   from Lotte Lehmann's *Midway in My Song* Copyright © 1938. Reprinted by Books for Libraries, Inc., 1970.

New Republic
   from review (March 8, 1969); from review by Josephine Jacobsen (1973); from review by James Walt (Oct. 20, 1973); from review by Claire Booth Luce (April 17, 1976); Copyright © 1969, 1973, 1976, *New Republic,* Washington, D.C.

New Statesman & Nation
   from review by Desmond Shawe-Taylor (June 25, 1938); from review by Annabel Farjeon (Oct. 29, 1959); from review by Arthur Marshall (Dec. 25, 1970); from review by Paul Johnson (Sept. 26, 1975); from review "Mirror, Mirror On the Wall" by A. S. Byatt (April 23, 1976); Copyright © 1938, 1959, 1970, 1975, 1976 New Statesman & Nation Publishing Co., London.

New York *Post*
   from review by T. L. Masson (Oct. 23, 1926), Copyright © 1926. Reprinted from the New York *Post.*

Publishers Weekly

from two brief excerpts from the *Publishers Weekly* Forecasts. Reprinted from the May 21, 1973 and August 30, 1976 issues of *Publishers Weekly,* published by R. R. Bowker Company, a Xerox company. Copyright © 1973, 1976 by Xerox Corporation.

G. P. Putnam's Sons

from *My Life* by Golda Meir, Copyright © 1975, G. P. Putnam's Sons.

Random House

from *Generations: A Memoir* by Lucille Clifton, Copyright © 1976, Random House, Inc.; from *With My Mind on Freedom* by Angela Davis, Copyright © 1975, Bantam Books; from *Among Friends* by M. F. K. Fisher, Copyright © 1971, Alfred A. Knopf, Inc.; from *Martha Graham* by Leroy Leatherman, Copyright © 1966, Alfred A. Knopf, Inc.; from *Haywire* by Brooke Hayward, Copyright © 1977, Alfred A. Knopf, Inc.; from *How it Was* by Mary Welsh Hemingway, Copyright © 1976, Alfred A. Knopf, Inc.; from *The Female Imagination* by Patricia Meyer Spacks, Copyright © 1975, Alfred A. Knopf, Inc.; from *The New Radicalism in American, 1889-1963: The Intellectual as a Social Type* by Christopher Lasch, Copyright © 1965, Random House, Inc.; from *Going Too Far* by Robin Morgan, Copyright © 1977, Random House, Inc.; from *Private Collections* by Jean Starr Untermeyer, Copyright © 1965, Alfred A. Knopf, Inc.

Saturday Evening Post

from review by David Brudnoy (May/June 1976), reprinted with permission from The Saturday Evening Post Company © 1976.

Saturday Review

from reviews by Helen Woodward (Dec. 19, 1926), Beulah Amidon (Dec. 28, 1935), Phyllis McGinley (Feb. 11, 1950), Josephine Lawrence (Sept. 16, 1950), Harrison Smith (March 24, 1951), Ernestine Evans (Feb. 13, 1954), Helen Bard Woodward (May 14, 1955), E. P. Monroe (Sept. 1, 1956), Quentin Reynolds (Nov. 29, 1958), dated (Nov. 28, 1959), Arthur Dareck (Nov. 25, 1967), Glendy Culligan (March 28, 1970), Thomas Gullason (Nov. 13, 1971), J. J. Cain (Nov. 15, 1975), Bruce Cook (April 16, 1976), Elaine Dundy (April 1977); Copyright © 1926, 1935, 1950, 1951, 1954, 1955, 1956, 1958, 1959, 1967, 1970, 1971, 1975, 1976, 1977 Saturday Review Magazine Corporation.

Charles Scribner's Sons

from *Cross Creek* by Marjorie Kinnan Rawlings, Copyright © 1942,

FOREWORD

First Person Female American is a cooperative project of scores of women and men, even more than will be mentioned here. The table listing "Entries and Contributors" includes the names of 114 women and men who have annotated 333 auto-biographical works by 224 American women. *FPFA* belongs to these contributors now. Any reader can tell from the entries the delight with which our editoral group received their work. We are affectionately indebted to each of them.

It is impossible here to enumerate all of the organizations and members of feminist networks who have provided spiritual support and practical help in this project. Salient among these networks, however, have been the members and supporters of the Faculty Women's Caucus at Old Dominion University. Although some of these women and men have not annotated any of the autobiographical works, their contribution to *FPFA* has been significant and is gratefully acknowledged.

We might not have had either our Caucus at ODU or this book if Sheila Tobias had not crystallized in us a sense of our worth as academic women and a determination to bring about proper recognition of that worth. Taking time from her summer holiday in 1973, she consulted with a delegation from ODU; she encouraged us to organize and to cooperate with each other in political and scholarly projects. Included in that delegation were Gail Adams, Tania Modleski, Zelda Silverman, and I, all of whom have been associated with *FPFA*. Then among the founding members of ODU's Faculty Women's Caucus (formally organized in 1974) were other contributors and facilitators such as Dorothy Johnson and Margy Moore and Velma Powell. This list would grow cumbersome if I tried to name every woman whose membership in the Caucus coincided with her aid to *FPFA*. I must, however, mention with special gratitude the devoted support of Eloise Word Skewis, whose feminist interests drew her into *FPFA* and led her to spend countless hours of proofing and library work.

Our involvement in the Faculty Women's Caucus and participation in feminist issues regionally, especially the Women's Caucus of the South Atlantic Modern Language Association, resulted in an invitation from *American Notes & Queries* to edit a special issue of that periodical on an aspect of women and literature. I chose the autobiographies of contemporary American women as our topic and began in 1975 to put together the special issue (September 1977) as well as a supplement to *AN&Q* which has become this work, *First Person Female American*. For those opportunities and for advice and aid, we thank John L. Cutler, Thomas B. Stroup, and Lawrence S. Thompson of *AN&Q*.

Early in 1976, we sent notices of our standards and purposes for *FPFA* to Women's Studies programs, Women's Caucuses, and Women's Professional groups, and they put us in touch with contributors from most of the academic disciplines. Our subsequent appeals for contributors included some made directly to a number of women and men attending the Conference on Women's History at the National Archives in Washington, D.C. (Spring 1976). And we found additional participants for *FPFA* among the women attending the Berkshire Conference at Bryn Mawr (June 1976). Thereafter our network of contributors spread rapidly from Alaska, through Washington, and California, to Florida and Maine and points between.

Dr. Mary Louise Briscoe's willingness to join our editorial group is truly an outstanding example of feminist cooperation. She had heard of *FPFA* from our routine mailing of notices about the project. At that time Coordinator of the Women's Studies Program at the University of Pittsburgh, Mary selected from her files for our use data on American women's autobiographies: data that she has been assembling since 1972 for her *American Autobiographies 1945-1980*. She convinced us that we were embarking on a project of far greater scope than we had realized, so that we narrowed our bases for selectivity; she also confirmed our optimistic notions that our impersonal calls for contributors would work as a means to find scores of people, most of them strangers, willing to volunteer time and skills.

And while on the subject of feminist cooperation, I want to thank Patricia K. Addis for exchanging information and suggestions with me about this work and her work tentatively called: *Her Story: An Annotated Bibliography of Autobiographical Writings by American Women.* These two women epitomize countless others who responded similarly: with no personal tie to the few of us who initiated *FPFA,* they joined in offering their research, their advice, and their skills, and we thank all of them.

A number of Old Dominion University's various research agencies as well as our English Department have arranged for funds and secretarial time to help produce *FPFA.* We thank John P. Broderick, Chair of the Department of English's Research Committee and the several members who twice provided grants for typing, travel, and library assistance. We are pleased also to note our appreciation to two of our colleagues who ultimately had to approve those grants and who encouraged our project in other ways: Dr. David S. Shores, Chairperson of the Departement of English, and Dean Heinz Meier of the School of Arts and Letters. The ODU Research Foundation provided absolutely vital assistance. We are pleased to express our gratitude to all of the members of their staff who worked with us and note especially the kindness of Jean B. Harrison, Maxine A. Lippman, Ernest Maygarden, Catharine Owen, and Robert Wolfe.

Our gratitude for help goes also to Dr. Cynthia Duncan of the Old Dominion University Library and to so many of her staff that we can only hope we have not omitted someone particularly vital as we try to list those who have spent long hours serving Women's Studies at ODU, while also fostering the work of *FPFA*'s local contributors. These generous staff members include: Audrey Amerski, Benjamin Clymer, Pat Curd, Elizabeth deBedts, Lucille Garner, Carl Hopkins, Ted Kruse, Robert Melanson, Jan Mitchell, Christine Poucher, Adrienne Schellings, and Cynthia Swaine.

When the editorial "we" has been used here it often involves four to whom I am wholeheartedly indebted. Associate Editor Mary Louise Briscoe, now Chairperson of the Department of English, University of Pittsburgh, has been noted above. My other Associate, Professor Ernest L. Rhodes, Department of

English at Old Dominion University is my dearest colleague as well as a kinsperson by marriage and temperament. The two other "we's" of us are our Assistant Editors, Dr. Margaret Moore Willen of Eastern New Mexico University, and Ms. T. Gail Adams, Emory University, ILA. More will be heard from these two fine young feminist scholars.

Carolyn H. Rhodes
Old Dominion University

PREFACE

The purpose of *First Person Female American* is primarily to provide a bibliographical tool that is needed immediately for women's studies. Courses and programs for such studies are vital to the research that is even now adding to bibliographies, reshaping theories, and redirecting scholarship about autobiography, about literature, and about the American culture.

Two standards for inclusion in *FPFA* are strict: an author of any work treated must be a woman, and she must have been alive after 1950. We decided to work with the autobiographies of women living after 1950 because *Notable American Women,* edited by Edward T. James, Janet Wilson James, and Paul S. Boyer (Harvard University Press, 1971), includes noteworthy women who died before 1951, and thus offers some guidance to the lives and writing of many who left autobiographical material. Although the purpose and scope of *FPFA* is such that we include many women who would not be considered for *NAW,* nevertheless we avoided much needless duplication of that monumental work by beginning with the autobiographies of women living after 1950. We anticipated other advantages by studying women living within the current quarter-century, such as the opportunity to consider the effect of the present feminist movement on the life stories of women.

Other standards have been applied with some flexibility. Autobiography is sweepingly defined: from lifetime life-narration to letters, diaries, journals, any writings telling a woman's own story in her own name or pseudonym, and in published form. *FPFA* does not include extant but unpublished autobiographical sources, oral or written. *American* can mean native born or naturalized to citizenship in the United States, and some American authors are treated whose books deal more with foreign experience than with life in the United States.

Another basic requirement for inclusion in *FPFA,* an important standard but one that has been very flexibly applied, is that the writing show some significance for women's studies. The reasons for significance are as intricate and multiple as the convictions, interests, and probably even the idiosyncracies of *FPFA*'s contributors and editors. For an annotation to be included the contributor had only to show that the book contained matter which a teacher of Women's Studies might want to be aware of; the teacher's use for the book could be positive or negative: for example, she might use it to present role-models or to show life-patterns to be avoided, to show strong women as they grow into their strengths or to show forces adversely shaping personality, to explore literary techniques within the life-narrative genres, or to find examples of countless topics of interest.

The format for *FPFA* has not been rigidly prescribed. We suggested a sequence for each entry: 1) a content summary, 2) an evaluation of the book's usefulness for women's studies, and 3) a survey of the book's critical reception, if noteworthy comments on it appeared at the time of publication or later. Yet we encouraged contributors to treat the three subdivisions in whatever order or combination they found effective. Contributors who were annotating multi-volume autobiographical works were especially likely to vary and combine the subdivisions. And some contributors, after reading a number of reviews, found none worth citing and consequently omitted that subdivision.

We have included "A List of Topics of Interest to Women's Studies." Each contributor, that is, has prepared such a list of topics for each of the entries annotated in *FPFA.* We have drawn these topics together, noting the numbers of the entries in which these topics are discussed by the authors of the life records we have included in this work.

FPFA began in part with the wish to discover whether reading about the lives of real women as told by themselves might not counterbalance some of the negative images of women which are so prominent in the fiction traditionally assigned for students to read. All too often the women characters in fiction are shallow, passive, confined by circumstance. Even the bold and perceptive women in fiction often break from the stereotypes only in self-defeating ways, such as moving beyond rage to madness, beyond frustration to suicide. Autobiographies, too, can record such downward paths to violence or to wisdom, even if self-destructive. But autobiographies far more often record triumphs, small winnings or great ones, triumphs over stereotypes as well as over circumstances.

Although our calls for contributors were oriented to teachers of women's studies and members of academic women's caucuses, we never set any ideological or gender-based limitations on the acceptability of contributors. Men have been welcome. Ideally, we would have been delighted to find them all feminists in the John Stuart Mill tradition, but no tests were discovered to apply to women or men for proving "true feminism," so we applied the same criteria for both sexes: these were simply the willingness to read thoughtfully and the effort to write clearly about books they chose from our list or suggested as appropriate additions to *FPFA*. We were pleased when contributors had special interests or expertise about their subjects, and we made special efforts to match the skills or backgrounds of a contributor with the women she annotated. But for most of the entries no such matching worked out. Indeed, we required no previous experience in scholarly publication, and are pleased that a number of our contributors will see here their first published writing. Yet we are equally pleased and proud to have entries from well-established scholars, some of them writing about women whose works they have studied in depth, or whom they have known professionally or personally.

FPFA draws together and provides a key to the contents of more than 330 autobiographies, diaries, journals, collections of letters and similar first person accounts of 224 women living after 1950. Included are the life records of women in dozens of professions and from every stratum in society, for example: Bella Abzug (politician), Polly Adler (prostitute), Mary Ellen Chase (Biblical commentator, teacher), Alice Hamilton (physician, industrial health specialist, peace worker, Harvard professor), Shirley MacLaine (actress and activist), Martha Martin (diarist and pioneer in Alaska), Joyce Maynard (eighteen-year-old radio and television commentator), Pauli Murray (lawyer, civil rights activist, educator, Episcopal priest), May Sarton (poet, novelist), Phillippa Duke Schuyler (concert pianist, composer, linguist, writer, newspaper correspondent), Blanche Yurka (theatrical director), Mildred "Babe" Didrikson Zaharias (track star, professional golfer). The space devoted to each author included in *FPFA* has been determined in part by the annotator's and the editors' assessment of the importance of the woman's autobiographical writing to women's studies, and in part by the availability of other reference resources. For women prominent enough that their lives or their autobiographies have already been subject to study, we asked contributors to cite some selected works which would be useful for further study of the autobiographical writing, but not to attempt coverage of other works by their autobiographer.

In the writings annotated for *FPFA,* our contributors have noted comments on topics of interest for women's studies which range from abortion, adolescence, and alienation, through loneliness, marriage, male chauvinism, menstruation, and motherhood, to Zen and Zorastrianism. The books annotated include such salty aphorisms as those of Flo Kennedy ("Marriage is a crock. Why should you lock yourself in the bathroom just because you have to go three times a day?"), and such inspirational insights as those of Helen Keller ("Rights are things we get when we are strong enough to make good our claim to them. . . . Today women are demanding rights that tomorrow nobody will be foolhardy enough to question").

First Person Female American has manifold uses. Researchers in the sciences and particularly in the social sciences will find in *FPFA*'s index a wealth of topics which lead into psychological, sociological, and anthropological issues with the special sort of evidence that only personal records can provide. Certainly, the information and the feminist perspectives in many entries of *FPFA* suggest questions which need further scholarly attention, as well as new sources of evidence for questions now debated. Obviously, *FPFA* has also manifold uses not only for the teachers and students in Women's Studies and American Studies courses, but for any humanist disciplines when they treat the lives, thoughts, activities and achievements of Americans. Women's autobiography is especially needed in American literature courses, where the peculiarly masculine reflections of reality have

been exposed by Leslie Fieldler, Mary Ellmann, Carolyn Heil-
brun and others. As Lee R. Edwards and Arlyn Diamond point
out in *American Voices, American Women* (New York: Avon,
1973, p. 12) "much of what we traditionally see as American
literature is profoundly and self-consciously masculine, anti-
social, undomestic, concerned with neither social manners nor
social morality." The life records treated in *FPFA* are human,
social, sometimes domestic, and concerned regularly with manners and social morality. *FPFA* could therefore contribute to
correcting the widely-noted invisibility of women in the curricula
of traditional departments. (For an in-depth study see Lois
Banner's "Women in the College Curriculum," Princeton, N. J.:
The Princeton Report on Women in the College Curriculum,
1977).

The recognition of *FPFA*'s potential as a corrective for the
invisibility of women is the source of much of the enthusiasm
of many of our contributors and editors. But of even more
significance is *FPFA*'s potential as a corrective tool for the dis-
torted image of the few women who are sometimes visible in
the curricula of traditional academic disciplines. Teachers are,
we believe, almost always men and women of good will who
would like to see the status of women improve in our profession
and our world. Even so, all too many of our colleagues, women
as well as men, do not yet realize that the courses which they
design and teach are perpetuating warped, patriarchal, self-
serving values. The stories of women annotated in *FPFA* point
to the problem and inspire all of us who have participated in
shaping this bibliographical tool to believe that our work is a
part of the solution.

Carolyn H. Rhodes
Old Dominion University

CONTENTS

Abzug, Bella

1   *Bella! Ms. Abzug Goes to Washington.*
       Patti Renner-Tana

Adler, Polly

2   *A House Is Not a Home.*
       S. Ellen Emser

Allen, Florence Ellinwood

3   *To Do Justly.*
       Deborah Johnson

Alsop, Susan Mary

4   *To Marietta from Paris: 1945-1960.*
       Cynthia L. Walker

Alta

5   *Momma: a start on all the untold stories.*
       Diane Marting

Ames, Evelyn Perkins

6   *Daughter of the House.*
       Beverly Seaton

Anderson, Margaret C.

7   *The Autobiography: My Thirty Years' War: Beginnings and Battles to 1930.*

8   *The Autobiography: The Fiery Fountains: Continuation and Crisis to 1950.*

9   *The Autobiography: The Strange Necessity: Resolutions and Reminiscence to 1969.*
       Patricia L. Miller

Anderson, Marian
10 *My Lord, What A Morning.*
Marie R. Oesting

Anderson, Mary
11 *Woman at Work: The Autobiography of Mary Anderson as Told to Mary N. Winslow.*
Judith B. Herman

Angelou, Maya
12 *I Know Why the Caged Bird Sings.*
13 *Gather Together in My Name.*
14 *Singin' and Swingin' and Getting Merry Like Christmas.*
Liliane K. Arensberg

Anthony, Susan B.
15 *The Ghost in My Life.*
Zelda B. Silverman and Helen B. Phillips

Astor, Mary
16 *My Story: An Autobiography.*
17 *A Life on Film.*
Clara Delores King

Baez, Joan
18 *Daybreak.*
19 *Coming Out.*
Cynthia Swaine

Bailey, Pearl
20 *The Raw Pearl.*
Carolyn H. Rhodes

Baldridge, Letitia Katherine
21 *Roman Candle.*
22 *Of Diamonds and Diplomats.*
Connie C. Eble

Balsan, Consuelo Vanderbilt
23 *The Glitter and the Gold.*
Patricia Stringer

Bankhead, Tallulah

24   *Tallulah: My Autobiography.*
     Virginia Cox

Barrymore, Ethel

25   *Memories: An Autobiography.*
     Virginia Cox

Bates, Daisy Gatson

26   *The Long Shadow of Little Rock: A Memoir*
     Joyce Shaw Peterson

Baxter, Anne

27   *Intermission.*
     Diana Reep

Beach, Sylvia

28   *Shakespeare and Company.*
     Eleanor B. Mattes

Berg, Gertrude

29   *Molly and Me*
     Naomi Leventhal

Bernstein, Aline

30   *The Journey Down.*
31   *An Actor's Daughter.*
     Deborah M. DiCroce

Bogan, Louise

32   *What the Woman Lived: Selected Letters of Louise Bogan, 1920-
     1970.*
     Carol Shloss

Boulding, Elise

33   *Born Remembering.*
     Margaret McFadden-Gerber

Boulton, Laura (Craytor)

34   *The Music Hunter: The Autobiography of a Career.*
     Margaret McFadden-Gerber

xxviii *First Person Female American*

Bourke-White, Margaret
35 *Portrait of Myself.*
Margaret Moore Willen

Bowen, Catherine Drinker
36 *Family Portrait.*
Charlotte S. McClure

Boyle, Kay
37 *Being Genuises Together 1920-1930.*
38 *The Long Walk at San Francisco State.*
Peg Cruikshank

Braudy, Susan
39 *Between Marriage and Divorce.*
Sharon Davie

Brooks, Gwendolyn
40 *Report From Part One.*
Kathleen Callaway

Buck, Pearl S.
41 *My Several Worlds: A Personal Record.*
Sharon Davie

Burke, Billie
42 *With a Feather on My Nose.*
43 *With Powder on My Nose.*
Virginia Cox

Caine, Lynn
44 *Widow: The Personal Crisis of a Widow in America.*
Joanne McCarthy

Calisher, Hortense
45 *Herself.*
Sue F. Law

Carrighar, Sally
46 *Home to the Wilderness.*
Beverly Seaton

Contents xxix

Carroll, Gladys Hasty

47   *To Remember Forever.*
48   *Years Away From Home.*
        Kathy Lynn Emerson

Carson, Rachel

49   Brooks, Paul. *The House of Life: Rachel Carson at Work; with Selections from her Writings, Published and Unpublished.*
        Charlotte S. McClure

Chapelle, Dickey

50   *What's a Woman Doing Here?*
        Marie R. Oesting

Chase, Mary Ellen

51   *A Goodly Heritage.*
52   *A Goodly Fellowship.*
53   *The White Gate.*
        Eleanor B. Mattes

Chicago, Judy

54   *Through the Flower: My Struggle as a Woman Artist.*
        Margaret Moore Willen

Chisholm, Shirley

55   *Unbought and Unbossed.*
56   *The Good Fight.*
        Janelle L. McCammon

Cirile, Marie

57   *Detective Marie Cirile: Memoirs of a Police Officer.*
        Jean B. Palmer

Clark, Eugenie

58   *Lady with a Spear.*
59   *Lady and the Sharks.*
        Charlotte S. McClure

Clifton, Lucille

60   *Generations: A Memoir.*
        Sharon Davie

Cochran, Jacqueline

61   *The Stars at Noon.*
         Nancy Manahan

Cooper, Anna Julia

62   *A Voice From the South: By a Black Woman of the South.*
         Sharon Harley

Cornell, Katharine

63   *I Wanted to be an Actress.*
         Sharon Friedman

Crawford, Joan

64   *A Portrait of Joan: The Autobiography of Joan Crawford.*
         Virginia Cox

Davenport, Marica

65   *Too Strong for Fantasy.*
         Carolyn H. Rhodes

Davis, Angela

66   *With My Mind on Freedom: An Autobiography.*
         Mary Louise Briscoe

Day, Doris

67   *Doris Day: Her Own Story.*
         Virginia Cox

Day, Dorothy

68   *The Long Loneliness.*
         Dana Greene

De Angeli, Marguerite

69   *Butter at the Old Price.*
         Beverly Seaton

De Mille, Agnes

70   *Dance to the Piper.*
71   *And Promenade Home.*
72   *Russian Journals.*
73   *Speak to Me, Dance with Me.*
         T. Gail Adams

Densen-Gerber, Judianne

74 *Walk In My Shoes.*
 E. E. Davis, Jr.

De Rachewiltz, Mary

75 *Discretions.*
 Conrad Festa

de Trevino, Elizabeth Borton

76 *My Heart Lies South: The Story of My Mexican Marriage with Epilogue.*
 Diane Brodatz Rothenberg

Dillard, Annie

77 *Pilgrim at Tinker Creek.*
 Margaret McFadden-Gerber

Dixon, Jeane

78 *My Life and Prophecies.*
 Judith A. Johnson

Dorfman, Elsa

79 *Elsa's Housebook: A Woman's Photojournal.*
 Jill Janows

Draper, Ruth

80 *The Art of Ruth Draper.*
 Naomi Leventhal

Drooz, Irina Gross

81 *Doctor of Medicine.*
 Charlotte S. McClure

Dunham, Katherine

82 *A Touch of Innocence.*
 T. Gail Adams

Dykeman, Wilma

83 *Look to this Day.*
 Margaret McFadden-Gerber

Elliot, Elisabeth
84 *Through the Gates of Splendor.*
85 *The Savage My Kinsman.*
86 *Shadow of the Almighty.*
87 *These Strange Ashes.*
88 *Twelve Baskets of Crumbs.*
89 *Let Me Be a Woman: Notes on Womanhood for Valerie.*
   Versa Laska

Enters, Angna
90 *First Person Plural.*
91 *Silly Girl: A Portrait of Personal Remembrance.*
92 *Artist's Life.*
   T. Gail Adams

Evers, Mrs. Medgar
93 *For Us, The Living.*
   Diane Jefferson

Farmer, Frances
94 *Will There Really Be a Morning?*
   Suzette Henke

Ferber, Edna
95 *A Peculiar Treasure.*
96 *A Kind of Magic.*
   Elaine Reuben

Fisher, M. F. K.
97 *Among Friends.*
   Marie R. Cesting

Flynn, Elizabeth Gurley
98 *The Rebel Girl: An Autobiography, My First Life (1906-1926).*
99 *The Alderson Story: My Life as a Political Prisoner.*
   Elsa Dixler

Fremantle, Anne
100 *Three-Cornered Heart.*
   Leslie E. Gerber

Friedan, Betty

101 *It Changed My Life.*
Maryann Intermont Ustick

Frooks, Dorothy

102 *Lady Lawyer.*
Janis Forman

Garrett, Eileen Jeanette

103 *Adventures in the Supernormal: A Personal Memoir.*
Betsy Etheridge Brown

Geva, Tamara

104 *Split Seconds: A Remembrance.*
T. Gail Adams

Gibson, Althea

105 *I Always Wanted to Be Somebody.*
Jean R. Halladay

Gildersleeve, Virginia Cocheran

106 *Many a Good Crusade.*
Barbara Greene

Giles, Nell

107 *Punch In, Susie!*
Judith B. Herman

Giovanni, Nikki

108 *Gemini: An Extended Autobiographical Statement on My First Twenty-Five Years.*
Sandra Y. Govan

Gordon, Ruth

109 *Myself among Others.*
110 *My Side.*
Elsie F. Mayer

Graham, Martha

111 *The Notebooks of Martha Graham.*
Kathleen Woodward

Graham, Sheilah
112 *Beloved Infidel: The Education of a Woman.*
113 *The Rest of the Story.*
114 *College of One.*
115 *A State of Heat.*
116 *The Real F. Scott Fitzgerald: Thirty-Five Years Later.*
        Nancy Manahan

Guffy, Ossie White
117 *Ossie: The Autobiography of a Black Woman.*
        Kathleen Callaway

Hahn, Emily
118 *Times and Places.*
        Diane Marting

Hale, Nancy
119 *A New England Girlhood.*
120 *The Life in the Studio.*
        Margaret Moore Willen

Hamilton, Alice
121 *Exploring the Dangerous Trades: The Autobiography of Alice Hamilton, M.D.*
        Charlotte S. McClure

Hansberry, Lorraine
122 *To Be Young, Gifted and Black.*
        Frances A. Grimes

Havoc, June
123 *Early Havoc.*
        T. Gail Adams

Hayward, Brooke
124 *Haywire.*
        Cynthia Wise Henley

Hellman, Lillian
125 *An Unfinished Woman: A Memoir.*
126 *Pentimento: A Book of Portraits.*
127 *Scoundrel Time.*
        Timothy Dow Adams

Hemingway, Mary Welsh

128   *How It Was.*
      Linda S. Coleman

Heyward, Carter

129   *A Priest Forever.*
      Phyllis Roe

Hoffman, Malvina

130   *Heads and Tales.*
131   *Yesterday is Tomorrow.*
      Ken Daley

Holiday, Billie

132   *Lady Sings the Blues.*
      Sandra Y. Govan

Hoover, Helen

133   *A Place in the Woods.*
134   *The Years of the Forest.*
      Beverly Seaton

Horne, Lena

135   *Lena.*
      Frances A. Grimes

Howar, Barbara

136   *Laughing All the Way.*
137   *Making Ends Meet.*
      Peg Cruikshank

Hulme, Kathryn C.

138   *Undiscovered Country: A Spiritual Adventure.*
      Charlotte S. McClure

Humphrey, Doris

139   *An Artist First: An Autobiography.*
      T. Gail Adams

Hurst, Fannie

140   *Anatomy of Me: A Wonderer in Search of Herself.*
      Linda A. Wyche

Hurston, Zora Neale

141   *Dust Tracks on a Road.*
      Margaret N. Simmons

Isabell, Sharon

142   *Yesterday's Lessons.*
      Nancy Manahan

Jackson, Harrisene

143   *There's Nothing I Own That I Want.*
      C. Lynne Harrison

Jackson, Mahalia

144   *Movin' On Up.*
      Eloise Skewis

Jackson, Shirley

145   *Life Among the Savages.*
146   *Raising Demons.*
      Laura Moss Gottlieb

Johnson, Claudia Alta Taylor (Lady Bird)

147   *A White House Diary.*
      Joan Frederick

Johnson, Josephine W.

148   *Seven Houses: A Memoir of Time and Places.*
      Harold S. Whisman, Jr.

Keller, Helen

149   *The Story of My Life.*
150   *Midstream: My Later Life.*
151   *Journal, 1936-1937.*
152   *Helen Keller, her Socialist Years: Writings and Speeches.*
      Sara C. Withers

Kenmore, Carolyn

153   *Mannequin: My Life as a Model.*
      Karen J. Blair

Kennedy, Florynce

154   *Color Me Flo: My Hard Life and Good Times.*
      Joanne McCarthy

Kennedy, Rose Fitzgerald

155   *Times to Remember.*
      Cynthia L. Walker

Keyes, Frances Parkinson Wheeler

156   *Roses in December.*
157   *All Flags Flying: Reminiscences of Frances Parkinson Keyes.*
158   *Along a Little Way.*
      Connie C. Eble

Kimbrough, Emily

159   *How Dear to my Heart.*
160   *The Innocents from Indiana.*
161   *Through Charley's Door.*
162   *Now and Then.*
      Virginia Cox

King, Billie Jean

163   *Billie Jean.*
      Margaret McFadden-Gerber

King, Coretta Scott

164   *My Life with Martin Luther King, Jr.*
      Jonna Gormely Semeiks

Kingston, Maxine Hong

165   *The Woman Warrior: Memoirs of a Girlhood among Ghosts.*
      Joan Manheimer

Knef, Hildegard

166   *The Gift Horse.*
167   *The Verdict.*
      Jean R. Halladay

Laird, Carobeth

168   *Encounter with an Angry God: Recollections of My Life with John Peabody Harrington.*
      Diane Brodatz Rothenberg

La Roe, Else Kienle

169   *Woman Surgeon: The Autobiography of Else K. La Roe, M.D.*
      Kittye Delle Robbins

Lee, Gypsy Rose

170   *Gypsy: A Memoir.*
      T. Gail Adams

Le Gallienne, Eva

171   *At 33.*
172   *With a Quiet Heart.*
      Virginia Cox

Lehmann, Lotte

173   *Midway in My Song.*
174   *My Many Lives.*
      Freda F. Stohrer

L'Engle, Madeleine

175   *A Circle of Quiet.*
176   *The Summer of the Great-Grandmother.*
      Beverly Oberfeld Friend

LeSueur, Meridel

177   *Salute to Spring.*
178   *Corn Village.*
      Nancy L. Paxton

Levertov, Denise

179   *The Poet in the World.*
      James Van Dyck Card

Lewis, Faye Cashatt

180   *Nothing to Make a Shadow.*
      Elizabeth Cummins Cogell

Lindbergh, Anne Morrow

181   *Gift from the Sea.*
182   *Bring Me a Unicorn.*
183   *Hour of Gold, Hour of Lead.*
184   *Locked Rooms and Open Doors.*
185   *The Flower and the Nettle.*
      Elsie F. Mayer

Lone Dog, Louise

186   *Strange Journey: The Vision Life of a Psychic Indian Woman.*
      Cynthia L. Walker

Loos, Anita

187   *A Girl Like I.*
188   *Kiss Hollywood Good-by.*
189   *Twice Over Lightly: New York Then and Now.*
      Virginia Cox

Loud, Pat

190   *A Woman's Story.*
      Judith B. Herman

Luhan, Mabel Dodge

191   *Lorenzo in Taos.*
192   *Background* (Vol. 1 of *Intimate Memories*).
193   *European Experiences* (Vol. 2 of *Intimate Memories*).
194   *Winter in Taos.*
195   *Movers and Shakers* (Vol. 3 of *Intimate Memories*).
196   *Edge of Taos Desert: An Escape to Reality* (Vol. 4 of *Intimate Memories*).
      Selma Burkom and Margaret Williams

Lyons, Ruth

197   *Remember With Me.*
      Betsy Etheridge Brown

McCall, Dorothy Lawson

198   *Ranch under the Rimrock.*
199   *The Copper King's Daughter: From Cape Cod to Crooked River.*
      Joanne McCarthy

McCarthy, Abigail

200   *Private Faces/Public Places.*
      Dana Greene

McCarthy, Mary

201   *Memories of a Catholic Girlhood.*
      Kathleen Callaway

McCullers, Carson Smith

202 *The Mortgaged Heart.*
     Anne Rowe

MacDonald, Betty

203 *The Egg and I.*
204 *The Plague and I.*
205 *Anybody Can Do Anything.*
206 *Onions in the Stew.*
207 *Who, Me? The Autobiography of Betty MacDonald.*
     Joanne McCarthy

McGinley, Phyllis

208 *Sixpence in Her Shoe.*
     Jennie Farley

McGovern, Eleanor

209 *Uphill: A Personal Story.*
     Dana Greene

McKenney, Ruth

210 *My Sister Eileen.*
211 *The McKenneys Carry On.*
212 *Loud Red Patrick.*
213 *Love Story.*
214 *All About Eileen*
215 *Far, Far From Home.*
     Justin Paniere

MacLaine, Shirley

216 *Don't Fall Off the Mountain.*
217 *You Can Get There From Here.*
     Mary Louise Briscoe

Maiullo, Minerva

218 *A Tapestry of Memories.*
     Karen J. Blair

Mannes, Marya

219 *Out of My Time.*
     Caroline H. Tunstall

Martin, Martha [pseud. for Helen Bolyan]

220 *O Rugged Land of Gold.*
221 *Home on the Bear's Domain.*
 Beverley B. Bryant

Maynard, Joyce

222 *Looking Back: A Chronicle of Growing Up Old in the Sixties.*
 Margaret McFadden-Gerber

Mead, Margaret

223 *Blackberry Winter: My Earlier Years.*
 Laurie Newman Di Padova

Mehdevi, Anne Sinclair

224 *Persian Adventure.*
225 *From Pillar to Post.*
226 *Persia Revisited.*
 Cynthia L. Walker

Meir, Golda

227 *My Life.*
 Patti Renner-Tana

Miller, Ann

228 *Miller's High Life.*
 Virginia Cox

Millett, Kate

229 *Flying.*
 Sandra Hunt
230 *Sita.*
 Nancy Manahan

Mitchell, Suzanne

231 *My Own Woman: The Diary of an Analysis.*
 Betsy Baugess

Montgomery, Ruth

232 *Hail to the Chiefs: My Life and Times with Six Presidents.*
233 *A Search for the Truth.*
234 *Here and Hereafter.*
235 *A World Beyond.*
236 *Companions Along the Way.*
237 *The World Before.*
 Cynthia L. Walker

Moody, Anne

238　*Coming of Age in Mississippi.*
　　　Judith B. Herman

Morgan, Lucy C.

239　*Gift From the Hills: Miss Lucy Morgan's Story of her Unique Penland School.*
　　　Betsy Etheridge Brown

Morgan, Robin

240　*Going Too Far: The Personal Chronicle of a Feminist.*
　　　Margaret Moore Willen

Moses, Anna Mary Robertson

241　*Grandma Moses: My Life's History.*
　　　Linda Hedrick

Mountain Wolf Woman

242　*Mountain Wolf Woman.*
　　　Helen C. Rountree

Murray, Pauli

243　*Proud Shoes: The Story of An American Family.*
　　　Sandra Y. Govan

Nevelson, Louise

244　*Dawns + Dusks.*
　　　Margaret Moore Willen

Nin, Anais

245　*The Diary of Anais Nin* (Vol. 1, 1931-1934).
246　*The Diary of Anais Nin* (Vol. 2, 1934-1939).
247　*The Diary of Anais Nin* (Vol. 3, 1939-1944).
248　*The Diary of Anais Nin* (Vol. 4, 1944-1947).
249　*The Diary of Anais Nin* (Vol. 5, 1947-1955).
250　*The Diary of Anais Nin* (Vol. 6, 1955-1966).
　　　Ruth L. Mack and Liliane K. Arensberg

O'Keeffe, Georgia

251　*Georgia O'Keeffe.*
　　　Margaret Moore Willen

Origo, Iris
252 *Images and Shadows: Part of a Life.*
Bella Mirabella

Ovington, Mary White
253 *The Walls Came Tumbling Down.*
Harold S. Wilson

Painter, Charlotte
254 *Confession from the Malaga Madhouse: A Christmas Diary.*
Mary Louise Briscoe

Park, Maud Wood
255 *Front Door Lobby.*
Dorothy E. Johnson

Peterson, Virgilia
256 *A Matter of Life and Death.*
Judith B. Herman

Picon, Molly
257 *So Laugh a Little.*
Kittye Delle Robbins

Plath, Sylvia
258 *Letters Home: Correspondence 1950-1963.*
259 *The Bell Jar.*
T. Gail Adams

Polykoff, Shirley
260 *Does She. . .Or Doesn't She? And How She Did It.*
Frances Hassencahl

Porter, Katherine Anne
261 *The Collected Essays and Occasional Writings of Katherine Anne Porter.*
Anne Rowe

Powdermaker, Hortense
262 *Stranger and Friend: The Way of an Anthropologist.*
Diane Brodatz Rothenberg

Previn, Dory
263 *Midnight Baby: An Autobiography.*
Clara Delores King

Priest, Ivy Baker
264 *Green Grows Ivy.*
Robert Melanson

Proxmire, Ellen
265 *One Foot in Washington: The Perilous Life of a Senator's Wife.*
Karen J. Blair

Randall, Margaret
266 *Part of the Solution: Portrait of a Revolutionary.*
Jonna Gormely Semeiks

Rawlings, Marjorie Kinnan
267 *Cross Creek.*
Edna Saffy

Rich, Adrienne
268 *Of Woman Born: Motherhood as Experience and Institution.*
Janis Forman

Rinehart, Mary Roberts
269 *My Story: A New Edition and Seventeen New Years.*
Jean R. Halladay

Rivers, Caryl
270 *Aphrodite at Mid-century: Growing up Catholic and Female in Post-War America.*
Jean B. Palmer

Robert, Jane
271 *The Coming of Seth.*
272 *The Seth Material.*
273 *Seth Speaks: The Eternal Validity of the Soul.*
274 *The Nature of Personal Reality.*
Cynthia L. Walker

Roosevelt, Eleanor

275 *This Is My Story.*
276 *My Days.*
277 *This I Remember.*
278 *On My Own.*
279 *The Autobiography of Eleanor Roosevelt.*
    Sandra Hunt

Rosenberg, Ethel and Julius

280 *Death House Letters.*
    Ted Kruse

Rosenthal, Jean

281 *The Magic of Light.*
    Jean Klein

St. Denis, Ruth

282 *An Unfinished Life: An Autobiography.*
    T. Gail Adams

St. Johns, Adele Rogers

283 *Final Verdict.*
284 *The Honeycomb.*
    Tom Hamilton

Sanger, Margaret

285 *My Fight for Birth Control.*
286 *Margaret Sanger: An Autobiography*
    Patricia L. Miller

Sarton, May

287 *I Knew a Phoenix: Sketches for an Autobiography.*
288 *Plant Dreaming Deep.*
289 *Journal of a Solitude.*
    Carol Shloss

Schneiderman, Rose

290 *All for One.*
    Dorothy E. Johnson

Schuyler, Philippa Duke
291 *Adventures in Black and White.*
292 *Who Killed the Congo?*
293 *Jungle Saints: Africa's Heroic Catholic Missionaries.*
294 *Good Men Die.*
    Sharon Harley

Scott-Maxwell, Florida
295 *The Measure of My Days.*
    Pauline Rose Clance

Sekaquaptewa, Helen
296 *Me and Mine: The Life Story of Helen Sekaquaptewa.*
    Joan M. Jensen

Shaw, Anna Moore
297 *A Pima Past.*
    Joan M. Jensen

Sills, Beverly
298 *Bubbles: A Self Portrait.*
    Joan Frederick

Skinner, Cornelia Otis
299 *Family Circle*
    Virginia Cox

Smith, Lillian
300 *Killers of the Dream.*
    Bella Mirabella

Smith, Margaret Chase
301 *Declaration of Conscience.*
    Audrey A. Amerski

Stalvey, Lois Mark
302 *The Education of a Wasp.*
    Judith A. Johnson

Stern, Elizabeth
303 *My Mother and I.*
304 *I am a Woman—and a Jew* [Leah Morton, pseud.].
305 *When Love Comes to Woman* [Leah Morton, pseud.].
    Jean Tobin

Stern, Susan Harris

306 *With the Weathermen: The Personal Journal of a Revolutionary Woman.*
Frances Hassencahl

Suckow, Ruth

307 *Some Others and Myself.*
Patrice K. Gray

Tarry, Ellen

308 *The Third Door.*
Elizabeth Nunez-Harrell

Terasaki, Gwen

309 *Bridge to the Sun.*
Marie R. Oesting

Terrell, Mary Church

310 *A Colored Woman in a White World.*
Margaret N. Simmons

Thompson, Bertha [Box Car Bertha]

311 *Sister of the Road: The Autobiography of Box Car Bertha.*
Robert Melanson

Toklas, Alice B.

312 *Staying on Alone: Letters of Alice B. Toklas.*
Sharon Davie

Truman, Margaret

313 *Souvenir: Margaret Truman's Own Story.*
Elizabeth Cummins Cogell

Turk, Midge

314 *The Buried Life: A Nun's Journey.*
Judith B. Herman

Untermeyer, Jean Starr

315 *Private Collection.*
Agate Nesaule Krouse

Vorse, Mary Heaton

316 *A Footnote to Folly: Reminiscences.*
     T. Gail Adams

Walker, Margaret

317 *How I Wrote Jubilee.*
     Betsy Etheridge Brown

Waters, Ethel

318 *His Eye is on the Sparrow.*
319 *To Me It's Wonderful.*
     Margaret N. Simmons

Webster, Margaret

320 *Don't Put Your Daughter on the Stage.*
     Clara Delores King

West, Jessamyn

321 *To See the Dream.*
322 *Hide and Seek: A Continuing Journey.*
323 *The Woman Said Yes: Encounters with Life and Death.*
     Patrice K. Gray

West, Mae

324 *Goodness Had Nothing to Do With It.*
     Linda Hedrick

Whitney, Eleanor Searle

325 *Invitation to Joy: A Personal Story.*
     Judith B. Herman

Wilson, Edith Bolling

326 *My Memoir.*
     Edith James

Wolff, Sister Mary Madeleva

327 *My First Seventy Years.*
     Sister Marie Carolyn Klinkhamer

Wong, Jade Snow

328 *Fifth Chinese Daughter.*
329 *No Chinese Stranger.*
     Diane Jefferson

Yurka, Blanche

330　*Bohemian Girl: Blanche Yurka's Theatrical Life.*
Naomi Leventhal

Zaharias, Mildred "Babe" Didrikson

331　*This Life I've Led: My Autobiography.*
Margaret McFadden-Gerber

Zassenhaus, Hiltgunt

332　*Walls: Resisting the Third Reich—One Woman's Story.*
Jean B. Palmer

Ziegfeld, Patricia

333　*The Ziegfelds' Girl: Confessions of an Abnormally Happy Childhood.*
Janis Forman

Abzug, Bella (Savitsky) (1920-   )

Political Activist, Feminist, Civil Rights Lawyer

[1]   *Bella! Ms. Abzug Goes to Washington.* Ed. Mel Ziegler.
New York: Saturday Review Press, 1972. 314 pp.

    Bella! is a diary of Abzug's first Year in Congress, the Ninety-
second, in 1971. She states that she particularly represents women, young people, and minorities, and wants to change the national priorities to benefit poor people. In her personal swearing-in
ceremony she pledges to "use our country's wealth for life, not
death" (13). Accordingly she serves as "political midwife" (277)
in creating the National Women's Political Caucus and the movement to make New York City the Fifty First State. As idealistic
as Mr. Smith, but not as naive, she is a political gadfly to the congressional liberals who compromise on providing important human
necessities and are absent from the floor at key moments. Her
major effort that year was to end the Viet Nam War. She details
her involvement with the War Crimes Hearings, the anti-war demonstrations, and her losing battle to be assigned to the House
Armed Services Committee. She even resuscitates the resolution of
inquiry as a tool to make accountable those people conducting the
War. Prophetically she ends the book with the hope that the
American voters will impeach Nixon (295). Yet the book remains
relevant since there will be arguments over the proper use of available resources so long as people have different values. Abzug also
records her demanding schedule outside of Congress. Her relationship with her family, her efforts to turn her Manhattan Nineteenth
Congressional District Office into a problem-solving center, her
public anti-war speeches—all take their toil on her health. In her
local appearances she is frustrated by having to answer charges that
she, the first Jewish Congresswoman, is not a strong enough advocate of Israel.

    The book's content and style reveal a warmly human and
courageous woman. The reader gets to know more than just her

functions as a member of Congress. We learn of her concern for her sick mother, and her sensitivity to the effect her public endeavors have on her supportive husband and on the identity of her two college-aged daughters. Abzug includes personal exchanges which compliment and insult her, and is not ashamed to crow with delight when she gets an ovation from an unfriendly crowd. In this diary she addresses herself to the issue of feminism frequently, making it clear that she is for both women's rights and social change at the same time, not merely female power (204). Her political analysis of racism and "Pentagon chauvinism" roots them in the "masculine mystique" (101), and her excellent radar picks up the daily incidents of sexism she encounters. Whether she is listening to jokes or legislative debates she has a consciousness of herself as a woman and an awareness that her physical appearance is a factor in her professional interaction. Bellz Abzug labels herself as "activist," accepts the term "radical," and wants everyone to know she is "serious." Her tone shows she is pleased with her accomplishments.

Bella Abzug's book received widely-divergent reactions and not everyone interpreted her account positively. The most negative comments came from Stephanie Harrington in the New York *Times Book Review* (July 2, 1972, pp. 5, 14). While Harrington applauds Abzug's "statement of the goals for which she is suffering," she criticizes Abzug for being self-aggrandizing in her dedication to them and in her claims of political innovation: "She lets us know how much she is doing for us and how it is killing her. . . . In Bella's book, no one suffers like Bella." She also deprecates her literary ability. However, Harrington does tell the reader that her review is written from the perspective of a "Ryan supporter" (William F. Ryan defeated Bella Abzug in the following Democratic primary). On the other end of the spectrum, Jeanne Kinney highly recommended *Bella!* "for women in need of a liberated model and for anyone in search of the truth about the workings of our government" (*Best Sellers*, July 15, 1972, p. 181).

Patti Renner-Tana
Nassau Community College

Adler, Polly (1900-1962)

Madam

[2]   *A House Is Not a Home.* New York: Rhinehart & Co., Inc., Popular Library Edition, 1953. 288 pp.

A House Is Not a Home is the story of how Polly (born "Pearl") Adler, as a young girl, left her native Russia to come alone to "the Golden Land" of America. Instead of immediate wealth and happiness, she lived with cousins in the slums of Brooklyn and found work in a corset factory. After much hardship, including being raped by her foreman, followed by pregnancy and an abortion, Adler looked for other work. In her search she met new people, among them showgirls who occasionally turned to prostitution. Men began asking Adler for introductions and, in her own words, "It was in this informal, almost casual, fashion that I began my career as a madam."

From this beginning in the 1920's Adler became American's most well-known madam, running an elegant house, with beautiful girls and an exclusive clientele. Adler bitterly describes her problems with corrupt police and politicians, gangsters, prostitutes and some of her customers. The life of a madam lost its appeal for Adler and in the 1940's she gave it up to realize her girlhood dream: a good education. After completing the last two years of high school, she went on to college, primarily, she explained, to learn self-expression so that she could write her autobiography.

Most reviewers of *A House Is Not a Home* saw as its major value the insider's view of life within the brothel. Lee Rogow (*Saturday Review,* June 27, 1953, pp. 18-19) called Alder's book "a remarkable chapter in the life of the vice chairlady of New York." Phoebe Low Adams (*Atlantic Monthly,* July 1953, pp. 82, & 84) said it was "interesting as a criminal version of the classic American success story. Immigrant makes good, or from Ellis Island to Park Avenue." In a more positive review, Stanley Walker (New York *Herald Tribune,* June 7, 1953, p. 4) stated, "It is not too much to say that she not only tells the truth but that she adds many details which none of the investigations into the sordid side of New York life, and none of the trials of the miscreants, have been able to bring out."

S. Ellen Emser
Clark University

Allen, Florence Ellinwood (1884-1966)

Lawyer, Judge

[3]   *To Do Justly.* Cleveland, Ohio: The Press of Western Reserve University, 1965. 201 pp.

Florence Allen begins her autobiography, *To Do Justly,* by describing her early years growing up in Ohio and Utah. Her father seems to have been a strong influence. He had a variety of careers as a classical Greek scholar and teacher, as an assayer for a mining company, and as a member of the Utah legislature and a representative to Congress. Allen tells less about her mother although she was "the first woman admitted to Smith College" and an active church and community leader. Allen attended a school in Ohio run by her grandfather and later went to Western Reserve College. After living in Germany for awhile with her parents, she entered Chicago Law School. Moving to New York in order to work for the New York League for Protection of Immigrants, she completed her law training at New York University Law School. It was during her years at law school that Allen became involved in the woman's suffrage movement. Her suffrage activities continued when she returned to Ohio and when suffrage was won, friends in the Woman Suffrage Party asked her to run for a common pleas judgeship. She won but served in this position only a short time because she was elected to the Supreme Court of Ohio in 1922 and in 1934 Roosevelt appointed her to the Federal Court of Appeals for the Sixth Circuit. She was the first woman to serve in all three of these judgeships. During these years Judge Allen was an active public speaker on international affairs, especially "the outlawry of war," and on the Constitution. She published a book on the Constitution, *This Constitution of Ours* (1940), and a book dealing with the United Nations, *The Treaty as an Instrument of Legislation* (1952).

To Do Justly is of interest because of Allen's participation in the suffrage movement and because of the many public positions she has held. However, the work is not deeply psychological nor philosophical. Allen tends simply to record and describe important events and to tell anecdotes. She comments only briefly. The book may appeal to students who are interested in law and (Ohio) politics, for Allen does discuss many of her cases. The autobiography itself is only 152 pages. An appendix contains several of her speeches, one of her articles reprinted from *The Educational Forum,* and her opinion on the Tennessee Valley Authority case of 1933 (one of the most important cases of her judicial career).

Deborah Johnson
Rensselaer Polytechnic Institute

Alsop, Susan Mary (1918-   )

Diplomat's wife, Socialite

[4]   *To Marietta from Paris: 1945-1960.* Garden City, N. Y.: Doubleday and Co., 1975. 370 pp.

To Marietta from Paris traces Susan Mary Alsop's personal and social maturation during the fifteen years she was married to William Patten, U.S. financial and economic attache to Paris and ends with Patten's death from emphysema and her return to America. Consisting mainly of letters written to her friend, Marietta Tree, *To Marietta* is supplemented with occasional letters to others and brief summaries to fill in information not provided by the letters, as well as retrospective evaluations of individuals encountered and events experienced.

Much of the book's popularity is due to Alsop's association with the great and near-great—political figures as diverse as Adlai Stevenson and Ho Chi Minh, assorted Kennedys and princesses. However, her evolution as an independent woman, in thought and action, her growing ability to respond to hardships, particularly her husband's deteriorating health, provide the reader far more than an entertaining glimpse into a Parisian social calendar. By 1953 she can objectively evaluate Embassy entertaining as so outrageously expensive that"ambassadors have to dip into their own pockets and often leave Paris practically ruined." She is equally honest in judging her children. The letters from 1948 on are sprinkled with anecdotes recording the cute and clever things her children have done. At the same time she quite openly describes her daughter's inability to concentrate and details her resultant academic failures.

Lilla Lyon (New York *Times Book Review,* 14 September, p. 37) comments that Alsop's lifestyle is "surprisingly like that embalmed in James's novels"; one could argue that the personality revealed in *To Marietta* suggests those of James's heroines—strong, courageous, honest, dispassionate and equally admirable. Diana Rowan (*Christian Science Monitor,* 5 December 1975, p. 31) is more critical: "the over-all tone is curiously prim and self-conscious. . . . The reader searches in vain for the witty spontaneous charm of Madame de Sevigne." D. R. Murray (*Library Journal,* 15 September 1975, p. 1622) sums up the book as "a unique and engrossing footnote to a most important period of modern history."

Cynthia L. Walker
University of Alaska—Fairbanks

Alta (1942-   )

Activist, Author, Editor, Feminist, Publisher, Teacher, Television Producer

[5]   *Momma: a start on all the untold stories.* New York: Times Change Press, 1974. 76 pp.

If Alta's poems are graffiti, then *Momma,* her second prose work (after *True Story,* 1973), is a love letter to all mothers. She tells her own experience painfully, truthfully, describing her relationships with her children, with husbands, lovers, friends, and neighbors (because of the kids) and how those others related to her and her children. Often one finds a discussion of the writing itself (10): "this is unbearable. how can i write it. no wonder it is not written. or if it is written, not published. or if it is published, not recognized. no one could relate to such constant pain except another mother wishing to treat her children well & how often are mothers also publishers?" But Alta's optimism always overcomes the despair (16): "why bother to tell all this anyway? because I am sick of being alone!" Her thematic range is the personal/political reality of motherhood in its feminist immediacy rather than a utopia: she mothers foster children; introduces a second and third father to her daughters, and later, must share custody of them: she is a daughter, a housewife, a single mother and on welfare; she 'gives birth' to a women's poetry reading; has ambivalent experiences with women's groups; but most of all, Alta feels "overwhelming love" for her children.

Alta's voice in *Momma* may be singular in its idiom, but the isolation she felt hopefully is a thing of the past. Identification with the Women's Liberation Movement had meant alienation from her daily experience as a housewife, or the reverse. Self-respect was hard to muster. For that reason, the story of *Momma* had gone untold (30): "people hate housewives. youve probly noticed. jokes about us: we couldnt have any brains or we wouldnt be doing this. & the women themselves (who the hell do i think i am? *our*selves—) say 'o, i'm just a housewife'."

When all of your labor is donated to the house, the children, and every once in a while poetry, how do you fight becoming the female eunuch Greer described? What is it like to be a poet and have dirty dishes be considered your *real* work? In answer, Alta replies that the joining of love and independence are a paradox, that they may seem an absurd combination, but they are actually well suited to each other. She knows the two are not contradictory; contradiction lies in dependence masquerading as love, and this is true for husbands as well as children. In *Momma*, Alta writes with contrition of need for independence from her children, who don't always understand that need (9): "for the luxury of time alone i must feel guilty that i dont want loved ones with me all the time. & i must be lonely. heavy payments."

Marge Piercy, in the foreword to *i am not a practicing angel* (Trumansburg, N. Y.: Corssing Press, 1975), said Alta "doesn't say more—or less—than she means. . . . Not angelic or demonic, not grand or overinflated, not studious or posey, what she writes is as human and daily as good soup. She has a salty sense of humor. Poems of the kitchen, the bedroom, and the street, and of herself as character caught and speaking" (6). And this is true of Alta's prose as well. Adrienne Rich says of *Momma* [that] "the best Alta places her finger on the raw nerve of motherhood: loving one's children, defending them. . .'like a mother bear,' [and yet] we still find in them the nearest targets for our rage and frustration" (*Of Woman Born,* New York: Norton, 1976, p. 278).

Alta herself asks in Book III, the final poem of *Momma,* "& how right is it to shut her [Alta's daughter] out of the room so I can write about her?" She ends Momma in verse form (46) because: "poetry seems easier. you just capture the essence: you dont have to relate the daily details. & the pain, tho intense, just lasts the length of the poem. raising kids is both poetry & prose. thats why the story is just begun. no matter how much i write. this book is the photograph of a woman giving birth."

Diane Marting
Livingston College, Rutgers University

Ames, Evelyn Perkins (1908-   )

Writer

[6]   *Daughter of the House.* Boston: Houghton Mifflin, 1961. 241 pp.

Daughter of the House focuses on the married life of the author's parents, Henry and Olga Flinch Perkins. A sensitively written book, it opens as Evelyn Perkins Ames is cleaning out the family home, scheduled for demolition. The home, at 55 Forest Street, Harrtford, Connecticut, was one of the Nook Farm colony, where Mark Twain, Charles Dudley Warner, and Harriet Beecher Stowe lived in suburban luxury in the late nineteenth century. Her father (1973-1959), a physicist and one-time president of Trinity College in Hartford, had an active and successful professional life. The mother, a Danish-born actress and scholar, gave up her pursuits when she married. While Ames is the central observer and a character in the story, we follow the parents in their troubled marriage as they each turn to the daughter of the house, for love and security. A particularly poignant scene is the fiftieth wedding anniversary, with those in attendance limited to the parents, the daughter, and their servants, in which Ames observes that, above all, they have "come through" together.

While *Daugher of the House* gives an excellent picture of what married life demanded of Olga Flinch Perkins and women of her era, it also brings forth ideas about marriage and the general state of women. Ames is not critical of marriage from outside—in private life she is Mrs. Amyas Ames, wife of a banker and mother of four children. Instead we find an intimate, truth-telling portrayal of a troubled relationship endured by two brilliant, but different individuals who finally, in the author's estimation, rose above it all. The feminist reader isn't likely to be as sympathetic with the father as with the mother. And although the author does not appear to be particularly biased, she observes in one place that "a woman has so little to show for her life as it flows away behind her. How can anyone know what she does with it, really, least of all (perhaps) herself. It disappears, wholly, into other lives" (171). More specifically, Ames tells how her mother complained about the difference between her husband's fulfilled life and her own, "empty, unfilled, reverberating with hollow disappointment" (173). Between these two people was the daughter of the house, whose final message seems to be that we are all creations of our parents' marriage as well as their two bodies, and that the same is true for our children and their children.

Beverly Seaton
The Ohio State University—Newark

Anderson, Margaret C. (c. 1891-1973)

Woman of Letters

[7] *The Autobiography: My Thirty Years' War: Beginnings and Battles to 1930.* Vol. 1. New York: Horizon, 1969. 278 pp.

After dealing briefly with her privileged childhood in an upper middle class, middle western (Indianapolis) family, Anderson focuses on those years which made her famous: from 1914, when she founded *The Little Review,* to its demise in 1929. She and her co-editor Jane Heap, whom she regarded as the world's best conversationalist, moved this "Magazine of the Arts Making No Compromise with the Public Taste" from Chicago to California, to New York, and to Paris, taking with them physically or spiritually a host of writers, activists, artists, and musicians including Amy Lowell, Ezra Pound (their foreign editor), Theodore Dreiser, George Anthiel, Gertrude Stein, James Joyce, Mary Garden, Alexander Berkman, Emma Goldman, Ben Hecht, Sherwood Anderson, and the incredible Baroness Else von Freytag von Loringhoven. Largely anecdotal, the volume provides accounts of adventures often prompted by Anderson's chronically impoverished state, such as the summer during which she, her sister, and several friends lived illegally in tents on the shore of Lake Michigan. Having spent these years not only gliding from one financial crisis to another but also fighting for freedom of expression (e.g., Anderson and Heap were charged with obscenity for their serial publication of Joyce's *Ulysses*), Anderson remarks by 1930 that "For me challenge has always been the great impulse, the only liberation."

B
A548A

[8]   *The Autobiography: The Fiery Fountains: Continuation and Crisis to 1950.* Vol. 2. New York: Horizon, 1969. 242 pp.

This second volume explores what Anderson terms the elements of her personal universe: music, love, nature, ideas. Living mostly in France during the '30's and '40's in homes including a lighthouse and five chateaux, Anderson describes her disgust engendered by the French bourgeoisie and her devotion inspired by the teachings of the mystic Gurdjieff. The abstract, dreamy quality of the prose confirms her assertion that she lives "without memory of facts." At the center of this book is her 22-year relationship with the actress and singer Georgette Leblanc, including their struggles to flee France before the German advance, accompanied by Leblanc's "fairy tale nurse" Monique. Presenting their years together as a kind of spiritual ecstasy, Anderson reveals the fortitude with which Leblanc endures terminal cancer and the vibrant memories and sadness which Anderson herself experiences after her friend's death.

[9]　*The Autobiography: The Strange Necessity: Resolutions
and Reminiscence to 1969.*　Vol. 3.　New York: Horizon, 1969.　223 pp.

In the final volume, Anderson honors her closest friends and her
favorite music, art, and literature while deploring current trends in
the arts, among them "today's rancid sex books" and the tendency
to assume that "reality" means ugliness and brutality.　In an effort
to be concrete about matters of taste in a book laden with abstractions about Art, Life, and Beauty, Anderson provides a long list of
musical recordings, describing the qualities of these selections
which constituted the "concerts" she played for her friends.　In
many places the third volume recapitulates material presented in
the earlier volumes.　In almost Joycean epiphanies, she describes
those moments of greatest sadness or delight in her life as a "di-
lettante" (a term she wholly approves).　Her primary emotional
concerns are memories of her relationships with Georgette Leblanc
and Dorothy Caruso and her attempts to deal with her own loneliness and old age.　Reviewing her life, however, she concludes that
"The blessings I wanted were love and music, books and great
ideas and beauty of environment.　I have had them all, and to a
degree beyond my asking even beyond my imagining."

Of the three volumes, *My Thirty Years' War* received the most
attention, partly because Anderson was still in the public eye in
1930 and reviewers could fondly recall the years of *The Little Review* when "Miltons hung on every tree and the millennium was a
page and a half away" (R. N. Linscott, *Saturday Review,* June 14,
1930, p. 1123).　In a review addressed to Anderson herself, Sherwood Anderson's recollections of *The Little Review* "Crowd"
both attest to the accuracy of *The Little Review* editor's description and suggest the kind of asexual seductiveness which Anderson exercised over her friends and contributors.　Harriet Monroe,
on the other hand, accuses Margaret Anderson of making false
claims for *The Little Review,* failing to acknowledge the importance of *Poetry,* engaging in literary "banditry," all as a result
of either a faulty memory or sheer perversity (*Poetry,* November
1930, pp. 95-100).　Fascination with this period of literary hyper-
activity apparently leads Matthew Josephson (*Nation,* June 18,
1930, p. 707) and others after him to regret that Anderson's autobiography focuses on herself instead of on her *Little Review* contributors.　While he at first praises those women—Anderson,

Monroe, Amy Lowell, Isadora Duncan—who "rescued and nursed" the American modern movement, Josephson concludes that because of these "Amazons," the artistic revolution lost its purity "from being entangled with all sorts of 'causes,' such as birth control, Greek dancing, Lesbianism, and psychoanalysis."

Anderson generally is regarded by her reviewers as "a talker, not a writer" (Alfred Kazin, New York *Times,* August 16, 1970, p. 1), but beginning with the publication of *My Thirty Years' War,* she has been admired as a "magnificent literary impressario" who lives in "a state of continual spiritual inebriation that would have left a lesser soul limp in a week" (Linscott). From Louis Kronenberger (New York *Times, Book Review,* May 25, 1930, p. 2), who notes the "gusto" which characterizes *My Thirty Years' War,* to Alfred Kazin, who describes her autobiography as "a rambling but always highly charged, fascinatingly feminine monologue," Anderson has been praised for her personal fortitude and energy and for those parts of her autobiography which are narrative rather than lyrical, anecdotal and personal rather than abstract. In a favorable review of *Fiery Fountains* (New York *Times,* December 23, 1951), Robert Hillyer points out the weakness of Anderson's "gushing rhapsodies," a flow which, along with her "murky" descriptions of transcendental experience (Thomas Lask, New York *Times,* August 3, 1970, p. 29), every critic cites. Several also condemn her life, which they see as "a constant flight from reality" (J. M. Edelstein, *New Republic,* June 13, 1970, pp. 19-22) because she is not concerned with certain ugly realities such as slums. Geoffrey Wolff, however, describes her autobiography not as a record of escape but simply as "a geography of interior places" (*Newsweek,* May 25, 1970, p. 114).

Patricia L. Miller
University of Connecticut, Storrs

Anderson, Marian (1902-)

Singer

[10] *My Lord, What A Morning.* New York: Viking Press, 1956. 312 pp.

> *My Lord, What A Morning* traces the career of Marian Anderson from the poor neighborhood in Philadelphia where she first joined the Baptist Church junior choir at the age of six through her astonishing successes as a concert artist both in the United States and abroad.

What Anderson writes is fascinating and marvellous, yet the items she leaves out or passes by fleetingly are just as amazing. She writes chiefly about her musical career, only incidentally about her personal life. She would prefer to be remembered as a singer of Schubert's *lieder,* or at least for her rendition of Schubert's *Ave Maria.* Of the famous Easter Sunday concert at the Lincoln Memorial in 1939, Marian Anderson writes but a short, twelve page chapter. It started for her as just another concert date to be arranged under Sol Hurok's management. "It was only a few weeks before the scheduled date for Washington that I discovered the full truth—that the Daughters of the American Revolution, owners of the hall, had decreed it could not be used by one of my race. I was saddened, but as it is my belief that right will win, I assumed that a way would be found. I had no inkling that the thing would become a *cause celebre.* . . . I felt about the affair as about an election campaign; whatever the outcome, there is bound to be unpleasantness and embarrassment. . . . It would be fooling myself to think that I was meant to be a fearless fighter; I was not."

Her family—especially her mother—supported her in her early career and Anderson writes lovingly of home and church. She tells mainly about successes: taking voice lessons, winning contests, crafting concert programs, singing to packed houses in Scandinavia, recording contracts. She does not avoid a discussion of race prejudice, but she writes at more length of her struggle to learn German. Anderson only hints at some of the travails of being on tour in an intolerant America; she deals instead with the joys of singing in Japan or Finland.

The only music book included in the American Library Association's list of "Notable Books of 1956," *My Lord, What a Morning* received generally favorable—although unecstatic—reviews. In 1977, the year of her diamond jubilee, some of the original descriptions of her book as one by a woman of dignity, sincerity, graciousness, and modesty still seem fitting. Her career can be summed up as did one reviewer of her book (*New Yorker,* November 17, 1956), with the notation that *My Lord, What A Morning* "reveals, gradually and movingly, a generous, humble, and wholly dedicated woman, equally at peace with life and with her art."

Marie R. Oesting
Baraboo, Wisconsin

Anderson, Mary (1872-1964)

Labor leader

B
A5485

[11] *Woman at Work: The Autobiography of Mary Anderson as Told to Mary N. Winslow.* Minneapolis: University of Minnesota Press, 1951. 266 pp.

Mary Anderson, born on a farm near Goteborg, Sweden, emigrated to the United States in the Spring of 1889, at the age of sixteen, and devoted most of the remainder of her life and energies to improving the working conditions of women in this country. *Woman at Work* is the record of her activities as labor leader from the time she joined a union, "for companionship," at age seventeen, through her service for nearly twenty-five years as director of the Women's Bureau of the Department of Labor (1918-44).

Anderson's early experience in a Chicago shirt-waist factory taught her how employers exploit workers, especially women workers. Existing practices and laws, she came to realize, if not openly favoring men, discriminated against women. Becoming active in the Women's Trade Union League in the first decade of the century, she worked for the recognition of the rights of workers to strike, to set up arbitration committees, and to negotiate grievances. In 1918 she was appointed to serve in the Department of Labor and spent most of the rest of her life striving to establish national standards for the employment of women. There she worked toward securing for women such things as an eight-hour day and a forty-eight hour week; equal pay for men and women; a minimum wage rate to cover the cost of living for dependents and not merely for the individual; prohibition of women's employ ment in occupations especially hazardous to them, such as certain processes in the lead industries; prohibition of industrial home-work; establishment of personnel departments and appointment of women to supervisory positions (98). In 1944, Anderson re-tired from public life with fifty years of service in one capacity or another in the women's labor movement.

Although there is little of her personal life in *Woman at Work,* her book is of great interest to women's studies for the history it recounts. For example, when, in 1944, the International Labor Office in Philadelphia endorsed the principle of "Equal Pay for Equal Work," Anderson believed she had seen the beginning of a movement for real equality for women and regarded the interna-tional acceptance of the principle as a triumph (254). Another topic of continuing interest in *Woman at Work* is Anderson's account of the early history of the equal rights amendment and the conflicts it then caused among different women's groups. While the National Woman's Party supported the amendment as worded ("Men and women shall have equal rights throughout the United States and every place subject to its jurisdiction"), Anderson and others in the women's labor movement opposed it as a vague and unenforcable slogan which could upset the legal protection achieved for women workers through the years. Perhaps it is be-cause of the legal protection Anderson and others achieved for women workers that many women today can support the current version of ERA.

The many reviews of *Woman at Work* paid tribute to Anderson's distinguished career in public service, and praised her book as an inspiration to the young and an important document in the history of the movement for reform of working conditions for women.

Judith B. Herman
State College at Buffalo

Angelou, Maya (1928-   )

Dancer, Writer, Poet, Political Activist

[12] *I Know Why the Caged Bird Sings.* New York: Random
House, 1969. 281 pp.

The story of Maya Angelou's first sixteen years, *I Know Why
the Caged Bird Sings* is a simultaneously comic, candid and poignant documentary of an imaginative and highly sensitive Black
girl's rural and urban experience in the thirties and early forties.
As with her other two memoirs, *I Know Why* is developed chrono-
loically, but this one is especially rich in portraits of individuals
who are transmuted by Angelou's sharp wit and social awareness
into vivid types: Momma, her self-reliant and puritanical grandmother who owns the only Black store in Stamps, Arkansas; Vivian
Baxter, her street-wise, aggressive and immaculately beautiful
mother; Mrs. Flowers, the town's Black intellectual, who introduces Maya to her cherished world of books; Maya's brother Bailey
whose supportive presence and wise absurdity permit the impres-
sionable and lonely girl some respite from the demanding and in-
scrutable adults.

Weaving together these and other finely wrought portraits are
the descriptions of the rhythms of her different environments: the
grim realities of growing up Black in the segregated South; the supreme importance of school and religion to the rural Black community; the heady freedom of San Francisco in the throes of the
war effort. So too is the young girl's consciousness painfully and
meticulously interwoven and revealed: the guilt and loneliness
engendered by the early absence of Angelou's parents; the nagging
self-doubts concerning Maya's own physical attractiveness because
she is not only extremely tall and lanky but also non-white; the
physical and emotional neglect by her mother's St. Louis clan—
which culminates with Maya's rape at the age of eight.

Her escape into books and fantasy as a means of creating her
own stable domain in an otherwise chaotic world is introduced
in *I Know Why* with her youthful immersion in white and Black
literature; in her later books this same pattern of escape will be
translated into her interest in music and particularly dance. Her
nagging insecurity about her height and physical appearance, as

well as her sexual confusion and curiosity, are themes running through all three autobiographies, and in *I Know Why* is manifested by her speculations on her possible lesbianism which she resolves through her pregnancy and the birth of her son which concludes this volume.

I Know Why the Caged Bird Sings has drawn critical enthusiasm and acclaim. Robert A. Cross described it as "more than a tour de force of language." He finds it a "tribute to the courage, dignity and endurance of the small, rural Southern black community" (*Newsweek,* March 2, 1970, pp. 89-90). Alluding to Angelou's career as a dancer, one reviewer noted that Angelou "writes a graceful, pirouetting style that can switch to down-home blues in about one funky second" (*Life,* June 5, 1970, p. 12). Critical articles on *I Know Why* are just beginning to be published, and the continuing praise for this first book in particular augurs much more scholarship on Angelou in the future. Two of the articles are psychological in nature: Myra K. McMurray, "Role Playing as Art in Maya Angelou's *Caged Bird,*" *South Atlantic Bulletin* (May 1976, pp. 106-111), and Liliane K. Arensberg, "Death as Metaphor of Self in Maya Angelou's *I Know Why the Caged Bird Sings,*" *CLA Journal* (December 1976, pp. 273-291); one article skillfully places Angelou's first two autiographies within the Black literary experience: George E. Kent, "Maya Angelou's *I Know Why the Caged Bird Sings* and the Black Autobiographical Tradition," *Kansas Quarterly,* 7, No. 3 (1975), 73-78.

[13] *Gather Together in My Name.* New York: Random House, 1974. 214 pp.

This second volume of Angelou's memoirs is less richly textured than the first, although her style retains its imagistic and colloquial qualities. Picking up where *I Know Why* ends, and set in the up-tempo post-Second World War street world of California, *Gather Together* is interspersed with lyrics of the popular songs of that era. This episodic narrative follows Maya's restless teenage attempts at trying-on of roles: short-order cook, waitress, madam to a couple of lesbian prostitutes, applicant to the U.S. Army's Officer Candidate School, cabaret dancer, prostitute for a middle-aged pimp around whom she weaves Hollywood-inspired fantasies of romantic love and domestic bliss. Maya's burning search for self is as often frustrated as it is nourished and rewarded, leading to adolescent extremes of risk-taking, self-approbation and denigration. Angelou's mother and brother remain influential and supportive forces during this period, but her family members' characteristic independence and *laissez-faire* attitude, which Maya herself upholds, lead to personal rifts which further underscore Maya's emotional isolation.

Her own serious identity-quest is complicated, however, by Maya's inability to perceive the growing anger and loneliness of her small son as he is boarded for extended periods of time with various baby-sitters. After the harrowing kidnapping of her son by one of these baby-sitters, Angelou begins to understand not only the sacred otherness of her child, this once-perceived beautiful appendage to herself, but also the importance of her responsibility as mother and sole parent to him. Although she still reviles her "too-tall body" and "unpretty face," and fears that they will keep her from winning worldly success and a man, it is actually the caring and respect of a male friend that prevents her from falling into the mire of the drug underworld. If *I Know Why* is a metaphoric statement on the Black experience in America as lived by one girl, *Gather Together* is the particularized story of a young woman growing through maturity to regain her innocence. It is the story of one person's self-education.

Widely and favorably reviewed, *Gather Together* was seen as yet another stylistic triumph for Angelou. Comparing it to *I Know Why*, one reviewer noted that in *Gather Together* Angelou's style "has both ripened and simplified. It is more telegraphic and more condensed, transmitting a world of sensation or emotion or understanding in one image—in short, it is more like poetry" (New York *Times*, June 16, 1974, p. 16). Special praise was given to Angelou's ability to superimpose the comic, foolish and touching nature of a young woman's growing pains on the very real struggles and demands of the world and its many racial inequities (*New Yorker*, July 15, 1974, p. 87).

[14] *Singin' and Swingin' and Getting Merry Like Christmas.*
New York: Random House, 1976. 269 pp.

Concerning her twenty-third through twenty-sixth years,

Singin' is the account of Maya Angelou's birth as a performer. Her perfect ladies' magazine marriage deteriorates, and her adventurous spirit propels her first to a strip joint where she works as the shake dancer Rita, and soon thereafter to the legendary Purple Onion where she makes her debut as the regal and exotic calypso singer Maya Angelou. Offered the part of a featured dancer in the touring company of *Porgy and Bess,* Maya siezes the opportunity for international traval. Her voyage through Italy, France, Greece, Yugoslavia and Egypt becomes the rambling centerpiece of the book. Gone are the crystallized portraits of her earlier works; instead the star-struck Angelou presents an itinerary of performances, and the accompanying famous personalities and stage triumphs. Deeper relationships, especially with her mother and son, seem to be less important to Angelou than her heady journey towards fame. Indeed, it is her son's psychosomatic skin rash which brings her overseas journey to an end, and it is their anguished reconciliation which closes the book.

Containing Angelou's observations on her interracial marriage, wifehood, religion, war, motherhood, the European attitude toward Black Americans, and frequently livened by excerpts from popular, folk and calypso songs, this third volume is of uneven quality. No longer the child of *I Know Why* or the adolescent of *Gather Together,* who was more often acted-upon by life than acting herself, in *Singin'* the adult Angelou finally takes full control and responsiblity for her life. It is here, too, that Marguerite Johnson, Rite, Rita, and Mrs. Thos Angelos is renamed Maya Angelou, for good. But the depth, wise objectivity and rueful candor of her earlier books is missing. The celebration of her entrance into show business is still so closely felt by the older writer that *Singin',* read without the background provided by her earlier books, appears simply as yet another elbow-rubbing memoir of an artist's rise to success and recognition in her profession.

The generally mixed reviews on the publication of *Singin'* were usually based on what was left out rather than what was included. For example, Angelou details her courtship, and the first year of her marriage, but the second year is completely excised from her narrative. Likewise, the reason she marries—"Because he asked me"—leads June Jordan to speculate that "the starved sorrow of that response strongly suggests that there are dimensions to Angelou's life that she is not ready to share, yet" (*Ms,* January

1977, pp. 40-41). On the other hand, Linda Kuehl explains the irregular nature of a great portion of the book by describing Angelou as "a self-conceived picaresque heroine." If Angelou is "not an integrated personality," Kuehl continues, it is "because she is constantly growing, open to change, too alive to reduce herself to the polemical dilemna of a black career-woman-feminist-wife-mother" (*Saturday Review*, October 30, 1976, p. 46).

Liliane K. Arensberg
Emory University

Anthony, Susan B. (1916-   )

Grandniece of Suffragist

[15] *The Ghost in My Life.* New York: Chosen Books, 1971. 221 pp.

Susan Anthony, namesake and grandniece of the famous suffragist, was a sometime reporter, broadcaster, feminist, pacifist, and alcoholic. In *Ghost in My Life* she tells of being brought to public attention by organizations that wished to capitalize on her name. She also describes her early discovery of alcohol's exhilerating effects on her personality, her romances and marriages, her encounter with McCarthyism, and her finding salvation in religion.

Had her name been Mary or Jane, the second Susan Anthony may have had little occasion to reach the limelight. She played many different roles in her life, but only her name, an unfortunate addiction to drink, and her conversion to religion in middle age were unusual. *Ghosts in My Life* is the first publication of Chosen Books, which specializes in works of an evangelical nature (*e.g.* Charles Colson's *Born Again*).

The book was reviewed in *Best Sellers, Publishers' Weekly,* and *Christian Century* and was commended for competent writing and warmth.

Zelda B. Silverman, and
Helen B. Phillips
Norfolk, Virginia

Astor, Mary (1906-   )

Actress, Writer

[16] *My Story: An Autobiography.* Garden City, N. Y.: Doubleday and Company, Inc., 1959. 332 pp.

My Story, the first of Mary Astor's two autobiographies, begins by recounting the lives of her parents prior to her birth and then describes her life as a youngster on a farm in the Midwest. She writes of her loneliness and unhappiness as the daughter of a greedy, domineering father and a passive mother. Astor concentrates more upon her personal life than upon her life as a successful actress. She relates the histories of her four marriages and her life as the mother of two children. She includes her account of the scandal associated with her divorce from her second husband, but does not include the particulars. She reveals the pressures placed upon her as a wage earner for her parents, her children, and her husbands.

As she approached middle age, her awareness of herself, of her failing career, and of her growing problem with alcoholism increased. She attributes much of her learning to resolve emotional conflicts and to deal with her feelings of a lack of self-worth to her conversion to Catholicism and her deep faith in God. Although she records the major events in her career, the book is her statement of her difficult struggle to become a woman who is her own self, not an extension of others who seek to control the events of her life.

My Story is a frank book. Lewis Nichols (New York *Times,* January 11, 1959, p. 23) believes that "Miss Astor seems less interested in standing a reader's hair on end than in getting at the facts about herself." Hollis Alpert (*Saturday Review,* January 17, 1959, p. 65) observes that "*My Story* is. . .an account of a sorely beset and bewildered woman who managed in her maturity to find some serenity and self-sufficiency." Astor in her foreword to *My Story* describes the book as an "emotional catharsis."

[17] *A Life on Film.* New York: Delacorte Press, 1971. 245 pp.

This second of Mary Astor's autobiographies deals with her experiences as an actress in films and on stage, radio, and television. She explains her view and impressions of the making of movies. She includes technical data involved in the production of films and television. She gives her opinions about various actors, actresses, directors, and producers. Unlike her first autobiography, this one contains only vague references to the many problems which she encountered in her personal life during the first thirty years of her career. This book contains information of a "behind-the-scenes" nature which presents the life of an actress as time-consuming, tedious, demanding, and difficult.

Clara Delores King
Campbell College School of Law
Buies Creek, N. C.

Baez, Joan (1941-   )

Folk-singer, Activist

[18] *Daybreak.* New York: Dial Press, 1968. 159 pp.

Published when Baez was twenty-seven, *Daybreak* is a collage of remembered experiences, from her childhood fears and accomplishments through the time of her intense involvement in nonviolent protest of the Vietnamese War. Recollections of discrimination against her for being part Mexican, negative encounters with formal education, work with handicapped children, relationships with her spiritual mentor Ira, with her understanding mother and not-so-understanding father: all these facets of her life are revealed. This brash and talented folk-singer only briefly discusses her life as a performer, preferring instead to dwell on other experiences and feelings about herself and humanity.

Rarely generalizing about women as a group and never speaking on the issue of women's liberation, Baez evidences a genuine loving concern for women she met in jail, for her independent mother who was jailed along with her for civil disobedience, for her sisters, for school friends. (Married before the book was published, she makes no mention of that part of her life.) Allusions to sexual freedom add to the overall impression of Baez as an honest, open woman whose individuality and integrity are never sacrificed in her attempts to discover the direction in which she and her country are going.

[19] *Coming Out.* New York: Pocket Books, 1971.

Written with her husband, David Harris, *Coming Out* alternatively recounts each of their feelings during his imprisonment for draft resistance. It offers some insight into her marriage relationship, left undiscussed in *Daybreak*.

Although Robert Cole denounces *Daybreak* (*Atlantic,* October 1968, p. 136) as a "sloppy, confusing. . .failure of a book," other reviewers have been less harsh. Like Cole, Richard Goldstein in the New York *Times Book Review* (September 8, 1968, p. 64) criticizes the loose organization of the book, but others, including Henry S. Resnik (*Saturday Review,* September 7, 1968, p. 43), stress the vividness and honesty of Baez's writing, especially concerning the father-daughter relationship.

Cynthia Swaine
Old Dominion University

Bailey, Pearl (1918-   )

Entertainer, Singer, Actress

[20] *The Raw Pearl.* New York: Harcourt, Brace and World, 1968. 206 pp.

Edited from tape-recorded conversations, *The Raw Pearl* traces Pearl Bailey's life from childhood through her success as a singer on stage and in films. Chronological treatment of her show-business career is combined with chapters featuring such topics as a disastrous marriage and a later happy one, comments on other celebrities, and views on subjects ranging from her work to race relations and family life, including interracial marriage and adopted children. She urges readers to love humanity and trust in God. The first-person narrative is interspersed with comments both to readers and to people who are being recalled, whether living or dead. At times poems or poetic essays emphasize intense feelings.

Her autobiography presents Bailey as a strong and successful woman. Self-supporting since her teen-age years, she is glad to record the joys of her home and marriage along with her career. In her private life, she shows continuing concern for parents and siblings, and treats the pleasures of cooking and gardening. Her passing references to women include comments on their mutual hostilities and she once calls females "the deadliest of the species." Yet she shows great warmth as she traces relationships with her mother, with certain women friends and co-workers. Strained relationships involve men: the pattern in which Bailey recalls unhappiness consists of narration followed by retrospective forgiveness expressed toward the one who caused pain; those who receive such absolution are usually male.

The Raw Pearl was shortly and favorably reviewed in many newspapers and popular periodicals.

Bailey has published two subsequent books of short personal comments, including some verse and letters: *Talking to Myself* (New York: Harcourt, Brace, Jovanovich, 1971) and *Hurry Up, America, and Spit* (New York: Harcourt, Brace, Jovanovich, 1976). She discusses her private and professional life and her religious and political opinions.

Carolyn H. Rhodes
Old Dominion University

Baldrige, Letitia Katherine (c.1926-   )

Social Secretary, Public Relations Expert, Business Executive

[21]   *Roman Candle.*   Boston: Houghton-Miffling Company,
         1956. 308 pp.

The six-foot tall blond from Omaha—a graduate of Miss Porter's
School and Vassar, beneficiary of sixteen months of graduate study
abroad, and former social secretary to the American ambassador
to France—studied Italian every Sunday afternoon and at least one
hour a night and prayed for an opportunity that would take her
away from her government job in Washington and transport her
to Rome. *Roman Candle* is Letitia Baldrige's sentimental story of
her dream come true as social secretary to Ambassador-to-Italy,
Clare Boothe Luce.   From her office in the sixteenth century
Villa Taverna, Tish Baldrige managed the thousands of details
that would assure that the American ambassador would make a
bella figura, tasks from arranging the butler's funeral, to finding
a wet nurse for the poddle litter, to executing a flawless dinner
party for ninety, to tactfully answering endless petitions for
money, jobs, and favors. After her hectic fourteen hour work day,
the Ambassador's secretary led an active social life of her own, en-
joying the cuisine, wine, candlelight, and music of the little trat-
torie.   Americans could live well in Italy in the early 1950's; she
had a six-room apartment with a loyal housekeeper-cook and wore
custom-made shoes and designer-original clothes.

Letitia Baldrige belongs to that generation of Americans who
after World War II flocked to Europe to immerse themselves in
the history, art, music, politics, and philosophy of those Old World
cultures which had so recently escaped oblivion. Unabashedly and
enthusiastically she fell in love with Italy. And the love affair between the tall blond American and an entire nation was mutual.
Baldrige herself is intelligent, independent, and imaginative and
pictures her female "boss" as a beautiful, charming, effective,
policy-making executive.   Nevertheless, the pervasive "feminine-
mystique" attitude of the 1950's is evident in Baldrige's idealized
presentation of Italian men and of the honor and privilege enjoyed
by Italian women because of their sex.

[22]   *Of Diamonds and Diplomats.*   Boston: Houghton-Mifflin Company, 1968. 337 pp.

In her "simple recording of a happy life," Letitia Baldrige describes the series of glamorous jobs that ultimately led her to the head of her own firm and to a happy combination of career, wifehood, and motherhood. After her Vassar degree, study abroad, and a crash course in typing and shorthand, the energetic young Francophile became social secretary to Ambassador and Mrs. David Bruce in Paris, bounding into an ambassadorial residence required to function smoothly according to the strictest standards of protocol and good taste. After three glamorous years in Paris, 1948-51, she yielded to family pressure to return to a government job in Washington. In just two years she was headed back to Europe, this time as social secretary to the American Ambassador to Italy, Clare Boothe Luce. (See *Roman Candle* above.) She returned to the United States in 1956 as the first female executive and director of public relations for Tiffany's. Although she started at Tiffany's with a bare desk and no job description, her enthusiasm, hard work, and imagination soon turned her life into a whirlwind of press releases, fashion shows, photographic sessions for magazine layouts, and public relations tours. Almost one-half of *Of Diamonds and Diplomats* is devoted to reminiscences of Letitia Baldrige's next job, as social secretary to First Lady Jacqueline Kennedy. From her White House office, Baldrige engineered all the details of the First Lady's public schedule including the minute planning of such memorable functions as the state dinner for the President of Pakistan at Mount Vernon, Pablo Casals' first cello performance in the United States since his self-imposed exile, and the White House dinner for all Nobel Prize Winners in the western hemisphere. She was also responsible for all the personal and social aspects of the Kennedys' official trips. In the summer of 1963 Letitia Baldrige headed her career in still another direction, moving to Chicago to become a consultant for the Merchandise Mart, the central market for the home furnishings industry. Within a few years she set up her own public relations firm, Letitia Baldrige Enterprises. Shortly afterwards, at about the age of forty, she married and settled into the career of business executive-wife-mother with the characteristic energy, enthusiasm, optimism, and success with which she had faced evey challenge in life.

Of Diamonds and Diplomats is a happy book by and about a

genuinely happy, talented,and successful woman. Its strength
lies in the narration; the few instances in which Baldrige attempts
to philosophize about or interpret events are shallow. In the
course of the narration, however, she illuminates important fringe
areas of government relations which traditionally have been relegated to political wives, often without acknowledging their importance—gracious thank-you notes, appropriate gifts for foreign
dignitaries and other guests, well-groomed appearances at official
ceremonies, cultural events, charitable functions, etc. *Of Diamonds and Diplomats* is not gossipy and reveals nothing deroga-
tory and little new about the famous people whom Letitia Baldrige
met in her varied and glamorous career.

Connie C. Eble
University of North Carolina—at Chapel Hill

Balsan, Consuelo Vanderbilt (1877-1964)

Socialite, Philanthropist

[23] *The Glitter and the Gold.* New York: Harper and Brothers, 1952. 336 pp.

The Glitter and the Gold is the story of Consuelo Vanderbilt
Balsan's fantastically privileged life, from her youth in New York
in the 1880's to her hurried escape for Lisbon in 1940. Great-
granddaughter of Cornelius Vanderbilt, and only daughter of
William D. and Alva Smith Vanderbilt, Consuelo was forced by
her strong-willed, ambitious mother to agree to a marriage of con-
venience with the 9th Duke of Marlborough. At the age of eighteen, Consuelo left the United States to assume the Dutchess of
Marlborough's duties at Blenheim Palace in England. After eleven
years of baronial splendor and lavish entertainment (and the birth
of two sons), Consuelo and Marlborough separated, and Consuelo
began to devote much time and energy to philanthropic activities.

Balsan was particulalry sensitive to the problems of women
and children, and championed activities that ranged from support

of prisoner's wives to women's education and chilren's care. Not as militant a feminist as her mother, who had become involved with the women's suffrage movement, Consuelo was nevertheless an extremely visible, successful supporter of charitable activities for English women. Her divorce from Marlborough was followed by marriage to Jacques Balsan, a French airman with whom she spent many happy years in France. During the 1930's, she and her husband combined philanthropic activities with an active social life. With the beginning of World War II, they were forced to leave France, and it is at this point that the author rather abruptly ends her autobiography.

Too much of Balsan's story consists of short descriptions of people she knew, places she saw, and events in which she participated; but though there are huge gaps in the commentary, and though the commentary itself tends to be amateurish, *The Glitter and the Gold* is a worthwhile document. For those who study the history of feminism and more particularly, for those who want to know more about women who have championed feminist causes, the book provides a rare look at an unusual woman.

Several themes are of interest to women's studies. First, there is the mother-daughter relationship. This theme (one that has been ignored as often as women writers and women of achievement have been ignored) is treated in a tentative way, yet is noteworthy precisely because it involves women and because the women were themselves influential. The theme of women's rights—rights to education, to work, to adequate care for their children, to humane working conditions—is seen from the vantage point of the society matron for whom ceremonial high society events are an insufficient *raison d'etre*. Radical feminism vs. moderate feminism is another theme alluded to by Balsan when she mentions her mother's feminist friends and their insistence on female self-sufficiency; but as always, one is left to wonder what Balsan felt the limits of feminism were, and how strongly she felt about the injustices she fought. Through all the book, the reader is forced to supply missing pieces, to substitute conjecture for fact, since Balsan rarely betrays her motives or her personal feelings. Balsan's memoirs do not make profound personal revelations, but provide instead occasional flashes of insight and a rather superficial, but engaging, view of her life. Since Consuelo Balsan was, however, a rare individual who combined wealth and title, American citizenship and a life

abroad, involvement in both high-society and feminist philanthropic activities, her autobiography has distinct historical value and
may be read, if not as a major contribution to autobiographical
literature, at least as a footnote that illuminates the history of
women.

Patricia Stringer
Emory University

Bankhead, Tallulah (1903-1968)

Actress

[24] *Tallulah: My Autobiography.*   New York: Harper &
Brothers, 1952. 335 pp.

During the peak of her career, Tallulah Bankhead was known
for her colorful personality—her throaty laugh, her love of the
New York Giants, her independent and freewheeling life style.
She called everyone "Dahling," making the expression such a
household word that it is still associated with her. Although an
actress by profession, she is perhaps best remembered as a personality.

Her autobiography begins with the declaration: "I loathe acting
. . .It is sheer drudgery." Yet she never considered doing anything
else: "I was born an actress." That statement sums up her theory
of acting—it is instinctive and requires no formal training. She
never had any, and, by her own admission, gave "no more thought
to my best roles than I have to my worst." Her story supports
this theory. Her prize for winning a screen magazine beauty contest at fifteen was a trip to New York, where she immediately
checked into the Algonquin Hotel and remained until she was
twenty, at which time she sailed for London, with no prospects
in sight. She quickly became the toast of the town and stayed
for eight years, "the happiest years of my life."

This bravado is all the more remarkable because of her family
background. The Bankheads of Alabama were conservative and

distinguished gentlefolk. Her grandfather was a United States
senator and her father a congressman. Tallulah's mother died
when she was three weeks old, and her father, in her words,
"couldn't cope" with Eugenia, her older sister, and herself, so the
two lived as "gypsies" for the first fifteen years of Tallulah's life.

Tallulah continued to live as a gypsy until 1943 when she
bought "Windows," her home in Connecticut. Her description of
the pleasure she derived from renovating this property, while com-
muting to New York and Hollywood for professional commitments, stands second only to that of her London experiences in
emotional warmth and vividness.

The reviews of Miss Bankhead's autobiography, which appeared
when she was forty-nine and still very much a public personality,
tend to cite its unabashed frankness. For example, "Witty, pug-
nacious, and uninhibited in every department" (Charles Rolo,
Atlantic, October, 1952, p. 92); "written in a sophisticated, con-
ceited, incredibly brash manner" (R. L. Blakesley, Chicago *Sunday
Tribune,* September 28, 1952, p. 3); "Tallulah pretty much knows
whom she doesn't like, and says so without footnotes" (Lewis
Nichols, New York *Times,* September 28, 1952, p. 6). If these
comments suggest that the author is malicious toward the people
she mentions, they are unjustified. Implicit and explicit throughout are her devotion to her family and closest friends, such as
Estelle Winwood, and her praise of actresses like Ethel Barrymore
and Katharine Hepburn. She assumes total blame for the failure
of her brief marriage to actor John Emerson, and is humble in her
admiration of Lilliam Hellman's talents—the only person she said
she hated. The main object of her uninhibited candor is herself.
She admits that she is insecure, impetuous, unintellectual; loves to
drink and gamble; always lives beyond her means; and has had
several affairs. She also admits that she has encouraged the image
of herself as a loudmouth rouee: "I attract disorder. I provoke
controversy."

In light of the biographies that have appeared since Miss Bankhead's death, the following critique seems most fitting: "*Tallulah,*
for all its entertainment value, does have some shortcomings as a
memoir. In life, as in her acting, she has not the capacity to verba-
lize or analyze her experience. This is no guided tour of the
works" (Lee Rogow, *Saturday Review,* September 27, 1952,

p. 11). Be that as it may, the book shows that Tallulah Bankhead was something we haven't seen the likes of since her spotlight faded.

Virginia Cox
University of Wisconsin—Oshkosh

Barrymore, Ethel (1897-1959)

Actress

[25] *Memories: An Autobiography.*   New York: Harper & Brothers, 1955. 310 pp.

"A rather disappointing account of a phenomenally rich and glittering life" (C. J. Rolo, *Atlantic,* June, 1955, p. 78). This is unfortunately an accurate appraisal of the autobiography of an actress revered as the "first lady of the American stage" during her lifetime.

One reads in vain for insights into the art to which Ethel Barrymore brought so much distinction, or for her views on such matters as what makes a play, or playwright, great—morally, artistically, technically or otherwise. Most disappointing of all, the book contains little information of a personal nature, about her famous brothers, Lionel and John, or about her own feelings, except for her love for her three children. The answer to her reticence may lie in this passing observation: "Such is the powerful and lingering influence of my grandmother, our deepest feelings are never to be disclosed. They are our own private affairs, never to be paraded in public. Strong emotions. . .may be hurled with gusto at an audience. . .but an author's invention we leave at the stage door."

In any event, the autobiography of Ethel Barrymore is bland. It consists, for the most part, of descriptions of the many roles she played, of the cities she most enjoyed when touring, and of her social life in London as a young woman—the many notable people she met, the garden parties and balls, and her nostalgia for those days without telephones and motor cars. Barrymore is unfailingly generous and kind about those whom she chooses to discuss, particularly Charles Frohman, the legendary Broadway producer who died on the *Lusitania,* and her ex-husband, Russell Colt.

The most interesting part of the book concerns her childhood. She grew up in Philadelphia in the home of her maternal grandmother, Mrs. John Drew, matriarch of one of America's most remarkable theatrical families. Barrymore's father and mother were usually away on tour, so she rarely saw them. She spoke sadly of never having known her mother, who died when Ethel Barrymore was fourteen. The greatest single influence on her life was her grandmother, known as "Mummum" to the young Ethel and her brothers.

The autobiography concludes with an account of the birthday party which the Academy of Motion Picture Arts and Sciences gave to honor her at the age of seventy. This life story of a gracious and gifted performer has more to offer to historians of the theater than to women's studies.

Virginia Cox
University of Wisconsin—Oshkosh

Bates, Daisy Gatson (1920-   )

Civil Rights Activist, Newspaper Publisher

[26] *The Long Shadow of Little Rock: A Memoir.* New York: David McKay Company, 1962. 234 pp.

In September of 1957 Little Rock's Central High School opened its doors to nine Black students in accordance with a long-term integration plan designed to meet the demands of the Supreme Court's 1954 decision outlawing segregation in public schools. As head of the Arkansas state NAACP, and a Little Rock resident, Daisy Bates led the efforts of Little Rock's Black community to make integration a reality. This book is the story of two tumultuous years during which Daisy Bates struggled against the racist attempts led by Arkansas' Governor Faubus to prevent the Black students from attending school. She led the organized support of the Black community for the school integration effort and provided continuing support and encouragement for the nine young women and men who each day faced physical and verbal assaults and insults from the mobs gathered outside the school and from many of their fellow students within. Every day after school the students gathered at the Bates home to discuss the events of the day, vent their anger and hurt, share strategies for survival, and reemphasize the knowledge that they were pioneers in a new stage of the civil rights struggle and that what they did was of importance to all Black people. Psychologists who analyzed the source of the students' strength gave great importance to their conviction that they were part of "something meaningful and historic." Daisy Bates' courage and support helped keep that conviction alive.

When Bates was a baby her mother was raped and murdered by three white men. The lethal combination of sex, racism and violence deeply impressed upon her the situation of a southern Black woman. As a child she fought, with the help of her adopted father, against an intense hatred of white people and a bitterness that threatened to immobilize her. It was a successful struggle that released great energy into the struggle for social justice. As a young co-publisher with her husband of the *State Press,* she fought against police brutality and supported CIO organizing efforts among workers at a cotton oil mill, an effort which earned her a brief jail stay. Bates' life is in the tradition of strong, activist women who give little attention to any of the disabilities that sex might be expected to impose. Her story is one of deep personal independence combined with a cooperative marriage that involved a working partnership in running a newspaper. Her commitment to social justice was such that she felt capable of endangering that newspaper even without consulting her husband if circumstances warranted. During the Little Rock integration struggle, friends and supporters kept her house under constant armed guard, and she carried a gun to protect herself once brandishing it in the faces of three teenage boys who threatened her in her car. Her strength and independence seem unself-conscious. Where she sees herself as unusual it is in being willing to take a front line position in the civil rights struggle but not as an exceptional woman. There is reward in this story of a woman who simply sees a job that needs doing and does it, facing the consequences as they occur.

The Long Shadow of Little Rock was reviewed favorably for its addition to the literature of the civil rights struggle. Cabell Phillips (New York Times, November 4, 1962, p. 3) hailed Bates as someone that future historians would name among the "martyrs and fearless pioneers," and John Howard Griffin (*Saturday Review,* October 27, 1962, p. 38) found the book a "masterful recreation of the Negro's side of the 'Southern Experience'."

Joyce Shaw Peterson
Florida International University

Baxter, Anne (1923-   )

Actress

[27] *Intermission.*   New York: G. P. Putnam's Sons, 1976. 384 pp.

Intermission is the story of actress Anne Baxter's four year struggle to build a marriage and a home in the Australian bush. The book begins with her decision to marry an American who is trying to tame the Australian wilderness and develop a cattle station 180 miles north of Sydney. She gives up her career, leaves the world she has known, moves over 8,000 miles, and starts to bake bread, tear up linoleum, paint walls and extract frogs from toilets. The book is interspersed with memories of Baxter's Hollywood career which add insight to her tough, determined personality.

Baxter writes vividly of her physical struggle to handle the hardships of a modern pioneer life and her emotional and intellectual struggles to handle the total separateness of the male and female worlds in Australia. Her insistence one Christmas that the husbands and wives eat dinner together both shocks the native Australians and angers her husband who accepts the prevailing social customs.

She clearly delineates her handling of daily chores, the births of two daughters, the frustration of missing her career, and the pressure of a pervading loneliness. She does have many satisfying victories in her housekeeping efforts, along with a developing appreciation for the beauty and "fiery challenge" of the bush. But there is also a growing realization that she cannot achieve any true communication as an equal with her husband. She must literally "overhear" the limits and expansions of her life. When her husband decides, without consulting her, to give up the Australian venture and buy an undeveloped ranch in New Mexico, the four year struggle ends. Baxter can no longer accept the position of having no influence over the direction of her own life.

Deborah Elliott (*Library Journal,* June 15, 1976, p. 1411) criticized Intermission as "nothing more than the trials and tribulations of an everyday housewife." However, Louise Bernikow in the New York *Times* (September 19, 1976, p. 22) enthusiastically reviewed the book and said Baxter had produced a beautifully balanced work: "Had she transformed the material into fiction, someone would have compared Anne Baxter to Doris Lessing. It is Lessing territory she covers, piercingly."

Diana Reep
Holy Redeemer College

Beach, Sylvia (1887-1962)

Bookseller, Publisher, Translator

[28] *Shakespeare and Company.* New York: Harcourt, Brace and Company, 1959. 230 pp.

Shakespeare and Company focuses on the years when Sylvia Beach owned and operated the bookshop which gave her reminiscences its title, especially the years when Anderson, Stein, Hemingway, Gide, Pound, Joyce frequented the shop. It is primarily an account of the people Beach knew and did business with and only secondarily an autobiography.

The first chapters speak of Beach's family, her early years, and mention that during World War I she was a volunteer farm hand in France and Red Cross worker in Belgrade. But the book has primarily two subjects: the American and French writers whom Beach knew in the 'twenties, and major adventures of her life—the publication of *Ulysses*. She had "Worshipped" Joyce before she met him. The title of the chapter in which she describes the circumstances of her offer to publish *Ulysses*, "Shakespeare to the Rescue," reflects her sense of satisfaction in the mission, and the heart of the work is the account of the dedication of her energies and resources throughout the 'twenties to Joyce and his "great book."

The remaining chapters are anticlimactic for those interested primarily in the literary figures of the 'twenties, but they continue the story of Sylvia Beach. During World War II she refused to return to the United States and shared the restrictions on the Jews imposed on her Jewish friends. After the Germans forced her to dismantle Shakespeare and Company, she served six months in an internment camp, then spent the rest of the Occupation in hiding, continuing to visit her friend Adrienne Monnier's bookshop secretly. The book ends with a brief reunion with Hemingway at the liberation of Paris.

Reviews of *Shakespeare and Company* were largely favorable, welcoming the new glimpses of Hemingway, Gide, Pound, and the new perspectives on Joyce as man and writer. Comments on Beach's manner of presentation were also mostly positive: "humorous," "generous," "fresh," "vivid," although there were a few that spoke of "naivete," "silliness" and "sentimentality."

Alice B. Toklas was, however, the only reviewer who identified the primary interest for a feminist, when she stated that the "two best and longest portraits are of herself [Sylvia Beach] and James Joyce" (*New Republic*, October 19, 1959, p. 24). For, in spite of the "modesty" and "self-effacing" quality of the account that critics noted, there is at least the outline of an individual, very different from a Zelda Fitzgerald or a Gertrude Stein, but clearly an individual. According to Toklas, Beach was a "classical American beauty," but she made no capital of it. As "an American girl. . . who had always been free to do what I pleased" (152), she chose to set up a bookshop—in Paris rather than her first choice, New York, because Paris rents and living were cheaper. Recognizing

Ulysses' worth, she undertook its publication as "an infinite pleasure" (201), "undeterred by lack of capital, experience, and all the other requisites of a publisher" (47). To know where her "infinite pleasure" lay and to pursue it places her in sharp contrast with so many "free" women of the twenties who had no idea what to do with their freedom. And the work invites a further feminist inquiry: to go beyond these reminiscenses for a fuller answer to the question posed by her opening chapter title: "for Who-is-silvier—."

Eleanor B. Mattes
Wilson College

Berg, Gertrude (1899-1966)

Actress, Playwright

[29] *Molly and Me.* New York: McGraw-Hill, 1961. 278 pp.

Written by a woman who warns us that she is "not the confessing type," and in any case has no great sins or disappointments to reveal, these memoirs tell the story of Gertrude Berg's happy youth and successful acting career.

The first half of her autobiography focuses on her childhood, with much attention given to her grandparents, Eastern European Jewish immigrants. They set the standards for the traditional, religious homelife which gave Berg a strong sense of security and a positive self-image. When she was seven, her parents became the owners of a summer resort in the Catskill Mountains in New York, where she became the unofficial social director. She was a close observer of the guests there and shows a tolerant attitude toward the different life-styles they chose, including that of a woman whose "extended family" included two lovers as well as a husband and three daughters. As a teenager she wrote and acted in dramatic skits and met her future husband, Lewis Berg, an engineer. She married at nineteen and was strongly supported by him in her attempts to write and act professionally.

Molly Goldberg, the character she created first on radio, then on Broadway in *Me and Molly,* and finally on television, was a strong woman with a sense of personal dignity, much like Berg's own mother and grandmother, who held the traditional role of housewife and mother. Berg celebrates the common sense, patience, and understanding that make her the central figure in the family structure. After playing for many years and seeing both her real and fictional children grow up, Berg starred with Sir Cedric Hardwicke in *A Majority of One,* playing the role of a Jewish widow.

F. H. Guidry (*Christian Science Monitor,* May 11, 1961, p. 813) questions the "synthetic liveliness" of parts of Berg's story, but commends her "good-humored acknowledgemnt of the foibles of humanity." R. T. Bresler (*Library Journal,* June 1, 1961, p. 2090) also points out the "minimizing of problems," but again concludes that Berg's "surehanded sympathetic pictures of her family and background" make an affecting story.

Naomi Leventhal
State University College—Fredonia

Bernstein, Aline (1882-1955)

Stage Designer

[30] *The Journey Down.* New York: Alfred A. Knopf, 1938.
        305 pp.

It is always interesting, and at times enlightening, to read an account of a love affair from the woman's point of view, particularly if the man has immortalized the relationship in a fictional rendition. Such seems to be the appeal of Aline Bernstein's account of her love affair with Thomas Wolfe.

In nine episodes, Bernstein's *The Journey Down* tells the story of the love affair of a beautiful, experienced woman of forty and a young struggling writer from the time of their meeting on board ship to her illness following his desertion. The novel captures,

almost heroically, the insecurities of a strong woman whose greatest weaknesses appear to be that she is too compassionate, too selfless, and all too human. "Don't leave me ever, stay with me, dearest, and love me forever," says the young writer early in the novel
(68). And this is exactly what she does, even strangely enough,
after he has left her! She, in essence, devotes herself entirely to
the needs, wants, and temperaments of a soon-to-be-but-not-quite
artist. As a woman more than familiar with the theater, she plays
her role on his stage, giving it everything that she has and trying to
make herself and him believe that it is more than enough.

Critical comments of *The Journey Down* vary with regard to its
author's writing style and narration (New York *Times,* February
20, 1938, p. 7; *Springfield Republican,* March 6, 1938, pp. 7-8).
Many agree, however, that the theme of the love of an older woman for a younger man has "come alive" in Bernstein's "moving
and poignant" account (*Books,* February 13, 1938, p. 2). And, as
Helen MacAfee perceptively points out, "it is the pattern of the
story as Mrs. Bernstein lays it out, the little details with which she
brightens it. . .that give it a special flavor" (*Theatre Arts Monthly,*
May 1938, p. 389).

[31] *An Actor's Daughter.* New York: Alfred A. Knopf, 1941.

Born in December 1882, the aughter of actor Joseph Frankau,
Aline Bernstein's childhood was a constant shuffle between back
stage dressing rooms and theatrical boarding houses, first one run
by her aunt and later one run by her mother. From this world of
actors, actresses, art collectors and the like, Bernstein recounts in
An Actor's Daughter how she learned what it meant to be a professional—the strength required to keep one's weaknesses from
interfering with one's work. "Blunder ahead with your own personal view," Robert Henri, her painting teacher, advised Bernstein.
"Everything," he observed, "depends on those who go on anyway"
(222). One senses that this philosophy permeates much of the life
and career of Bernstein who became a brilliantly successful stage
designer and one of the directors of the Neighborhood Playhouse.

An Actor's Daughter was received well as a "narrative which is
written with a swift, light touch, with dashes of bright color, and
a happy undaunted spirit" (*Springfield Republican,* February 5,

1941, p. 10). According to Drake de Kay, the author emphasizes "the vivid and often humorous evocation of character and incident" (New York *Times,* February 9, 1941), p. 5).

Deborah M. DiCroce
Tidewater Community College

Bogan, Louis (1897-1970)

Poet, Critic, Teacher

[32] *What the Woman Lived: Selected Letters of Louis Bogan, 1920-1970.* New York: Harcourt Brace Jovanovich, Inc. 402 pp.

Louis Bogan's letters document her public life as a lyric poet and critic, as well as her private efforts to turn these intellectual and aesthetic pursuits into a dependable livelihood for herself and her daughter Maidie. Bogan is reported to have been a cool and formal reader of her own verse, but for the friends addressed in these letters—Edmund Wilson, Rolphe Humphries, Theodore Roethke, Morton Zabel, Ruth Limmer (who is also editor of the volume)—she reserved wit, taste, and a wry self-effacement about both her achievement and her domestic situation.

She recounts details of her personal life—being widowed, divorced, a single parent, having lovers, enduring meager financial security, suffering emotional breakdown—without self-pity and without shame. Along with these shared confidences, Bogan speaks broadly about the American cultural situation: about American distrust of formal lyric verse, her dislike of categorization in the arts (she had a "horror at corresponding with lots of female songbirds"), the talent of her contemporaires, her duties as poetry reviewer for the *New Yorker.* W. H. Auden called her the "best critic of poetry in America," and his judgment was confirmed by other formal recognition. She was the recipient of a Guggenheim Fellowship in 1933, a Fellow in American Letters of the Library of Congress, a member of the Academy of American Poets, the

American Academy of Arts and Letters, the National Institute of
Arts and Letters, the Consultant in Poetry to the Library of Congress in 1945. Despite these high honors, she remained detached
from the New York literary scene, preferring reading, friendship,
constant work, private judgment of partisan politics. To Ruth
Limmer, Bogan once wrote, "But one experience must be seized
and passed on to you." What is "seized and passed on" in these
letters is clear, fierce and remarkable intelligence, and a life in
which art is never detached from responsibility.

Carol Shloss
Wesleyan University

Boulding, Elise (Biorn-Hansen) (1920-   )

Sociologist, Pacifist, Writer

[33] *Born Remembering.* Wallingford, Pennsylvania: Pendle
Hill, 1975. 30 pp.

"Solitude is the most beautiful condition of the human spirit."
With those words, Elise Boulding sums up her brief spiritual autobiography, the description of her conversion from a "life of for-
getfulness" to a "rebirth of remembering" her otherness at age
fifty-one. The first half of the work recalls her early life and education in New Jersey, her pacifistic but unreligious Norwegian
parents, volunteer social service in New York, her conversion to
Quakerism, her marriage and five children. As the years pass, she
becomes increasingly involved in the peace movement (helping
found the Women's International League for Peace and Freedom)
and in peace research (working in irenology studies at the university level).

But the conflict between suburban comforts and the Vietnam
War, between starving Indians and "spiritual" Quakers meetings,
precipitates her inner crisis, the real story of this work. She reads
the great mystical writers, makes a retreat at a Catholic monastery,
fasts, prays as she tries to work out her own spiritual needs. Finally, after more than a year of intense struggle, she resolves her crisis

by a decision to spend most of her time for a year working in her hermitage—a simple one-room cabin in the Rockies—where she can begin to translate what she has learned in solitude to a reaching out and fuller participation in society. Throughout, Boulding tries to reconcile her longings for the spiritual and physical structures of Catholicism with her belief in the unadorned individual forms and community of the Society of Friends.

Missing in this short work is an analysis of conflicts Boulding may have felt between career and family, or any discussion of the important sociological study she has done on women in developing countries.

The work might be useful in an examination of women's spiritual autobiography—treating works ranging from St. Theresa to Anne Morrow Lindbergh and Anne Fremantle.

Margaret McFadden-Gerber
Appalachian State University

Boulton, Laura (Craytor) (-   )

Ethnomusicologist, Educator, Lecturer

[34] *The Music Hunter: The Autobiography of a Career.* Garden City, New York: Doubleday & Co., 1969. 513 pp.

Boulton's title states the matter precisely; this work is not really the story of her life but rather the "autobiography of a career." In that sense the book is correctly catalogued—it is found in the ethnomusicology section, not with autobiography.

In 1929, Laura Boulton, then a vocal music student, joined her first expedition to Africa; in the thirty-five years after that she made twenty-eight expeditions to remote places, recording the traditional music of peoples, many of whom had never encountered a white woman nor a tape recorder. This book is a report of those extraordinary travels, as Boulton describes a variety of cultures, the sorts of music and musical instruments used, the similarities in both songs and instruments among diverse peoples, the difficulties she faced with her unsophisticated recording equipment, her meetings with famous religious and governmental leaders.

Boulton structures the book geographically and only roughly chronologically, dividing her story into sections on different areas of the world (Africa, The East, The Americas). She gradually becomes most interested in religious and liturgical music and sets out to record the music of all of the world's great religions, as well as many of the traditional tribal religions.

The book brims with anthropological detail. For women's studies students, the most interesting is probably Boulton's account of an *efundula,* the coming-of-age ceremony for young women of the Ovambo tribe of South West Africa. This ceremony lasts for many days and includes various dances, rituals, and ordeals. Remarkably, in one phase, the young women are symbolically changed into men. For several days they assume all the male prerogatives of the tribe, insulting, beating, degrading others especially the chosen husbands, venting all their pent-up resentment against males, in preparation for their life-long submission to their husbands.

One of the great collectors in ethnomusicology, Boulton has not chosen to reveal any of her inner motivations in this book. Of the impact of major historical events or of events in her personal life we have only tiny hints. Thus the book is less life-writing than chronicle or travelogue.

The Music Hunter was reviewed in musicology and anthropology journals, as well as in standard library reviews. General reviews were more favorable than the specialized ones. David McAllester, in the *American Anthropologist* (October 1969, pp. 1005-6), criticizes both Boulton's method and her theory, claiming that music is not a universal language to be seized and collected everywhere, but it is "inextricably bound to its culture at every point." He finds Boulton's language revealing of her method, as she speaks of "primitive music" and the "rounding up" of musicians.

Still, one cannot help admiring the dedication of Boulton in preserving these musical artifacts before transitor radios and

Western music had effectively contaminated all traditional music.

Margaret McFadden-Gerber
Appalachian State University

Bourke-White, Margaret (1906-1971)

Photojournalist, Author

B
B774

[35] *Portrait of Myself.* New York: Simon and Schuster, 1963.

Margaret Bourke-White spent her adult life making her child-hood dreams of "doing all the things that women never do" come true. Largely recounting her career, she describes the many assign-ments that were often dangerous and mostly considered unsuitable for a "lady photographer." Starting out as an industrial and ad-vertising photographer, Bourke-White became one of the best photojournalists in the world. In her work for *Life* and *Fortune* magazines, she perfected the genre of the photo essay, and those not familiar with her name will recognize her work. The auto-biography is illustrated with her best photos of the Dust Bowl, post-war Germany, Cleveland steel mills, the South of the share-cropper, the Nazi attack on the Kremlin, and India in violent transition. Bourke-White more than just recorded the crises of the mid-twentieth century, she learned from them and shows great insight and humanity when writing about them. The final chapters deal with Bourke-White's struggle against Parkinson's disease.

On a more personal level, Bourke-White discusses the "double standard" she encountered in her career and the roles that men and marriage played in her life. She writes of being "slapped down" by male competitors and constantly having to talk her way into photographing situations where men were automatically per-mitted. Bourke-White considered marriage to be a possible threat to her career, explaining that she needed an "inner tranqullity" since she had created an outer life of excitement and tension. (She had second husband Erskine Caldwell sign a marriage contract designed to help protect her inner peace.) Though thoroughly devoted to her career, Bourke-White says at the end of her book that had she had children, she could have shaped her work to them, drawing from them inspiration.

Portrait of Myself was widely reviewed and praised as a spirited and courageous account by a woman whose career and life had been just that. Only one reviewer was critical of "Maggie's" devotion to her career, calling her self-centered, agressive, and "deceptively feminine." (Homer Bigart, New York *Times,* July 7, 1963, p. 7) Reviewers generally liked her "simple, accurate, and breezy" style.

Margaret Moore Willen
Eastern New Mexico University

Bowen, Catherine Drinker (1897-1973)

Writer, Biographer

[36] *Family Portrait.* Boston: Little, Brown and Company, 1970. 302 pp.

Published after writing several biographies of musicians and of outstanding men as well as two books on biography, this book is Catherine Drinker Bowen's attempt to probe, in the people closest to her, some eternal human questions. Speaking little of herself but revealing much of the quality of her innermost being, she writes of the drive in men and women to develop their lives, of the influence of parents and siblings and the environment on their lives, and of old age and meeting death.

Bowen's narrative begins when at eight she becomes aware of her place as the youngest (four brothers and a sister) of the six children of the president of Lehigh University. Out of the diaries, journals, and letters of the family, and along with her own, she recreated the major events of a pattern of life that included: education at home and in private schools, summer months at a New Jersey beach house, the grand tour of Europe and the Orient with her parents and sister Ernesta, her marriage and two children;

then her divorce and her writing about long-lived successful men.

Between these events, she writes chapters about her relationship to her father (distant) and to her mother (intimately encouraged to develop her own essence); to her strong brothers, whom she emulated and who always urged her to excel as they did; to her sister, to whom this book is dedicated and for whom beauty was her fate; and to Aunt Cecilia, a portraitist, whom Catherine did not particularly like but who represented the image of a woman as artist.

Throughout this self-effacing narrative ("the Drinker reticence," p. 176), Bowen urges the full development of girls and women according to each one's "essence." The remark, "First of all we are women," is for Bowen a dangerous doctrine that implies a coy acceptance of captivity in a male-dominated environment. Through her focus on her brothers and Aunt Cecilia, she achieves objectivity in her exposition of the stress resulting from traditional male-female roles (pp. 6, 46-47, 60-61, 127-28, 145, 159, 162, 176, 229).

Marcia Davenport (New York *Times*, June 7, 1970, p. 6) calls the book an "autobiography only in periphery" but also designates it as Bowen's achievement of the goal her brothers insisted she strive for—parity with the masculine mind. While J. M. Carroll (*Library Journal*, June 1, 1970, p. 2138) notes Bowen's understatement in revealing the character of her family and herself, N. W. Ross (*Saturday Review*, June 13, 1970, pp. 31-32) claims it is clear that Bowen saw her work cut out to survive the curse, even in an intelligent and devoted family, of being born a female in a world dominated by males.

Charlotte S. McClure
Georgia State University

Boyle, Kay (1903-   )

Novelist, Short Story Writer

$\mathcal{B}$
Mll4ab.

[37] *Being Genuises Together 1920-1930.* New York: Double-
        day, 1968. 373 pp.

The original version of this book, by Robert McAlmon, published in 1938, is an account of an American writer and his expatriate friends in Paris. One of them, Kay Boyle, revised and
shortened the book in 1968, adding to McAlmon's text alternate
chapters of her own reminiscences. An important figure in the
literary revolt of the twenties, McAlmon published and supported
many avant garde writers before they became known. He is
entertaining except when reliving numerous drinking bouts, and
presenting his unflattering portraits of Joyce, Stein, and Hemingway which suggest envy of their fame. By contrast, Kay Boyle
writes more affectionately of these and lesser-known people of the
"lost generation." Her parts of *Being Genuises Together* are more
reflective than McAlmon's, more self-revealing, and more self-
critical.

In 1922, when she was nineteen, she left a secretarial job in
Cincinnati to go to New York, where she married a French engineer, Richard Brault. Her account of their impoverished life in
Le Havre is one of the most vivid sections of the book. In the mid-
twenties she wrote her first novel and fell in love with Ernest
Walsh, who edited a magazine for new writing called *This Quarter.*
When Walsh died, Boyle's grief for him was intense. She gives few
details about this experience, however, or about her decision to
leave her husband, or about her emotional life generally. She
joined a group which had formed around Raymond Duncan,
Isadora's brother, and ran one of his shops in Paris. As the book
ends, she is living with Lawrence Vail, a painter.

Mentioned throughout this autobiography is Kay Boyle's
mother, a creative and independent-thinking woman whose influence on her daughter's intellectual development was strong not
only in Boyle's youth but in later years as well.

Without romanticizing the artists and writers she knew in Paris,
Kay Boyle makes their frantic, bored, and disillusioned lives seem

appealing. They were intensely serious about their work: once when McAlmon mocked a poetry anthology Boyle was planning, she angrily threw a stein of beer at him. Her own unsettled life in the twenties she describes candidly. Of her concerns as a woman and as a woman writer she says little, but she does admit: "I had come to demand a great deal of women, and more of women writers than I was able to express" (169).

Reviewers liked the device of alternating chapters in *Being Genuises Together*. They judged Boyle a better writer than McAlmon but said more about him in their reviews. The last part of Mario Puzo's review epitomizes the condescending treatment male critics often give women writers. After praising Boyle's "feminine charm," Puzo adds: "To show how extraordinary Miss Boyle is, she even has a genuine liking for other women" (Chicago *Tribune Book World*, June 9, 1968, p. 3). Saul Maloff calls Kay Boyle "tender, deep going, rich and full of feeling and idealism" (*Newsweek*, July 8, 1968, p. 70).

[38]   *The Long Walk at San Francisco State.* New York: Grove Press, 1970. 150 pp.

The title of the longest essay in this collection alludes to the picket line of students and faculty at San Francisco State during the strike of 1968-69. Kay Boyle was on the faculty as a creative writing teacher. She tells a harrowing story of her experiences before and during the strike. With a novelist's sense of complexity and fondness for detail, she describes the clash between freedom and tyranny which she witnessed. Scenes of police brutality and invasion of the campus are neatly counterpointed to quotations from her students' poetry and anguished questions French and German students ask her when she meets with them during crises at their own universities. Boyle portrays S. I. Hayakawa as a blustering, despotic, and confused old man. She aptly calls the administrators and faculty who are unsympathetic to student demands "interchangeable men" (26). "Men" is a key word, for the breakdwon she chronicles is the breakdown of a male structure. "We were opposing a nation's fear," she concludes, "a fear that has brought us to the passing of ruthless judgments on our own children" (63).

While the moral fervor and sense of urgency of this essay make

it very different from *Being Genuises Together,* one statement
in the earlier work foreshadows Kay Boyle's intense commitment
to the San Francisco State strikers: a declaration that the America
she felt loyal to in her expatriate years was not the country
that executed Sacco and Vanzetti but creative, artistic America,
exemplified for her by William Carlos Williams, Ernest Walsh, and
her mother.

Reviewers called *The Long Walk at San Francisco State* an eloquent work, one which illustrates Boyle's versatility as a creative
writer.

Peg Cruikshank
G.N.E.S., San Francisco, CA

Braudy, Susan (-   )

Journalist

[39] *Between Marriage and Divorce.* New York: William Morrow and Co., 1975. 252 pp.

"We struggle and suffer to reconquer our solitude." Susan
Braudy chooses Albert Camus' words to preface *Between Marriage
and Divorce,* an account of her struggle to move from marriage—
and a lifelong assumption that female self-worth is dependent on
marriage—into a state of separate and strong individuality. Braudy
writes about trying "to reconquer. . .solitude" not in the sense of
attempting to deny the importance of relationships with others,
but in the sense of trying to recover a relationship with herself.
"Marrying was a way out," she writes, "a way to find an identity
for myself." Much of *Between Marriage and Divorce* examines
what happens when both she and her husband begin to find their
identities confined by their marriage, begin to outgrow the static
roles they've adopted with each other. Those roles are as tight as
skin, and when they begin to tear (as they must, when the growing
self pushes through), there is pain. Braudy captures that pain, and
the fear that accompanies it, vividly: "Sometimes I wake up in the
middle of the night in terror because I can't remember who I am
or which character in my dream I am supposed to identify with."

What carries Braudy's account beyond the territory marked out by her title is her insistent and probing honesty in examining both the background and present ramifications of her predicament: her sex-role stereotypical upbringing; her sexual guilt and ignorance; the passivity, learned early, that carries over into her professional life; her intense need for male approval; her late-found but invaluable recognition of the strength women can draw from each other.

V. K. Musmann in *Library Journal* praises Susan Braudy's "passionate candor" (October 15, 1973, p. 1912). Karen McGinley suggests that *Between Marriage and Divorce* "is only incidentally. . .about marriage and divorce," its major focus being the process of "taking stock and surviving both despite and because of the varied everyday horrors which disguise their true nature in the context of routine living" (*Best Sellers,* December 1975, p. 274). Alix Nelson faults Braudy's style and content, viewing the former as "heated, introspective, flat-footed," and the latter as too narrow (New York *Times,* November 9, 1975, pp. 24, 26). While serious and thoughtful, Nelson's review seems to me essentially wrong-headed. She overlooks, in her criticism of Braudy's style, the author's own direct discussion of the entries which "were overheated, but. . .represented my responses at the time." The reviewer's most serious misrepresentation, however, concerns the breadth and depth of subject matter covered in the journal. Far from restricting herself to an examination of "sexual infidelity and boredom," Braudy offers commentary on a wide range of subjects related to her emerging sense of self. The most resonant of these concerns her experiences on the male-dominated staff of *Newsweek;* her increasing experimentation with a more personal perspective in her journalism; her encounters with Jill Johnston, radical feminist and lesbian; and her exploration of an emotionally close, nonsexual relationship with a man. Alix Nelson's judgment about Susan Braudy's feminism is specious: Braudy does not represent herself as an ideal of feminist—if such exists. She does present herself, convincingly, as a woman who is involved in the process of learning to know and like herself. And her words invite us to share in that process: "I tell this story, my story, because its outline and emotional content are common ones. In the ordinariness of my own private fellings, I hope other women can see their own. We are unsurprisingly not alone."

Sharon Davie
University of Virginia

Brooks, Gwendolyn (1917-   )

Poet, Activist

[40]   *Report from Part One.*   Detroit: Broadside Press, 1972.
215 pp.

Report from Part One is not a neatly chronological narrative of
Gwendolyn Brook's life.   It begins with lengthy prefaces, one by
poet Don L. Lee, another by the critic George Kent, both of whom
concentrate on the political implications of being a Black American
Writer in the present.   Lee also notes in passing the problems of
being a Black American Female poet and insists that Brooks has
never fit the stereotype of the "Negro Lady Poet" that some would
wish her to be.   Though Brooks herself is not so explicitly political
as those two essayists, their themes are constantly recurring issues
throughout the *Report.*   As Toni Cade Bambara observed in her
review, (New York *Times,* January 7, 1973, p. 1) the *Report* "is
all of a piece and readable and memorable in unexpected ways.   It
documents the growth of Gwen Brooks."   Both Lee and Kent have
been her collaborators in that growth, and they sound themes
that motivated the autobiography.

Brooks begins her autobiography with an account of her childhood in a closeknit middle class family in Chicago.   She offers
loving portraits of her parents: her father's tender nursing care, her
mother's gift for amateur theatricals; and she tells much about her
extensive family relations: favorite aunts who taught her the
Charleston, sewed dresses for her, and sent her special treats.
Among the documents and family photographs, she even includes
an essay by her mother about Gwendolyn's childhood, letting her
mother say in her own words much that was important about their
relationship.   Throughout this portion of the *Report,* her characterization of family members bespeaks great affection but equal reserve and regard for the privacy of others, as when she leaves the
details of her children's lives for them to tell or when she deftly
alludes to the fact of her divorce after thirty years marriage.   She
treats her relations with other writers such as Margaret Danner,
Don L. Lee, Amiri Baraka, Dudley Randall, Sterling Brown with
similar tact.   Her *Report* is emphatically not confessional, though
it is unmistakably personal.

Of great interest to most readers is her account of discovering her Blackness. She begins the *Report* by remarking that she had no idea as a child that her color would ever be called beautiful and confesses in more than one passage that had she died at fifty, she would have died a Negro. She credits the change in her consciousness to her contact with younger writers, in classes, workshops and at one memorable conference in 1967 at Fisk University. That event she narrates in three different parts of the *Report,* each time with great humor and self irony, and each time revealing more about the process of developing political consciousness as a writer.

Closely linked to her increasing political awareness are the fragments on Africa included in the *Report.* Written as a travel journal, these pieces record her varying impressions of a journey to Africa, mainly Kenya and Tanzania, undertaken to discover for herself the meaning of being an Afro-American.

Throughout the *Report,* in narrative, interviews, and sketches, Brooks makes observations on her role as a writer. She explains that in her childhood she developed very early a conviction that she had to be a poet, and that conviction was nurtured by her mother who was convinced that she should be the "Lady Paul Lawrence Dunbar." She writes at length of the importance of writers' workshops, such as that established in Southside Chicago in 1941 by Inez Cunningham Stark, or those developed by Brooks herself with such unlikely groups as the Blackstone Rangers, a Southside Chicago street gang. She also insists throughout on the importance to writers of tangible public support through prizes, fellowships, and vehicles for publication. Herself the winner of the Yale Younger Poets Award, numerous honorary degrees, and a state poet laureateship, she emphasizes the effect of such reinforcement to writers. She also explains some of her efforts through the Broadside Press to make poetry more accessible to her reading public. Indeed, she discusses the possibilities of involving a non-reading public in the creation of poetry. In interviews in the *Report,* she admits that she can teach very little to poets. Indeed, she describes her role as a teacher with a kind of musing wonder at her success. Nevertheless, she has included for the use of her readers and other teachers of poetry an appendix of notes on her poems.

Though some reviewers were critical of her experiment in

assembling the *Report* in so anomalous a form, (rather than writing a chronological narrative of her life), and though others were disappointed at her reticence in treating her divorce and her personal friends, on the whole, reviewers responded positively to the theme of pride in her work—pride in being a woman, a writer, and an Afro-American in our time.

Kathleen Callaway
Florida International University

Buck, Pearl S. (1892-1973)

Novelist, Humanitarian

[41] *My Several Worlds: A Personal Record.* New York: The John Day Co., 1954. 407 pp.

Pearl Buck's *My Several Worlds* may not appeal to readers who like autobiographies to be personal in perspective, intimate in tone, and contemporary in subject. But, even though I usually seek those qualities, by the time I had finished Buck's narrative of her life, I had come to feel genuine warmth and deep respect for this woman of another generation, another world—indeed, as the title suggests, several other worlds. The writing is uneven, with some passages of remarkable vividness and others that are plodding and pedestrian. Yet Buck's book as a whole is powerful. She brings a sensitive and humane perspective—as well as an eye for color and an ear for sound—to her story: her childhood in the China of the 1890's and early 1900's; her growing, painful awareness after the Boxer Rebellion of the irrevocable split between her white and Asian worlds, her teaching career and involvement in the Chinese literary world in Nanking; her close escape from Communist soldiers in Nanking in 1927; the pains and pleasures of immigrating to her foreign homeland, the United States, in 1934. Her record of the next twenty years in this country never achieves the depth, the breadth, the resonance, of her depiction of her years in China. Her perspective here is that of a wondering outsider, yet one whose identification and concern with the United States as a nation is the more deep because of her early physical separation from it.

Above all during these years she tries to bring her two countries, her two worlds, together. She creates Welcome House, an adoption agency for American-Asian children; she supports the East/West Association, which sponsored Asian visitors to American communities; and she writes. *The Good Earth* (1931) was but one of the works cited by the committee that awarded Pearl Buck the Nobel Prize in 1938. Her biographies of her missionary mother and father, *The Exile* and *Fighting Angel: Portrait of a Soul*, received special mention. It seems likely that Buck received the Nobel Prize not so much for the "literary value" of her books, in the narrow sense of that phrase, as for the welding of extraordinary experiences and unusual insight that marked her life as well as her art.

My Several Worlds would be of particular interest to those students who wish to explore the experience of women in Asian countries; immigrant literature; or the female social novelist. An illuminating project in a women's studies course would be a comparison of Buck's autobiography with Maxine Hong Kingston's *The Woman Warrior*. These women bring widely differing perspectives to related experiences: the older American woman stresses her roots deep in China, its land, history, politics, literature, while the younger Chinese-American focuses on the rich but painful intersection of her American and Chinese identities. Buck's book, like Kingston's, emphasizes the difficult struggle for identity shared by women from vastly different cultures. In a book that frustrates with some of its omissions of purely personal details (about her marriages, for instance), Buck does discuss her personal isolation as a woman writer, both in China and America. None of the reviewers of *My Several Worlds*, writing in the fifties, mentions this stress on female experience. The reviews are very favorable, even those which mention the uneven quality of Buck's prose. Elizabeth Janeway praises Buck's "candor, simplicity, sincerity," and perceptively links the form and content of her autobiography to her work as a social novelist (New York *Times*, November 7, 1954, pp. 4, 32). Margaret Parton's review is equally sensitive and well-written, but stresses Buck's depiction of the "strange, dual world of the missionary child" (*The Saturday Review*, November 6, 1954, p. 17). Florence Haxton Bullock, writing in The New York *Herald Tribune*, is one of the few reviewers to stress Buck's comments on American culture—marriage, divorce, childrearing, the family, social service agencies (November 7, 1954, p. 18).

Biographies of Pearl Buck which discuss *My Several Worlds* or re-
tell its story include Irvin Block's *The Lives of Pearl Buck: A Tale
of China and America; Pearl Buck,* by Paul A. Doyle; Theodore F.
Harris's *Pearl S. Buck: A Biography;* and Celin V. Schoen's *Pearl
Buck: Famed American Author of Oriental Stories.* Buck's *A
Bridge for Passing* (1961) acts as a final chapter to *My Several
Worlds,* chronicling a physical journey to Japan and an emotional
journey back to herself after her second husband died. Fanny
Butcher's words in her review of Buck's *My Several Worlds* can
stand as a closing salute to that unusual book: 'It is not personal
in the sense of being outspokenly revealing. . .but [it is] surprisingly intimate in its revelation of man's relation to man" (Chicago
Sunday Tribune, November 7, 1954, p. 1). And I would add, of
woman's relation to woman, to man, and to her world.

Sharon Davie
University of Virginia

Burke, Billie (1886-1970)

Actress

[42] *With a Feather on My Nose.* New York: Appleton, Cen-
tury-Crofts, 1949. 272 pp.

[43] *With Powder on My Nose.* New York: Coward-McCann,
1959. 249 pp.

Anyone who has seen *The Wizard of Oz* will remember Glinda,
the lovely but slightly daffy Good Fairy. Few people, however,
remember that Billie Burke, who played Glinda, was once a celebrated stage ingenue, first in London and then in New York.

Christened Mary William Ethelbert Appleton Burke, she was the
daughter of Billie Burke, an internationally acclaimed clown with
Barnum and Bailey's circus for many years. She assumed her
father's name when she began her acting career. At the height of
her popularity on Broadway, she married Florenz Ziegfield, against

the advice of almost everyone, including her mother, the biggest influence on her life, and Charles Frohman, the "Great Ziegfield's" fellow entrepreneur. As Burke put it: "I chose my husband over my career." Much of her first volume of memoirs concerns her marriage to the fabled showman, whose reputation as a ladies' man proved well deserved. After the Wall Street crash of 1929 ruined Ziegfield, Miss Burke resumed her career, this time in Hollywood. She soon became type-cast: "And so I began to do my silly women . . .birdwitted ladies."

Burke's personality, as revealed in her autobiographies, bears no resemblance to these silly, birdwitted characters. Her philosophical interjections both delight and surprise. On fame: "Don't envy people who get their names in lights. . . . They just worry about how to keep it shining." On stage mothers: "Someone ought to do a piece of scholarly research on the number of girls who have become stage and movie stars because their mothers pushed them." On herself: "Some fantastic things have happened to me. . .but I might as well face it. Even today I am the clining vine type. I'm not an enterprising woman. I *enjoy* clinging."

With Powder on My Nose, although interspersed with personal anecdotes, is more a "how to" book for women, written, according to the author, to correct the problem of "a revolt among women themselves *against being women.*" It contains advice on infidelity ("act as if you don't know what's going on"); personal grooming (slip out of bed before "he" awakens and spruce up); being an "MIL" (mothers-in-law should be seldom seen and almost never heard); learning to manage money (she never did, until after her husband died, leaving enormous debts); remarriage (do it only for love, never out of desperation); becoming an actress (it's hard work); and similar matters. The book clearly shows that Burke held "old-fashioned" values, but they were born of the tough-minded realization that hers was a man's world. Because men could get away with being vain and self-centered, women were forced to learn how to keep marriage and family together. Being female may be hard work, she suggests, but it has its rewards: "Some of the happiest, most worthwhile women in the world are spinsters—Old Maids. They can be the best friends boys, girls, young men, ever have. They fulfill themselves as mothers. It is impossible for an old bachelor to feel like a father."

Neither autobiography received what could be called critical acclaim, but the reviews were polite and favorable.

Virginia Cox
University of Wisconsin—Oshkosh

Cain, Lynn (c.1929-   )

Publicist

[44] *Widow: The Personal Crisis of a Widow in America.* New York: Morrow, 1974. 223 pp.

Caine's autobiography covers a period of less than five years, from the first suspicion of her husband's illness through the fourteen months of his dying and the emotional chaos which followed. She speaks openly of the inadequacy she felt as a single mother, financial fears (although she held a well-paying job), sexual frustration, and the danger of becoming a "professional widow." In a fine analysis of grief, Caine emphasizes that the emotion which the widow experiences is a healing process whose inevitable stages (numbness, "craziness," denial, anger) can be prepared for by the reader. She offers practical advice based on her own mistakes: how to write a will, make financial and funeral arrangements in advance, and prepare children to deal with the trauma of death (talk about it). Since one of every six American women over twenty-one is a widow, Caine's purpose seems to be to help other women survive, rather than succumb.

A few reviewers see *Widow* as a how-to-do-it book. However, others like Walter Clemons (*Newsweek,* June 10, 1974, pp. 90, 93) praise Caine's honesty and candor: "[She] is particularly eloquent on the dangerous feelings neither partner allowed to surface during . . .the final months." Eugene L. Linehan, S. J., writing in *Best Sellers* (July 15, 1974, pp. 182-83), seems to miss the whole point, suggesting that the book should serve as a reminder of the Biblical injunction to "take care of widows." By far the most thoughtful and encompassing review comes from Annie Gottlieb in the New York *Times* (June 9, 1974, p. 7), who focuses on Caine's real message, "a strong incitement to women—single, married, divorced or widowed—to make lives and identities for themselves."

Joanne McCarthy
Tacoma Community College

Calisher, Hortense (1911-   )

Author, Teacher

[45] *Herself.* New York: Arbor House Publishing Co., 1972. 401 pp.

Hortense Calisher's autobiography, termed "an account of a life in progress," is written with all the brio of her celebrated fictional style: experimental in form, but always lucid. Among other things, the book encompasses a narrative of her early life, reflections on faculty living, and a critical analysis of male homosexual writers, shifting from one subject to the next, and from first person to third without loss of cohesion. Calisher observes a refreshing rectitude about her personal affairs with the self imposed rule: "Except for where it appertains to the work, keep your private life out of it" (121); but she does not withhold relevant information, including a private journal written for her lover on her travels for the State Department in the Far East. She is unembarrassed by an awareness of fashion; she is observant of clothes, jewelry and fine cars without attaching undue importance to any of them.

In her communications on male-female problem areas, Calisher does not tolerate what she perceives as foolishness in either sex, stating that "women who complain of injustices done to them as women are not in reality angry at the different or inequitous treatment of women but at the difference *between* men and women— which of course is ineradicable" (362). At the same time, she impales male values and the demanding restrictions placed on women:

As artists, women can also. . .be made to feel that the honesty of their work is impugned by their effect as women

—particularly if it's a good one; dare they have beauty, style or the vanities approved as womanly, or must they bloomerize. Historically. . .men and women have dressed to show the fashion of their convictions; after which women usually get the credit for the fashion, and men for the convictions. (363)

In her somewhat unusual position as "a woman artist with a family and a conventional family setup," she is amusedly aware of the unconscious conformity of nonconformists who have, she says, "the same failure to distinguish the inner and outer ways of life" as do the bourgeoisie. And she flatly states "anything monosexual to me is a bore" (365).

Of particular interest to women's studies is Part IV, "Pushing Around The Pantheon," where she presents a thoughtful consideration of American women writers. She insists the position of the writer is that of androgynous artist (357-58) recognizing at the same time that American society supports the concept of the so-called "ingrainedly feminine-masculine" characteristics of the intellect. Speaking of the women who would not be confined in "sensibility writing," she says "they are not going to be trapped into speaking for women only. . .and in this, like any artist who avoids category, they are right. . . . [The woman artist] knows her own capacity for the universal and will not have it contaminated by the particular—if the particular is feminine." Calisher regrets that in order to avoid categorizing, early women writers "had belittled their experience, or hunted in male terms" (377). Her own solution is clearly set forth in her balanced, polished style: "What would enlarge me as a writer is what would enlarge any woman, any man, any one—the right to do and be, without scorn or sneer" (393).

Sue F. Law
Old Dominion University

Carrighar, Sally (-   )

Writer, Naturalist

[46] *Home to the Wilderness.*   Boston: Houghton Mifflin,
        1973. 330 pp.

Dominating this story of the childhood and early years of
Sally Carrighar is the character of her mother. The author's birth
was a difficult one, in which forceps were used and her mother's
coccyx broken. A result of this was apparently a lifelong psychotic
reaction to the child Sally by the mother. The true relationship
between the mother and the daughter was revealed to Sally
through psychoanalysis after an attempted suicide when she was
in her thirties. The father was a gentle and sympathetic man who
simply was not around to see what was happening; but Sally was
not without help from many older friends whom she calls "proxy
parents." her early ambition was to be a concert pianist, but she
did not have the physical stamina for such a pursuit. Her two years
at Wellesley were marked by illness, which eventually forced her to
give up college. She drifted to Hollywood, where she worked in a
movie studio and had a chance at being a professional dancer,
which her mother refused to allow. She went to San Francisco
where she worked at a variety of depressing journalistic jobs.
Finally she found her salvation in writing about animals and living
close to them. The book ends with the publication of *One Day
on Beetle Rock* (1944).

The importance of this autobiography for women's studies lies
in its fascinating revelation of the mother-daughter relationship.
Carrighar illustrates the book with a few photos, including one of
her mother taken before the daughter's birth when, according to a
friend, "She would never again be so beautiful" (10). While not
dwelling on it, Carrighar suggests that vanity about her good looks
was involved in her mother's trauma. Among the many tortures
inflicted on her by her mother was a distrust in her own sexuality,
but the author was able to free herself from this problem. Even so,
she never was able to feel comfortable "trapped" in a human relationship, as she explains when telling about an eight-year-affair
from which she withdrew. The mother-daughter theme is most
touchingly illustrated in a scene that Carrighar views of a confrontation on a street car in which a daughter argues viciously

with her mother. At that moment Carrighar decides that she will never risk having a daughter of her own (179).

Beverly Seaton
Ohio State University—Newark

Carroll, Gladys Hasty (1904-   )

Author

[47] *To Remember Forever.* Boston: Little Brown and Company, 1963. 306 pp.

To Remember Forever is subtitled *The Journal of a College Girl 1922-1923* and is gleaned from the author's writings—a journal, letters, and college newspaper articles—of her sophomore year at Bates College in Maine. There is no attempt to be retrospective, only to capture the emotions and experiences she went through at nineteen. The book covers her rural home life, her unexpectedly early scholastic successes at college, and her responses to a variety of situations. There is a scarlet fever epidemic, for example, during which for a week she is completely isolated to avoid catching the disease. And there is her growing awareness of the development of her mother's individuality after the deaths of a grandfather and a strong willed aunt leave her mother in charge of her own household. Throughout the journal, however, it is clear that Gladys Hasty's dual goals are family security and literary success. As members of her own family die, she replaces them emotionally with members of her college family, and ultimately with her fiancé; but she does not change her desire to emulate the success of another Maine woman, Sarah Orne Jewett.

Gladys Hasty's Maine heritage made her independent and confident. She felt Bates women had always influenced their husbands and their students. "We intend to do that," she wrote in August, 1922, "but we shall be active in politics too, and in civic improvement of all kinds. Those of us who don't marry can give our whole lives to public service." Her account of 1922-1923 provides an accurate picture of a Maine college girl of the day, but also portrays those elements in Gladys Hasty which eventually enable her to write successfully about Maine people in numerous novels and histories.

[48] *Years Away From Home.* Boston: Little, Brown and Company, 1972. 373 pp.

Although the first seventy pages of this book cover much the same material as *To Remember Forever,* Carroll's intention is to show the controlling influences of home on her life. The remainder of *Years Away From Home* traces her development as a writer from the first rejection slips in the mid-1920's to the success of her novel, *As the Earth Turns,* in 1933.

Of particular interest to women's studies is the account of Carroll's unsuccessful attempt to publish realistic girls' stories in the late 1920's. She wrote to an editor that "girls under ten will read about dispositions and treasures if that's all that is put before them. . .girls over that—intelligent girls—won't." He agreed with her, but a girls' page for *Household Magazine* which included book reviews was the most the time would allow. She decided to leave the juvenile field because there were no outlets "for what I wanted to say to and about young girls and the feelings and thoughts I knew they had." The result was a novel not so much about "a girl who had both head and heart and used them," as about a breed of folk the author knew well—the Yankee farmers of home.

Kathy Lynn Emerson
Wilton, Maine

Carson, Rachel (1907-1964)

Biologist, Ecologist, Writer

[49] Brooks, Paul. *The House of Life: Rachel Carson at Work; with Selections from her Writings, Published and Unpublished.* Boston: Houghton Mifflin Company,

1972. 350 pp.

Forty percent of this biography is composed of Rachel Carson's published and unpublished letters and writings, producing a semblance of an autobiography of the very private person that was Rachel Carson. Paul Brooks has arranged alternate chapters of narrative about her life, drawn from her letters and from reminiscences about her by friends and co-workers, with chapters consisting of excerpts from her books and articles. This arrangement reveals in Carson's own words much of her intense feeling for all human beings' relationship to the living world around them. The major episodes and influences of her life included: her mother's early encouragement to be aware of the beauty and mystery of the natural world; the influences of her women college professors who helped her to merge her imagination and insight as a creative writer with a scientist's passion for fact; her support of her mother and two nieces; her conflict on a federal job between making a living and the desire to write; her books and articles on the natural world that preceded *Silent Spring* (1962); her handling of adverse criticism developing from the controversy over pesticides; her mothering an orphan nephew; and her fatal illness.

House of Life presents Carson as a paradoxically shy, assertive, modest, successful woman. She nurtured her parents and relatives and enjoyed friendships with men and women (pp. 321-22), but showed little interest in cooking and indoor activities. She celebrated life reverently and scientifically, and viewed it wholly without reference to male/female roles.

Even in 1972 with ecology and environmentalism prominent, *House of Life* received but little attention. David McCord in *Saturday Review* (March 25, 1972, pp. 108-109) noted Carson's paradoxical personality and her "stunning germinal stream of letters flowing down the years." Edward Weeks (*Atlantic,* April 1972, p. 124 noted the "admirable but guarded account" of Carson's life with emphasis on her "accumulating force as a writer and conservationist." The New York *Times Book Review* (April 30, 1972, p. 30) and the *Library Journal* (April 1, 1972, p. 1313) emphasized the book's message on conservation more than its autobiographical elements.

Charlotte S. McClure
George State University

Chapelle, Dickey (c.1919-   )

Photographer, Journalist, Author

[50] *What's A Woman Doing Here?* New York: William Morrow and Company, 1962. 285 pp.

From a skinny kid who loved airplanes to a veteran war correspondent, Dickey Chapelle traces her life through wars and revolution. Already a seasoned air show writer and photographer before Pearl Harbor, Chapelle parlayed a photographic assignment to "cover what women were doing in the Pacific" into front-line reporting of the assaults of Iwo Jima and Okinawa. Here insistence on going "as far forward as you'll let me" led her into the alternately hurried and bored world of combat soldiers. After World War II, Chapelle joined her husband in covering the refugees of Europe from Poland to Iran for the American Friends Service Committee and other humanitarian agencies.

About a third of the book deals with her fifty-two days of captivity in Hungary, having been caught while reporting the smuggling of pneumonia-preventing penicillin to Hungarians about to flee to Austria during the Hungarian Revolt. The most touching portion of *What's a Woman Doing Here?* dwells on the last two weeks of her confinement spent in a cell with eight other women— the "Murderess" gently dressing each woman's hair, the gentle "serat lak" I-love-you kisses from her cellmates on Chapelle's release day. Chapelle additionally photographed Algerians fighting French rule, she landed with the U.S. Marines in Lebanon, and she crossed the Santiago golf course no-mans'-land to report on Castro two years before he finally succeeded in his overthrow of the Batista regime.

Reviews were generally positive although not enthusiastic. For example, the *Library Journal* (May 15, 1962) observed, "This fast-paced book, though not distinguished for its writing, will interest girls who are looking for the sort of adventure usually reserved for men."

Marie R. Oesting
Baraboo, Wisconsin

Chase, Mary Ellen (1887-1973)

Novelist, Biblical Commentator, Biographer, Essayist, Teacher

[51] *A Goodly Heritage.* New York: Henry Holt, 1932. 298 pp.

A Goodly Heritage recounts Mary Ellen Chase's early years in Maine. The title, chapter headings and prologue all establish that the focus is on social influences rather than inner feelings, and Chase states that her autobiography is valuable because it describes typically American rather than exceptional experiences. It opens with accounts of her mother's and father's family and other relatives, family chores, parties, pets. These are followed by descriptions of the three traditions—the Puritan, the seafaring, the classics-based educational—which developed the strength of character, the breadth of vision, the intellectual discipline Chase views as "a goodly heritage." The emphasis throughout is on ideas, ideals, influences of other minds. She states: "Even the love affairs of the academy were promoted and fostered by interests intellectual as well as social" (270). In the chapter on life at the University of Maine the five other freshman girls and fraternity house parties are merely mentioned; only the teachers are individualized. Although Chase notes in the epilogue that "experience is its own end and goal," she also emphasizes the "process of brain-building by which we are, each of us, what we are" (295).

[52] *A Goodly Fellowship.* New York: Macmillan, 1939. 305 pp.

A Goodly Fellowship has a similar focus on ideas and ideals. It is "the story of a life spent in teaching" (xi), in a one-room school in Maine, a progressive boarding school in Wisconsin, a fashionable school for girls in Chicago, a public school in Montana, then at the University and the College of St. Catherine in Minnesota, and at Smith College. The dramatic highlights are encounters with pupils, teachers, academic employers. "Life in Montana" indicates that Chase went there because she had tuberculosis and did recover; but there is little mention of her feelings in fighting what was then an often fatal disease. Instead the chapter focuses on what she read and wrote, on the principal and the pupils of the school in which she taught. She states that at twenty-eight she "was far younger than most of that age" (179), but only to explain why she wrote children's stories rather than the novel she hoped to write. Nowhere does the work mention close friendships with fellow students or colleagues, although Chase had these, especially at Smith. The warm expressions of affection and appreciation are for her teachers and administrators: they are the memorable characterizations. And the autobiography closes, not with Chase's own conclusions, but with William Allan Neilson's final address as President of Smith College, in which he in turn is quoting from Matthew Arnold.

[53] *The White Gate.* New York: W. W. Norton, 1954. 185 pp.

The White Gate, published twenty-two years after *A Goodly Heritage,* deals with the period of Chase's childhood and many of the same people and places described in that earlier book. There is, on the one hand, more concern with inner experience: accounts of epiphanies, and of a recurrent dream of emptiness, abandonement, aloneness and ultimate nothingness. But these are carefully alternated with character sketches of aunts, uncles and other relatives and descriptions of routine rural chores like cleaning lanterns. So this work reads more like a volume of essays than an autobiography.

Reviews of both *A Goodly Heritage* and *A Goodly Fellowship* were favorable but included no penetrating analyses. *A Goodly Heritage* was termed "reminiscences of a New England girlhood" in the *Saturday Review;* and it was commended for preserving "the nicest New England innate modesty" in *Commonweal. A Goodly Fellowship,* on the other hand, was praised for being "refreshingly honest" (*Saturday Review*). Perry Westbrook draws repeatedly on Chase's autobiographical works for material to illustrate the points he would make about her literary achievements and chhracteristics (*Mary Ellen Chase,* New York: Twayne, 1965). He observes that her autobiographical works belong in the twentieth century Humanist tradition identified with her fellow women novelists Cather, Glasgow, and Fisher.

The feminist finds in them a different significance. She sees

A Goodly Fellowship as revealing the characteristics of the woman teacher-scholar of the 'twenties through the 'forties who provided the model for the many students whom she influenced, some now themselves senior teacher-scholars, with the strengths and limitations they inherited. To enumerate these characteristics: 1) Chase without questioning accepts men and women writers and scholars as equals. Cather is her example of the author who best ties the moderns and the ancients in American literature, and she cites a woman as the outstanding student in their graduate seminar on the novel. 2) But she also accepts the existent discrimination in the educational system. She enjoyed being one of the first women students to enter the University of Maine, but she left the University of Minnesota because she saw that its attitude toward the promotion of women would prevent her from reaching the top of her profession, as she could at Smith College. 3) She is proud of her independence, writing of her "desire to complete my experience in a position which. . .should also allow me to feel that I had reached the goal set for myself by myself" (286). 4) She makes much of ideas, little of emotions and cultivates impersonality, merely mentioning a "chimerical love affair" of her adolescence (34) and having nothing to say about the deep affection for men and women (other than teachers) which she is known to have experienced.

A Goodly Fellowship is therefore important for feminists and women's studies both for what it has to say and what it leaves unsaid. It reveals an influential and representative teacher-scholar of her time, who gave her students the confidence that women were the equals of men, but also implicitly led them to accept the status quo of discrimination and to move into only those avenues of advancement that were open. She encouraged them to cultivate rather than to question independence and impersonality—both antithetical to the concept of sisterhood. Finally, she taught them to assume that "we are, each of us, what we are," primarily because of the process of "brain-building." *A Goodly Fellowship* is an important key to our understanding of the ideas and ideals that many older scholars today, feminists included, were taught to value.

Eleanor B. Mattes
Wilson College

Chicago, Judy (1939-   )

Artist, Feminist, Educator

[54]   *Through the Flower: My Struggle as a Woman Artist.*
New York: Doubleday, 1975. 226 pp.

In documenting her struggle as a woman artist, Judy Chicago
has also documented the formation of a feminist art community;
the feminist heritage in art and literature; and development of her
own open marriage. Growing up in a family of political radicals
seems to set the stage for the change Chicago later undergoes,
from woman artist to feminist artist. Her radicalization comes
about after a series of painful encounters in the academic and professional art establishments, encounters after which she is obliged
to suppress expression of her femaleness in her art.

Chicago comes to realize that her accomodation is self-defeating, and that to break out of her schizophrenic artist-woman role,
she must develop a woman's art community, a community concerned with not only the making of female art, complete with
female imagery and female crafting, but the teaching, selling,
distributing, criticizing, and historical study of women's art by
women. As she describes the development of this feminist community, Chicago's autobiography becomes a history of Woman-
house and the Woman's Building in Los Angeles, and the women's
art studies programs at Fresno State College and at the California
Institute of the Arts. (A result of research into the feminist heritage, one entire chapter is devoted to a survey of women artists
and writers.)   The autobiography ends with the spring of 1974
and the recording of a breakthrough in her art. At last able to express those once suppressed images and thereby express her values
and attitudes, Chicago feels that she is now able to affect society.
In this way, all women, she says, can move "through the flower"
to heal the "great gulf between masculine and feminine."

Through the Flower aroused emotionally charged criticism
among reviewers. Feminists hailed it as "remarkable and original
autobiography" with great social implications (Adrienne Rich,
Partisan Review, Winter, 1975, p. 156); others found fault in its
expression and showed open hostility to its ideas. Christopher
Lehmann-Haupt labels the prose insensitive in this "autobiography

manifesto" (New York *Times,* March 10, 1975, p. 27); while Lucy R. Lippard found the tone of alternating effusiveness and "curious deadpan brevity" to be peculiarly female and a writing break-through (*Ms.,* August 1975, p. 42). Reviewers' sympathies were most evident as they reacted to Chicago's self-conscious and psychoanalytic analyses of her own work. Vivien Raynor expressed disgust and spoke of "soggy-core porn" (*The New Leader,* May 26, 1975, p. 27); but Lippard praised Chicago's imagery, finding a glowing symbolism.

Margaret Moore Willen
Eastern New Mexico University

Chisholm, Shirley (1924-   )

Politician, Educator

[55] *Unbought and Unbossed.*   Boston: Houghton Mifflin Company, 1970. 177 pp.

328. 73
C5412 u

Unbought and Unbossed begins with Shirley Chisholm's impressions of her early childhood in Barbados living with Grandmother Seale and of her later childhood in Brooklyn after being reunited with her parents. It is to the experiences of these years that Chisholm attributes many of the qualities that guided her later life: the exercise of strong self-discipline, the belief in hard work, excellence as a student, and a sense of black pride and responsibility.

While a student at Brooklyn College during the mid-1940's Chisholm received the first encouragement to enter politics. But this option was deferred for serveral years while she successfully pursued a career as an educator. Chisholm discusses frankly the factors that led to her becoming the first Black woman from Brooklyn to serve in the New York State Assembly and the first Black woman to be elected to the U.S. Congress. From this point on, Shirley Chisholm has attracted much attention because she has refused to accept many of the norms of the House of Representatives and of the prevailing political climate.

In *Unbought and Unbossed* Chisholm explains her views about the shortcomings and possibilities of the Congress, featuring the issues which are of particular importance to her. She outlines her opposition to the war in Vietnam, and discusses her ideas about responsive government, as well as some difficult questions regarding abortion, the role of black politicians, and women's movement; and the utilization of America's youth.

[56] *The Good Fight.* New York: Harper and Row, 1973. 206 pp.

The Good Fight is a reflection of another phase of Shirley Chisholm's career as a public figure: her development and achievements as she sought the Democratic Party's presidential nomination in 1972. Candor is paramount in this brutally honest analysis —even when the candor results in the revelation of a disorganized Chisholm campaign, sexist attitudes on the part of Black leaders of national importance, and hypocrisy in the ranks of McGovern's liberal staff.

Students of women and politics will find this book particularly interesting not only for what it tells about the political system and both the first woman and the first Black to seek the U.S. Presidency, but also for what it reveals about the role of organized women's groups (from traditional church groups to radical feminist groups) in coalition politics.

Almost without exception, the reviews of *Unbought and Unbossed* and *The Good Fight* make mention of the straightforward, candid, and idealistic approach with which Shirley Chisholm analyzes the current political system and her role in it (*Kirkus,* August 1, 1970, p. 835). The view of the author which emerges is that of an honest, effective, intelligent, gutsy, fascinating, Black woman (Patricia Schuman, *Library Journal,* November 15, 1970, p. 3901).

Clearly the Shirley Chisholm of *Unbought and Unbossed* uses her position in the Congress to deliver needed benefits to her constituents in the 12th Congressional District in Brooklyn and, where possible, to her two national constituencies—Blacks and women (Elizabeth Kolmer, *Catholic World,* February 1971, p. 203). The purpose of her presidential candidacy, as explained in *The Good*

Fight, was to "shed light on political campaigns" and to "shake up and help eliminate the status quo" (Janet Price, *Library Journal,* September 15, 1974, p. 2307). Thus she hoped "to prepare the way for some future woman, black or white, who might conceivably win the Presidency" (*Publishers Weekly,* April 9, 1973, p. 59).

Criticisms of *Unbought and Unbossed* focus on its simple, uncomplicated writing style resembling that of a "school primer" (New York *Times,* November 1, 1970, p. 22). The strongest attack comes from Barbara Mahone McBain who describes Chisholm as being "confused" about some fundamental issues: whether she has suffered greater discrimination as a black or as a woman, whether legal abortion is in reality an attempt to reduce or extinguish black population growth, and others. Because of this "confusion," McBain generally rejects the favorable evaluation of Shirley Chisholm, the person, found in most other reviews (*Black World,* August, 1971, pp. 84-86).

The Good Fight is praised as an "honest" (New York *Times,* October 21, 1973, p. 20) even "blunt memoir" (Norman Lederer, *Best Sellers,* July 15, 1973, p. 175) of Shirley Chisholm's campaign for the democratic Party presidential nomination, written with "direction and wit" (Janet Price, *Library Journal,* September 15, 1974, p. 2307). The last third of *The Good Fight,* where Chisholm "focuses pragmatically upon the failure of the McGovern campaign and the role of minorities in politics," is viewed as perhaps the most valuable contribution of the book (*Library Journal,* May 15, 1973, p. 1588).

Janelle L. McCammon
Washington, D.C.

Cirile, Marie (-   )

Police Officer

[57] *Detective Marie Cirile: Memoirs of a Police Officer.* Garden City, New York: Doubleday and Company, 1975.

222 pp.

Detective Marie Cirile is a detailed description of almost twenty years as a New York City police officer. The book opens in 1973, while Cirile is on sick leave, confined to her apartment. With nothing else to do, she shares with us her reasons for becoming a police officer and her adventures in a series of flashbacks through her career.

In recruit training school in the 1950's where "women were tolerated or worse yet treated as pets," Cirile fights to learn self defense, judo and all that men are taught. Through sheer force of will she learns more than most women were permitted. Upon graduation she was automatically assigned to the policewomen's bureau.

As Cirile began her career, the work allowed to her was "bascially the same as the 1890's:" Matron duty or the strip searching and guarding of all female prisoners; guarding female prisoners detained in hospitals; guarding female material witnesses; operating lost children's centers; full dress uniform assignments at public functions; (more a PR stint than police work); and finally, searching the bodies of "dead-on-arrivals" to remove things for safe keeping. Soon after Cirile's start, work at the women's bureau was widened under the leadership of a particularly forceful woman and opportunities for accomplishment increased. Cirile's experience included the gypsy squad; the Broadway Squad; Special assignments; the degenerate squad; the pickpocket and confidence squad. After almost eight years Cirile obtained her Detective shield. The book also explores having and raising two children while holding a demanding position, and describes in detail her disintegrating marriage.

Cirile's enthusiasm, her ambition, her unceasing eagerness to do her job well, and her lack of bitterness at the way women officers were treated during the 50's and 60's make the book a worthwhile, candid discussion of the vocation of policeofficer for women. Her story is particularly appropriate for younger women exploring vocational alternatives.

Michele Slung's review in *Ms.* magazine (April 1976, pp. 45-47) was neutral: "the breezy and extroverted Marie Cirile has concocted an autobiographical police memoir that is liberally sprinkled with hard boiled pizza. . . .This is not a terribly introspective or analytic book, although Cirile has strongly held opinions and is consistently vocal on the subject of equal responsibility for women cops." And, "Detective Marie Cirile minces no words as she describes the demands and satisfactions of the cases she has worked on" (*Library Journal,* May 15, 1975, p. 1003).

Jean B. Palmer
Stoneham Public Library, Stoneham, Mass.

Clark, Eugenie (1922-   )

Marine Biologist

[58] *Lady with a Spear.*   New York: Harper & Brothers, 1953. 243 pp.

An informal but scientifically accurate memoir of the author's adventures in pursuit of knowledge, *Lady with a Spear* narrates the experiences of a "typical American girl" participating in an atypical occupation—deep sea diving and classifying fish, especially poisonous ones. In a series of chronologically ordered anecdotes, set in the matrix of her accurate observations about fish, Clark discusses: the influence of her devoted Japanese mother; supportive college professors; her decision to work for a Ph.D. in zoology; incidents of prejudice against ancestry and her sex; her brushes with danger; the cooperation of government officials and natives in areas in the South Pacific and the Red Sea. Her childhood curiosity about fish in aquariums evolved into a serious study of evolution, focusing on the reproductive behavior of fishes and the sexual isolating mechanism of certain fish that prevents hybridization. Her line drawings of fish and of spearfishing equipment enhance her descriptions of them. Her success as an ichthyologist was marked by assignments with the Navy, various marine laboratories, and a Fulbright scholarship.

Reviewers recognized Clark's motivation to write informally for a popular reading audience. Two reviewers, both divers, praise her

nontechnical but accurate volume (Gilbert Klingel, New York
Times, July 19, 1953, p. 3) and "her warm, live, and informative
account (John S. Douglas, *Saturday Review,* July 25, 1953, p. 10).
Douglas misses in her book the weird color of the undersea world
of Cousteau and the high adventure expressed in books by other
divers.

[59] *Lady and the Sharks.* New York: Harper & Row, 1969.
269 pp.

Beginning where *Lady with a Spear* ended, Clark adds twelve
more years to her memoir of a marine biologist. During the years
from 1955 to 1966, she develops and manages the Cape Haze
Marine Laboratory near Sarasota, Florida, directing basic research
projects on sharks and fish while raising four small children. Here
she emphasizes her curiosity about a symbiotic relationship between human beings and fish (250). She stresses the interaction
and the cooperation needed to avoid pollution of the environment. Severing her managerial ties with the Laboratory in 1966,
and ending her marriage, Clark began a somewhat new life (256),
teaching ichthyology at the Univeristy of Maryland.

Clark's vision of the world is holistic and synergistic: all crea-
tures come in different sorts and within the species a particular
creature has individuality and character. Her attitude in managing
her own life at first made her doubt that she could provide to the
Cape Haze Laboratory the necessary direction to make it useful
and respected. The book demonstrates how she worked out her
vision with the assistance of many people.

This sequel to *Lady with a Spear* attracted fewer reviews, but
the book's scientific accuracy and readability, its drama and
humor, were praised (*Choice,* 1970, p. 1774; *Publisher's Weekly,*
August 18, 1969, p. 73). Daniel M. Sims (*Library Journal,* September 15, 1969, p. 3077) points out the way that children fit into
the world of the marine laboratory as a mainstay of the story.
Mary Richie, herself a participant in whale study expeditions,
admires the unsensational tone with which Clark recounts the
shark-training experiments that captured worldwide attention and
the author's wondering and yearning to understand how everything in a given creature actually works (Washington *Post Book*

World, November 23, 1969, p. 4).

Charlotte S. McClure
Georgia State University

Clifton, Lucille (1936-   )

Poet, Author of Children's Books

[60] *Generations: A Memoir.*   New York: Random House, 1976. 79 pp.

Like a poem or a song or a folk tale—and it has affinities with all of these—*Generations* contains certain significant refrains that are repeated again and again.   None is more significant than "Get what you want, you from Dahomey women," spoken by her great-great-grandmother.   For Lucille Clifton's *Generations* is about identity, and about freedom, and how the two are intertwined. "Slavery was a temporary thing, mostly we was free," Clifton's mother tells her.   And Clifton tells us—in prose that is often poetry, in written words that capture the cadence of living, spoken language—that that freedom was rooted in a self-respect which grew out of deeply-felt connections to a line of strong female forebears stretching back to the Dahomey women in Africa. These forebears are not distant to Clifton: her great-great-grandmother Caroline Donald Sale, Dahomey woman from Africa sold into slavery, raised Lucille Clifton's grandfather and then her father, passing down stories to him that he passed on to her about

The woman called Caroline Donald Sale
born free in Africa in 1822
died free in America in 1910

Lucille Clifton weaves *Generations* like a tapestry out of the facts, legends, the lives that she grew up hearing about; and those lives she had known firsthand, her "magic-wisdom" Mama and her "story-teller Daddy."   Despite her closeness to them, Clifton never sentimentalizes the lives she recreates for us. We hear about the pain the family members share, and cause each other. And Mama's assertion that "mostly we was free" is balanced by Daddy's words about slavery as he struggles to comprehend that Mammy Ca'line's husband was a wedding present to someone: "It ain't something in a book, Lue. Even the good parts was awful." Yet the final thrust of *Generations* is not to mourn injustice and pain, but to celebrate the maintenance of identity despite them: "Things don't fall apart. Things hold. Lines connect in thin ways that last and last and lives become generations made out of pictures and words just kept."

Generations is illuminating as a work of Black female history, of autobiography, and as background for those who read the fine poetry of Lucille Clifton. It would add depth to the reading list of a course in autobiography as a genre, twentieth-century women authors, or Black writers; and would be relevant to a program in American studies or women's studies.

The reviews of *Generations* were consistently favorable. M. H. Murphy is typical in lauding Clifton's "moving and vibrant" portrait of "strong dynamic characters" (*Library Journal,* March 15, 1976, p. 805). An unsigned review in *The New Yorker* stresses the suggestive, evocative nature of the "spare, fluid, lyrical" prose: "like the handful of blurred, cracked photographs that accompany the text, the book frequently suggests more than it tells" (April 5, 1976, p. 138). Reynolds Price wishes that the "gaps" in the stories were filled in, yet praises Clifton's "lyrical rapture," her "power to touch and move," which he links to a long tradition of black oratory (The New York *Times,* March 14, 1976, p. 7). None of the reviewers stress Lucille Clifton herself as the underlying focus of the work, however, and I think she is. For *Generations* is ultimately about Black female identity, about Lucille Clifton's identity, about what made Clifton who she is: a poet, a woman with vision, a woman who is strong enough to translate that vision into language we can share.

Sharon Davie
University of Virginia

Cochran, Jacqueline (c.1910-   )

Aviator, Business Executive

[61]   *The Stars at Noon.*   Boston: Little, Brown and Company, 1954. 272 pp.

Jacqueline Cochran's autobiography is a rags to riches story. Told with husband Floyd Odlum as "wingman," it describes her impoverished childhood in the South and her rise from a Georgia cotton mill community at age eight to owning a large cosmetic firm and being chosen Business Woman of the Year. Her real passion, however, has been flying. She has set distance, altitude, and speed records (first woman to break the sound barrier) and has made many contributions to aviation by experimenting with new aerodynamic equipment. She organized and directed the Women's Airforce Service Pilots (WASP) in World War II and traveled widely, meeting and speaking her mind to VIP's from the Pope to Mao Tse-tung. With appealing ingenuousness, Cochran portrays herself as a woman who "without special advantages" did anything she set her mind to. While she is grateful to those who helped her and is acutely aware of sexism in the military and in aviation, her basic message is that with energy, determination, and faith in God, anyone can be successful.

When *The Stars at Noon* was published, Cochran was a national celebrity. *Atlantic Monthly, Vogue,* and *Life* carried excerpts from the book. *Atlantic Monthly's* cover (October, 1954) featured her climbing into her airplane. One note of criticism was Lucy B. Johnson's complaint (*Saturday Review,* November 6, 1954, p. 18) that Cochran is "quick to feel resentment at anyone who, accidentally or on purpose, holds her back in any way." Paradoxically, Johnson was the only reviewer to mention the prejudice Cochran battled in her efforts to organize women pilots during the war.

Nancy Manahan
Napa College

Cooper, Anna Julia (1859-1964)

Educator, Community Activist, Author

[62] *A Voice from the South: By a Black Woman of the South.* Xenia, Ohio: The Aldine Printing House, 1892. 304 pp.

After graduating from Oberlin College in 1884 and receiving an honorary master's degree from that institution in 1887, Anna Julia Cooper moved to Washington, D.C. to begin her teaching career in the District of Columbia Public Schools which lasted more than forty years. Shortly after her arrival in Washington, D.C., she published *A Voice from the South, By a Black Woman of the South,* her major work.

Cooper, as an early advocate of women's equality, made several significant observations concerning women: first, Black women could make important contributions to the uplift of the race. Second, Black progress depended on the full utilization of the skills and reasoning of educated women. Third, education was important in improving women's status in American society. Fourth, women as well as men should have an opportunity for higher education. She denounced the view that education would automatically "unsex" women. Cooper felt that it was essential for females to articulate their views and not have males speaking for them. It was her belief that men would never be able to accurately describe the needs and concerns of women. She criticized those educated Black men who lacked an awareness of the true condition of women.

In *A Voice,* she referred to the unique experiences of Black women who faced the double burden of sexism and racism and cited several instances in which she and other Black women were discriminated against by whites, both males and females. She discussed the roles Black women played in both the women's struggles and the Black race's movements which went virtually unnoticed. For example, she mentioned her own attendance at the 1891 National Women's Council meeting held in Washington, D.C.

Although it was written in 1892, *A Voice* deals with many of the concerns of present-day feminists: the need for women to speak for themselves and to fulfill their own desires and goals in life. Cooper implored females to stop suppressing their aspirations and goals merely to make themselves more pleasing to males.

Segments of several favorable reviews are included in Monore A. Major's *Noted Negro Women: Their Triumphs and Activities* (1893, pp. 284-287). Of particular interest is a critique from the Chicago *Inter-Ocean* which stated that "It is not often that the question here raised has been discussed more candidly, more earnestly and intellegently, and in a better spirit than in the volume before us." The authors of *The College of Life; or, Practical Self-Educator, A Manual of Self-Improvement for the Colored Race* (1895, p. 101) referred to Cooper's book as probably the best book "ever written by a colored *man* on his race."

Sharon Harley
University of the District of Columbia

Cornell, Katharine (1893-1974)

Actress, Actress-Manager

[63] *I Wanted To Be An Actress.* New York: Random House, 1939. 379 pp.

Written at the height of her career, this narrative by Katharine Cornell, as told to Ruth Woodbury Sedgwick, is less a memoir than a discursive account of the growth of an actress.

Cornell devotes the first pages of her book to her family's involvement in the theatre, a tradition passed on through the male line. Her grandfather, a friend of John Drew, was reputed to be a gifted amateur actor and director; her father gave up his medical practice to enter professional show business as a theatre manager in Buffalo. Although the men in Cornell's family introduced her to the theatre, it was the actress, Maude Adams, starring in the magical *Peter Pan,* who stimulated her earliest inclinations to devoter her life to the stage. The book traces her career beginning with minor roles in productions by the Washington Square Players in New York and in the summer stock company of Jesse Bonstelle, an actress-manager. Bonstelle was one of Cornell's most important teachers and, undoubtedly, a role model as well. Despite her father's lack of confidence in his daughter's seriousness and ability, Cornell eventually attracted critical attention for her portrayal of Sydney in *A Bill of Divorcement* (1921). She finally achieved fame for her role as Iris March in *The Green Hat* (1924). It was during her tour with Bonstelle that Cornelle came to know the young director, Guthrie McClintic, whom she later married against the adivce of her father and of Bonstelle. Contrary to their negative expectations, Cornell describes her marriage as a successful and creative union. In 1931, Cornell and McClintic formed their own company—she as actress-manager, and he as director and producer. They made their debut with Besier's *The Barretts of Wimpole Street* in which Cornell played Elizabeth Barrett Browning, the frail poetess constrained by her overbearing and possessive father.

Throughout the book Cornell discusses her values concerning the theatre. Disliking the "star" system, she regards her art as a craft, and the play as a collective venture. This egalitarian spirit is reflected in the events which she selects as highlights of her career: e.g., the benefit performance for Chicago school teachers during the Depression and her transcontinental tour of 1933-1934 when she played 77 cities. Written simply, almost humbly, though with minimal introspection, Cornell's autobiography gives the reader glimpses of the emotional investment required of an actress. It is evident that she valued her work as essential to her life. Indeed, when Cornell speaks of her marriage, it is in the context of her work; she observes that success in marriage is as important to a woman as success in her profession.

As one might expect, *I Wanted To Be An Actress* was reviewed generally in terms of its significance for those interested in the theatre. One should note the stereotypical attitudes toward actresses and celebrated women implicit in the following critiques: Mina Curtiss of *The Nation* (May 6, 1939, p. 537) observes that Cornell expresses "none of the 'stylized exhibitionism' typical of so many of even the greatest actresses," and *Time* (April 3, 1939, p. 23) comments that the actress is "virtually all smiles. About nothing, about no one, is she pert, meddlesome, unexpected. Compared to the First Lady of Broadway, The First Lady of the Land Eleanor Roosevelt is six days a week, a purveyor of shuddersome scandals."

Sharon Friedman
Temple University

Crawford, Joan (1908-1977)

Movie Actress

[64] *A Portrait of Joan: The Autobiography of Joan Crawford.* Garden City, New York: Doubleday, 1962. 239 pp.

Joan Crawford was spotted in a New York chorus line at seventeen and invited to go to Hollywood for a screen test. She had no dramatic training and, for that matter, no acting ambitions. She was young, flightly, insecure, and loved to dance. But inept as she may have been at the beginning of her career, she listened carefully to criticism and worked hard to overcome her deficiencies, which included an Oklahoma accent and her name, Billie Cassin.

She was born Lucille LeSueur in Texas, but her father left the family when she was six weeks old. Her mother moved to Oklahoma, where she married Henry Cassin, from whom Lucille acquired her second name. This stepfather eventually disappeared too, and the family fell on hard times. Along with her mother and older brother, Lucille/Billie struggled to support the family by working in a laundry—scrubbing clothes, ironing, and at the same time tried to keep up her studies in convent school. The diligence and self-discipline she learned during these years never left her. Nor did her sense of intellectual inferiority or her consuming desire for a family of her own ever leave her. She divorced her first husband, Douglas Fairbanks, Jr., because she outgrew him—he loved endless rounds of parties while she preferred quiet evenings at home reading and discussing books. She married her second husband, Franchot Tone, because of his cultured intellect. After their divorce, and unable to bear children, she adopted a boy and a girl. After divorcing her third husband, Phillip Terry, she adopted twins. This was in 1945, the year she won an Academy Award for *Mildred Pierce*.

In *A Portrait of Joan,* Crawford described her professional struggles, such as fighting for her release from studio contracts to secure good roles; her friendship with crews and co-stars like Clark Gable, Spencer Tracy and Robert Montgomery; and her awe of actresses like Katharine Hepburn, Greta Garbo and Judy Garland. She obviously approached her career seriously and worked hard at it. But above all, she took motherhood seriously. The most impassioned parts of the book deal with her emotions for her children: "Can you imagine what it meant to me to be surrounded by four warm young lives? To come home to their confidence and love, their chorus of 'Hi Mummie—dearest!'. . .Four little faces, changing daily as they responded to each new filament and fragment of living. Four pairs of hands reaching to clasp mine. They changed my life, these children, gave me a whole new world."

The book concludes with an account of her very happy fourth marriage, to Alfred Steele, president of the Pepsi-Cola Company. Athough his death meant a deep loss for her, she was able to recover because of the positive philosophy of life she developed down through the years: "Essentially I'm interested in the future . . . . Tomorrow is my destination. I'll wake to it as I wake to each new day of my life, with this prayer, 'Thank you, God, for this lovely day. What can I contribute to it?' "

My Way of Life, although based on personal experiences, is more of a book of advice for women (on beauty care, entertaining, wardrobe, and the like) than an autobiography.

Neither book received serious critical attention.

Virginia Cox
University of Wisconsin—Oshkosh

Davenport, Marcia (1903-   )

Novelist, Biographer

[65]   *Too Strong for Fantasy.*   New York: Charles Scribner's
Sons, 1967.   483 pp.

Tracing her life chronologically, Marcia Davenport begins *Too
Strong for Fantasy* with a sketch of the immigrant family of her
mother, Alma Gluck, and the history of her mother's early career
as a singer.   Through the book she continues to explore her mother's character and their closeness to each other and to discuss
the world of music and musicians, showing special homage to
Arturo Toscanini.   From her childhood, sometimes joyous and
sometimes lonely, Davenport developed her capacities for solitude
and for literature.   She began writing for a living after the early
break-up of a teenage marriage left her with a child to support.
She emphasizes the partnership roles in her second marriage, to
Russell Davenport, and the intensity of her later love for Jan
Masaryk.   In connection with these men, she discusses political
matters, such as the campaign of Wendell Willkie and Communism
in Czechoslovakia.   A number of literary figures appear, including
her editor, Maxwell Perkins, and her friend Marjorie Kinnan Rawlings.   And she discusses the processes of her own writing, her
biography of Mozart and some of her novels.

As the title suggests, *Too Strong for Fantasy* surveys a vivid
life through a record that strives for truth.   One feminist concern
which Davenport takes up (without that label for it) is the conflict
which can arise in a mother betwen self-expression and devotion
to children's needs.   She sums up her mother's veiw (62) and her
own (134, 160, 306-308) and illustrates the practices of both in
part.   Her comments on settings and people who were transmuted
into her fiction note that reviewers sometimes read in parallels
which were invalid.   Some topics which she develops recurrently
are the need for ambition, thoughts on aging, the importance to
her of retrospective recall and solitary selfhood, her responses to
music, to literature, and to cherished places: houses and cities—
European and American.

With an occasional objection to her emotional passages, reviewers praised Davenport's skill at characterizing the many note-

worthy people whose lives she shared. A few commented on the oddity of her failure to discuss her daughters; for example, Ellen Moers observed that "puzzling over what Mrs. Davenport did with her children after they were born can add zest to the very few dull stretches of her autobiography" (New York *Times,* October 22, 1967, p. 4). And a few others were critical of her treatment of history and of political events with which she was closely associated, especially the controversial death of her beloved Jan Masaryk in Czechoslovakia in 1948 during the Communist's struggle for domination. Arthur Dareck liked her "resonance and glow" when she wrote of her mother, Toscanini, and Maxwell Perkins; and Darack notes that "one can understand and sympathize with Mrs. Davenport's anti-communism, but," he believes, "her autobiography is marred by it" (*Saturday Review,* November 25, 1967).

Of particular interest to women's studies is Elizabeth Janeway's treatment of Davenport's autobiography (*Harper's,* November 1967, p. 120) with that of Edith Sitwell and the biographies of Isak Dinesen and Svetlana Alliluyeva. Under the title, "More Tragic than the Male," Janeway observes:

> These women have lived and worked in the great world as much as any man has. They are all able, all capable of decision and action. They have fought to be responsible for themselves; and yet not one of them has controlled her own life in the way that men of equal talent expect to do. When they acted, it was out of necessity. The decisions they made resolved dilemmas instead of being arrived at by free choice. Not one of them made a "successful" marriage, though each loved one man deeply and passionately. All of them outlived their lovers, two of whom died violently. There is very little humor and much tragedy in these books, and above all a sense of struggle.

Carolyn H. Rhodes
Old Dominion University

Davis, Angela (1944-   )

Activist

[66] *With My Mind on Freedom: An Autobiography.* New
         York: Bantam Books, 1975. 399 pp.

In the Preface to her book, Angela Davis writes: "I was not
anxious to write this book. . .I felt that such a book might end
up obscuring the most essential fact: the forces that have made my
life what it is are the very same forces that have shaped and mis-
shaped the lives of millions of my people. . .I was also unwilling to
render my life as a personal 'adventure'—as though there were a
'real' person separate and apart from the political person." Remarkably, Davis has managed to render a personal view of her
developing commitment to a political cause, and whether or not
she wants to admit it, this process is exactly what makes her unlike most Black women in America. Her political commitment demands that she deny the importance of her individuality, but
readers can easily discover the unusual quality of her life in spite
of her depersonalized narrative style.

She was not a typical Southern Black child in a typical Southern
Black family. Her mother, a teacher, had worked on the Scottsboro case in the thirties; her family was the first to move into a
White Birmingham neighborhood which later became known as
Dynamite Hill; her family frequently had communist friends,
some of whom helped to arrange for Angela's escape from the
provincial South to New York's Elizabeth Irwin High School.

It was at Elizabeth Irwin that Angela first read the *Communist
Manifesto:* "I read it avidly, finding in it answers to many of the
seemingly unanswerable dilemmas which had plagued me. . .like
an expert surgeon, this document cut away cataracts from my
eyes. The eyes heavy with hatred on Dynamite Hill, the roar of
explosives, the fear, the hidden guns, the weeping Black woman
at our door, the children without lunches, the schoolyard bloodshed,. . .the back of the bus, police searches—it all fell into place.
What had seemed a personal hatred of me, an inexplicable refusal
of Southern whites to confront their own emotions, and a stubborn willingness of Blacks to acquiesce became the inevitable consequences of a ruthless system which kept itself alive and well by

encouraging spite, competition, and oppression of one group by another. Profit was the word: the cold and constant motive for the behavior, the contempt and the despair I had seen." Although this statement seems to describe a completed conversion, there were many years of intervening experience before Davis paid her first fifty cents dues to join a Black Communist Party unit in Los Angeles.

Her interest in Marxism led to her interest in philosophy, which she studied as an undergraduate at Brandeis and a graduate student at the University of Frankfurt. Her description of these years suggests a sense of displacement. She excels in her studies, has educational opportunities unavailable to most Americans, but is continually troubled by the fact that she has somehow escaped her lot. Returning to America in the late 1960's, she experienced with hundreds of other Americans the erosion of her intellectual life, and like hundreds of others, she attempted to combine her intellectual life with political activism. Her denial of self in the narrative of this book has much to do with the shock of being thrust so quickly into the headlines of history. She had not aimed for heroism, but for a more meaningful connection between her thoughts and actions. she was simply not prepared for the burden of leadership in the eye of the storm called political revolution.

She was also not prepared to go to jail. The opening chapter, "Nets," describes the shock that any middle-class American woman would experience were she suddenly jailed. In this chapter, as throughout the book, Davis is relentless in her attacks against racism and capitalism. Her rhetoric sometimes becomes only that, especially when she allows it to dominate her recollections of childhood and adolescence. But in jail for the first time, the rhetoric is overpowered by her physical and psychological responses to imprisonment—the stench, the confinement, the reduction of all humanizing factors of ordinary life, and the shock that she is there. After "Nets," she writes of her childhood ("Rocks"), her college years ("Waters"), the development of her political activities from 1967 ("Flames")—the year many Americans remember as the long, hot summer, the months of prison and difficult litigation ("Walls"), and finally her legal victory and her attempt to continue her work against racism and for what she believes is the greater good for all Americans ("Bridges").

What we see throughout the book is a clear picture of the ways in which her intellect controls her outrage over social injustice, channeling her emotional energies into political organization. She avoids sullen immobility, cynicism, and madness by attempting to find constructive uses for her energy. Although she is often shocked by her experience, the general organization of the book reflects Davis's guarded optimism.

Reviewers have criticized the book for being political propaganda, and for presenting an impersonal self-portrait. As Elinor Langer said, writing this book "was not an act of self-discovery: it was an act of political communication" (New York *Times,* October 27, 1975, p. 5). The book offers descriptive detail about radical Black politics in the late 60's, but it also is an intense portrayal of political commitment in a woman of unusual strength and will.

Mary Louise Briscoe
University of Pittsburgh

Day, Doris (1924-   )

Movie Actress, Singer

[67] *Doris Day: Her Own Story.* New York: Bantam Books, 1976. 362 pp.

Doris Day wrote her autobiography because she wanted to correct her image as "Miss Goody Two-shoes," America's freckle-faced virgin, with a song in her heart, a smile on her lips and a glass of buttermilk in her hand.

She gained this reputation through her highly successful thirty-year career, beginning as a singer with big bands like Bob Crosby and the Bobcats and Les Brown's Band of Renown and continuing through a series of movies with co-stars like Rock Hudson, James Garner and Cary Grant.

The public image grew out of this career, but Day never sought

success. It came, it seems, in spite of her efforts, not because of
them. Her dream, from the time she was little Doris Kappelhoff
growing up in Cincinnati, Ohio was simply to be a huasfrau, surrounded by home, hearth, and husband. But this was not to be.
Her story is one of betrayal by men.

When she was eleven, her father had an affair with her mother's
best friend, and her mother divorced him. When Doris was seventeen, she married Al Jorden, a musician who turned out to be a
sadistic psychopath. Although she remained with him only until
the birth of her son, the scars were permanent. At nineteen she
married again, this time to George Weidler, another musician,
with whom she moved to Los Angeles to settle down. But he left
her after eight months because of male ego. As he explained to
her: "You're going to be a star and I'm never going to be anything
more than just a side man in a band." Day's third marriage, to
Marty Melcher for seventeen years, ended with his death, at which
time she learned that he had lost in foolish investments the millions she had earned, leaving her without assets.

Day sued the attorney who had advised her husband and won a
landmark decision of nearly $23,000,000, the highest amount
ever awarded in a civil suit in California history. But the question
of Melcher's motives remains unanswered.

After being a devout Christian Scientist for many years, Day
began to question its beliefs and develop a personal religion, which
eventually led her to leave the church. "Que Sera, Sera," a song
for which she is famous, summed up her philosophy and apparently sustained her during the many long nights of despair when the
Miss Goody Two-shoes image didn't fit.

One reviewer called Doris Day's story "candid, and at times
moving" (*The Booklist*, January 15, 1976, p. 660), but another
said: "The basic facts are few and unexciting" (Donald McCor-
mich, *Library Journal*, February 15, 1976, p. 632). John Updike's
comments were by far the most perceptive. In comparing the
actress to the late Errol Flynn, who played her husband in an early
movie, he said: "Both brought to the corniest screen moment a
gallant and guileless delight in being themselves, a faint air of
excess, a skillful insouciance that, in those giant still dreams projected across our Saturday nights, hinted at how, if we were

angels, we would behave." ("Susy Creamcheese Speaks," *New Yorker,* February 23, 1976, p. 114).

Virginia Cox
University of Wisconsin—Oshkosh

Day, Dorothy (1897-   )

Social Activist, Journalist, Publisher

[68] *The Long Loneliness.* New York: Curtis Books, 1972. 318 pp.

The Long Loneliness is a personal confession, the tale of a woman whose life was, as her friends expressed it, haunted by God. Day reminisces about a pious and happy childhood in an Episcopalian family, her later rejection of religion as an opiate during her years as a student at the University of Illinois, and her desire for social justice which led her to write for the socialist-oriented New York *Call* and to participate in strikes and demonstrations which often ended in jailing. The pivotal event of her life, however, was her conversion to Roman Catholicism. As she tells it, this event led to her separation from her common-law husband by whom she had a daughter, as well as to conflict among her anarchist, socialist, and pacifist principles.

Day admits that her desire for justice and her religious peity were given direction only when she met Peter Maurin, a dynamic French peasant with whom she subsequently founded the Catholic Worker Movement. Jointly they published the *Catholic Worker,* a newspaper which propounded a philosophy of Christian anarchism and pacificism, and set up a House of Hospitality in which the poor and dispossessed of New York City were housed and fed. For Day, the greatest achievement of the Movement was that it created an enduring community. Love, born of community, was the solution to the long loneliness which had pursued her for so many years. In it she found fulfillment and meaning both as a woman and a Christian.

Dana Greene
St. Mary's College of Maryland

De Angeli, Marguerite (1889-   )

Writer, Illustrator

[69]   *Butter at the Old Price.* Garden City: Doubleday, 1971.
          248 pp.

A distinguished writer and illustrator of books for children, de
Angeli tells of her life from her birth through her fiftieth wedding
anniversary.   Born to a middle-class family with many children,
she had a happy and secure childhood. At twenty-one she married
John de Angeli, a salesman, and the couple had six children. After
ten years of marriage, she decided to take art lessons, and soon she
was illustrating professionally.   Her first children's books were
written in the thirties, and she seems to have become quite well
known by the early forties, winning the Newberry Medal in 1950.
Her career has spanned forty years, as she continues to publish in
the seventies. For years the de Angelis were not well off, with
work difficult to find and many children to care for. Tragedies
(the death of her daughter Catherine) and a breakdown are only
lightly touched upon.   In a sense, this book seems written for
youth, although it would be of doubtful appeal to young readers
(a point mentioned by several reviewers). There is little analysis
or feeling communicated, beyond a sort of cheerful the-show-
must-go-on attitude.   Yet there is an admirable display of spirit
here, and her successful combining of marriage and career is instructive.

Throughout her book, de Angeli insists that her marriage and
family come first. But they did not deter her from achieving her
goals for a career, which they might easily have done. Never a person to enjoy housework, she disciplined herself by thinking of her
own happy childhood: "Perhaps *this* will be one of those days my
children will remember. I'd better make it a *good* one!" (163).
Her parents did not encourage her to develop any identity outside
the home; as a young woman she held a job in a store for one day
before realizing that Papa was right. " 'Now,' Papa said, 'you see
what we mean. You are much more suited to helping Mama, who
needs you' " (44).   Further, when she had developed her fine
contralto voice and was offered a position in an opera chorus, with
the company soon to go on an international tour, instead of rejoicing with her, her parents pointed out that a career had little to

offer a woman. Her life would "have more meaning" if she stayed home and married her fiancé as soon as possible. Oddly enough, she immediately saw that they were right (one wonders if it was so immediate as she remembers). Nevertheless, she kept on singing in various church choirs, usually as one of the hired professionals. But when her father protested about her decision to take up painting after ten years of marriage, she pointed out that she had proven herself for ten years and felt she could be trusted. So began her illustrating and writing, which was to make a good deal of money for the de Angelis and take them all over the world on research trips. Never does she say that her husband himself had any doubts about her career, and throughout the book he is portrayed as gracious and understanding. One should point out that he too was a musician.

Beverly Seaton
Ohio State University—Newark

De Mille, Agnes (1909-   )

Dancer, Choreographer, Writer

B
D38 1

[70] *Dance to the Piper.* Boston: Little, Brown and Company, 1952. 342 pp.

Dance to the Piper is the first of three autobiographical books by de Mille that span the years from the mid-1920's to the mid-40's. In this work, as in the second, de Mille writes in the first person and the narrative develops chronologically from her ancestral background (her mother, Annie, was the daughter of economist Henry George; her uncle was Cecil B. de Mille) through her choreographic success with the works *Rodeo, Oklahoma, One Touch of Venus* and *Carousel.* Skillfully woven into her family history are chapters such as "Ballet and Sex," discussing dance history and the ballerinas who "literally and profoundly. . .wed their work" (57), while also explaining her father's opposition to his daughter's choice of dance as a career.

Introduced in *DTTP* are themes to which de Mille will return in later works: the difficulty of having talent and intelligence passed over for physical appearance—particularly characteristics in body shape that preclude a standard career in ballet; the seeming impossibility of a woman successfully combining marriage, family and career; and the need of support and encouragement from family and friends for those dedicated to the dance and its rare rewards.

De Mille's parents were divorced when she was graduated from college, and for some time her mother was her companion. In *DTTP* her attitude toward her mother is ambivalent, while in the later works she writes with increasing gratitude and love in acknowledging debts owed both emotionally and financially. For example, see her touching foreword to her mother's biography of Henry George. In this short piece, she clearly delineates her mother's character and explores their relationship, which was a source of strength for the daughter despite its tensions.

Dance to the Piper drew favorable reviews, such as Carl Van Vechten's comment that "this dancer has written a great autobiography" (*Saturday Review,* January 26, 1952, p. 17). M. C. Scoggin, however, felt that most readers would dislike the nonnarrative elements when the book becomes "too involved with the author's ideas about the dance's relation to sex and religion" (*Horn Book,* April 1952, p. 126).

D38/a   [71]   *And Promenade Home.*   Boston: Little, Brown and Company, 1958. 301 pp.

De Mille covers the same years and events but pushes forward into the late 1940's in her second autobiography, *And Promenade Home.* In it, she addresses more directly those questions about marriage and career that plagued her in *DTTP.* She sums up her thoughts and decisions on the position of the creative-artist-wife-mother in Chapter XIII, "The Milk of Paradise" (213-31). Although her statements are directed primarily toward women in the arts, they widen to include all women who seek to work toward a fullfillment of self. The book ends with her return from working in England to reunite with her husband in America and to await the birth of their child.

The author's inclusion of a love interest was emphasized by many reviewers, as in the comment in *Kirkus Review* (August 15, 1958, p. 634) that *APH* "seems more of a woman's book than its predecessor." Margaret Lloyd, dance historian and critic, observed of de Mille that in *APH* "she is a woman who understands women" (*Christian Science Monitor,* October 9, 1958, p. 7).

[72] *Russian Journals.* New York: Dance Perspectives Foundation, 1971. 57 pp.

Partly in diary form, these journals cover trips to Russia in 1966 and 1969 as a member of cultural exchange groups. De Mille surveys aspects of contemporary Russian dance, and certain Russian views of trends in American dance. Reviews may be found in *AB Bookman's Weekly* (March 15, 1971, p. 806), and in *Dance* (July 1971, p. 82).

[73] *Speak to Me, Dance with Me.* New York: Popular Library, 1973. 404 pp.

De Mille returns in this book to England during the depression years when she was beginning her concert career. The work is comprised of excerpts from letters written by de Mille to her mother, which alternate with retrospective prose passages in which de Mille writes of what was really happening. A tragic love story, never before hinted at in previous works, emerges; and de Mille becomes more human, more understanding, as gaps in time are explained in this account of her intense emotional involvement with a dying man, Ramon Reed. An interestingly uneven, yet moving work, *Speak to Me* shows how autobiographies are changed and made more deeply textured, enriched, when intense feelings are finally confronted after suppression.

Like de Mille's other autobiographical writing, this book received wide and favorable attention. Yet R. L. Coombs, while specifying it as "one of the more intelligent" celebrity memoirs, also summed up its content and style rather condescendingly: "glittery theatre, trivia, gossip-column, name-dropping (Porter, Lawrence, Coward, et al.), and a good deal of rapid, emotional, introspective rambling" (*Library Journal,* February 15, 1973,

p. 561).

T. Gail Adams
Emory University, ILA

Densen-Gerber, Judianne (1934-   )

Psychiatrist, Lawyer

[74] *Walk In My Shoes: An Odyssey Into Womanlife.* New York: Saturday Review Press, 1976. 289 pp.

In *Walk In My Shoes* Judianne Densen-Gerber discusses her ideas about "being" and "becoming" in relation to five concepts of "womanlife;" her concepts are important because she believes that a woman can understand her "becoming" only when she can adequately define her "being." Using the major political, social, psychological, sexual, and familial events of her life as examples, Densen-Gerber demonstrates how a woman, as she reaches an understanding of her being, can become a truly self-actualized person. Only self-actualized women can achieve true equality with men and lead the way in exposing and eliminating the false justifications, the hypocrisies, the rationalizations, and the stereotyping prevalent in the attitudes of both sexes. Though Densen-Gerber is a professional woman of the upper class, she also deals with the problems of lower class women (particularly prostitutes and runaways) through her recollections of her work as executive director of Odyssey House.

Densen-Gerber states several times that she is not seeking to present a careful ordering of facts from which to build a case, nor is she constructing a highly reasoned and scholarly polemic; rather, she is purposely writing as emotion and memory dictate. This technique not only gives the book a conversational quality, but also effectively underlines her defiance of a rigid and sometimes coldly brutal society. Densen-Gerber is not afraid of her emotions, whether anger, fear, joy, pity, or love. Nor is she afraid to direct her sharp wit, as she so effectively does, at society, men, women, her family, and herself. She balances the humorous and the serious, sometimes even the tragic, and ultimately expresses hope, despite the problems of modern society. Thus despite its seemingly random sequences, the book maintains an underlying unity which relates Densen-Gerber's personal odyssey into womanlife to the larger concept of human liberation.

One reviewer (*Booklist,* July 1, 1976, p. 1498) has criticized Densen-Gerber for "lack of focus" but acknowledges "some astute insights about equal relationships now and for the future." Another reviewer (*Publisher's Weekly,* May 10, 1976, p. 78) notes that her "perceptions transcend current militancies, cut through old notions and stereotypes and get down to basic human values." Finally, Laurie Johnston (New York *Times,* October 8, 1976, p. C24) finds the book "outspoken" and "disorganized." Though she praises Densen-Gerber for "a stimulatingly unorthodox feminism," she deplores what she considers a light treatment of the drug problem and an "all but total" avoidance of the question of abortion.

E. E. Davis, Jr.
Old Dominion University

De Rachewiltz, Mary (1925-   )

Daughter of Ezra Pound and Olga Rudge

[75] *Discretions.* Boston: Little, Brown and Company, 1971. 312 pp.

Mary De Rachewiltz is the daughter of the poet Ezra Pound and the concert violinist Olga Rudge. Only days after her birth she was given into the care of a tender, loving German woman who nursed her and raised her as her own child in a peasant cottage among the beautiful Tyrolean mountains ninety miles north of Venice. In 1940, Mary was sent away to a boarding school in Venice. During the war, she continued her formal schooling, but her real education was directed by her father. By the end of the war, Mary was working as a practical nurse, tending the wounded and acting as a secretary and comforter to her distracted father. Shortly after the war, she married a young Russian-Italian, Baron Boris De Rachewiltz, heir to a Russian title. The young couple purchased a run-down seventeenth century castle located just a few miles from the Tyrolean village, Gais, where she had spent her childhood. Although Mary has lived extended periods of time in America, she still maintains the castle, Brunnenburg, as her home.

Aside from the interest kindled by the comments of a person close to many of the twentieth century's literary giants, by far the greatest interest in this book is the author's search for identity. Mary's earliest memories center on those situations in which conflicting demands and desires made her unsure of who she was. At a very early age, no more than three years old, she knew that she was not only a part of her foster parents' family, but that she also had other parents who, though remote and vaguely mysterious, visited her from time to time and seemed to be honored by her foster parents. By the time she was five, she was spending several weeks out of the year with Olga and Ezra in Venice. The contrast between the Tyrolean cottage and the fashionable Venetian apartment could not have been more striking; in a sense they were mutually exclusive, yet both in their own ways were attractive to her. Until she was fourteen years old, for nine months of the year she assumed the role of a peasant farm girl (keeping goats, chickens, bees, and a small garden) and a daring hoyden among her playmates. When living in the city, however, she was rigorously trained to be an intellectual, cultured, "finished" young lady whose playmates were the adult friends of her parents. In addition to the conflict of those demands, she also felt, as did many other Tyroleans, a divided sympathy for Italy and Germany; but for her the matter was further complicated by a loyalty she felt she owed to America, a land represented by her mother and father even though one she had never seen. Perhaps the most critical problem Mary had to resolve, however, was created by having two mothers. The contrast between her foster mother (simple, direct, strong) whom she loved warmly and Olga Rudge (complex, cultured, rigid, temperamental) whom she respected and admired was so great that she felt the need to choose one or the other as a model for the role of woman and mother which she herself would become.

The strongest influence in her life, however, was Ezra Pound— the great man to whom all in her acquaintance deferred. He was a stern but loving and generous taskmaster. Under his guidance,

Mary became an accomplished linguist, translator, and creative artist. Her devotion to her father and her conviction that he is the great man of twentieth century letters has led her to devote much of her professional life to the literary works and reputation of her father. One senses throughout the book her strong desire to support her maligned father, even to the extent of putting that business before any of her other interests.

Through the entire autobiography runs an unspoken theme of the individual's need for personal integrity, courage, and faith. One is finally left with the impression that though her life has demonstrated adversity as a constant condition, achievement of a sense of beauty, of calm, and of truth is possible.

Conrad Festa
Old Dominion University

de Trevino, Elizabeth Borton (1904-   )

Journalist, Author

[76] *My Heart Lies South: The Story of My Mexican Marriage with Epilogue.* New York: Thomas Y. Crowell Company, 1972. 252 pp.

When Elizabeth Borton was sent by the city editor of the Boston newspaper for which she worked to do a story on Mexico in the 1930's, she did not know the trip was to change her life. The first Mexican she met, Luis Trevino, fell quickly in love with her and embarked on a subtle, culturally specific Mexican courtship which totally eluded "Eleesabet" until some time after she had been accepted as his intended bride by both his family and by the provincial Monterrey society in which the Trevino life was based. With little trepidation about the difficulties of cross-cultural marriage, Elizabeth Borton accepted the proposal of marriage and began the unfamiliar process of becoming a Mexican wife. To this experience she brought the attitudes of an emancipated North American women, along with personal flexibility, an apparent sense of humor, a desire to accomodate herself to her new world, and a growing love for her Mexican family and for Mexican life. It was taken for granted that one's primary concern was the welfare of the members of the extended family upon which one's happiness and well being depended, and that relationships with the world in general were governed by the self-regulating question: "What will people think?" The result, as she observed it, was a harmonious caring for others, which insured that no one within the family was neglected, abused or ignored. Her satisfaction with these benefits far outweighted the discomfort she felt at the social inequality of men and women, the emotional manipulations between the sexes, and the total restraint on individual behavior, all of which she not only accepted, but came to rationalize to her own satisfaction. The final chapter in the 1972 edition, the only addition to the original version published in 1953, brought the family history up to date and emphasized that, in spite of radical social and economic changes in Mexico during the intervening years, the centrality of the family has remained unchanged, and continues to distinguish the Mexican way of life.

Appreciative reviews greeted the publication in 1953. The reviewers applauded both the insight of Trevino's observations and the chatty, easy way in which the information was advanced. Jean L. Ross (*Library Journal,* September 15, 1953, p. 78) felt that the book "demonstrated that admiration, respect and affection can build an effective bridge between two cultures. . .it is delightful entertainment." In contrast to the review by Dan Wickenden in the New York *Herald Tribune* (September 20, 1953, p. 6) which observed the "intimate and intensely feminine" quality of the analysis, V. I. Warren (New York *Times,* October, 11, 1953, p. 3) stressed the analytic quality of Trevino's work, the "professional detachment," the analyses of "ritualistic patterns of courtship" and of the "history of the city which does much to explain its character in the most palatable way." The 1972 edition was critically ignored, which while not surprising, leads one to wonder how a feminist orientation might influence contemporary critical evaluations of *My Heart Lies South.*

Diane Brodatz Rothenberg
Encinitas, California

Dillard, Annie (1945-   )

Poet, Essayist, Naturalist

[77] *Pilgrim at Tinker Creek.* New York: Harper's Magazine
Press, 1974. 271 pp.

A solitary walker, a solitary seer—such is Annie Dillard's profession in *Pilgrim at Tinker Creek,* not so much autobiography as it is
spiritual introspection based on an intense communion with nature. In form the book transcribes a year of the changing seasons
in a small area of the Blue Ridge Mountains south of Roanoke,
Virginia.

Dillard searches for—and finds in unself-conscious instants—
the vision of the "tree with lights in it" that the newly-sighted
child sees when its bandages are first removed. "Seeing" is a mission for Dillard; it can be sought, but the vision itself is a matter
of grace, a gift to be grasped only in fleeting epiphanies. Thus her
"journal" is a meditation, at times almost mystical and liturgical,
of the glory and terror of creation. Fascinated by insects, she reveals how the giant water bug sucks the frog's life-blood; how the
mindless tracking instincts of pine caterpillars can lead to starva-
tion; how the praying mantis eats her mate as he is coupling with
her. Such episodes occasion Dillard's reflections on the eternal
question of the goodness of creation.

Dillard's writing is lyrical, precise, exciting. The excitement is
that of stalking a muskrat or a heron or a sudden change of light
on the mountain. No human relationships, no conversation,
nothing is heard but Dillard's solitary voice. Her search is richly
informed by borrowings from Heraclitus, Merton, Teale, Heisen-
berg, Dinesen, Blake and more. She says, "I bloom indoors in the
winter like a forced forsythia; I come in to come out. At night I
read and write, and things I have never understood become clear"
(38). Thus, the writing and reading help her make sense of the
intricacies, fecundity, violence, and horror of nature. At other
points she reflects on how self-consciousness separates one from
the experience itself, but is necessary in order to remember it and
understand it.

Pilgrim at Tinker Creek was widely and lengthily reviewed, mostly favorably, many comparing it to *Walden.* Hayden Carruth (*Virginia Quarterly Review,* Fall 1974) sees Dillard's view as comparable to Thoreau's of "plain old-fashioned optimistic American transcendentalism" (639). Several reviewers, while praising the writing and tough-minded insights, note that Dillard fails to consider at all what human beings have done in and to nature, thus finding the book essentially escapist (Eva Hoffman, *Commentary,* October 1974, p. 88) and dangerously nostalgic (Carruth). Eudora Welty (New York *Times,* March 24, 1974, pp. 4-5) faults Dillard for being sometimes overly dense, for neglecting the necessary relationship between writer and reader.

As a book of "literary ecology," Dillard's life-writing can take an honored place beside Thoreau, Anne Morrow Lindbergh, and Colin Fletcher (*The Man Who Walked Time*).

Margaret McFadden-Gerber
Appalachian State University

Dixon, Jeane (c.1917-   )

Prophet, Astrologer, Writer, Real Estate Agent

[78] *My Life and Prophecies.* New York: William Morrow & Company, 1969. 219 pp.

Whatever else they do, prophets are expected to remain persons of mystery, living beyond the grasp of Time. And Jeane Dixon, convinced of her own prophetic powers, is not about to about to burst the mystery bubble that surrounds her.

Dixon's autobiography tells us less about the woman Jeane Dixon than the New Testament tells us about the boy Jesus. We learn nothing about her formative years (except that she was given a crystal ball at eight). We learn little about Dixon the success in real estate (except how she manages to "find" an extra 217 working days per year more than the rest of us). Instead of a chronology of events, the Dixon autobiography is, as one reviewer stated, "a jumble of anecdotes, reflections on prophecy and practical theology" (Thomas Garret, *Best Sellers,* September 15, 1969, p. 221).

As a feminist, Dixon is either two hundred years ahead of her times, or two hundred years behind: she gives no thought or attention whatever to female/male roles or relations. (One might comment, why campaign for a woman president when you can "see" one coming along?) Dixon is a prophet in our times who happens to be a woman. If it is difficult to see her in feminist garb, the problem may not lie in Dixon's visions but in our own, concentrated as they are on the Present.

As the personal record of a phenomenal person, the Dixon autobiography deserves attention, providing (as one suspects) that it is not a crime to write for popular consumption without literary pretensions while at the same time attempting to rub historic elbows with Ezekiel and Isaias and Anna. Few reviewers gave the book more than passing notice. E. T. Smith, in the *Library Journal* (October 15, 1969) called the contents "gloomy . . .replete with preaching"—not altogether an unfair comment: after all, the book was written by a prophet.

Judith A. Johnson
Old Dominion University

Dorfman, Elsa (c.1939-   )

Photographer, Writer

[79] *Elsa's Housebook: A Woman's Photojournal.*   Boston: David R. Godine, 1974. 78 pp.

The *Housebook* chronicles the visits of a host of colorful characters to Elsa Dorfman's Cambridge, Mass., household. In what has become a kind of contemporary "salon" are welcomed assorted literary figures, local friends and family. This collection of eighty black and white photos transcends mere snapshots to become portraiture. Dorfman aims to appreciate her friends, including

Allen Ginsburg, Robert Creeley, and Hannah Green—more than to flatter. Her efforts to capture what is casual and direct in their personalities balances beautifully a tendency to underexpose shots and thus create a faintly nostalgic mood. The accompanying auto-biographical text provides both picture references and emotional glimpses of the photographer, who calls each photograph "an exquisite metaphor, a delicate haiku of memory" (52).

The *Housebook* is concerned with independence and intimacy, mothers and daughters, work, family, nurturing and growth. The author's candor is revealing, in particular her contradictory wish through photography to pretend that nothing changes—"we'll never get any older and we're always going to be friends" (10)—as well as to record change in her environment. What is intriguing is the exchange of roles that emerges in the book. Poets and friends are creative models for Dorfman, who in turn inspires readers as an imaginative, receptive woman herself. The conflicts and joys of single womanhood are especially well-presented, as the author struggles with conventional versus unconventional values.

Reviewers praised the *Housebook* for its warmth, sensitivity, and humanness. Barbara Ehrlich White called Dorfman's unique-ness "the unselfconscious manner in which she presents her subjects, a manner that can be described as caring, empathetic, and sympathetic" (*The Feminist Art Journal,* Summer 1975, p. 32). In *Women's Studies,* Vol. 3, No. 2 (1976), Annette Kolodny noted Dorfman's innovation on the female tradition of creating journals of household affairs (pp. 215-16). The reviewer also stressed the *Housebook's* importance in recording complex and daily realities of female existence. "For the feminist, this insistent recording of un-exceptional experience has a peculiar and timely importance" (p. 217). Jayne Kantor's enthusiasm in the same issue was some-what qualified. She prefers "those individual images that are most honestly self-conscious" (p. 219). But she believes that the book works as a whole, and credits Dorfman with revealing "her painful awareness of the complicated dilemmas all women face" (p. 221).

Jill Janows
The Women and Literature Collective

Draper, Ruth (1884-1956)

Actress, Dramatist

[80] *The Art of Ruth Draper.* Garden City, New York: Doubleday and Company, 1960. 373 pp.

Although not an autobiography, this volume is a useful guide to the life and work of an accomplished woman of the theater. It includes thirty-five dramatic monologues written and performed by Draper and a substantial memoir by Morton Dauwen Zabel which quotes from her unpublished diary. The memoir describes Draper's comfortable childhood in New York City and her fifty-year career. As a child, she was influenced by her German governess who introduced her to the world of art and literature and encouraged her to develop her natural ability to mimic character. In her twenties, Draper's social position as the granddaughter of Charles Dana enabled her to form friendships with such figures as Henry Adams, Henry James, and Paderewski, who encouraged her to begin a professional career. Performing her monologues, she toured the world and won wide respect and many honors, including that of the Commander of the Most Excellent Order of the British Empire.

Believing that she could best portray characters which she knew completely, Draper wrote all the material she performed. Her monologues show that without any formal training as a writer, she could create realistic, sensitive portraits of many types of women, from debutantes and society matrons to working women and immigrants. Her compassion and gentle use of irony enabled her to avoid sentimentalizing or burlesquing her characters.

Ruth Chatterton in the New York *Times* (May 29, 1960, p. 17) questions the literary value of the monologues, calling them "commonplace and corny." Others, however, including the reviewer in the *Times Literary Supplement* (May 6, 1960, p. 286) and Edward Barry in the Chicago *Sunday Tribune* (May 22, 1960, p. 3) generally praise them, with Barry calling the best of them "touchingly human."

Naomi Leventhal
State University College—Fredonia

Drooz, Irina Gross (1913-   )

Physician and Neuropsychiatrist

[81] *Doctor of Medicine.* New York: Dodd, Mead and Company, 1949. 308 pp.

Written the year she was qualified as a specialist by the American Board of Psychiatry and Neurology, Irma Gross Drooz's autobiography traces her dream of becoming a doctor from her memory as a five-year-old of breaking a thermometer while attempting to take her doll's temperature. With clarity and objectivity she describes courses in the medical curriculum in the late 1930's and early 1940's, her reactions to medical experiences, her patients' responses to her, and her marriage to a fellow neurologist based on common interest and love.

Drooz's training took place during war time when the need for doctors was enlarged. Hence her narrative contains few references to specific problems of a woman attempting to become a doctor.

Reviewers remark on the usefulness of this autobiography for the potential medical student because of its details about medical school courses, and demands. Mary Ross (New York *Herald Tribune,* August 7, 1949, p. 12) points to Drooz's intellectual and emotional satisfaction gained in the relationship with patients and colleagues and in the excitement of pure research, while I. W. Voorhees (New York *Times,* June 26, 1949, p. 12) praises the witty and humorous style.

Charlotte S. McClure
Georgia State University

Dunham, Katherine (1910-   )

Dancer, Choreographer

[82] *A Touch of Innocence.* New York: Harcourt, Brace & World, Inc., 1959. 312 pp.

In a note to the reader Dunham advises that "this book is not an autobiography. It is the story of a world that has vanished, as it was for one child who grew up in it." To heighten this fictive quality, Dunham uses the third person. With the exception of a sombre mood-setting first chapter, the narrative follows a chronology that spans memories from the author's birth to age eighteen.

In this tortured family history, Dunham tells of the effects caused by her mother's death, her father's abandonment of his children, and a bitter custody battle over Katherine and her adored older brother. She attributes any stability in her life to her stepmother, but notes the limitation of such support because of the acceptance by her stepmother of the traditional husband/wife roles. Dunham's idealistic worship of her brother is arresting, and her father's overreaction to her embrace of her brother is a foreshadowing of Dunham's father's own incestuous longings toward her, whom he compares to his deceased first wife. A harrowing near-molestation by a tramp, and a later physical advance made by her father, underscore Dunham's ambivalence toward men. Realizing her aloneness and not able to confide in her stepmother, Dunham ends this memoir with her bid for freedom and autonomy through employment, oblivious in her innocence to the forces of race prejudice that surround her.

Women, whose lives are controlled by men, by forces of race, economics, and paucity of spirit, comprise one of the central themes of this autobiography which was widely and favorably reviewed. Fanny Butcher (Chicago *Sunday Tribune,* October 25, 1959, p. 4) wrote of Dunham's style: "By the device of always speaking of herself as Katherine. . .she gives the 'feel' of fiction which intensifies the impact of the fact." Annabel Farjeon felt that "Miss Dunham has overdone her literary style a little, writing of herself in the third person as 'the girl;' yet there is power and atmosphere in every sentence. This is a horrifying history of an American half-caste's upbringing" (*New Statesman,* October 29, 1959, p. 60). Elizabeth Janeway (New York *Times,* November 8, 1959, p. 54) terms *A Touch of Innocence* "one of the most extraordinary life-stories I have ever read."

T. Gail Adams
Emory University, ILA

0

Dykeman, Wilma (1920-   )

Novelist, Essayist, Biographer, Historian

[83] *Look to this Day.* New York: Holt, Rinehart & Winston,
       1968. 342 pp.

Like her novels, biographies and histories, Wilma Dykeman's
autobiography presents her region's traditions and lore. In *Look to
this Day,* Dykeman reflects upon her family, travel, and Southern
Appalachia. Consisting of short essays (some of which were newspaper columns originally) treating a period of eighteen months,
the book discusses widely various topics, from sorting magazines
to a visit with Robert Frost. With Thoreau's dictum, "Only that
day dawns to which we are awake" as her epigraph, Dykeman seeks
to reveal the importance of those small awarenesses mediated by
the five senses.

Except for the essays on travel and her own childhood, this is
not Dykeman's best writing. Her sensitive and accurate portrayals
of the folkways and speech patterns of Appalachian people are
absent. Nor do we find a strong female voice like that created for
Lydia McQueen in *The Tall Woman* or Ivy Cortland in *The Far
Family.* There is little here of a strictly feminist concern, for
Dykeman is less interested in her own self-consciousness as a
writer and woman than in recording personal responses to the tex-
tures of everyday things. Her relationship with her husband, poet
James Stokely, is only hinted at, and the difficulties encountered
in a two-career family are barely mentioned.

The excellent pieces on a European journey and her relationship
to her parents reveal how intensely *familial* a creature Dykeman is.
Her own reactions to Siena or Carcassone are conditioned by those
of her mother and teen-age sons who accompanied her. While
some might find travel with a three-generation family burdensome,
Dykeman welcomes the enrichment it bestows. For her, creativity
is the product of family stability. She was not, she says, "helped"
to become a successful writer by parents who ignored their child
or hated each other, thereby giving raw material for successful
fiction and drama. Though her parents knew suffering and horror,
"they made their home a refutation, not a replica, of the world's
frequent tawdriness, conflicts, prejudices" (151), and thus

Dykeman was supported in her creative development.

Look to This Day was reviewed only briefly, though favorably, in the standard library publications.

Margaret McFadden-Gerber
Appalachian State University

Elliot, Elisabeth (1926-   )

Missionary, Biographer, Theologian

[84] *Through the Gates of Splendor.* New York: Harper & Brothers, 1957 and 1965. 258 pp.

Through the Gates recounts Elliot's experience with five young missionary families in southeast Ecuador in the 1950's. The men including Elliot's husband James were all killed in an attempt to penetrate the territory of the hostile Auca tribe.

[85] *The Savage My Kinsman.* New York: Harper & Brothers, 1961. 159 pp.

Kinsman, with photographs by Elliot and Cornell Capa, deals with her life after the traumatic experience in *Through the Gates.* She decided to carry on the legacy of her husband James and his four companions. She learned some of the Aucas' language and with her three and a half year old daughter, Valerie, and Rachel Saint, sister of the missionary pilot killed with James Elliot, she entered the Auca community. She records in words and photographs the differences in daily living (housing, tools, cooking) that might be expected and comments on the sometimes stunning mutual reactions to less tangible matters. Elliot's perception of the most subtle nuances in behavioral patterns opens up heretofore unknown vistas in the psyche of primitives. While she was with the Aucas she transposed their language to writing.

[86] *Shadow of the Almighty.* New York: Harper & Row, 1958. 256 pp.

In *Shadow,* Elliot draws upon her recollections as a wife to reconstruct the life of her husband James from his diaries and letters.

[87] *These Strange Ashes.* New York: Harper & Row, 1975. 144 pp.

Ashes is the recollections of the author's stay among the Colorado Indians of Ecuador. During her stay, flood demolished the mission station and all her notes were stolen. She observes that "to be a follower of the Crucified means, sooner or later a personal encounter with the Cross" (p. 129). In this same work she says (pp. x-xi): "It was here that I was introduced rather suddenly to the serious business of people being born and people dying, to a great height of joy and a great depth of depression, and to the severe tests of living with a variety of alien humanity. . . . We see through a glass darkly. But it is worth our looking."

[88] *Twelve Baskets of Crumbs.* Chappaqua, New York: Christian Herald House, 1976. 173 pp.

Crumbs is the title of a collection of essays by Elliot about "the things I have seen" as a missionary, mother, wife, teacher, lecturer, writer (p. viii).

[89] *Let Me Be a Woman: Notes on Womanhood for Valerie.* Wheaton, Illinois: Tyndale House Publishers, Inc., 1976. 190 pp.

Let Me Be a Woman draws together Elliot's experiences and her observations about a life of religious study and service as the basis for advice to young women about to marry. The work is Elliot's analysis of Christian womanhood. Her thesis is that, while intellectually and spiritually women and men are equal in the home (as in the church), women must carry out the divine mission established by the word of God. This type of submission, she believes, is by no means a weakness, only obedience to the voice of God (pp. 145-47).

Elisabeth Elliot may be described as "one of Christendom's most able and articulate writers." She is the author of numerous articles dealing with theological questions and the application of Christian principles to the daily life and behavior of women. Several appeared since 1957 in *Christianity Today* (for example, "Prayer of the Five Widows" January 7, 1957; and "Why I Oppose the Ordination of Women," June 6, 1975). Articles written by her appeared in *Life* (November 24, 1958 and April 7, 1961), and she is the subject of articles appearing in *Life* on two occasions (January 30, 1956 and May 20, 1957). *Reader's Digest* condensed and published *Through the Gates* (August 1956) and *Kinsman* (November 1962). Her life demonstrates that women are equal to men in the strenuous world of the Christian missionary. Her attitudes about women and feminism have been shaped by her religious beliefs, by her complete immersion in her faith, with her spiritual eye focused on an ultimate Christian nirvana.

Elliot's books have been translated into nine or ten foreign languages and widely reviewed. She "writes simply, forthrightly. . . . The religious tone is fundamentalist; the mood is calm," according to a *Library Journal* review (June 1, 1957) of *Through the Gates*. The *Library Journal* (May 1, 1961) describes her *Kinsman* as "a real contribution towards understanding between peoples of different cultures," and says that she "ranks with the great missionary women of the past." The *Christian Century* observes (March 19, 1975) of her later work, *These Strange Ashes* ("with a hint of a love story"), that "Ms. Elliot, who gained a following of millions for her writings after the Auca tragedy in 1956, is not likely to run out of a market."

Versa Laska
Regis College

Enters, Angna (1907-   )

Dancer

[90] *First Person Plural.* New York: Stackpole Sons, 1938. 386 pp.

> *First Person* covers only a brief period in Enters' career and is described by Muriel Rukeyser (*New Republic,* January 26, 1938, p. 346) as "a series of impressions, diary notes, descriptions of places, scenes and dances, lacking intimate background and cloying egotism usually found in dancer's writings." Enters mentions few personal details but notable among these are her receipt of two Guggenheims and a nervous breakdown in 1935 (350). She also defends both Women's clubs and magazines against charges of triviality, citing their support as contributing to her success as an artist (244).

[91] *Silly Girl: A Portrait of Personal Rememberance.* Boston: Houghton Mifflin Company, 1944. 322 pp.

> Written in the third person and following a straight chronological narrative from Enters' birth to her departure from Paris in 1938, *Silly Girl* provides much of what was omitted from Enters' earlier *First Person Plural. Silly Girl* is at once a story of a life developing, and an artistic life in development. Although she writes in early chapters of a tyrannical grandmother and of a mother betrayed by a philandering husband, the bulk of the writing is devoted to Enters' struggles to begin a career in dance and maintain independence. Because of her dual artistic interests, there is much discussion on the relationship between painting and dance, and because of the unusual nature of her dance-mime-tableau-vivant compositions, almost all her performances featured woman. Enters is a seminal figure in American dance drama and her literary works received, for the most part, favorable reviews, albeit with debate over their genre. Isabel Peterson for instance (*Theatre Arts,* June 1944, p. 382) advised that "*Silly Girl* is not an autobiography. It is the story of an artist's life seen through the long perspective."

[92] *Artist's Life.* New York: Coward-McCann, Inc., 1958.
447 pp.

Enters' third book, *Artist's Life,* is again primarily concerned
with "the portrait of one life in the arts" (8). She uses the same
format as in *First Person Plural* and some of the material from that
work. The narrative, spanning the period from the early 1930's
to 1956, covers Enters' work in Hollywood as a costume designer,
her career as a painter, her work on her novel, *Among the Daughters,"* and her entrance into teaching. Most reviews commented
upon the absence of intimate touches, the impersonal quality of
Artist's Life. Fitzroy Davis, for example, praises the work as a
chronicle of a career in dance but noted that "Still, there is no
denying there will be some who will not know where to look for
Angna herself in this book" (New York *Times,* October 5, 1958,
p. 6).

T. Gail Adams
Emory University, ILA

Evers, Mrs. Medgar (-   )

Civil Rights Leader's Wife

[93] *For Us, The Living.* New York: Doubleday and Company, Inc., 1967. 378 pp.

Writing after the assassination of her husband, civil rights leader
Medgar Evers, and after her move from Mississippi to California,
Mrs. Medgar Evers tells of life as a middle class Black in Mississippi.
Although she writes of her adolescent years and gives a valuable
picture of southern Black women in the fifties, she emphasizes her
years with Medgar Evers. Indeed, she writes as *Mrs. Medgar* Evers
rather than as Myrlie Evers indicating not only her self-image, but
her perspective as well. She discusses her late husband's regional
background and examines her compulsion to rectify the racism of
Mississippi, stating that his dedication to his cause and the NAACP,
and his absence from her and from their children were difficult to
accept, but that she herself came to a similar dedication after

some years.

For women's studies this autobiography gives valuable insights into the experience of southern Black womanhood. The section of the book dealing with the trial of Medgar Evers's assassin is the most moving because it epitomizes all the aspects of racial prejudice in the South that Medgar Evers strove to overcome. For example, when his wife requests that she be called "Mrs. Evers" rather than "Myrlie" during the trial, the reader realizes that Mrs. Evers is demanding the respect Black women have been long denied, and one cheers for the dignity afforded by that simple formality when her request is carried out.

Diane Jefferson
San Luis Obispo, California

Farmer, Frances (1914-1970)

Actress

[94] *Will There Really Be a Morning?* New York: Putnam's, 1972. 318 pp.

Frances Farmer was a Hollywood Cinderella who soared to stardom in the "Golden era of the silver screen." She enjoyed a brilliant, meteoric career until alcohol, overwork, and isolation drove her to a nervous breakdown. *Will There Really Be a Morning?* gives a chilling account of her struggle to survive in a macabre and Kafkaesque world. Jailed for a traffic violation, Farmer was removed to a sanitarium, then placed in the custody of a mother whom she despised. She was sent to a state mental institution as punishment for her "insolence" and kept there for refusing to act lady-like and demure. She endured grotesque tortures in the form of insulin shock, hydrotherapy, brutal beatings, and sexual assaults. Stripped of civil rights and human dignity, she survived five years in a violent ward through "cunning and dogged determination." Released to nurse her aging parents, she was kept in servitude by the perpetual threat of another commitment. Only after her parents' death did she find inner peace. She was supported for ten years by the selfless friendship of Jean Ratcliffe, a woman who rescued Farmer from alcoholism and lovingly cared for her through the final ravages of esophageal cancer.

Although Farmer is not consciously a feminist, she deals with topics that are clearly relevant to women: the traumatic impact of her mother's hysteria; the debilitating effects of her affair with Clifford Odets; the escape offered by two loveless marriages; the treatment of women in mental institutions; the guilt she feels about her Hollywood abortions; the comforts of female friendship; and the social pressures that revolve around fame, beauty, and artistic creativity.

Most critics reviewed Farmer's work as an "appalling and moving posthumous autobiography" (*Publishers' Weekly*, April 17, 1972, p. 57). The New York *Times*, called it "a ghastly tale, not easy to forget" (August 20, 1972, p. 20). Gavin Lambert felt that the chapters describing her asylum incarceration were "flamboyantly written" ("The Star that Failed," *Books and Bookmen*, June, 1974. p. 24). And the *Times Literary Supplement* condemned the book's "Circumstantial description of a lesbian encounter culminating in cunnilingus with onomatopoeic effects," neglecting to mention that the scene is a Lesbian rape witnessed by Farmer (June 14, 1974, p. 628). *Will There Really Be a Morning?* was unjustly dismissed as a Hollywood memoir and quickly went out of print. It ought to be reclaimed as a valuable addition to women's studies.

Suzette Henke
SUNY Binghamton

Ferber, Edna (1885-1968)

Novelist, Dramatist, Short-Story Writer

[95] *A Peculiar Treasure*. New York: Doubleday, Doran & Company, 1939. 398 pp.

Only once in twenty-three published volumes had she used a

portion of the substance of her own life as the subject of a book, and, because "it is the lot of the imaginative creative writer always to look on, never to participate," Ferbert says, she had rarely been able to voice her sympathy with a cause, a movement or a belief in her fiction, only sometimes in "a straightaway article, factually written." *A Peculiar Treasure* was to be such an honest, informative work, about a middle-class American Jewish family in the past half-century, the family she knew best: her own. As Nazism ravages Germany and the civilized world does little to stop Hitler or to save itself, Ferber feels the impulse to take stock, perhaps to escape, to document an epoch that is ending. She introduces this autobiography as an expression of concern for the fate of world Jewry; its Biblical title recalls Gods's conditional promise to Israel, and suggests the similar promise Ferber had seen in the American experience.

The first portion of *A Peculiar Treasure* is Ferber's tribute to her family and the experience of growing up in the Midwest at the turn of the century. Essentially a chronological narrative covering her first twenty years, the book is structured by the Ferber family's moves. Edna's father takes the household from their Chicago "base," the home of her lively, dramatic maternal grandparents, to Kalamazoo, to Ottumwa and to Appleton, pursuing the opportunity he had come to America seeking; Edna goes alone to Milwaukee at nineteen to follow her career as a newspaper reporter. When illness forces her back to Appleton she begins writing fiction as part of her recuperation, and discovers the work that will engage her for the rest of her life.

A Peculiar Treasure continues to the moment, thirty years later, when Ferber is responding to readers of the autobiography's prepublication magazine serialization. In this "success story" portion of the book, cross-country and international travel experiences alternate with major writing projects as they did in the pattern of her life. Disassociating herself from the soul-baring school of autobiography, Ferber says she will (and she does) write about herself, her family, "and America, and Jews, and Writing, and the Theatre, and Fun, and Friends, and Work, and Food, and Hope, and Hate, and Ambition," but would not "Tell All." If she had intimate, i.e. sexual, relationships, they are not hinted at here; if anything she could be said to have been married to her work. On this subject Ferber seems most vulnerable: proud of her popular and continuing appeal as a novelist, irritated that her novels have not been treated more seriously by American critics. Although she cites some classically sexist reviews of her early fiction she does not name them as such, and herself later balks at taking on the research that would become *Cimarron* because it is "a man's job."

Ferber's closest friends appear to have been male, but the major figure besides herself in the autobiography is her mother, Julia, whom she admires greatly and with whom she lived and travelled for many years after her father's death. Ferber's sister, Fanny, is also presented with affection and respect, and Fanny's daughters were to be companion/proteges; it is to her nieces that *A Peculiar Treasure* is dedicated.

The book was well received. The New York *Times* gave it page 1 of the February 5, 1939 *Book Review*, and publications from *Time* to the London *Times Literary Supplement* similarly responded to it as newsworthy. Most reviews reflect appreciation of "Edna Ferber," a character whom they find to be worthy of her creator; she is praised for energy, integrity, generosity, humor and for her love of family and country; her story may be enjoyed as an instance of small town girl making good. *TLS* (May 6, 1939, p. 267) sees the autobiography as having the reportorial strengths of Ferber's fiction without her novelist weaknesses, but *Time* (February 2, 1939, p. 26) and *Forum* (April, 1939, pp. 210-215) use the occasion of the autobiography to snipe at Ferber's best-sellerdom. Except for interviews with Ferber and reminiscences by her friends, the only later evaluation appears to be one by Leon Spitz, "Edna Ferber: An American-Jewish Self-Portrait," The Chicago *Jewish Forum*, Winter 1954-55, pp. 100-104.

[96] *A Kind of Magic.* Garden City: Doubleday & Company, Inc., 1963. 335 pp.

As Ferber acknowledges, *A Kind of Magic* is a "haphazard" book, elaborating on *A Peculiar Treasure* and celebrating the living —and knowing one is alive—of her second quarter century as a writer. The work of writing is a major topic throughout, as is the diversity of America experienced in her travels and reflected in her novels' various regional settings. Much space is devoted to the building of a home and "lady farming" in Connecticut, activities interrupted by work for the Writers' War Board, celebrity War Bond tours and a European reporting assignment that produces some of the strongest passages in *A Kind of Magic*. (Quite different, but similarly memorable as a setpiece, is Ferber's eulogy for James Dean, whom she encountered while filming *Giant*.) Consistent, perhaps, with her focus on public rather than private self, Ferber reports her mother's death from cancer in a brief passage, and does not explore any connection between that event and her subsequent decision to sell Treasure Hill and return to New York apartment living.

Among the mini-essays interspersed in the narrative (itself interspersed with opinions and asides) is a chapter lauding the strengths of American women and deploring the "female" role and status that prevent such potential from being fulfilled. The reader is reminded of an earlier chapter on Ferber's formative influences in which she credits four women (and four men) with having broadened her social sense and shaped the conduct of her life: Jane Adams, Ida Tarbell, Lillian Adler and Julia Ferber.

Reviews of *A Kind of Magic* were less enthusiastic than those for the first volume, and the least enthusiastic is the most sexist: "Well written, honest, informative, Edna Ferber's autobiography . . .will appeal to most men about as much as an Amy Vanderbilt column; many women will find it lovely," says *The Critic* (October-November, 1963, p. 81), concluding that the book is not bad, "but it belongs next to the lustre cream." The most enthusiastic review is almost as sexist, however: Edward P. J. Corbett compares the book favorably with Moss Hart's *Act One,* saying "Women especially, will adore it. . . . There must be a feminine streak in my make-up, too" (*America*, November 9, 1963, pp. 592-93).

Elaine Reuben
University of Maryland

O **Fisher, M. F. K. (1908-   )**

Author, Gastronome

[97] *Among Friends.* New York: Alfred A. Knopf, 1971. 306 pp.

Mary Francis Kennedy Fisher—or, as she signed her more than a dozen books on gastronomy, M. F. K. Fisher—writes here not of mere food but of childhood sustenance in a family perhaps a touch more peculiar in its way than are most families. Father has an abiding love for a hard luck story and for the bum-tramp-saint who tells it. Mother, generally pregnant, is reading English novels while propped on her couch. Grandmother, a primly corsetted Victorian, entertains an assortment of sane and not-quite-sane ex-missionary ladies. Most interesting to any little girl are the "batties"— the odd flotsam of humanity bumping into her life as hired girls, neighbors, circus acrobats. Fisher writes that her schoolteacher "was so used to my mother's odd ideas of regular attendance that she never questioned my absences, and I was probably the only child in Penn Street School who never needed a 'written excuse' "—quite a useful arrangement when the circus was in town.

The family was middle-class, not quite welcome into the upper echelons of society but not entirely at home either with the largely Mexican-Catholic inhabitants of "jimtown."

Among Friends, as its title implies, does deal with living in a community of Friends (capital *F* as in Quaker). Non-Quakers, such as Fisher's family, were accepted but not considered quite "proper" by the prevailing in-bred, inward-looking and somewhat closed society of the Whittier, California, Friends. There were little incidents of childhood intolerance such as are meted out to any child who does not quite fit the community norm, but *Among Friends* does not award such acts with a greater importance than they deserve.

Most of *Among Friends* deals with loving, rich childhood memories, especially of the women of the family and neighborhood. The loving portrait for example of "Aunt Owen," the neighbor, is capped by Fisher with a recipe for Aunt Owen's Fried-Egg Sandwiches, whose "prescription" is: "To be eaten on top of a hill at sunset, between trios of 'A Wandering Minstrel, I' and 'Onward, Christian Soldiers,' preferably before adolescence and its priggish queasiness set in." Or there is the memory of wandering through the house of the invalid Mrs. Chaffee, "as if we were in the most intimate secret apartment of Queen Glinda Esmeraldina, which perhaps we were, for we saw Mrs. Chaffee herself only one time, and then she was as if made of cobwebs on an enormous bed, nourished perhaps by three peeled grapes a day and a sip of yellow wine."

Fisher is most renowned for her translation of Brillat-Savarin's *Physiology of Taste.* Over the space of more than twenty years she has also written a dozen books on cooking; probably her most famous is *How to Cook a Wolf. Among Friends* received scant critical attention, possibly because in it she was breaking out of her traditional sphere of writing.

Marie R. Oesting
Baraboo, Wisconsin

Flynn, Elizabeth Gurley (1890-1964)

Labor Organizer, Writer, Activist

[98] *The Rebel Girl: An Autobiography, My First Life (1906-1926).* New York: International Publishers, 1973. 351 pp.

Elizabeth Gurley Flynn completed what she assumed would be the first volume of her autobiography during her trial for conspiracy. Along with other prominent Communists, Flynn was accused and convicted of advocating the overthrow of the government. While she was in prison editors prepared the manuscript and gave it a title: *I Speak My Own Piece* (New York: Masses & Mainstream, 1955). But Flynn would have called her book *The Rebel Girl,* after the song I. W. W. troubador Joe Hill wrote for her. The recent re-issue bears the new title, and has been revised according to suggestions made by Flynn before her death.

The Rebel Girl describes the political education of one of America's most effective radical speakers and agitators. Although Flynn eventually became the most visible woman in the American Communist hierarchy, her autobiography covers the period before she joined the Party. (The second volume, detailing Flynn's life as a Communist, was never written.) Like many radical autobiographies, *The Rebel Girl* is more political than personal. Flynn writes a lively history of the American labor movement in the early twentieth century. Her book is full of information about the free speech fights of the Industrial Workers of the World, about the many strikes in which Flynn participated—notably Lawrence in 1912 and Paterson in 1913—and about the political prisoners, including Sacco and Vanzetti, whose freedom she campaigned for. It includes capsule biographies of important leaders of the American left: Mother Jones, Ella Reeve Bloor, Vincent St. John, Bill Haywood, Eugene Debs.

Although Flynn's focus is political, she also tells us about the strains in the career of a woman radical. Flynn learned her socialism from her father and her feminism from her mother. Annie Gurley Flynn, an Irish immigrant and a fervent suffragist, taught her daughter determination. Flynn married Jack Jones, a miner and I. W. W. organizer she met on a Western speaking tour when she was 17. Jones resented his young wife's insistence that she continue to travel, agitate, and go to jail. They eventually separated, just before the birth of their son. Annie Flynn enabled her daughter to continue her political career by caring for her grandson. From 1912-1925 Flynn lived with Italian anarchist Carlo Tresca. She struggled to balance the demands of her son, her lover, and her political work, but *The Rebel Girl* makes it clear that the work came first.

The Rebel Girl is written in serviceable if not elegant prose. Both in style and in content it provides a contrast and a corrective to the more widely read autobiography of Flynn's contemporary, Emma Goldman.

[99] *The Alderson Story: My Life As A Political Prisoner.* New York: International Publishers, 1963. 223 pp.

The Alderson Story records Elizabeth Gurley Flynn's experiiences as a Smith Act prisoner in the Women's House of Detention in New York City and the Federal Penitentiary for Women in Alderson, West Virginia, between 1955 and 1957. Flynn is particularly sensitive to the lives of women in prison, speculating about the differences between men and women prisoners and discussing lesbianism. The book closes with several of the poems Flynn wrote at Alderson.

Flynn's autobiographical writings were generally ignored by reviewers when they were first published, except in the left-wing journals. But her work has been appreciated by scholars discussing twentieth century feminism; for example, see June Sochen, *Movers and Shakers: American Women Thinkers and Activists 1900-1970* (New York: Quadrangle, 1973) and *Women and Literature: An Annotated Bibliography of Women Writers,* 3rd ed. (Cambridge, Mass.: The Women and Literature Collective, 1976).

                                                    Elsa Dixler
                                Signs, University of Chicago Press

Fremantle, Anne (1910-   )

Novelist, Journalist, Educator, Historian

[100] *Three-Cornered Heart.*   New York: Viking Press, 1971. 316 pp.

Only a remarkable personality could sustain the several public *persona* which Anne Fremantle has displayed to Americans since she became a U. S. citizen in 1947. But that personality does not gain full expression in *Three-Cornered Heart.* The book's design is partly responsible, for Fremantle recounts her mother's childhood and adolescence before turning to her own story. The volume thus ends with Fremantle's marriage in 1930, though hints about her later career are sprinkled throughout. To be sure, her mother's early life holds much fascination. The daughter of Mountstuart Grant Duff, "Tiny" Huth Jackson grew up near the political and cultural center in Victorian England. A liberal MP of impeccable breeding, Mountstuart fraternized with Brown-

ing, Arnold, Newman, Darwin, Marx, Cobden—the list of luminaries seems endless. Tiny's world was shaped not only by this
milieu but by all the "above-stairs" conventions of her social
class: colonial experience, governesses, finishing school, coming
out, stalking a proper husband.

In narrating her own first quarter century, Fremantle suppresses
more than she reveals. While we do learn something about her religious concerns, responses to World War I, and struggles with Victorian sexual repressiveness, she rather completely distances herself from the reader. Always speaking of herself in the third person, she intimates almost nothing about her courtship, early political attitudes, or feelings towards her father. Her preoccupation is
with reminiscing about the "greats" she has encountered: Waugh,
Lady Gregory, Einstein, Auden, etc. Yet the book does contain
vigorous and accomplished writing, a marvelous chapter on how
Oxford treated its few female students in the 1920's, and excellent
anecdotes of all sorts.

Fremantle won much praise from critics, who generally were
caught up in the book's revelations about notorious characters.
Anne O'Neill-Barna found the work so "pellucidly candid as to be
virtually libelous" (New York *Times,* November 29, 1970, p. 52).
But Glendy Culligan also sees in it the theme of self-liberation from
a male dominated Victorian world (*Saturday Review,* December
12, 1970, p. 35). In terms of Women's Studies, *Three-Cornered
Heart* might well form an adjunct reading in a course treating
generational conflict about female roles during the interwar period
in England. Fremantle has produced a fine study of George Eliot,
and her most recent book, *Women's Way to God* (1977), treats
various female "pilgrim souls," pioneers of spirituality, like
Dorothy Day, Simone Weil, and Mary Baker Eddy.

Leslie E. Gerber
Applachian State University

Friedan, Betty (1921-   )

Feminist, Writer

[101] *It Changed My Life.* New York: Random House, 1976.
    388 pp.

Published thirteen years after her first book, *The Feminine
Mystique,* which spurred the revival of American feminism in 1963,
It Changed My Life is an intermingling of personal and social history. A collection of Friedan's articles and speeches since 1963,
each preceded by "memories of surrounding circumstances,"
this book weaves into a coherent whole the developing women's
movement and Friedan's personal experiences as activist.

Beginning with a description of her life as a suburban housewife
when the feminine mystique "really hit" in 1949, Friedan recounts
the changes in her life which have paralleled the changes in the
movement she initiated. Her role in founding the National Organization for Women (NOW) in 1966, her activist years as president of NOW from 1966-1970, her withdrawal from the movement
from 1971-1973 "to come to new terms with the political as personal" in her life, and her participation in the International Women's Year Conference in Mexico City in 1975, are all unified by
her driving search for acceptance. Throughout the book, Friedan's
message to the women's movement echoes her own personal need—
to remain in the mainstream of American life, to change the system so that talented and ambitious women like herself need not
be outcasts.

Friedan is criticized for her "failure of penetration and analysis" and lack of feminist philosophy by Sara Sanborn in *Saturday
Review* (July 24, 1976, p. 26). Other reviewers have challenged
the accuracy and criticized the redundancy of the book. Jo Ann
Levine in the *Christian Science Monitor* (August 3, 1976, p. 22)
calls it a "grab bag of dire predictions, vast distortions and indisputable truths about the women's movement," while lamenting the
brevity of Friedan's personal insights.

The underlying theme of most reviews is that *It Changed My
Life* attempts to be both history and autobiography and does
neither quite well enough. Yet the feminist periodical *Spokes-*

woman (July 15, 1976, p. 18), while chiding Friedan for her "un-willingness to face issues," sounds a recurring theme among re-viewers. Friedan is "a sort of senior stateswoman" who with her "sharp observations" and "quick and colorful style" can remind American women "how far we have come and how much we have to lose if we only slide back a little."

Regardless of the criticism of some reviewers, *It Changed My Life* is an invaluable collection of source materials and must be consulted by historians in the future.

Maryann Intermont Ustick
St. Leo College

Frooks, Dorothy (1899-   )

Lawyer, Writer, Social Reformer

[102] *Lady Lawyer.* New York: Robert Speller and Sons, 1975. 201 pp.

Dorothy Frooks traces the development of her career as a law-yer, dramatizing and summarizing the key events of her public life from the time of her speechmaking as a young suffragette to her involvement in international law as an elder woman lawyer. In the first third of the book she dramatizes her defense of Catherine Deninno, accused of murdering a man who had raped the young woman during childhood, and considers how this case stimulated her interest in promoting laws to protect widows and orphans.

From the start Frooks underlines her central theme: her com-mitment to defending the rights of the unfortunate and to main-taining high ethical standards in her work. In chapter seven she re-traces her activity in the suffrage movement, introducing a broad social historical perspective on women's fight for the vote, and sketches in her childhood. Then she turns to her earliest profes-sional activities, her work as a lawyer for the Salvation Army and her efforts to support the creation of a small claims court in New

York.

A chapter follows on her defense of a woman lawyer falsely accused of withholding funds from a male law associate and subsequently condemned by a corrupt judge. In her discussion of this case, she reflects on the obstacles women lawyers faced in working for recognition within their profession. In the last third of her book, she focuses on her journalism, her political writing and her work as editor of a local New York paper, *Murray Hill News.*

Janis Forman
Goucher College

Garrett, Eileen Jeanette (1893-1970)

Medium, Publisher

[103] *Adventures in the Supernormal: A Personal Memoir.* New York: Creative Age Press, 1949. 252 pp.

Adventures in the Supernormal is the most comprehensive of Eileen Garrett's autobiographical writings, although she wrote other, more specialized accounts of her mediumistic experiences. This volume is a revised and expanded version of an earlier memoir, *My Life as a Search for the Meaning of Mediumship* (New York: Oquaga Press, 1939), extending her story beyond her paranormal experiences to her activities as an American businesswoman and philanthropist. An Irish orphan reared by a loving uncle and a cold, aloof aunt, Garrett experienced supernormal perceptions from earliest childhood; they included clairvoyance, clairaudience, and the perception of the auras of objects and people. Her childhood was a difficult one, since those around her, especially her aunt, accused her of deception and dismissed her experiences as the products of a diseased or overactive imagination. Afer a disastrous marriage and the death of two children, she was involved in several business ventures while devoting most of her enegy to an investigation of her unusual powers. Dissatisfied with work as a trance medium, she took a scientific approach to supernormal phenomena, unusual in the early part of this century, and worked with a number of English and American scientists in an attempt to test and understand her "gift." Eventually settling in America, she founded *Tomorrow,* a magazine devoted to "creative living," and the Creative Age Press. She also established the Parapsychological Foundation, devoted to research and the publication of scholarly books and monographs.

Much of Garrett's memoir is devoted to careful description and analysis of her supernormal experiences; her attempt to understand and explain her gift has led one reviewer to describe her memoir as "a lesson in the art of self-examination" (New York *Times,* October 23, 1949, p. 51). Just as interesting as her supernatural experiences are her memories of a traumatic childhood and young adulthood: the lack of understanding from her aunt, the disillusionment with education and religion, the dissatisfaction with her role as wife, the difficulties of her career as a businesswoman. Garrett's life and career became more settled after her arrival in the United States, where she eventually became known as "Lady Bountiful of Parapsychology" because of her support of research and experimentation in psychic phenomena. Garrett's career has been evaluated in a biography by Allen Angoff (*Eileen Garrett and the World Beyond the Senses,* New York: Morrow, 1974) and in a more scientific study by Dr. Jan Ehrnewald (*Telepathy and Medical Psychology,* New York: Norton, 1948). Her autobiography was widely reviewed and praised for its candor and objectivity. The volume is of interest to women's studies because it is a searching account of an unusual life that, nevertheless, reveals many of the same patterns as do the lives of other women.

Betsy Etheridge Brown
Pennsylvania State University

Geva, Tamara (c.1907-   )

Dancer, Actress

[104] *Split Seconds: A Remembrance.*   New York: Harper & Row, 1972. 358 pp.

Using a chronological first person narrative, *Split Seconds* traces Geva's life from her childhood in Leningrad to her triumph as lead dancer in the American musical *On Your Toes*. The illigitimate daughter of an aristocrat and a dancehall chorine whose "beauty was her meal ticket" (4), Geva was fearful of her mother's manic-depressive swings, and in awe of her father whom she rarely saw. The birth of a brother and eventual heir, when Geva was six, made the marriage of her parents possible. Soon after this union, the Russian revolution began and the author's father lost his money, position, and his wife's affections. During these years of poverty, Geva's relationship with her mother deteriorated, and she was witness to her mother's infidelity with another man.

At twelve, she was accepted as a ballet student in the Petrograd Theatre School, and there at age fifteen met George Balanchine, whom she married a year later. The couple left Russia in 1924 and soon after, the marriage failed, for Geva did not like the role of "dancer-wife" in which she was cast and "began developing. . . a strong compulsion to be accepted" for herself (335). For a time after this, the dancer was "kept" by a Marquis but notes "It was inevitable that the situation would remind me of my mother's life" (345) and so she ended the affair. On tour in America, Geva decided to remain in this country and renewed her friendship with Balanchine, appearing in his *Errante* at the first performance of the American Ballet Theatre (now the New York City Ballet).

The most lasting influence on the dancer, "a relationship which would never be duplicated in (her) life," (36) was her governess, Fraulein Rosalie who acted as mother, teacher, sister and friend; and in the end, literally gave her life for Geva's future. The few reviews of *Split Seconds* ranged from lukewarm to negative, with the *Library Journal* noting that it was "of special interest to dance lovers" (October 1, 1972).

T. Gail Adams
Emory University, ILA

Gibson, Althea (1927-   )

Athlete, Tennis Player

[105] *I Always Wanted to Be Somebody.* Ed. by Ed Fitzgerald. New York: Harper & Row, 1958. 176 pp.

I Always Wanted to Be Somebody covers a period from Gibson's birth in Silver, S. C., in 1927 through 1957. It outlines her childhood in Harlem where she was constantly in trouble of one kind or another; for example, truancy and fighting (her father gave her boxing lessons and wanted her to become a prize-fighter). With her introduction to tennis in her adolescence, her talent soon became obvious to various Black tennis experts, and she was virtually adopted by Dr. Hubert Eaton of Wilmington, N. C., and Dr. Robert W. Jackson of Lynchburg, Va. She lived alternately with the families of these two men, attended high school in North Carolina, and eventually went on to college. The book outlines her gradual rise through the world of Black tennis, her breakthrough into the world of white tennis (earning her the sports reporters' nick-name: the Jackie Robinson of tennis), her world travels with a group of young tennis players as an American ambassador of good will, climaxing with her becoming the first Black woman to win the Wimbledon tennis crown in August 1957. As the book ends she is contemplating a show business career as a musician.

I Always Wanted to Be Somebody is of value to those in women's studies interested in race relations and sports. The book is filled with lengthy quotations from news accounts of Gibson's important tennis matches. Gibson is open about her childhood, equally candid in regard to relationships with friends; for example, her "two doctors" and their families, Sugar Ray Robinson and his wife Edna Mae who encouraged her interest in music. She is however much more reticent about more intimate relationships.

The reviewers of *I Always Wanted to Be Somebody* were divided in their opinions as to the relationship of Ed Fitzgerald to the book. Quentin Reynolds, however, wrote that the book "is 'edited,' not 'ghosted,' by sports writer Ed Fitzgerald—and an excellent job he has done. The language is the language Althea uses" (*Saturday Review*, November 29, 1958, p. 16). Another reviewer speaks of the work as a "peculiarly innocent book. . .written with a simple and rather tough honesty which makes it extremely appealing" (Barbara Klaw, New York *Herald Tribune Book Review,* February 22, 1959, p. 8). Allison Danzig writes, "This absorbing story of Althea Gibson's rise from the streets of Harlem to acceptance in the highest social circles, might be judged a valuable social document on the advancement of the Negro despite segregation, restrictions and discrimination" (New York *Times,* December 7, 1959, p. 3).

Jean R. Halladay
Old Dominion University

Gildersleeve, Virginia Cocheran (1877-1965)

Educator, World Peace Activist

[106] *Many a Good Crusade.* New York: The Macmillan Company, 1954. 434 pp.

Dean of Barnard College for thirty-six years and active internationalist for twenty-seven, Virginia Gildersleeve writes in her autobiography of many efforts, "generally vain, to reform and improve the world." Although she did not explicitly promote feminist causes, she accomplished much in expanding educational and career opportunities for women.

Gildersleeve describes herself in her early years as slow to develop, shy, unsocial, snobbish and solemn. Her mother, the single most influential figure in her life, was a strong determined woman who encouraged her to develop her mind and body fully and pushed her toward college in spite of her own reluctance. In her years as dean, Gildersleeve acted on her belief that a college must be active in the world. Through World War I and II and in the years that followed, her involvement centered increasingly upon efforts to build peace through international understanding and tolerance. Through work with the International Federation of University Women she built close ties with women in other countries and achieved world-wide distinction. She served as the only female delegate from the United States at the United Nations founding conference in 1945 and in 1946 she flew to Japan with the United States Education Mission to help chart that Country's democratization of its school system. Her autobiography shows extensive understanding of conditions and viewpoints of others and then occasionally reflects her insulated position of upper middle-class power and privilege.

Many a Good Crusade received generally favorable reviews, the most comprehensive of which was written by Gildersleeve's friend and fellow educator Mildred MacAfee Horton (*Saturday Review,* October 30, 1954, p. 21). Horton lauds book and writer for an interesting history of Barnard and for the depth of crusading fervor revealed. She makes note of Gildersleeve's many friendships with men as well as women and describes her as a proponent of full responsibilities for women without expecting or demanding special favors for them. The New York *Herald Tribune* (November 7, 1954, p. 3) found Gildersleeve's account of her "journey out of a Victorian childhood into a most responsible position" to be "extraordinarily interesting." Several reviews praised the book's uninhibited frankness, and the *Booklist* (December 15, 1954, p. 174) finds its chief interest to lie in its discussion of women's education, the place of women in the scholarly world and in national and international affairs.

Barbara Greene
Norfolk, Va.

Giles, Nell (c.1920-   )

Novelist, Newspaper Columnist

[107] *Punch In, Susie!* New York: Harper and Brothers, 1943. 143 pp.

In 1943 Nell Giles, by profession a reporter, took a job at a General Electric factory that made parts for Air Force planes. *Punch In, Susie!* is the series of articles she wrote for the Boston *Globe* describing her life as a woman factory worker during World War II.

Attempting to perform all the tasks assigned to her with utmost care, cheerfully accommodating herself to different shifts, accepting the factory decorum for women (no black metal lunch boxes, only bags; no stockings, only leg make-up), Nell Giles felt great pride in her contributions and those of women factory workers everywhere to the war effort. A sincere patriotism sustained her and her co-workers as they served in what she calls this "second front."

Mainly a series of autobiographical articles written to encourage other women to join the war effort, *Punch In, Susie!* is nevertheless of interest to women's studies for its view of women's work. Giles stresses the vital contribution women factory workers were making, but always in terms of service to "the boys at the front." Women workers (usually supervised by men) are shown to be carefully and proudly fitting out the planes for the male pilots to fly. On the other hand, those men at home who suggested that women were perhaps doing "men's work" were assured by Giles and others that the change was only temporary and that the women planned no takeover (127). The experience in the factory, as Giles describes it, seems to have effected no significant change of consciousness in herself or in the women she writes about. She does conclude, however, with a desire to revise her role somewhat from being a manicured white-collar worker to being what she calls "a more *essential* [her emphasis] woman" which consists in learning "how to mend an ironing cord and repair a leaky faucet and make bread" (142-43).

Judith B. Herman
State College at Buffalo

Giovanni, Nikki (1944-   )

Poet, Teacher

[108] *Gemini: An Extended Autobiographical Statement on My First Twenty-Five Years.* New York: Viking Compass Edition, 1973. 149 pp.

Nikki Giovanni's *Gemini* is an autobiographical account bound
to engender mixed reactions. Some will experience discomfort
with it because it violates form and is not "true" autobiography.
More reasonable readers will applaud it for what it is—a vibrant extended fictionalized autobiographical statement of the artist's first
twenty-five years.

Gemini is a mix of genres. Structurally, the first five chapters
introduce us to the poet and the major influences of her life: her
grandmother, her mother, her sister, and her son. The fifth chapter, "Don't Have a Baby till You Read This," is hilariously warm
and descriptive as Giovanni recounts the physical and emotional
trauma of having her child and learning how to care for it.

Chapter six is pivotal as it moves between personal statement
(a Black woman travels in Haiti) and political statement (observations about Angela Davis). Chapters seven through twelve use a
different stance and voice and are overt social and political commentary on people (Lena Horne), places (Africa, America,
Europe), ideas (Black art, aesthetics, relationships between men
and women, whites and Blacks), books (*The Sound of Soul*), and
aspects of culture. A first reading would indicate, seemingly, that
in these chapters Giovanni employs some specious socio/historical
analysis; a second reading could lead one to concur with June
Jordan who sees these chapters as "entertaining, high-spirited raps"
(New York *Times,* February 13, 1972). In fact, Jordan views all
of *Gemini* as a "collection of essays" seemingly unrelated; but the
structure of the book dispels that theory.

Chapter thirteen returns us to the personal voice of the poet:
Giovanni comments on why she became a poet, what her intellectual influences had been, how she achieved her emotional
growth. She also comments on productive Black artists, those
"who are persistently exposing (their) insides and trying to create
a reality" (143). Her comments on the actions of white women
should be of more than passing interest to feminists.

One of the things *Gemini* does best is illustrate the warmth,
strength, and stability of Giovanni's family in the teeth of recent
sociology stereotypes about the decline of the Black family.
Poignant glimpses of a Black folk culture and the rhythms of an
oral tradition suffuse the work, particularly in its personal mo-

ments. The conversational tone is consistent throughout.

Initial response to *Gemini* is not worth repeating. Suffice it to say that most reviews were by white males who, apparently, could not stand Giovanni's direct approach and who resented her political observations about revolution. Perhaps they overlooked the obvious symbolism of the title.

Sandra Y. Govan
Emory University

Gordon, Ruth (1896-   )

Actress, Playwright

[109] *Myself among Others.*   New York: Atheneum, 1971. 389 pp.

Myself among Others enables the reader to follow Ruth Gordon's career spanning nearly sixty years. In 1914, equipped with her father's telescope should she ever need something to pawn, Ruth Gordon (Jones) left Wollaston, Massachusetts, for New York to pursue a career on the stage. In so doing she moved from obscurity to fame, which she enjoyed continuously up to the time of publishing this, her quasi-autobiography, at the age of seventy-four.

In a volume almost exclusively restricted to her theatrical life, Gordon devotes the opening pages to Alexander Woollcott, her early mentor, the drama critic for the New York *Times;* his 1915 review of *Peter Pan,* in which she starred as Nibs, launched her on a meteoric rise to fame. Taking Woollcott's advice, "If you want to make sure you know what you're talking about, talk about yourself" (30), Gordon narrates her experiences in stardom, experiences which she shared with scores of luminaries: Thornton Wilder, Katherine Cornell, George Kaufman, Vivien Leigh, Ethel Barrymore, Helen Keller, and Laurence Olivier, to name a few. Comfortable with both sexes and seemingly free of sexual hang-ups, Gordon narrates anecdotes involving her dealings with celebrities, flashbacks to her days as an aspiring actress, brief accounts of trivia, and still briefer passages of intospection. Sometimes whimsical, sometimes lyrical, but always absorbing, her experiences run the gamut from celebrating New Year's Eve with Somerset Maugham to suffering through the final days of Jeanne Eagels' life.

Although disjointed and discontinuous, *Myself among Others* is unified by Gordon's personality, whose off-beat mannerisms cannot disguise her *joie de vivre*. Pround of her performances in such productions as *The Matchmaker* and *Rosemary's Baby* and hopeful of continued success in her late years, Ruth Gordon reveals herself as totally immersed in the theatre. So strong was her determination from youth to become an actress that a vote of no confidence given her at the American Academy of Dramatic Arts failed to dissuade her. The alternative to a theatrical career, she remarked to her father, was suicide, and since she prized life, she was left with no choice.

In a profession long noted for its overemphasis of feminine sexuality as a criterion for success, Ruth Gordon, harboring no illusions of personal beauty and acknowledging her commonness, forced her critics' attention away from sexual stereotypes in favor of her talent.

[110] *My Side.* New York: Harper & Row, 1976. 488 pp.

B
G664a

In her youth Ruth Gordon's parents wanted her to become a nurse, a secretary, or a physical culture teacher, but the voice to which Gordon responded belonged to Hazel Dawn, who while starring in *The Pink Lady,* sang out "Dream." Gordon's dream, to reach the zenith of stardom, and its accompanying struggles are traced in her autobiography. Emphasizing events rather than the principal's internal life, this book, whose organization is loosely chronological with frequent flashbacks and stream of consciousness passages, records Gordon's career beginning with her experiences as a struggling ingenue and ending with her avowed determination to remain active in the theatre as an octogenarian.

Without influence or experience but endowed with ambition and self-confidence, Gordon narrates the troubles and dreams of a spectacular but difficult career. Discipline and disappointment she learned early from touring the Midwest in a mediocre production of *Fair and Warmer* and from unsuccessfully hounding the New York agencies for a theatrical part, be it ever so small. After her first success in Peter Pan (1915) there followed over the years a string of brilliant performances in such plays and films as *The Matchmaker, Ethan Frome, The Country Wife, Harold and Maud,* and *Rosemary's Baby,* but among them were the failures. Throughout Gordon reveals a resilient spirit, inherited from her parents, that enabled her to learn the lessons taught by failure as well as by success.

Gordon also learned from turmoil and suffering. She tells about her happy marriage to actor and tutor Gregory Kelley, which ended in tragedy when he died from a heart attack. And she reports with candor the anxiety occasioned by her abortions. Gordon writes about her side of a four-year love affair with producer Arthur Hopkins, and her affair with producer Jed Harris which forced her to live in Paris until after the birth of their son Jones. Her story touches upon her loneliness before marrying Garson Kanin, her anxiety about debts, and her guilt at leaving her infirm mother. These and other difficulties all support Gordon's claim that troubles as well as dreams and success have characterized her life.

Agreement is rare among reviewers, but such is the case with the reviewers of Ruth Gordon's *Myself among Others,* who find fault with its form and content. Pointing to its disjointedness, reviewers object to Gordon's failure to weigh and explain the significance of her experiences. For Julius Novick, Gordon's book is "a grab-bag of anecdotes" (New York *Times Book Review,* June 12, 1971, p. 6), while for Edward Weeks it is "a jackdaw nest" (*Atlantic Monthly,* August 1971, p. 95). Under fire is Gordon's name-dropping, the emphasis on the "Others" of her title. According to Novick, names are strung together, but the people remain lifeless (p. 6). Novick compares this book to Bennett Cerf's "nameless literary genre" except that some of Gordon's stories are not supposed to be funny (p. 6). Novick concludes that there is a better book inside Gordon.

That better book is Gordon's autobiography *My Side.* John Houseman (New York *Times,* October 10, 1976, pp. 6-7) notes Gordon's obsession with stardom, and admits that the book may have greater appeal to readers deeply involved in the theatre than those not so infected, but argues that the latter will find interesting Gordon's varied experiences and the glamorous places she frequented. Houseman recommends *My Side* for its "surprising qualities of warmth and human understanding" (p. 7).

Elsie F. Mayer
Henry Ford Community College

Graham, Martha (1894-   )

Dancer, Choreographer, Inventor, Actress

[111] *The Notebooks of Martha Graham.* New York: Harcourt Brace Jovanovich, 1973. 464 pp.

793.22
G74/n

In what could more fittingly be called the *Notebook* of Martha Graham, we find an unedited record, never intended for the public, of her mind at play, dreaming works which have never been brought to the stage or film, and creating many of her nearly one hundred and fifty original theatre/dance pieces from *Deaths and Entrances,* first performed in 1943, to the recent *Mendicants of Evening* (1973). As she tells us in *Publisher's Weekly* (November 5, 1973, p. 33), the *Notebooks* are the result of a habit developed some twenty to twenty-five years before, the practice of sitting up in bed before going to sleep and writing her thoughts down in a series of stenobooks. Like Ezra Pound's *Cantos,* whose sense of time and spirit of romance Graham shares, these pages are a chaotic swirl of telegrams to herself, musings, choreographic jottings, and fragments of countless quotations from a largely Western literary tradition including Emily Dickinson, Shakespeare, David Daiches on Virginia Woolf, the Bible, Rilke, and Marianne Moore, to name only a few. This volume is not a confessional autobiography nor even an intermittent diary of domestic events; for instance, she never mentions her close personal and professional relationship with her longtime accompanist and musical director Louis Horst, her break with her lead male dancer Bertram Ross after many years, or even her associations with such artists as Noguchi or Merce Cunningham. Graham reveals instead a woman who conceived of herself first as an artist and *only* as an artist. Although the act of writing was certainly a way of composing the self ("What is the beginning? Perhaps when we seek 'wholeness'—when we embark on the journey toward wholeness," 305), dance was always primary; hers is not the self-conscious search for identity shown, for example, in Nin's *Diary*. Rarely in fact, does the word "I" appear in these 464 pages. One of the few such passages offers a glimpse of a formative childhood event. Catching her in a verbal lie revealed by her body, her father explained that "Movement never lies" (270); this truth found expression in her life and career.

The *Notebooks* received scant and mixed reviews. "Graham's mind is infinitely more fascinating than this anthology of scholarly jottings suggests, and the publication unhappily reinforces the present-day image of Graham as that of a bookish lady who puts on dances," wrote Arlene Croce in the *New Yorker* (May 6, 1974, p. 3). Only Marcia Siegel in the New York *Times* (December 16, 1973, p. 3) commented on the volume from a feminist point of view: "In her versions of mythic events we've always heard told from a male point of view the women are at the center. More than just creating roles for herself, for fifty years Graham has been probing the feminine psyche to a depth few other artists, and probably no Americans, have ever done." Since Graham is "the first woman in the history of drama East and West to have contributed a huge and amazingly varied body of work to the theatre" (wrote L. Leatherman in what is still the best, but non-feminist essay on Graham, *Martha Graham*, Knopf, 1966, p. 32) and since she presents women as her central characters, she deserves more attention by feminist critics.

How Graham's mind transforms the well-known stories of Clytemnestra, Mary Queen of Scots, Joan of Arc, Hester, Phaedra, and Pocahontas, among others, is the dominant action of the *Notebooks;* her comments at times break into a passionate lyricism. The myth of Eve "might be a dream confessional of any woman/Any woman is Eve" (290). Alcestis is "fully the equal of masculine lovers" (44). And Clytemnestra is "the woman whose creative instinct—her child Iphigenia—has been killed by her husband. . .(her woman's nature has betrayed her)" (258). Graham's vision of woman is essentially Jungian; women are associated with the night, imagination, and intuition. To triumph in a man's world, her heroines must be tragic. As Graham writes, "I will not be released from this bondage until I have released myself. No man can do it for me" (206).

Kathleen Woodward
University of Wisconsin—Milwaukee

Graham, Sheilah (c.1908-   )

Journalist

[112] *Beloved Infidel: The Education of a Woman.* New York: Henry Holt and Company, 1958. 338 pp.

ß
G74182

Beloved Infidel, the first of five autobiographical works, covers the years from Graham's birth to the death of her lover, F. Scott Fitzgerald, in 1940. Graham movingly describes her resourceful rise from an impoverished and humiliating childhood in a London slum to fame as a Hollywood columnist. She also reveals the story of her turbulent romance with Fitzgerald during the last four years of his life, sharing the pleasures and horrors of loving a gifted alcoholic. Her's is the story of a woman with intelligence, ruthless ambition, and charm.

Reviews of *Beloved Infidel* varied from qualified praise to caustic condemnation. Many reviewers saw value in the third of the book which deals with Fitzgerald but were impatient with Graham's life story. The New York *Herald Tribune* (November 3, 1958, p. 3) called the book "a Cinderalla story written for Victorian servant girls."

[113] *The Rest of the Story.* New York: Coward-McCann, 1964. 304 pp.

Graham, continuing her autobiography from 1941 to 1963, re-emerges strong after the shattering death of Fitzgerald. She wrangles a war correspondent assignment to London, marries twice, rears two children, has her own radio and television shows,

and achieves her goal of earning what the top film stars make:
$5,000 a week. Graham records, but she does not explore in
depth, the conflicts of a woman enmeshed in the values of the
Fifties: the working woman and mother dilemma, ambition and
love, success and guilt.

The Rest of the Story, a gossipy and fragmented book clogged
with trivia, drew predictably negative reviews.

[114] *College of One.*   New York: Viking Press, 1967.   245 pp.

Graham re-tells the story of her early life as backdrop for this
description of the two-year college education F. Scott Fitzgerald
designed and conducted for her. She for years lived in dread of
making a slip which would betray her eighth grade education.
Fitzgerald's crash course in history, literature, philosophy, religion, music and art made it possible for her to be at ease among
the Hollywood literati with whom they associated. Graham, in
summarizing each segment of the course, conveys the excitement
of her intellectual awakening.

Reviewers focused on what *College of One* reveals about Fitzgerald as a pedagogue and intellectual and showed little interest in
Graham except to call her learning superficial. One exception was
the *Times Literary Supplement* (June 29, 1967, p. 567) which
complimented Graham's touching earnestness and noted that Fitzgerald succeeded in his campaign to "improve her mind. . .[and]
make her a better writer."

**[115] *A State of Heat.*   New York: Grosset & Dunlap, 1972.
244 pp.**

Graham gives yet another run-through of her life in this rambling, explicit history of her sexual adventures, which she had
omitted from previous volumes. She brags of having had "success
. . .money, fame, great love, proposals by the score, and hundreds
of propositions" (1). She recommends that a woman learn to project a sexual "state of heat" in order to win a man and "use him to
get what she wants from life" (5). If she is ever without a man, she
consoles herself with overeating and with her favorite fantasy, rape.

A State of Heat received little critical attention. Nora Ephron (New York *Times,* April 23, 1972, p. 38) called the memoir "close to being unpublishable" because of its tasteless candor.

[116] *The Real F. Scott Fitzgerald: Thirty-Five Years Later.* New York: Grosset & Dunlap, 1976. 282 pp.

Graham's rationale for writing yet another autobiographical account stems from the recent re-awakened interest in Fitzgerald. "Perhaps with a more probing analysis of his whole personality and mine, and a fuller account of our relationship, I shall finally dispel some of the irritating errors that have been printed" (12). Writing with less gossip, more maturity, and greater self-respect, Graham portrays Fitzgerald as a compelling romantic, afraid of disillusionment, idealizing women as either angels or whores. She was angelic when he was sober, whorish during his binges. Graham also includes a short story and part of a play she wrote with Fitzgerald's help.

The Real F. Scott Fitzgerald received even less attention than *A State of Heat.* Reviewers agreed with Pauline J. Earl (*Best Sellers,* September, 1976, p. 196) that in bringing out another book on Fitzgerald, Graham's eye may have been more on the cash register than on setting the record straight.

Nancy Manahan
Napa College

Guffy, Ossie White (1931-   )

Mother, Activist

[117] *Ossie: The Autobiography of a Black Woman.* New York: Norton, 1971. 213 pp.

At the time she published her autobiography, Ossie Guffy was a mother of eleven children, living with her husband in Watts and working vigorously in the anti-poverty program. Because her book includes such facts of a life of poverty as hunger, rape, poor medical care, crowded housing, unemployment, drugs, and gambling, it is frequently compared by reviewers to other confessional autobiographies of poor Black Americans, such as Maya Angelou, Piri Thomas, or Claude Brown. Ossie differs from the others in its expression of folk culture even in an urban environment. Though she grew up in Cincinnati and moved eventually to Watts, the precepts around which she organized her life and which illuminate her story are those shared with her by her rural southern grandparents. Most of the chapters, for example, begin with folk sayings or aphorisms, such as "Like sometimes happens when you've reached the end of the road, another one opened up for me," or "You gotta make do with what you got." Against the assaults on her identity and the threats to her children that modern urban life poses, she musters her folk wisdom and folk ways. Because of her lack of formal education, the narrative lacks polish and abstract generalizations, and throughout Ossie calls herself "the dumbest nigger around." That epithet, though, comes to have a double edge, for she shows consistently that she is a resilient and resourceful person by choice, capable of analyzing the forces that impinge upon her and determined to forge solutions to the difficulties that confront her.

Her narrative is of particular interest to feminists, for she has selected from her life incidents that exemplify only too clearly the double oppression that afflicts Black American women. She demonstrates in the episodes of her life the effects of the sexual double standard, discriminatory employment, and the class biases of the medical profession. In spite of the degrading situations that confront her, she maintains a bouyant and life-giving philosophy which she expresses eloquently in the book. She views the birth of each of her children, for example, not as financial disaster (as she is encouraged to do by well-meaning doctors and social workers or even her upwardly mobile sister), but rather as a gift expressing more life. She does much to reveal the attitudes of her class and race and sex toward child rearing, sexuality, and family life, underlining again and again the conflict between her generous emotions and the economic conditions of her life.

Though some reviewers complained of her characterization of Black men as weak or ineffectual, she attempts to balance that picture of the absent or deserting lover or husband with portraits of her own father and her present husband. She also consistently explains the failures of men in her life in terms of their circumstances rather than in terms of personal weakness. She admits, though, more than once in the book that she perceives a definite difference between the way that Black men and Black women cope with the same problems. She says, for example, that if some people trust God to provide, then for many Black men, God must be a Black woman. Through all the crises of her own life, her determination to sustain herself and her children is supported by other Black women: neighbors, friends, mother, grandmother, aunts.

She says in her introduction that she hopes to let others know what it is like to be Ossie. In her autobiography, she lets us know not only about Ossie but about a great many other people like her, for throughout she emphasizes her ordinariness, her "commonness," her shared experience of life.

Kathleen Callaway
Florida International University

Hahn, Emily (1905-   )

B
H148   Essayist, Biographer

[118] *Times and Places.* New York: Thomas Y. Crowell Company, 1970. 303 pp.

Times and Places is a hodge-podge of anecdotes and opinions. In it Hahn treats her family life—with her parents and later her children—in the Belgian Congo, the British Museum's Reading Room, Japan and Shanghai; she tells of overcoming opium addiction, attempting suicide, battling sexism in the academy and the office. Amusing reading it is, but so uneven that its use for a feminist classroom is limited. Yet, Hahn is an independent woman, and all the stories reflect her strength, even though her ethnocentrism and aversion to collectives of any kind lead to a preference at times for the trivial. As Helen Mears said of an earlier book of Hahn's, *China to Me,* "From the evidence. . .she is an extreme individualist, wholly apolitical in her interests, 'bemused' by life, with a great zest for experience—for its own, or art's sake" (*New Republic,* January 15, 1945, p. 92).

Rebellion Reconsidered could be the subtitle to "Be Not the First," an amusing story in *TaP* which treats the issue of women's clothing. Emily's mother, in an attempt to prevent damage to dresses from after-school activities, substituted knickers for her two daughters' usual school attire. The notoriety and embarassment which followed provoked Emily into fighting back against friends, teachers, newspaper reporters, the school principal and even the state legislature, which regretted that it could not prevent her from wearing knickers since she was "decently covered." Such a tale could be useful for Women's Studies classes, at least at the high school level, since it shows that any one of us, perhaps for reasons beyond our control, could be forced to have a day in knickers so that others will be able to take for granted what we won at a price. Nevertheless, the title warns that pain awaits the frontrunner, and negates Emily as a role model.

In "B.Sc." Hahn dared to circumvent university regulations about taking a certain science course: she declared a major in mining engineering, with the intention to change back to the humanities curriculum once the course ended. But when told by professors, fellow (and I mean "fellow") students, and engineers that women were not capable of making it in the field, she knew she had to prove that she could. Emily Hahn became the first female graduate in mining engineering at the University of Wisconsin. Her struggle to succeed makes interesting reading and yet one curses the cost to Hahn's life—she didn't really like mining engineering. Hahn's point of view is that of a white, middle-class woman: intelligent, observant, and wry, but anti-analytical and rarely aware that the leisure she enjoys has causes and effects.

Janet Freedman was partially correct when she wrote, "While some of the anecdotes [in *TaP*] are merely amusing, most contribute to an extraordinary self-portrait of a determined woman who refused to let her sex or society's conventions block her aspirations" (*Library Journal*), December 15, 1970, p. 4252). The book should be read for the determination and courage Hahn displays, but one will have to resist the impulse to lay it aside in frustration because of its clear implication that if we are going to fight battles, we must fight like ladies.

Diane Marting
Livingston College, Rutgers University

Hale, Nancy (1908-   )

Author

[119] *A New England Girlhood.* Boston: Little, Brown & Company, 1936. 232 pp.

Nancy Hale collects under one title a series of previously published essays for this "affectionate re-creation of things past." Not attempting to write a factual autobiography of her early years, Hale blends fact and fantasy to write stories that record the flavors of early twentieth-century Boston, the events and feelings in the life of a New England debutante, the maverick world of her artist parents, and all the "reverberations from childhood that sometimes make it seem as if the first few years of all our lives constitute the riddle which it is a lifework to solve." This last Proustian attitude is reflected in Hale's style, which borrows the salient features of Proust's narrative without achieving its depth.

New England Girlhood was well-received by the critics. All found it "delightful" and "gracious," and noted its value as a period recreation. Only Jean Holzhauer pointed out the lack of profundity, the absence of the "hard thrust of surviving permanent emotion," especially as compared to Mary McCarthy's *Memories of a Catholic Girlhood* (*Commonweal,* July 11, 1958, p. 9).

[120] *The Life in the Studio.* Boston: Little, Brown & Company, 1957. 209 pp.

Though writing primarily recollections of her artist parents, Hale inevitably reveals much of her own childhood and development of her adult values. Most touching and honest are her descriptions of her relation to her mother. Of particular interest,

"The Other Side," "Journeys," and "My Mother's Solitudes" show a discovery of her mother who overcame a Victorian upbringing to enjoy an equal marriage and to develop true expression in her art.

Not as widely reviewed as the earlier *New England Girlhood, Life in the Studio* was, however, sensitively reviewed by poet-novelist May Sarton in the New York *Times*, (July 27, 1969, p. 7). Sarton noted the loving descriptions of the private world of the artists and the role their only child played in it. She underscored the dominant role given to the accomplished "rare, remote, elusive" Lillian Westcott Hale who was artist first, and wife and mother second.

For further and more detailed work by Hale writing on a woman artist, see her *Mary Cassatt* (New York: Doubleday, 1975), in which Hale characterizes Cassatt's career as a struggle for equality against biological determination.

Margaret Moore Willen
Eastern New Mexico University

Hamilton, Alice (1869-1970)

Physician: Industrial Doctor, Social Scientist, Peace Worker, Teacher

[121] *Exploring the Dangerous Trades: The Autobiography of Alice Hamilton, M. D.* Boston: Little Brown and Company, 1943. 433 pp.

Published when Alice Hamilton was seventy-four *Exploring the Dangerous Trades* records seven decades of a full life set against a national and international backdrop of idealism growing into disillusion. The book treats parts of her life as a child and student; a physician and social worker in and outside of Hull House; a surveyor of industrial disease in Illinois and across the nation; a worker for Peace in Europe in 1915 and for rehabilitation in 1919; an assistant professor of industrial medicine at Harvard Medical

School, "the stronghold of masculinity against the inroads of women" (252); a social scientist studying social trends for President Hoover and a medical consultant to the General Electric Company on less obvious hazards in industry such as fatigue, light, noise and vibration; a student of conditions in Germany in 1933 and in 1938; an observer of health and conditions in Russia and for the League of Nations; and her "retirement" to Hadlyme, Connecticut, in 1935 when Harvard made her a Professor Emeritus, a "great honor" pleasantly ignoring her sex (405). Throughout these activities, Hamilton studied the causes and effects of diseases resulting from smelting, painting, mining, explosives, air hammering, and match-making. Interspersed are her indignation at employers' ignorance and indifference and the workers' acceptance of their lot, her praise of employers who did improve the physical and psychological conditions of the workers; her gentle assertiveness in the face of opposition to her industrial investigations and the logic of her suggestions for improvement.

The influences and achievements of women abound in this autobiography. Hamilton recalls her mother's lack of possessiveness and her insistence on every woman's right to privacy and her obligation to do something about the wrongs in society. The author describes the uncompetitive atmosphere in her family of four sisters and one brother and her father's insistence that any statement must be supported by logic and evidence. Hamilton presents scores of examples of leisured women supporting each other and taking interest in and action on public issues.

Exploring the Dangerous Trades is an historical and somewhat hopeful record, from a woman's point of view, of more than sixty years of America's struggle to become more democratic. Reviewers praised the quality of Hamilton's life as well as her narration of it: "A serious, often indignant history of a woman's pioneering in a new medical field" (*Booklist*, April 15, 1943, p. 331); a "straightforward story lit with humor and thoughtful understanding gives a glimpse of a breadth of living that few men or women have the capacity to attain" (Mary Ross, New York *Herald Tribune*, April 11, 1943, p. 6); a Cellini-like autobiography of "high accomplishment and truth" (Frances Perkins, *New Republic*, April 19, 1943, p. 514).

Charlotte S.McClure
Georgia State University

Hansberry, Lorraine (1930-1965)

Playwright

[122] *To Be Young, Gifted and Black.* New York: Prentice-Hall, 1969. 266 pp.

Stitched together and published posthumously by Lorraine Hansberry's husband and literary executor, Robert Nemiroff, *To Be Young, Gifted and Black* is the life story of Hansberry, told in her own words from letters, speeches, notebooks, diaries, and plays. From a pastiche of chronologically disordered scenes and excerpts, interspersed with selected photographs and drawings by Hansberry, emerges a sharply defined account of people, places, and events affecting the playwright's life: her family and her middle-class upbringing on the Southside of Chicago; her two years as a fine arts major at the University of Wisconsin and her opportunity to voice opinions about "revolutionary" causes and "radical" ideas to responsive, if not always agreeing, subjects; her flirtation with the theatre and her acclaim when her first play, *A Raisin in the Sun,* won the new York Drama Critics Award for "The Best Play of the Year" (1959); her involvement in the Civil Rights Movement and the inspiration she offered young people; her illness with cancer and her impending death.

Though Hansberry at one point demonstrates her support of women's liberation by spiritedly attacking a fellow college student from Africa for his "medieval" ideas about the proper behavior for women, she offers her best defense for woman's place in society by adopting for herself and for others a view of life which celebrates the human spirit: "I think that the human race does command its own destiny and that that destiny can eventually embrace the stars." It is this all-encompassing spirit that permeates the better portion of her life and writings. Her description of that spirit as "happy and defiant" when she announced her forthcoming marriage to Nemiroff seems never to have been dampened in the union: she continued to write, apparently in seclusion whenever she wished, lecture, travel, maintain happy associations with family and friends, and involve herself in causes with little to hamper her.

Because the book *To Be Young, Gifted and Black* was published after the successful staging of the play by the same name, substantial assessments of the presentation of Hansberry's life have been directed toward the performance of the play rather than the printed word. The book itself, however, through an introduction by James Baldwin ("Sweet Lorraine") and a foreword and postscript by Nemiroff, manages to provide a measure of criticism on its contents.

Frances A. Grimes
Hampton Institute

Havoc, June (1916-   )

Actress, Dancer

[123] *Early Havoc.*   London: Hutchinson & Company, 1960. 313 pp.

Early Havoc covers only the first fourteen years of the author's life. Set primarily in a 1930's marathon dance hall, the narrative utilizes the experience of a first marathon as the lead-in to flashbacks of her past as a vaudevillian child-star. Billed as "Baby June," then later as "Dainty June," Havoc was managed by the indomitable Rose Hovick, famous as the quintessential stage mother in the musical comedy *Gypsy*—a piece based on the memoirs of Havoc's sister, Gypsy Rose Lee.

In recounting her childhood, Havoc tells of a bizarre existence on the edge of disaster. She received little formal education and had no stability other than that provided by the presence of her mother and sister. Fathers (four of them) drifted in and out of her life, and Havoc notes "Men just didn't seem to last" (30). Although she lived in the squalid conditions imposed by a touring circuit, Havoc was essentially innocent, with little knowledge of the realities of sex. Her mother's main instruction was that "God cursed them [men] by adding an ornament" that grew "everytime they so much as think of a woman." She went on to advise her daughters that nearly all men had syphilis. Havoc reports that her mother regularly warned that "Men are all selfish. They all want to separate us, but no one will ever do it" (31).

June's elopement at age thirteen earned her Rose Hovick's implacable enmity. Then less than a year after the marriage, Havoc separated from her husband and, desperate for employment during the Depression, found work as a dance marathon "horse." She reports that both her mother and her sister turned her away when she completed her first dance marathon. With no prospect for employment, she entered another marathon and, at fourteen, became a professional "horse."

Havoc concludes this fragment of her life with the observation that "Mother was right about one thing, marriage is difficult to understand. I had learned all about that angle of life, so I wouldn't have to waste much more time on men or marriage. As for my uncomfortable age, well, I only had to be fourteen for a year" (275).

June Havoc went on to set records as a marathon dancer and later achieved some success as an actress. This autobiography was adapted for the stage as *Marathon '33* and produced in 1962 with Julie Harris in the lead role as June. Rose Feld of the New York *Herald Tribune* (May 24, 1959, p. 4) was particularly impressed by Havoc's narrative technique. Typical of most reviews was the one in the *Library Journal* (March 15, 1959, p. 846) which found *Early Havoc* "a remarkable human document. . .that inevitably recalls the autobiography of her sister Gypsy Rose Lee," which was turned into the musical *Gypsy* with its portrayal of a driving managing mother.

T. Gail Adams
Emory University, ILA

Hayward, Brooke (1938-   )

Model, Actress

[124] *Haywire.* New York: Alfred A. Knopf, 1977. 326 pp.

Brooke Hayward's *Haywire* records the poignant history of a theatrical family. She speaks of her book as a personal memoir which also surveys "carelessness and guilt, and the wreckage they can make of lives" (3). She indicts her parents, Leland Hayward, theatrical agent and producer, and Margaret Sullavan, actress and homemaker, for the pernicious influence they had upon the lives of their three children, Brooke, Bridge and Bill. Hayward begins with a dramatic account of Bridget's death, possibly suicide, concluding this first chapter with the disconsolation: "I, Brooke—I would never be able to forget this—almost literally. . .I. . .held in the palm of my hand the singular and now irretrievable opportunity to save my sister's life" (31). Yet her sister's death, like her mother's death nine months earlier, was not clearly suicidal. Hayward avoids strict chronology and uses digressions, foreshadowings, and a sprinkling of memories related by such family friends as Henry Fonda, Jimmy Stewart, and Tom Mankiewicz. Enriching the descriptions of the family homes in California and Connecticut are nostalgic anecdotes of sibling rivalry, parental warmth as well as "carelessness and guilt," laced with the "opulent trappings" of the 1930's and 40's. The story ends with a chapter recounting the death of Hayward's father, Leland. It is a chapter marked by the author's maturation and understanding as she, her brother Bill, and Leland Hayward's wife, Pamela, join in the decision to "sever Father's lifeline" at the hospital and take him home to die "surrounded by the people who most loved him, in his own bed, in his own house" (310-11).

Hayward discloses very little about her adult life as fashion model, actress, and mother. To a friend she states " 'I'm the daughter of a father who's been married five times. Mother killed herself. My sister killed herself. My brother has been in a mental institution. I'm twenty-three and divorced with two kids' " (59). She repeatedly takes this tone of endurance as she describes the members of her family and how each affected the other. Although Hayward says in her introduction that her emphasis is on herself, Bridget, and Bill, and that the memoir "is not primarily about my parents' lives, except as they bore directly upon our own" (3), Margaret Sullavan emerges as the dominant figure. As an actress, at home as well as on stage, she was captivatingly energetic and critically demanding of herself and of her family. Hayward resents her mother's domination, glorifies her sister's eccentricity, bemoans her brother's neuroses, and protects her father's reputation.

Of particular interest to women's studies is *Haywire*'s depiction of the relationships that hold and tear a family of privilege, begotten of wealth and fame.

Not all reviewers reacted to *Haywire* as Elaine Dundy who feels that "underneath the book's sometimes flip, sometimes plodding exterior, there is not a shred of talent—or humanity" (*Saturday Review,* April, 1977, p. 30). Andre Sarris in *Harper's* finds the memoir to be a "lugubrious saga of family misfortune" (June, 1977, p. 77); and Charles Michaud observes that Hayward's "portraits of her parents and her sister are vivid and sometimes penetrating" (*Library Journal,* February, 1977, p. 482). Lois Gould (New York *Times,* March, 1977, p. 2) points to the "pain. . .the deceptive simplicity, the complex hidded machinery and, above all, the terrible cost" chronicled in Hayward's story.

Cynthia Wise Henley
Old Dominion University

Hellman, Lillian (1905-   )

Playwright

B
H477

[125] *An Unfinished Woman: A Memoir.* New York: Bantam, 1974. 244 pp.

The first third of the first volume in Lillian Hellman's trilogy of memoirs follows a first person chronological narrative. Later the author uses diary entries from the 1930's and 1940's and supplements these with flash-forwards, flash-backs, and parenthetical asides. The final three chapters are mini-biographies, sketches of four people who were central to the playwright's life: Dorothy Parker, her closest woman friend; Helen and Sophronia, two Black women who for Hellman became one identity; and Dashiell Hammett, with whom she lived for over thirty years. These last portraits serve as a transitional bridge in style and structure to the second autobiographical volume, *Pentimento.*

An Unfinished Woman begins with an account of Hellman's childhood in New Orleans and New York and in this section she introduces the family which was later to figure in her play *The*

Little Foxes. As an only child, the author early was aware of the power she held over her parents, and she writes of her relationship with Sophronia, the one person her father felt could control his daughter. Hellman establishes an early intimation of "sadness, a first recognition that there was so much to understand that one might never find one's way and the first signs, perhaps, that for a nature like mine, the way would not be easy" (9). Her nature, she later informs, was given to rages and rash acts, motivated by a strong sense of social injustice; yet brusqueness and anger were often simply the covering faces for an inner feeling of vagueness and indecision.

She writes briefly of her college experience at New York University, and of her first job, with Liveright Publishing Company, where she belonged to a generation of young women who felt that "the fight for the emancipation of women, their rights under the law, in the office, in bed, was stale stuff" (29). Hellman discusses an abortion in which her attitude is simultaneously admired as bravery and seen as coldness. She treats sketchily her marriage to Arthur Kober and describes her move to Hollywood where she began to write short stories secretly. Her marriage failed and soon after she entered into a life-long relationship with the writer Dashiell Hammett, the "strong teacher" she felt she needed to direct her life. In 1936 Hellman became involved in Spanish Civil War activities and she cites this as "the root-time of my turn toward the radical movements of the late thirties" (101). The portion of her memoirs that document her trip to Spain, and later trips to Russia, are filled with asides that reflect Hellman's thoughts on the unreliability of documents as a source of the true past: "In those five months I kept diaries of greater detail and length than I have ever done before or since, but when I read them last year, and again last week, they did not include what had been most important" (111).

Chapter twelve of her first memoir is a recapitulatory flashback of all that occurred during the McCarthy era and after, given in the form of a recollection of a conversation with a Russian friend. Hellman mentions her appearance before the House Un-American Activities Committee, Hammett's imprisonment, her blacklisting, loss of reputation and money, Hammett's illness and death. In this chapter she fleetingly notes that she underwent psychoanalysis with Gregory Zilboorg.

Throughout the memoirs, Hellman's work in the theatre is for the most part ignored, the exclusion explained in these terms: "I know as little as I knew then about the conflict that would keep me hard at work in a world that is not my world, although it has been my life" (63). She feels that the cause for this ambivalence might stem from the fact that she is "not good at collaboration, the essence of the theatre" (63).

The portraits of Parker, Helen, Sophronia, and Hammett are most intriguing, for Hellman uses these sections for implicit statements about her ideas of character, courage, and strength. Of Parker she notes the unlikelihood of "two such difficult women" being friends, yet adds "I enjoyed her more than I have ever enjoyed any other woman" (186). Helen and Sophronia "became in effect," according to one reviewer, "a model for an entire lifestyle, a direct, astringent way of facing up to things (meaning trouble), with so little nonsense and sentimentality that at times it almost became a kind of sentimentality itself" (Robert Kotlowitz, *Harper's Magazine*, June 1969, p. 88). But both women, for Hellman, represent "a need in many of us for the large, strong woman who takes us back to what most of us have always wanted and few of us ever had" (206). Her long complicated relationship with Hammett is never fully explained, but the author stresses "the continuing interest" in one another that proved more durable than any notions of romantic love.

Winner of the 1970 National Book Award, this memoir was widely, and for the most part, favorably reviewed. But Kotlowitz noted "an over-fastidiousness at work in *An Unfinished Woman,* as well as a fondness for self-mockery that in the end deprives us of some of the things we want to know about" (88). Other reviewers mentioned in particular the lack of treatment of her own life as a creator and a writer. "Free Women," a review essay by Patricia Meyer Spacks, (*Hudson Review,* 24, Winter 1971-1972, 559-573), is even more severe concerning Hellman's reticence, suggesting that her "central effort has been to create for her own benefit as well as others, a character to meet masculine standards," and citing a life of "constant action" as one of the masculine accomplishments sought by Hellman. Spacks' review, which compares this work to Anais Nin's diaries and Doris Lessing's novels, juxtaposing the three against the autobiographical writings of Colette, finds a trait "peculiarly feminine" in all of the works: "the obsessiveness of its

implicit or explicit concern with the question of freedom, psychic
and social, and the nature of its revelation about freedom's limitation for women" (564).

[126] *Pentimento: A Book of Portraits.* New York: New American Library, 1973. 245 pp.

B
H4772

This second volume of the autobiographical works of Lillian
Hellman is a carefully structured series of seven portraits of people
and events in the author's life. All of these reveal for Hellman "an
old conception, replaced by a later choice. . .a way of seeing and
then seeing again," and reveal to the reader "a picture of a woman
and writer in the making" (James Walt, *New Republic,* October 20,
1973, p. 27). These portraits span a loose chronology that links
stages of development in Hellman's life, each section giving hints
and indications of the portraits to come. A mini-Seven Ages of
Woman, the portraits begin with two figures from Hellman's early
childhood and adolescence: "Berthe," is the story of an aunt who
disgraced herself for love; "Willy," was Hellman's first love in
which "the mixture of ecstasy, as it clashed with criticism of myself and the man was to be repeated all my life" (61). "Julia,"
is the story of Hellman's childhood friend who was killed for anti-
fascistic activities in pre-World War II Vienna.

Hellman's theatre work is covered in a separate chapter that
follows her playwriting career chronologically. She advises that
ten of her twelve plays were connected to Hammett and his most
direct influence was on *The Little Foxes.* She again admits to a
basic incompatibility with a field in which she is the foremost
American woman practitioner. "Arthur W. A. Cowan" is an attempt to reconstruct the life of a mystery man, one who has "become a game of true or false" (187). "Turtle" is a remembrance
of an episode from the past triggered by Hellman's near-drowning
which focusses primarily on her earlier attempts to come to terms
with life and death. And the final chapter, which shares the book's
title, takes place after Hammett's death and relates the author's
attempts to reconcile herself to his loss. Helen, the Black maid
introduced in *An Unfinished Woman,* figures prominently in this
piece. "Everybody else in this book is dead" states the author in
explaining why she should not relate the tale of the young man
Jimsie, but this statement is belied by the vibrant presence of

Lillian Hellman herself.

Pentimento is a carefully constructed autobiography which utilizes biographical techniques. Chapter by chapter the author reveals her development and growth as a person. One dissenting critic faulted Hellman's spare prose style, indicating that "the writing often recalls Gertrude Stein's stonier prose—obdurate, flat and mannered" (Martha Duffy, *Time,* October 1, 1973, p. 114).

[127] *Scoundrel Time.*   Boston: Little, Brown and Company, 1976. 155 pp.

Hellman's most recent autobiographical piece is an examination of her life during the McCarthy period of the early 1950's. "Carefully limiting her text to what she herself experienced, thought, said, and did, this memoir," according to Bruce Cook, "nevertheless applies directly to the essential experience of her time—in other words to history" (*Saturday Review,* April 16, 1976, p. 28). After an introduction by Gary Wills, Hellman's slim memoir is written in first-person, fairly straightforward chronology with occasional flashforwards.

In *Scoundrel Time* Hellman establishes her roots of political rebellion by citing Sophronia's gift of "anger, an uncomfortable, dangerous, and often useful gift" (46). The author later advises that she was astounded at Clifford Odets' indecision about testifying and claims "It's all been decided so long ago, when you are very young, all mixed up with your childhood's definition of pride or dignity" (98).

Subpoenaed in 1952 to appear before the House Un-American Activities Committee to testify concerning her involvement in alleged communist organizations, Hellman agreed to answer questions concerning herself but refused to testify against others. Her letter to the HUAC advised "I cannot and will not cut my conscience to fit this year's fashions, even though I long ago came to the conclusion that I was not a political person and could have no comfortable place in any political group" (93). This action was followed by years that "took a heavy penalty" (113). Unable to work regularly in her profession, Hellman took a series of lesser film writing assignments, was forced into selling the farm she and

Hammett had developed, separated from him and entered into a destructive affair. "I was evidently driven to find another kind of villain and another kind of punishment" (113). She worked for a time under an assumed name as a clerk in a department store until a legacy from an aunt provided rescue. The year prior to Hammett's death in 1961 saw the production of *Toys in the Attic,* which was a financial success. Hellman cites her thesis in *Scoundrel Time* as "simply, then and now, I feel betrayed by nonsense I had believed" (40) and adds "I had believed in intellectuals" (153). She points to those who did not speak out against the HUAC as indicative of the intellectual timidity that led America into future conflict and political scandal.

"An unpleasant part of [her] life," *Scoundrel Time* ends with Hellman's statement that although recovered in a sense, she does "not believe in recovery. The past, with its pleasures, its rewards, its foolishness, its punishments, is there for each of us forever, and it should be" (155).

This particular past has been highly debated. The best known attack on her last memoir is William F. Buckley's "Scoundrel Time and Who is the Ugliest of Them All?" (*National Review,* January 29, 1977, pp. 101-106), a piece characterized by nasty malice. Accusing Hellman of being as guileful as any of her fictional creations, he writes, "It's another case of Germaine Greer, filibustering against male chauvinism, while strip-teasing her sexual biography across the magazine racks" (102). His pertinent political points are lost in ad hominem argument. Fortunately a number of more balanced analyses of Hellman's interpretations of the decade are available. Chief among these is Nathan Glazer's "Answer to Lillian Hellman, (*Commentary,* June 1976, pp. 36-39), in which Glazer examines the "new truth" that is emerging in writings about post-war, cold-war America. Other questioners of Hellman's historical version of the 1950's include William Phillips, Melvin Lasky, Hilton Kramer, Irving Howe and Murray Kempton. Even initial reviews were sharply divided in opinion with many praising Hellman's autobiographical formula while criticizing her political naivete.

Timothy Dow Adams
University of Arkansas

Hemingway, Mary Welsh (1908-   )

Journalist, Writer, Writer's Wife

[128] *How It Was.* New York: Alfred A. Knopf, 1976. 537 pp.

Although Mary Hemingway's autobiography, *How It Was,* covers her life from childhood through the time of the book's writing, it is for the most part the story of her life with writer/ husband Ernest Hemingway. Opening chapters quickly run through her childhood in Minnesota, her abbreviated college career, and her successful and interesting days as a reporter and war correspondent (Chicago *Daily News,* London *Daily Express,* and *Time/Life*). Her first two marriages, one an extremely brief college-days marriage and the second a short wartime marriage to journalist Noel Monk, are given sketchy, superficial treatment. The purpose of the book seems to emerge in chapter four with the entrance of Hemingway, whom she meets in London during World War II. The remaining twenty-eight chapters detail Mary's days as the wife and then the widow of Hemingway. They moved to Cuba in 1945 where she spent her time entertaining, hunting and fishing, working, playing, and loving. The last years before Ernest's suicide were spent traveling through Europe, Africa, and the U. S. After his suicide in 1961, in their home in Ketchum, Idaho, Mary became her husband's literary executor, turning all of her attention to the work involved with the estate and trying to reconstruct her life without the pivotal figure of the past seventeen years. This book was part of her effort.

How It Was is the story of a successful, independent career woman who becomes the wife of an already famous writer. Which part of her life Mary Hemingway sees as the more important is reflected in the fact that only four of the thirty-two chapters treat her life before Ernest. She does write a long, close, loving section on her father and their early days together in the wilds, revealing an attachment to him and the outdoor world he introduced her to. And, her chatty recollections of her days as a journalist and war correspondent, breaking new ground for women reporters, have a lively style which grows out of pleasant memories. But when she married Hemingway, she very clearly became Mrs. Ernest Hemingway, even as she consciously recognized that "I had been an entity; now I was an appendage." She became hostess, caretaker, decorator, protector of Ernest's time, and companion. Even the diaries from which much of the book is drawn were kept because she thought "Ernest might find them useful."

As might be expected of the autobiography of a woman married to a noteworthy author, many of the reviewers of this book focused on the value of it for Hemingway studies. The comment made on Mary's style was most often negative, for example, V. S. Pritchett in the *New Yorker* (November 1, 1976, pp. 161-64) says "Mary Hemingway was trained to note 'how' it was rather than what it was or what it felt like." The book was also criticized by the *National Observer* (October 9, 1976, p. 25) as "deeply boring, dreadfully written, scarcely coherent, smug, fatuous, complacent, mildly racist, inept, and extremely stupid." One of the more interesting comments made, and one of the few which really focused attention on Mary herself, came from Russell Davies in the *Times Literary Supplement* (March 18, 1977, p. 290): "She may have resembled one [a liberated woman], for she hunted, shot and fished with the best of them—Ernest, naturally—but this can now be seen as no more than her (successful) attempt to be Ernest's most submissive wife so far."

Linda S. Coleman
University of Wisconsin—Milwaukee

Heyward, Carter (-   )

Priest, Educator, Activist

[129] *A Priest Forever.* New York: Harper and Row, 1976. 146 pp.

A Priest Forever is an intelligent and moving account of one woman's life struggle to affirm her selfhood as a woman and her vocation as a priest. Carter Heyward was one of eleven women "irregularly" ordained to the priesthood of the Episcopal Church, a church which had never allowed women to enter the full priesthood. Her ordination, on July 29, 1974, in Philadelphia, caused one of the most heated controversies the denomination had ever faced. It was partially resolved in September 1976 (five months after the publication of her book) when the Episcopal Church in its General Convention, passed a resolution permitting the ordination of women to the full priesthood.

In *A Priest Forever* Carter writes of growing up as a Southern woman in the Episcopal Church. She reflects on her childhood yearings to be a priest, her subsequent years of college and seminary, and her experiences in psychotherapy and women's consciousness-raising groups. The account relates Carter's increasing awareness of her own strength and her vocational call to the priesthood.

Essentially an autobiography, *A Priest Forever* is interspersed with Carter's poems and with documents (personal letters of support and condemnation, official communications with bishops, records of ecclesiastical decisions) which reveal the political process within the Episcopal Church as it fought bitterly over the ordination question. These sections vividly portray the agonizing split within the Church as well as the personal and emotional cost to Carter as she wrestled with her own role in the controversy.

The book has become a valuable personal document for women in religion as well as an articulate historical and theological reflection on a dramatic period in religious history. It should become a landmark in feminist literature within the religious context. *A Priest Forever* will be of primary interest to women in the field of religion, but as the personal account of one intelligent and passionately committed woman it could be read with profit by anyone interested in the changing role of women in society.

A Priest Forever did not receive major critical review, unfortunately. Library journals, however, were enthusiastic and commented on the high literary quality of the book. One reviewer described the book as "a cogent personal statement by an intelligent, articulate and passionately committed woman whose own religious call has meant a Gospel-inspired fight for women's right" (*Kirkus,* February 15, 1976, p. 234). For other reviews see *Library Journal,* April 15, 1976, p. 1029 and *Publisher's Weekly,* February 16, 1976, p. 86.

Phyllis Roe
Emory University,
Candler School of Theology

Hoffman, Malvina (1885-1966)

Sculptor

[130] *Heads and Tales* (British title: *A Sculptor's Odyssey*). New York: Charles Scribner's Sons, 1936. 416 pp.

[131] *Yesterday is Tomorrow: A Personal History.* New York: Crown Publishers, 1965. 378 pp.

Malvina Hoffman perhaps belonged to another social era, but she most certainly ranks as a major artistic force among twentieth century women. She was born to parents who had already broken from society's mold: her mother, Fidelia, and her father, Richard, eloped when her mother's parents refused to allow their daughter to marry a musician and public performer who consorted with such personalities as Jenny Lind. The Hoffman family lived in a brownstone on Forty-third Street not far from Broadway and the growing theatre district, and so Malvina's early life was filled with the independence of many artistic personalities. Her father encouraged her artistic sensitivities and her love and admiration for him are quite pronounced. Two weeks before he died she completed her first major work, his bust in marble.

After her father's death, Hoffman and her mother embarked for Paris where Hoffman determinedly sought out Rodin. Impressed with her forthright desire and spirit, Rodin admitted Hoffman to his atelier where she continued to study for over a year. By 1912 Hoffman had her own Paris studio, was taking classes at the Academy, receiving weekly critiques from Rodin, and learning the intricacies of bronze from Emanuel Rosales. Her Parisian years were filled with the exciting awakening of a renaissance as she encountered the magnetism that Paris held for all the arts at that time.

Hoffman became especially close to Pavlowa who was the "muse and inspiration" for much of her early work. Several bronzes involved Pavlowa and her partners, the most ambitious of which was a frieze of twenty-six panels interpreting the *Autumn Bacchanale* by Glazounoff. A most revealing aspect of the spirit in which Hoffman encountered her life and work are two episodes in which she describes dancing. In the first she recalls studying with Pavlowa for several months to prepare herself for the work on the frieze. Hoffman actually danced a private performance of the *Bacchanale* with Pavlowa's partners, and exerted such passion that she fainted as the curtain fell after the last act.

Rarely does Hoffman recount any difficulties in becoming acknowledged as a sculptor in what was a totally male dominated art form. Ivan Mestrovic, with whom she studied in 1928, told her that she would have to learn the principles and techniques of her work better than most men just to be able to start on an equal basis to gain credibility and recognition. Her reputation gradually grew and in 1930 Hoffman received a commission to complete 101 sculptures for the Hall of Man, a project originated by Marshall and Stanley Field for the Field Museum of Natural History. The bulk of *Heads and Tales* concerns Hoffman's five year trek around the world, with her husband and entourage, modeling figures of the world's races for this, her major work. She amusingly tells of her persuasion of Stanley Field and his board of trustees first to allow her to be the only artist involved in the project and second to invest in the more endurable and expensive bronze rather than plaster for which she had originally contracted. Hoffman speaks only in complimentary terms about her husband, Samuel Grimson, although she reveals, in *Yesterday Is Tomorrow,* her divorce from him.

Hoffman writes much of other personal relationships in *Yesterday Is Tomorrow,* including her friendships with Marianne Moore who stimulated her to write the volume, and Ignace Paderewski who encouraged her to write *Heads and Tales.* Hoffman published one other book, *Sculpture: Inside and Out* (New York: Bonanza, 1939) in which she explains her work technically. Generally, all of her books were favorably reviewed. Edward Weeks, writing in the *Atlantic* (December 1936), praised Hoffman's *Heads and Tales* as a "live book about art" and complimented her as observant, spirited and with a "neat" turn of prose. Marianne Moore reviewed *Yesterday Is Tomorrow* for the New York *Times* (November 7, 1965), and cited it as "a kind of true allegory in which a Mr. Valiant like the one in Bunyan's dream, encounters beings of similar valor, with a strength 'to see, to find, and not to yield,' princes of the spirit—some poor and anonymous, some a-glitter with honors and insignia of achievement" (p. 30). Moore concluded her review by writing that "in the battle of life (Malvina Hoffman) behaves. . .as if the dead had eyes; as if she had wings and carried a torch" (p. 34).

Ken Daley
Old Dominion University

0

Holiday, Billie (1915-1959)

Singer

[132] *Lady Sings the Blues.* With William Dufty. New York: Lancer Books, Inc., 1965. 191 pp.

Billie Holiday observes in her autobiography, *Lady Sings the Blues,* that "Mom and Pop were just a couple of kids when they got married. He was eighteen, she was sixteen and I was three" (5). This unsentimental and candid book holds the captured reader as it reveals the author's rough childhood and her all too know-ledgeable adolescence (7, 16-19, 22-31). It exposes the physical and emotional conditions which shaped the blues she sang, dis-cusses the limited job opportunities for poor Black women—maid service or prostitution (24), and comments on the street education that supplemented her fifth grade education. The book also traces the development of her career and records her not infrequent harsh contacts with the law as well as her bouts with drug addiction.

The autobiography follows Holiday from infancy through her mid-forties and closes as she prepares to face drug charges in court in her mid-fifties. The section covering the period from the 1930s through the early 1950s reads something like a *Who's Who* of the entertainment world with emphasis on the jazz scene. Her descrip-tion of the vagaries of hotel, night club, and one-night-stand circuit is often painful.

Holiday's indictment of American racism is implicit in the social conditions she describes. Her haunting "Strange Fruit," for instance, grew out of a southern tour with a white band and the shock of witnessing the aftermath of a lynching—the victim still dangling from a tree. Her indictment of the treatment of drug addicts is explicit (126-30, 157-58).

Lady Sings the Blues is a little too early to reflect the women's consciousness movement; nevertheless the work has several sensitive portraits of women and the relationships between women. She describes the warm relationship she had with her mother and her grandmother, and the hostile relations among other female members of her family. She discusses lesbians she has had to deal with and the relationships she observed among women while she was incarcerated in several correctional institutions.

Of course, not all of Holiday's observations are about women. She speaks of the love she and her mother bore her father, a musician who went on the road. And she speaks of many male musicians and Louis McKay, the man she loved. She discusses both racial and sexual roles, for Blacks and Whites and makes some perceptive observations about exploitation. She does not emerge from the book as the stereotype of the strong and enduring Black woman but as a woman with failings as well as strength.

The reviewers, apparently all male, were sometimes hostile, sometimes given to backhanded compliments, and sometimes admiring and applauding.

Sandra Y. Govan
Emory University

Hoover, Helen (1910-   )

Writer, Naturalist, Metallurgist

[133] *A Place in the Woods.* New York: Knopf, 1969. 292 pp.

In *A Place in the Woods,* Helen Hoover tells how she and her husband gave up their jobs in Chicago and moved to the Minnesota woods to live. A research metallurgist, she gave up her job with International Harvester, while her husband, Adrian, gave up his job as promotional art director for a publishing house. After many difficulties, they found new careers, she as a nature writer, he as an illustrator. He illustrated all of her works including two published previous to this one, *The Long-Shadowed Forest* (1963) and *The Gift of the Deer* (1966), in which she focused on animals and descriptions of nature.

Throughout *A Place in the Woods*, Hoover reveals herself as a woman comfortable in her female identity. Her marriage is a happy one, with the two sharing their lives in a heartening way. While her early career was an unusual one for a woman, she does not comment on that at all. In fact, there is a refreshing lack of remarks about womanly weakness; when she isn't big or strong enough to lift something, for example, that is simply accepted. She moves back and forth between strenuous outdoor activites and traditional feminine activities—baking her first loaf of bread, doing needlework while her husband reads aloud.

[134] *The Years of the Forest.* New York: Knopf, 1973. 318 pp.

This work chronicles the adventures of Hoover and her husband in the years following the events told of in the first book. Human relationships, improvements to the property, and financial achievements are all part of the story, as the Hoovers live out their dream of a life in the woods. But "progress" comes to their area, and in the end they have to leave the place to the deer hunters, bulldozers, and power lines. One of the reviewers pointed out that the book was written in Taos, New Mexico. As in *A Place in the Woods*, the reader is struck by the close partnership between the author and her husband. In both of these volumes we meet in Helen Hoover a person of great charm and ability. One wishes she would write about her childhood and youth.

Beverly Seaton
Ohio State University—Newark

O **Horne, Lena (1917-   )**

Singer, Actress

[135] *Lena.* New York: Doubleday, 1965. 288 pp.

Lena, an autobiography "as told to" Richard Schickel, represents Lena Horne's having come to terms with herself as a person. She chronicles her life with accounts of her unsettled childhood marked by brief periods spent with grandparents, one divorced parent or the other, or a hastily appointed guardian. She tells of entering show business as a chorus liner at the Cotton Club at the age of sixteen in order to support her mother and step-father. And she continues her story through her achievement of recognition and success in nightclubs, films, television, and the theatre.

In describing the struggle to find her personal freedom, the attractive Lena Horne, who in the early stages of her career was called the "chocolate chanteuse" and the "cafe-au-lait Hedy Lamarr," inevitably sets in focus many of the issues confronting women in general as they seek liberation. Pursuing a career as a performer, she faces the problems of employers and agents who habitually take personal and contractual advantage of female employees and clients; Horne tells of the difficulty of combining the roles of wife and of mother with career aspirations in her first marriage; and she gives her account of the estrangement from relatives and unkind treatment from others over her choice of a white man as her second husband. Combined with the general indignities associated with racial prejudice, Horne's many problems might have proved overwhelming for her had it not been for the sure, if frequently strained and interrupted, contact she had experienced in her formative years with her strong-willed, activist grandmother.

Lena, while focusing on its subject, also provides fresh insight into many well known personalities of the entertainment world. Roderick Cook (*Harper's,* November, 1965, p. 130) notes the book's "earnest and modest tone" and calls it "much less gossipy" than other celebrity autobiographies.

Frances A. Grimes
Hampton Institute

O
Howar, Barbara (1934-   )

Washington Celebrity, Television Personality

[136] *Laughing All the Way.*   New York: Stein and Day, 1973.
298 pp.

Laughing All the Way is a well written but not very deep book
about Howar's life before, during and after she was a Washington
hostess and intimate of Lyndon Johnson.   The subjects are the
author's girlhood in Raleigh; her unusual closeness to a mother
who lived vicariously through her; early work as a reporter; her
marriage to a rich Syrian and subsequent divorce from him; the
private life of a president and his family; her affair with an un-
named senator and resulting scandal which caused the Johnsons
to drop her; two years as a talk show hostess in Washington (a job
she quit because the hosts received much higher salaries); a disastrous talk show venture in New York; and her response to her
mother's death.

Laced with anecdotes and gossipy items about the famous, the
book is nonetheless serious in explaining the important role social
life plays in Washington politics and in treating the author's own
shortcomings honestly.   There are fascinating portraits of LBJ
and Henry Kissinger and shorter sketches of such figures as Eugene
McCarthy, Lady Bird Johnson, and Joan Kennedy.

Laughing All the Way has a satirical tone but an ambivalence
not usual in satire: Howar makes fun of herself but also seems
pleased by her notoriety; she loathes some aspects of Washington
life but loves it, too; she respects the women's movement but
wants to get her "sense of being real" from a man.

An intelligent and clear-sighted woman, Howar touches on
many subjects of interest to feminists—her sense of self-hatred;
her mother's alcoholism; "feminine conditioning;" politicians'
hypocrisy on abortion; sexism in the television industry; psychia-
trists' oppressive attitude towards women; depression; and the
desperate unhappiness of political wives who have destroyed their
own identities for the sake of their husbands' careers. But since
none of these topics is developed, the book probably would not be
useful in a women's studies course.   And the author's breezily

contemptuous remarks on lesbians may offend some feminist readers.

Laughing All the Way received mixed reviews. The fact that it was treated far more sympathetically and thoroughly by female critics than by males suggests that creative work by women must be judged by women. Charlotte Curtis noted that while Howar is not a thinker, she has a good eye for detail (New York *Review of Books*, May 20, 1973, p. 4). Other perceptive reviews were written by Nora Magid (*Commonweal*, October 26, 1973, pp. 89-92) and by Nora Ephron (*Esquire*, August 1973, pp. 52-53).

[137] *Making Ends Meet.*   New York: Random House, 1976. 369 pp.

Making Ends Meet uses the same material as *Laughing All the Way* (some passages from the earlier book are barely rewritten for the second) but the attempt to turn autobiography into fiction is not successful: *Making Ends Meet* is a memoir posing as a novel. It probably would not have been published if Howar were not a celebrity. The book is far too long, and the mid-life crises of her heroine, Lilly Shawcross, rather tedious. Her situation is interesting, however, since she struggles to find her own identity rather than to live through men. But the author brings little sense of complexity and no talent for fiction to the exploration of this crucial modern problem. For a more favorable assessment of this novel see Susan Braudy's review in *Ms.*, June 1976, pp. 95-96.

Peg Cruikshank
G.N.E.S., San Francisco, CA

Hulme, Kathryn C. (1900-   )

Writer, United Nations Administrator

B
H915

[138] *Undiscovered Country: A Spiritual Adventure.* Boston: Little, Brown and Company, 1966. 306 pp.

Written after her two previous books, *We Lived as Children* (1939) and *The Wild Place* (1953) had provided specific details of earlier portions of her life, this book is Kathryn Hulme's attempt to unify the different stages of her varied and intensely lived life and to reveal the spiritual goal that she—a soul "hungry for something more"—attained.

Her narrative begins in the Paris of the Thirties where she met the Russian mystic, George Ivanovitch Gurdjieff. Over the years, she learned from him the principle of separating one's inner life—one's "undiscovered country"—and one's in-life activities (294). She writes her autobiography with that separation evident in her emphasis on Gurdjieff and other people as much as on herself. Taught by Gurdjieff to make contact with her inner animal nature and with the outer world's struggles, Katie accepted his name for her—Crocodile—as both the problem and solution of her life-long attempt to know herself and to deal with circumstances. After an unsuccessful marriage, she became the companion and guide of a wealthy milliner on a trip abroad and gathered material for her first three books. Her hunger for something more took her from travel and writing to welding liberty ships to administering the readjustment process of displaced Poles and Hungarians under the aegis of the United States. She describes how Gurdjieff's teachings guided her in friendships with women, in relating to working class men and women, in dealing with bureaucrats and displaced persons. On the death of her mother and of Gurdjieff and through her friendship with a Belgian nurse, she became a convert to the Catholic church.

E. T. Smith (*Library Journal,* November 15, 1966, p. 5600) complains of too much attention to Gurdjieff, a gross man interested in eating and platitudes, and not enough to Hulme. Conversely, Anne Fremantle (New York *Times,* November 20, 1966, p. 10) praises the detail of the steps of Hulme's "work on the self" prescribed by Gurdjieff, who is brilliantly evoked.

Charlotte S. McClure
Georgia State University

Humphrey, Doris (1895-1958)

Dancer, Choreographer

[139] *An Artist First: An Autobiography.* Middletown, Connecticut: Wesleyan University Press, 1972. 305 pp.

Published posthumously, *An Artist First* owes much to the skillful editing and arranging of Humphrey materials by Selma Jeanne Cohen, who was selected for the task by Humphrey's son, Charles H. Woodford. All reviews of the book praise Cohen's contribution and Deborah Jowitt (New York *Times,* February 18, 1973) is particularly laudatory.

An Artist First is divided into two main sections. Part One, Humphrey's own autobiograhical sketch, was published previously under the title "New Dance" as a separate issue of *Dance Perspectives* (25, Spring 1964). This piece follows a straight first person chronological narrative from 1898 to 1930, when Humphrey left the Denishawn dance troupe to form a company in partnership with Pauline Lawrence and Charles Weidman. She died of stomach cancer in 1958 leaving the remainder of her life unwritten.

Part Two picks up from 1930 with Cohen's chronological narrative, interspersed with excerpts from letters and journals kept by Humphrey, her family and friends. The editor skillfully balances material concerned with Humphrey's concerts, teaching at Bennington and Julliard, involvement with the Dance Unit of the Federal Theatre project, her communal living arrangments with Lawrence, Weidman, and Jose Limon; relationships with other dancers (St. Denis, Martha Graham, Hanya Holm); and her reaction to decreased abilities as a performer. Of particular interest is Humphrey's relationship with her mother, and her unorthodox, yet stable and happy marriage to Leo Woodford, a seaman. She wrote: "I don't know I have a husband as he is never here to enter into any of the life or problems" (160). Leo noted: "When she's a woman she's with you, but you run a poor second when she's an artist" (148). Humphrey's juggling of career, marriage and motherhood, provides interesting, funny, and touching moments. Because of the communal living, her son ("my biological composition," 121) was cared for by all the dance members; Pauline Lawrence the surrogate mother; Weidman and Limon taking the place of the boy's father who was at sea for months at a time.

Cohen treats sensitively Humphrey's bitterness about the crippling effects of arthritis of the hip that cut short her performing career, and her determination to overcome its effects. The editor also examines the dancer's courage during her terminal illness when she was bed-ridden in great pain and trying to finish both her autobiography and her book on theory of dance. But of primary importance in this "striking autobiography-biography" (*Library Journal,* March 1, 1973) is the placement of Doris Humphrey as pivotal figure and an inspiring innovator for modern American dance chorerographers; this book pays her a deserved honor. Included are a complete index-chronology of performances, and a bibliography of Humphrey's writing on the theory and philosophy of dance. Her *The Art of Making Dances,* also published posthumously, is the definitive work on the choreographer's craft.

T. Gail Adams
Emory University, ILA

Hurst, Fannie (1889-1968)

Short Story Writer, Novelist

[140] *Anatomy of Me: A Wonderer in Search of Herself.* Garden City, New York: Doubleday and Company, 1958. 367 pp.

Anatomy of Me is Fannie Hurst's account of her attempt to become socially and professionally independent and successful. Her chronicle does not rely upon dates, but upon events in her life and the effect of these events on her feelings and actions. Because of this, one gets the impression that Hurst views her life as a timeless story.

The Hurst family's life in the writer's formative years is retold with candor which reflects both love and sorrow. Fannie became the only child after the early death of her younger sister, and consequently the sole object of her parents' love, and conflicting expectations. Her mother's major concern seemed to be to shape a daughter who would marry well and rear a family; education was nice, but smart girls couldn't catch husbands. Fannie's father continually stressed for his daughter that "knowledge is power." However, in confrontations, the mother's desires for Fannie took precedence over the father's wishes for their daughter. As Fannie Hurst matured, her independence and determination were unable to mollify her parents' bickering; she is painfully honest in discussing her feelings of confusion and guilt, that she was a disappointment to both her parents, despite her success as a writer and her personal happiness in her marriage to pianist Jacques Danielson.

In an era when proper young ladies did not leave the shelter of their homes until they married, Fannie Hurst moved from St. Louis to New York City to pursue a career as a writer, to lead a life of her own choosing. For Hurst, learning about herself and accepting herself for both her good points and bad were necessary in her growth as a person and a writer. Throughout her life, she was overweight, and she recounts how she came to accept her physical self because she believed that true beauty was an internal matter, not an external one. She is honest about her love for Danielson and explains why she wanted for five years to keep secret her marriage to him, an atypical union that apparently thrived because it did not rely upon traditional role playing. One feels that the fact their marriage was childless strengthened the bond between them. Regularly, Hurst writes of her experiences in such a way as to communicate a love for humanity, a sensitivity to the human condition and a compassion for all people.

One reviewer (*Kirkus*, August 1, 1958) finds "the chief distinction of" an *Anatomy of Me* "is its value as a human document, of a woman who chanced to be a successful writer." Iola Haverstick (New York *Times*, October 5, 1958, p. 7) reflects the attitude of many critics, writing that some of Hurst's "mental and spiritual processes—particularly her revelations about her parents and early life—are, for all the vigor of her style, self-conscious and tedious. This does not mean that. . .Hurst's autobiography is entirely dull," Haverstick adds. *Anatomy of Me* is a study of learning about one's self, of recounting a life lived according to the needs of particular woman rather than a life lived according to the commonly accepted patterns of a particular society.

Linda A. Wyche
Old Dominion University

Hurston, Zora Neale (1901-1960)

Writer, Anthropologist, Folklorist

[141] *Dust Tracks on a Road.* Philadelphia: J. B. Lippincott
Company, 1942. 294 pp.

Blog
H966

Beginning with the history of her birthplace, Eatonville, Florida,
the first incorporated Black town in the United States, Hurston
presents, frequently in colorful Black vernacular, her long struggle
to achieve success. A sensitive, inquisitive, but stubborn child, she
refused to be molded into a docile, doll-playing little girl. Often
wandering alone for long periods into the swamps and forests, she
brazenly and defiantly ventured into probing the cosmic mysteries
of life. Her actions gained her a reputation for being difficult and
sassy, and while her minister-father attempted to break her spirit,
her understanding mother exhorted her to "reach for de stars."

When seven years old, Hurston experienced for the first time a
recurring vision where "like clearcut stereopticon slides, I saw
twelve scenes flash before me. . .a preview of things to come." The
book is in large part a revelation of how each prophecy came true.
The first of these, the death of her mother and permanent separation of the seven children when she was nine, profoundly altered
Hurston's life; it meant the loss of her only ally, that she was now
unloved, homeless, and in poverty. Her spirit remained undaunted.
Although her formal education was interrupted by her mother's
death, Hurston records that she continued to read voraciously
while supporting herself as a maid, later as lady-in-waiting to an
opera singer in a touring company, and then as waitress.

Returning to school at eighteen, she went from night school
and high school in Baltimore, to Howard University where her
literary career began. Aided by a scholarship, she entered Barnard
College and earned the B.A. degree in Anthropology. The book
recounts the years she spent in reserach into folklore and in organizing and sponsoring folk recitals and concerts. In addition to
being a vivid account of her personal struggle and triumphs, the
autobiography is a repository of Black folklore—Music, Religion
and Voodoo.

In a chapter on "Love," Hurston comments on her brief marriage to her college sweetheart, but focuses mainly on her long and tempestuous relationship with the one man she truly loved and admired.   His strenuous objection to her career caused a painful severance of their relationship which she recaptures in her novel *Their Eyes Were Watching God* (1937).

Hurston pays tribute to three women with whom she had warm rewarding relationships, Fannie Hurst, whom she served as private secretary, Ethel Waters, a close personal friend, and R. Osgood Mason who encouraged and financed her research.

The autobiography does not treat the serious aspects of Black life in America. Of her early association with the Harlem Renaissance movement, she provides only a brief glimpse. She passively accepts racial discrimination, at times attempting to rationalize her non-resistance while criticizing Black activists. She expresses the belief that Blacks used race as an explanation for any shortcomings and states that she saw "no curse in being black. . .skins were no measure of what was inside people." With this philosophy, her intelligence, and determination to "reach for de stars," Hurston became a successful anthropologist and a writer of exceptional merit. In addition to numerous short stories, she published six novels.

Of the autobiography, *Booklist* (December 1, 1942, p. 120) calls its language "occasionally vulgar," while *Library Journal* (November 1, 1942, p. 950) feels that the "literary crudity may have been chosen to heighten effect." Phil Stong in *Saturday Review* (November 28, 1942, p. 6) calls it a "fine, rich autobiography . . .heartening to anyone," and although he sees it as "more a summary than. . .autobiography," he maintains that "it is told in exactly the right manner." Arna Bontemps in *Books* (November 22, 1942, p. 3) says of Hurston's work, "it has great material, and she knew how to make the most of it."

Margaret N. Simmons
Hampton Institute

Isabell, Sharon (1942-   )

Writer

[142] *Yesterday's Lessons.* Oakland: Women's Press Collective, 1974. 206 pp.

> *Yesterday's Lessons* is a blunt powerful account of a young lesbian's struggles through years of painful experiences, the "lessons" of the title. With little encouragement from family, school, or even from her friends, Sharon Isabell survives to communicate in nicely understated prose her rage on behalf of all powerless people. Of special interest are her army experiences and her participation in a women's ball team. Here is a voice not often heard in print: working class, poor and lesbian.
>
> While *Yesterday's Lessons* received positive reviews in lesbian-feminist publications, it was ignored by the established press. As Kathy Hruby noted (*Amazon Quarterly,* November 1974, p. 40), *Yesterday's Lessons* is "an expression that has no validity in male culture."

Nancy Manahan
Napa College

Jackson, Harrisene (1941-   )

Nurse, Activist, Mother

[143] *There's Nothing I Own That I Want.* Englewood Cliffs, New Jersey: Prentice Hall, 1974. 168 pp.

> Harrisene Jackson's story is an often brutal and horrifying account of her struggle to escape the ghetto. She expresses her love for her mother, whom she had seen murdered when she was six years old. As a child, she grew up in the homes of different members of her family. She discusses the difficulties of growing up in the ghetto without becoming involved with drugs or becoming a prostitute. At sixteen, she became pregnant and married the

baby's father, who became one of the few Black officers in the Army. She tells of the housing discrimination they encountered, as well as the brutality and neglect she suffered at the hands of her husband. After her divorce, she was left alone, with an overwhelming concern to give her children a decent life and a set of values to live by.

One of the topics of concern to women that is dealt with in Jackson's book is mental illness. Faced with the mental breakdown of her oldest daughter, she fought doctors and hospitals in order to obtain proper care for Coretta. Another concern is abortion. In order to retain custody of her children while she was divorcing her husband, Jackson was forced to have an abortion, which she found a terrible experience because of her strong Catholic faith.

The style and frankness of Jackson drew favorable comments from reviewers. The *Library Journal* (October 15, 1974, p. 2596), stated that, "She talks as though she's at your kitchen table pouring out the terrible sorrow, bitterness, terrible struggle, and occasional great joy." *Publisher's Weekly* (August 12, 1974, p. 55) stated that, "This black woman's history owes much of its clout to her style—a frank outpouring rather than a sober narration." The same review noted that, "The book is horrifying but bracing because its author will never say die."

C. Lynne Harrison
Old Dominion University

Jackson, Mahalia (1911-1972)

Concert Gospel Singer

[144] *Movin' On Up.* Hawthorne Books, 1966. 212 pp.

With Evan McLeod Wylie, Mahalia Jackson tells in straightforward and un-selfconscious fashion of her life as a singer of gospel songs. "I was singing almost as soon as I was walking and talking. . .I was raised with music all around me. . .ragtime music, jazz, and the blues." She tells of "Movin' on up" to God as well as moving up in her career as concert singer.

Beginning her story in New Orleans where her Mother's family settled after leaving the plantation on which her great-grandparents were slaves, Jackson tells of the "richness" of her childhood, of growing up slowly, happily—but not freely. At sixteen Jackson moved to Chicago into the crowded home of an aunt and weathered the Depression of the 1930's by the first of her public singing and also by being a laundress and maid and by starting her own hair-dressing shop. As her fame spread, there were concerts in cities all over the United States as well as in Europe. Having confidence in her own God-given-gift, she refused formal voice training. She said, "First of all you've got to get the rhythm until, through the music, you have the freedom to interpret it."

With great patience and no bitterness, Jackson tells of how it was to be Black, especially before 1956, and especially in the South. "There was no place for us to eat or sleep on the main highways. Restaurants wouldn't serve us. Some gasoline stations did not want to sell us gas and oil. Some told us that no rest rooms were available." Jackson recounts the great part which railroads played in American life, pointing out the contribution they made to Negro men who were hired as cooks and porters and who saw the wonders of America from coast to coast.

Moving' On Up praises Negro women for their strength and dignity. Jackson is of course speaking from experience: left motherless at five, she was raised by one of her mother's seven sisters, "Aunt Duke" Paul. The singer points out that because Negro men were weakened by not being able to get jobs with prestige or advantage, Negro women began to assume the responsibility for the family. Jackson comments, "the Negro woman has helped make the colored world decent and strong—she has stood by and raised her children alone when the hurt and frustration her husband suffered weakened him and drove him to leave his family. It was usually the Negro mother who had to keep a certain dignity in the family." She notes that "today fifty percent of Negro business, North and South, is run by Negro women." The theme of a matriarchal society is found throughout the book.

Reviewers found Jackson's lack of bitterness and her affirmation of life the remarkable qualities of this autobiography. "For all the bitter facts, there is no bitterness in the telling. Jackson tells her story as eloquently as she sings the gospel music that has made her famous. Unlike most aubobiographies of great performing artists, this one is no disappointment" (New York *Times,* March 5, 1967, p. 46).

Eloise Skewis
Norfolk, Virginia

Jackson, Shirley (1919-1965)

Novelist, Short Story Writer

[145] *Life Among the Savages.* New York: Farrar, Strauss and Young, 1953. 214 pp.

[146] *Raising Demons.* New York: Farrar, Strauss and Young, 1956. 310 pp.

One learns little of Shirley Jackson the person or writer from her two autobiographical works (*Life Among the Savages* and *Raising Demons*). Written in the housewife-humorist style of Jean Kerr and Erma Bombeck and based squarely in the 1950's, these anecdotal books deal exclusively with Jackson's life as the harried but happy mother of four young children. Much of the humor in the books rests upon acceptance of common sexist assumptions about the separate roles of men and women, and about competition between women. Jackson recounts amusing incidents involving her dealings with moving men, pets, kids, Little League baseball, hand-me-downs, her husband's female students, and other mothers. She shows herself enlisting her children's help to deceive her husband when she has had a car accident or has spent too much money. Her husband is depicted as being marginal to the day-to-day operations of the household, and is apparently the only one in the family entitled to a room of his own. As one might expect from such books written in such a time, Jackson shows no feminist interest or consciousness; and the themes of paranoia, horror, and terror which pervade the novels and short stories for which she is better known do not appear here.

Many reviewers welcomed these revelations of Jackson's sunnier side. They praised her writing style, her sense of humor, and the casual family life described in her books, but also pointed out the repetitiousness and lack of structure in them. Margaret Long (*Saturday Review*, June 27, 1953) gushed: "Shirley Jackson. . . has written herself a darling novel about herself, her husband and her young." *Women and Literature* observed, wryly one suspects, that Jackson "amused a wide audience with autobiographical accounts of 'womanly' pursuits" (p. 65). Jean Campbell Jones (*Saturday Review*, January 19, 1957) wrote that "somehow one expects more of Miss Jackson, who has after all, in her pre-Little League days, done some memorable short stories. . . . Is this the new momism?"

Laura Moss Gottlieb
West Virginia University

Johnson, Claudia Alta Taylor (Lady Bird) (1912-   )

First Lady, Businesswoman

[147] *A White House Diary.* New York: Holt, Rinehard & Winston, 1970. 806 pp.

A White House Diary is Lady Bird Johnson's day-by-day account of the five tumultuous years she spent as America's First Lady. Edited from tape recordings she made during her White House tenure, the *Diary* begins with that fateful November day in Dallas in 1963 and concludes with the Johnsons' arrival back at the LBJ Ranch after the Nixon Inauguration. The *Diary* is crowded with names, places, and events—sometimes overwhelmingly so. But always present is the self-portrait of a woman struggling to help her husband cope with the most demanding of jobs and the most trying of times, to guide and support her two daughters through adolescence, courtship, marriage, and motherhood, and to maintain her own sense of roots, self, and worth. As the *Diary* unselfconsciously reveals, Lady Bird Johnson was remarkably successful in meeting these challenges.

A White House Diary has much to offer the student of women's studies. Marya Mannes observes (New York *Times Book Review,* October 25, 1970, p. 1) that the *Diary* "is an intensely personal document that reveals a woman who describes herself as 'terribly average—something like litmus paper,' but who, in fact, is not average at all. Lady Bird is remarkable for the range and depths of her loves—fierce loyalties as well as small delights—and for a physical and spiritual stamina which bore her through ordeals which would have drained lesser humans." Johnson's *Diary* was also well received abroad as a detailed portrait of a truly American woman in a uniquely American position. The London *Times Literary Supplement* (November 27, 1970) states that "her achievement is to have described in strongly personal and moving terms what it was like to have been the wife of a President." "What seems to be missing the most is candor" (*Library Journal,* December 1, 1970, p. 4165). Like it or not, most of the First Lady's life is taken up with just such "dull" responsibilities as planning state dinners, meeting innumerable statesmen, politicians, and private citizens. *A White House Diary* demonstrates that the amazing achievement of Lady Bird Johnson is that in the midst of official duties, which she performed so admirably, she was able to preserve her family's closeness, maintain her sense of humor, and become a stronger woman for the experience.

Joan Frederick
James Madison University

Johnson, Josephine W. (1910-   )

Writer

[148] *Seven Houses: A Memoir of Time and Places.* New York: Simon and Schuster, 1973. 159 pp.

Seven Houses, Josephine Johnson's account of her childhood and early marital years, is organized around seven houses that "shaped and sheltered her existence." The memories of time and

place, of events and episodes, of family, friends, and nature in-
voked by each house are the book's essential ingredients.

   Johnson begins with the important houses in her hometown of
Kirkwood, Missouri: a school and the homes of her parents, maternal grandparents, and a group of aunts. While discussing these
houses, she lets us know about her father, the tenderness she felt
for other family members, especially her maternal grandfather,
and her admiration for an early teacher named Blanche Byars. She
also shows her close observation of and devotion to the larger
world of nature. From Kirkwood she moves to the most fondly
remembered childhood house, Rose Cottage. This home of two
aunts in Columbia, Missouri, is rich in its memories of rural farm
life. Then Johnson turns her attention to Hillbrook, her parents'
retirement home outside St. Louis. Even though she spent twenty
years in this house and evidently began her writing career here
(winning a 1935 Pulitizer Prize for her novel *Now in November*),
she mentions it scantly. Instead, she moves on to the last and to
her most important house, the Old House in Newtown, Ohio. The
first home ever owned by Johnson and her husband, Grant Can-
non, its memories prompt her to write a glowing tribute to the
man and their marriage. In discussing the ten years lived here, she
also describes their three children and her feelings about motherhood. At times motherhood seems wonderful and the children are
like "a priceless and unbreakable treasure" while at other times the
"grease grows suddenly cold and gray in the dishpan and the baby
cries out with pure meanness."

   Seven Houses: A Memoir of Time and Places received favorable
reviews. Phyllis Meras found it "a treasure chest of the joyousness,
the awe, the laughter, the fragrances, light, and shadow of country
living" (New York *Times,* May 13, 1973, p. 16).

Harold S. Whisman, Jr.
Old Dominion University

Keller, Helen (1880-1968)

Essayist, Lecturer, Humanitarian

[149] *The Story of My Life.* Edited by John Albert Macy. New
        York: The Century Company, 1903. 441 pp.

Famous from the time she was ten, Helen Keller seems to have
radiated vitality all her life, and, deprived of the two primary
senses, she nevertheless turned outward, with the help of Anne
Sullivan, toward knowledge, ideas, and other people. These qualities are apparent in *The Story of My Life,* written when she was
a student at Radcliffe.

Many of the chapters were originally written to fulfill college
composition assignments, and were later revised for serial publication in the *Ladies Home Journal;* thus, each rather short chapter
focuses on some important event or recollection: Helen's illness
which left her blind and deaf at nineteen months, the arrival of
Anne Sullivan, the indispensable "Teacher" whose guidance enabled Helen to develop her intellectual gifts, Helen's first realization (from having water poured on her hand) that all things have
names, her first conscious Christmas, her first visit to the Perkins
Institute for the Blind in Boston, and so on in largely chronological
order through the various stages of her education and increasing
mastery of language and general knowledge.

Obviously, the importance of Anne Sullivan's role in the development of Helen Keller can hardly be over-emphasized, and, in
one sense, Helen Keller's book is the story of two women of extreme sensitivity and intelligence (especially in verbal skills), incredible determination, and extraordinary independence.

That Helen was warm and loving, and also fun-loving, is apparent; and although she admits to periods of anger and frustration, there is no self-pity. In addition to Sullivan, Helen had close
relationships with her parents, with her younger sister, and one
of few sorrows of her early years was the death of her father.

Among her pleasures at Radcliffe was associating with girls of
her own age. She also had friendships with many of the famous
people of her day, most of them men, such as Mark Twain, Edward

Everett Hale, and Alexander Graham Bell.

A selection of Helen's letters is included in the autobiography, showing her development in language and concepts from her childhood to her early twenties. The final sections of the book are Anne Sullivan's account of Helen's education and of her literary style.

Contemporary reviews of this book were mostly laudatory.

B [150] *Midstream: My Later Life.* New York: Doubleday, Doran, 1930. 362 pp.

K29am

Midstream continues the story of Keller's life from the time she was a student at Radcliffe until her mid-forties. Generally, though not strictly, chronological, each chapter is an account of a specific experience, friendship, idea or belief. Among these may be mentioned her financial struggle after college which led her to undertake a two-year stint in vaudeville, and an autobiographical movie, the latter a financial and artistic disaster. She describes her many lecture tours which were motivated not only by the need to support herself and her household, but also by her wish to bring before the public the cause of the handicapped, especially the blind. Her efforts in behalf of the blind, and for the prevention of blindness, she regarded as her life work. Keller gives a touching description of her one experience of romantic love, which, though it ended in sadness and misunderstanding, remained a precious memory to her. (She and a young man temporarily serving as her secretary had actually applied for a marriage license when the affair was discovered and broken off by Keller's mother.) Keller also comments discreetly on the break-up of the marriage between John Macy and her teacher. He had been influential and intellectually stimulating to Keller, and one senses the pain involved for all when he left the household.

Deeply religious, Keller was a Swedenborgian, and, in politics, a socialist, profoundly concerned for the welfare of the working classes. She was interested in the cause of woman suffrage, and mentions attending a demonstration in Washington, D. C. just before Wilson's inauguration in 1913.

Like her first volume of autobiography, *Midstream* received mostly laudatory reviews.

B
K29

[151] *Journal, 1936-1937.* Doubleday, Doran, 1938. 313 pp.

Written as a kind of outlet for her grief after the death of Anne Sullivan Macy, the *Journal* is the most intimate and personal of Keller's autobiographical writing.

[152] *Helen Keller, her Socialist Years: Writing and Speeches.* Edited by Philip S. Phroner. New York: International Publishers, 1967. 128 pp.

Feminists will be interested in this work because of an essay in which Keller expresses the following views on the rights of women (p. 65):

> There are no such things as divine, immutable or inalienable rights. Rights are things we get when we are strong enough to make good our claim to them. Men spent hundreds of years and did much hard fighting to get the rights they now call divine, immutable and inalienable. Today women are demanding rights that tomorrow nobody will be fool-hardy enough to question. . . . The laws made by men rule the minds as well as the bodies of women. The man-managed state so conducts its schools that the ideals of women are warped to hideous shapes.

There is, as yet, no standard biography of Helen Keller, nor is there serious scholarly assessment of her autobiographical writing. The work of a woman who was regarded as a miracle in the nineteenth century, and who is still the only deaf-blind person to make an outstanding contribution to society is naturally a subject for praise and for inspirational commentary. It is now time for analysis.

Sara C. Withers
Gallaudet College

Kenmore, Carolyn (-   )

Model

[153] *Mannequin: My Life as a Model.* New York: Bartholo-
mew House Ltd., 1969. 313 pp.

Carolyn Kenmore does not present a full account of her life,
but rather she elaborates on her career as a New York fashion
model. Dispelling the myth that a pretty face is all you need to
earn three hundred dollars a day and grace the covers of national
magazines, she tells about the Spartan discipline required in the life
of a young woman who wants to be a successful beauty vendor.
Food, drink, drugs, exercise, and late parties must all be measured
in careful doses. Even birth control pills are suspect, for bloating
will endanger the shapeliness that the camera demands. Versatility
is also required, because the catalog poses, fashion shows, television
commercials and high fashion shots, in the studio and on location,
call for varied talents.

Sufficiently detailed to serve as a guide-book for potential
models, *Mannequin* outlines the mysteries of agencies, make-up
classes, wig rentals, and shooting sessions. Simultaneously, the
book documents the dependence of a model on the taste· ᵔf the
agencies, whims of the clients, the talents of her cameraɨ.ian, the
willingness of her colleagues to teach her the intricacies of applying false eyelashes, and her ability to make contacts at parties.
Kenmore is most successful at portraying the precariousness of a
model's status. She emphasizes the free lance nature of her assignments, the absence of fringe benefits like sick leave, and the in-
calculable demands of each job. When a broken fingernail, failure
to bring along the perfect clothes or accessories, or a too-sexy hair
color rinse can determine one's eligibility, the work is unpredictable rather than glamorous.

Of particular interest to feminists is Kenmore's discussion of
"Crotch Politics," or the ever-present nature of sex in her job.
Men whistle, snicker and gesture at models even more frequently
than they do at other women. Contemporary advertisers demand a
model's nudity to sell their products. Kenmore insists that it is
possible to rise the top of the modeling world without sleeping
with the clients, agents, and cameramen. However, she describes

so many opportunities that were available to her, that had to be declined with tact, and resulted in dismissal from a job, that no mother would send her daughter to the Big Apple for a modeling career if she were acquainted with this account. A model can expect to be inspected for flaws before she gets a bubblebath or bra account. She may be asked to do an underpants fashion show topless, in order to give the lingerie buyers a laugh. She will be invited to decorate the parties of rich and powerful advertisers and to sleep with them for promotion.

Kenmore does not express rage at the sexism. Her beauty has won her the attentions of so many men that she has come to expect little else from them. She mentions that an attempt was made to rape her at age four. In her teen years, her father beat her when he learned that she had been in the basement with two boys. Her New York beau, whom she portrays as a gallant, understanding IBM executive with an admirable tolerance for her irregular schedule, nevertheless escapes as an old-fashioned boss. (" 'Ball' was one of the four-letter words David wouldn't let me use.") The sex that she stands for is simply part of her job, like the cold criticism of her appearance by the buyers: "Darling, you're not pretty enough for us." It hurts, but Kenmore tolerates it for the short-lived fame she finds satisfying.

Karen J. Blair
California Institute of Technology

Kennedy, Florynce (1916-   )

Lawyer, Political Activist, Author

[154] *Color Me Flo: My Hard Life and Good Times.* Englewood Cliffs, New Jersey: Prentice-Hall, 1976. 177 pp.

Florynce Kennedy is not an ordinary woman; neither is this an ordinary autobiography. The first portion of the book contains statements of her political and social philosophies; the rest is autobiography interspersed with newspaper clippings, transcripts of speeches, essays, and countless photographs of Kennedy at demonstrations, speaking engagements and occasionally under arrest. She describes herself as "just a loud-mouthed middle-aged colored lady with a fused spine and three feet of intestines missing, and a lot of people think I'm crazy." Like a fox.

Born in Kansas City, Missouri, Kennedy early learned her own worth. Her mother "always treated us like precious people. . . . And of course Daddy was ready to shoot somebody and kill him to keep our house." Kennedy did domestic work while in high school, then opened a hat shop with a friend. Later she went with her sister to New York, where she worked for the Treasury Department and began night school at Columbia University.

In 1948 she applied for admission to Columbia Law School ("all I had to do was to look at lawyers and then look at mothers to know which I would rather be"), but was refused because she was a woman. She threatened to sue on charges of racial discrimination and was promptly accepted. In three years she managed to graduate "at the bottom" of her class, but by 1954 she had her own Madison Avenue law office. Kennedy and her partner successfully defended singer Billie Holiday and later handled her estate and that of jazzman Charlie (Bird) Parker. In spite of her frequent pronouncements against marriage ("Marriage is a crock. Why should you lock yourself in the bathroom just because you have to go three times a day?"), she married an alcoholic Welsh writer ("terribly damaged merchandise") who died a few years later of cirrhosis.

In 1966 Kennedy set up the Media Workshop to attack racism and sexism in media and advertising. Her speaking career began spontaneously in 1967 at a Montreal anti-war convention. A member from its inception, she began to feel NOW was "retarded" and left it in 1971 to found the small but vocal Feminist Party, which backed Shirley Chisholm's candidacy for President.

To read Kennedy, one must learn a whole new vocabulary—— "jockocracy," "Pentagonorrhea," "fetus fetishists"—though she insists: "I don't use foul language. . . . I use White House language . . .what's good enough for Nixon is good enough for me." Her basic commitment is to social change: "In order to turn this country one degree, you might as well get ready to die." When she went to Boston in 1974 to speak during the school integration riots, she was ready; she told her sisters, "If I don't come back from Boston, it's okay."

Flo Kennedy is always ready to lay it on the line, and she does not mince words: "It's important that women organize around the things they agree on, and to those that say, 'I'm not for women's lib,' my position is if you can't say the whole word. . .do us a favor and get out of the way."

Kennedy's reviewers agree on the impact of her language and personality upon her writing. Louise Bernikow (New York *Times*, January 2, 1977, p. 6) calls her "basically a street-fighter against racism and sexism" and generally praises the book, though pointing out that structurally it is a "hodgepodge." The reviewer for *Publishers Weekly* (August 30, 1976, p. 328) examines her militancy and concludes that Kennedy "has assuredly been one of the most effective fighters for the rights of the individual in modern times."

Joanne McCarthy
Tacoma Community College

Kennedy, Rose Fitzgerald (1896-   )

Daughter, Wife, and Mother of Famous Men

[155] *Times to Remember.* Garden City, New York: Doubleday & Company, Inc., 1974. 536 pp.

Although technically an autobiography, *Times to Remember* is also a history of the Kennedy and Fitzgerald families from their arrival in America to the early 1970s. While aware that many readers are interested primarily in personal accounts of her famous sons' formative years, Rose Kennedy adheres to her literary intentions and writes her own autobiography, devoting as much space to her own childhood and adolescence as she does to her children's.

Times to Remember is Franklin's *Autobiography* in drag. Like Franklin, Kennedy is fully aware that she is both an exception and

an example and writes accordingly. Few women are mayors'
daughters, millionaires' wives and Presidents' mothers, so she
describes the special experiences that these positions have afforded her. Yet many women will rear children and confront the
tragedies of mental retardation and early deaths of family members: Kennedy quite consciously offers her own experiences as
guidance to others. And like Franklin, Kennedy provides plenty
of homely advice: "I believe in keeping interested, growing and
learning. Sedentary people are apt to have sluggish minds: A sluggish mind is apt to be reflected in flabbiness of body and in a dull-
ness of expression that invites no interest and gets none." Understandably enough, Kennedy firmly believes in the American success dream; her family, from her Irish immigrant ancestors to her
sons, are proof of its validity, as was Franklin's own life.

At one point Kennedy states that she would rather be a senator's mother than a senator, and although readers might not share
her choice, they are obliged to admire her autobiography, not just
as a monument to her remarkable family, but as a monument to
all women who choose the "confines" of marriage and motherhood
and flourish within them.

Cynthia L. Walker
University of Alaska—Fairbanks

Keyes, Frances Parkinson Wheeler (1885-1970)

Novelist, Biographer, Journalist, Political Wife

[156] *Roses in December.* New York: Doubleday and Company, Inc., 1960. 328 pp.

Keyes' first volume of autobiography spans the period of almost nineteen years from her birth in President James Monroe's
house in Charlottesville, Virginia, to her reception as the bride of
a prominent New Englander twenty-three years her senior in her
family's Vermont ancestral home. Left fatherless by the death of
John Wheeler, the brilliant young professor of Greek at the University of Virginia, Keyes was brought up by her class-conscious

mother in an atmosphere of wealth and gentility in Vermont and Boston. Her adored older half-brother, usually away at school, moved West after his Harvard graduation; her kindly step-father, an influential Boston lawyer, was lost by divorce.

Keyes' education was strictly supervised by her mother and to a lesser extent by her paternal grandmother, who taught her to read at age four, beginning with the first word of Genesis. Keyes' formal education began at a day school for girls in Boston and was supplemented by dancing and riding lessons. Sometime in these early school days she did her first writing, a pageant enacted with her playmates in the parlor. At age ten she spent a year in Europe with her mother and attended school in Geneva. Keyes returned to Vermont with a German governess and spent the next few years happily in the company of family and friends and in studying, reading, and riding. At fourteen she entered Miss Winsor's Day School in Boston, and for the first time in her life felt alienated and rejected. However, she soon made life-long friends and entered easily into the social whirl of luncheons, dances and young gentlement callers. The summer before her final year at Miss Winsor's she became secretly engaged to Henry Wilder Keyes, former captain of the Harvard crew and a member of the New Hampshire legislature. Both families opposed the marriage, and Keyes' mother whisked her off to Europe in an unsuccessful effort to end the romance. But in the end Frances Parkinson Wheeler was married in an elegant ceremony with all the preparations and conventions required by polite society.

Roses in December provides a detailed description of the life, concerns, and physical surroundings of an upper-class American girl around the turn of the century. Two women figure prominently in Keyes' story. Her mother, twice-married and once-divorced, was exceedingly gracious and charming and for many years attracted the attention of younger men. Her grandmother, the first Frances Parkinson Wheeler, had worked her way through Mount Holyoke as a special student and had later taught her son the Latin irregular verbs at age seven. It was this intelligent and pious Congregationalist who enkindled in Keyes her first religious feelings. Although Keyes' mother devoted much time and expense to her daughter's education, she would not consider sending her to college—an opinion which Keyes' future husband shared. As for her daughter's efforts at writing, she expressly forbade them and threatened dire consequences if Keyes persisted in scribbling verses. But the young writer continued to develop in secret the talent which satisfied her creative impulses and which later brought her fame.

[157] *All Flags Flying: Reminiscences of Frances Parkinson Keyes.* New York: McGraw-Hill Book Company, 1972. 655 pp.

This second volume of autobiography covers the years from Keyes' marriage in 1904 until 1931 and was published after her death virtually uncut and unedited, with a foreword and afterword by her son Henry W. Keyes. The first fourteen years of marriage were spent at her husband's Pine Grove Farm in New Hampshire as mistress of a large household (including in-laws), as a young mother and teacher of three sons, and as the wife of a state congressman and later governor who was often away from home. During these years—and throughout her life—she was beset by health problems ranging from severe burns from an accidental household fire to complications from childbirth and surgery. She was also beset with financial worries and was often made to feel guilty that she had not brought her husband a fortune as had the wives of his brothers. As the wife of a senator in the nation's capital she handled her official social responsibilities with confidence and ease, making 650 obligatory calls in a season and providing Washington hostesses with an excellent dinner guest. She began writing professionally during this period and soon authored "Letters from a Senator's Wife," a regular monthly feature in *Good Housekeeping* for fourteen years. She championed the Sheppard-Towner Bill for the Protection of Maternity and Infancy (the first women's rights legislation) and soon as a journalist was covering various government conferences and the national political conventions. In 1923 *Good Housekeeping* sent her to Rome for the congress of the International Suffrage Alliance, and while in Italy she got her first scoop, an interview with Signori Mussolini. For the next several years she travelled on assignment to such far-flung places as the Great Wall of China and Patagonia, recording everything and everyone in great detail—a travelogue which occupies two-thirds of this book. She took as official secretary one of her older sons, each of whom had learned shorthand on the side at Harvard for just this purpose.

This second volume of autobiography contains a frankness not found in her earlier work, particularly about her relationship with her mother, mother-in-law, and her husband. She cannot forget that her husband's derision of her early writing efforts forced her to write in secret and with no moral support from him and that she was forced to provide the financial resources to clothe herself as befits a senator's wife, to buy a car, and to educate their sons. Nonetheless, she recognizes that her husband's position as United States Senator (almost as much as his former position as captain of Harvard's crew) opened doors that furthered her writing career, sending her off on world tours with letters of introduction fom influential ambassadors and senators and even the President of the United States. Unfortunately, *All Flags Flying* ends before her conversion to Roman Catholicism and before the time of Keyes' greatest productivity as a writer, covering the publication of only the first four of her fifty-one books. Keyes' life reads much like one of her novels—exotic settings, a sense of history, generations of the same family preserving important family property or traditions, financial reversals. And Keyes could easily be one of her own heroines—well-born, genteel, intelligent, self-reliant, and strong willed.

[158] *Along a Little Way.* New York: P. J. Kenedy & Sons, 1940. 83 pp.

Throughout her life Keyes was a reverent reader of scripture and naturally inclined to prayer and meditation. As a child, she found the expression of faith of her Congregationalist elders lacking in joy and warmth and at age fourteen chose to be confirmed in the Episcopal church. Through her travels Keyes became attracted to the mode of worship in Catholic countries and especially appreciated the custom of leaving churches open night and day for private devotion. Although the process of becoming more and more at home in Catholic churches was gradual, the decision to convert came as a sudden inspiration while Keyes was praying at the shrine of St. Anne de Beaupre. Knowing that her action might cause sorrow to others, she quietly studied, prayed, and sought counsel. Several years later Keyes was confirmed in Lisieux, France, where she lived while writing the life of St. Theresa. It was an occasion of great joy and splendid pomp and ceremony in which townspeople as well as members of religious orders and the hierarchy participated. Five poems of prayer written at various times in her life are included in this spiritual autobiography.

Along a Little Way makes no attempt to be rational or theologically or dogmatically persuasive; neither is it emotionally unrestrained or zealous. It is simply personal, tactful, and very readable.

Connie C. Eble
University of North Carolina at Chapel Hill

Kimbrough, Emily (1899-   )

Writer, Editor, Lecturer

[159] *How Dear to My Heart.* New York: Dodd, Mead & Company, 1944. 267 pp.

[160] *The Innocents from Indiana.* New York: Harper & Brothers, 1950. 229 pp.

[161] *Through Charley's Door.* New York: Harper & Brothers, 1952. 273 pp.

[162] *Now and Then.* New York: Harper & Row, 1972. 176 pp.

In *How Dear to My Heart,* Kimbrough describes the first eleven years of her life, growing up in Muncie, Indiana, "when automobiles were new and farmers shot at them." *Innocents from Indiana* deals with her childhood after her family moved to Chicago. In *Through Charley's Door,* Kimbrough portrays her four years at Marshall Fields Department Store, first as fashion editor and then as editor of the store's magazine. *Now and Then* contains miscellaneous reminiscences of her twins as they were growing up. In all of these works, and in the eleven travel books she has written, Kimbrough reveals a gracious personality and a curious mind, but the works provide little of substantial interest for women's studies.

Virginia Cox
University of Wisconsin—Oshkosh

King, Billie Jean (1943-   )

Professional Tennis Player, Publisher

[163] *Billie Jean.* New York: Harper and Row, 1974. 208 pp.

BIOG   Billie Jean N.Y.: VIKING PRESS   1982 220 pp.
K522

Billie Jean King hates to write. In her monthly publisher's column for *Women Sports,* she says that "putting pen to paper is one of those painful experiences which I avoid at all costs." Thus, her "autobiography" is not written by her, but spoken into a tape recorder. Kim Chapin, the "editor," does not rewrite but leaves in all the clichés and slang of King's speech. The result is a sloppy book, interesting more for the insights into professional tennis and King's super-star status than for literary value as an autobiography or for usefulness for women's studies.

It is instructive that King claims never to have kept a diary or journal; she is not introspective, and most often makes no attempt to draw out the generalization from her experience. What she does do, and do well, is chronicle the history of women's professional tennis and the revolution that it has brought for women in professional sports. Billie Jean King has been at the very center of that revolution, and the political machinations of how it came about are fascinating reading.

A chapter on "Women's Lib" reveals King's less-than-radical attitude toward the movement with which she often has been associated (mainly because of the Bobby Riggs tennis match). She there explains her much-touted abortion and her becoming a spokesperson for women athletes. She has put her energies toward equalizing pay and opportunity for women in professional sports— here she has had some success—but about radical change in the family or society as a whole she has nothing to say.

Charles Shapiro in *The New Republic* is typical of reviewers who fault the book for its failure to reveal anything of the author's inner life. He also sees King as an "unpleasant opportunist who uses the women's movement" (June 8, 1974, p. 28).

Billie Jean records the development of a star tennis player—important matches are described, point by point—and chronicles its author's fight for equality for women athletes. Unfortunately, it

fails to deal with many of the paradoxes inherent in that very life—
a major athletic tournament sponsored by a cigarette company or
King's contradictory notions about competition and equality.

Margaret McFadden-Gerber
Appalachian State University

King, Coretta Scott (1927-   )

Lecturer, Concert Singer, Civil Rights Leader

B
KS 34K

[164] *My Life with Martin Luther King, Jr.* New York: Holt,
Rinehart and Winston, 1969. 372 pp.

The title of this book reveals its focus. Coretta King was
twenty-eight when Rosa Parks refused to give up her bus seat to a
white passenger, thus launching in 1955 the Civil Rights Movement in Montgomery, Alabama; the bulk of this book concerns
itself with the struggle against racism from that year to 1968, when
Martin Luther King was assassinated. We get very brief—and
fascinating—glimpses of Coretta's childhood, young adulthood,
and courtship by King. She was the daughter of land-owning,
ambitious Black parents, who wanted her to have the education
that they themselves did not have. Her mother didn't want her to
have to depend on anyone, not even her husband, for a living.
Coretta and her sister Edythe were the first Black students to attend Antioch. From there, Coretta went to the New England
Conservatory of Music. Intending to be a singer, she had nearly
graduated when she met Martin Luther King, who was openly
looking for the right kind of wife. Edythe advised her to marry
him in 1953, adding that she would have a career with him, if not
the kind she had desired and planned for: King was clearly not an
ordinary young minister.

Fifteen years, four fatherless children and countless battles
later, Coretta King is convinced she made the the right decision.
At the Nobel Peace Prize award in 1964, she explained that her
role had always been simply to give King support: "It was the most

important thing I could have done, and I had wanted to do it."
Yet her role was larger than this sounds. She was a concert singer,
performing in many benefits for the Movement, and a public speaker much in demand; she served as a spiritual and political advisor
to her husband; she was a delegate to the 1962 atomic-test-ban
talks in Geneva; and somehow, between those lectures in Chicago
and concerts in San Francisco, she bore and raised four children.
She needed to be strong. From the Montgomery Bus Boycott to
the Freedom Rides, from the confrontation with Eugene (Bull)
Connor to Birmingham to those with Wallace's men in Selma,
there were beatings, bombings and murders that had to be accepted, that had to be explained to the bewildered supporters of
the Movement. What held her and her husband up was the belief
that "unearned suffering and personal sacrifice were redemptive"
and that they were always fulfilling a special destiny they'd begun
to glimpse in the earliest years of their marriage.

The religious cast to that destiny is mentioned by Richard
Neuhaus as being often ignored by the media (*Commonweal*,
December 5, 1969, p. 317). He says Coretta King's book, though
far from critical, does "depict the man moving to the promised
land under the shadow of the cross." Adele Silver comments that
one of the flaws of the book is that its author hardly ever reveals
herself (*Saturday Review*, October 11, 1969, p. 33)—exceptions
are the brief descriptions of childhood and the courtship scenes,
where Martin Luther King emerges as something of a sexist. For
the most part, the real man and the real woman remain hidden, in
Silver's words, behind Coretta King's "genteel and stately prose."
She continues, "Her calm tone, her judicious choice of words, is
unfaltering"—during all the murders, all the beatings, even during
her husband's assassination. "What has it cost her," Silver concludes, "to speak with such firm faith?"

We never learn. We don't get to see the personal woman; Coretta King avoids the kind of intimacy and confessional tone we've
begun to expect from our writers and poets, even sometimes our
politicians. Scenes of domestic life are rare. Doubts over her *own*
life, her own career, apparently ceased when she married; apparently, too, there were no marital conflicts. (Only two or three times
in the book does mild criticism of King surface, usually having to
do with his or his followers' male chauvinism.) Rereading her
journals at one point in this book, she muses, "I see myself now as

an eager, vulnerable young girl I'd almost forgotten." We witness how increasingly invulnerable, although never insensitive, she becomes by virtue of her great faith. It arms her against personal fear, uncertainty and tragedy that could crush those of less faith. Her narrative increasingly moves from worldly concerns to spiritual commitment and purification. The reason this book isn't critical, isn't personal, is that Coretta King was unconsciously creating, as she lived and as she wrote, a myth; and myths are curiously impersonal, devoid of particularizing facts. All the materials were there; King consciously patterned his life after Christ's and Ghandi's, and the book is made richer by its religious imagery. The Kings knew early what fate awaited this courageous and revolutionary minister; when the shot finally came, Coretta King was shocked not at it, but at her own surprise and at how hard it hit her.

Jonna Gormely Semeiks
Queens College, CUNY

Kingston, Maxine Hong (-   )

Author

[165] *The Woman Warrior: Memoirs of a Girlhood among Ghosts.* New York: Knopf, 1976. 209 pp.

Maxine Kingston's *The Woman Warrior* boldly violates the conventions of its genre. Describing a life athwart two cultures, the book is casual about chronology, ignores the traditional bias which favors reality over fantasy, and transcends the conventional egoism of the genre. Kingston conceives the story of her life as the stories of the striking female figures, real and imagined, who haunt her: an aunt whose name was obliterated from family records after she killed herself and her illegitimate child; a fantasy of a woman who is honored as both avenging warrior, and wife and mother; another aunt who goes mad attempting to complete the journey from the world of China to America; a young Chinese girl who remains mute in an American school; and Kingston's mother, Chinese midwife, American laundress, who harrasses her daughter and gives her the gift of story.

Kingston's autobiography implicitly argues the existence of a powerful matriarchy deep within patriarchal culture. A hidden lineage, however, is a source of limitation as well as power. Many of the figures who constitute Kingston's "matriarchy" are among the "ghosts" of the book's subtitle; and the label suggests the harsh reality resonant at the autobiography's center: that the Chinese and American cultures both deprive women of the fullness of life. Kingston's act of memory is, in one sense, a query: how wrest life from a culture which hurls epithets like "maggots" at your sex? or one which offers you pompons instead of power? Kingston's book suggests an ambiguous reply: the rage which energizes the tribute to her dead aunt; and the celebrative attentiveness which allows her to describe an origami soldier, whose fingers, mere wisps of paper, dance to her breath.

The Woman Warrior, Kingston's first book, has won the National Book Critics Circle award for nonfiction and bcome an unexpected best seller. Critical response to this fantasy-memoir suggests that Kingston, like the Chinese culture hero Fa Mu Lan whom she admires, has achieved significant power: "As an account of growing up female and Chinese-American in California it is anti-nostalgic: it burns the fat right out of the mind. As a dream—of the 'female avenger'—it is dizzying, elemental, a poem turned into a sword" (John Leonard, New York *Times,* September 17, 1976, p. 21). Diane Johnson also celebrates Kingston's success, but raises disturbing questions about its implications as she locates the book in the tradition of female autobiography: "In writing, as in mourning, it sometimes appears that women have reserved or been assigned the duty of expressing human resentment, leaving men to fashion the consolations. . .wisdom and 'adjustment' are often qualities of the masculine tone, and women since Margery Kempe have tended to write in tones of protest and madness" (New York *Review of Books,* February 3, 1977).

Joan Manheimer
Vassar College

Knef, Hildegard (1925-   )   Neff, Hildegard

Actress, Singer

[166] *The Gift Horse.*   New York: Dell Publishing Company,
Inc., 1972.   Translated from the German by David
Anthony Palastanga.   384 pp.

The Gift Horse covers the years from Hildegard Knef's childhood in Germany to 1970.   It begins with a "Declaration of Love
for a Grandfather" in whose home she spent her earliest childhood
as a result of her father's suicide.   Knef describes her education and
early theatrical training in Hitler's Germany, and her own war experiences.   Her description of the fall of Berlin to the Russians
(during which she disguised herself as a man and went with her
lover to join the fighting) and her own capture and imprisonment
by the Russians is particularly compelling.   During the post-war
years she married an American soldier, Kurt Hirsch, thereby losing
her German citizenship.   In the early 1950's she became an American citizen.   She gives a two-leveled account of her life in America
during the late 1940's and 1950's.   At the personal level she describes the difficulties of relationships between herself and her
Jewish husband's family who thought of her always as a Nazi.
At the professional level she describes her experiences in Hollywood (where producers changed her name to "Neff") and her
gradual rise to stardom in America.   She devotes approximately
seventy pages to a description (much of it hilariously funny) of the
production of the Broadway musical *Silk Stockings* in which she
starred with Don Ameche.   There is also much discussion of the
film and stage world in Germany.   With her marriage to Hirsch
ended in divorce, in 1962 she married an Englishman, David
Anthony Palastanga, becoming at that time a British subject.   In
1968 she gave birth to a daugher, Christina.   The baby, seven weeks
premature, was delivered by caesarean section, an operation complicated by a series of illnesses and injuries going back to Knef's
childhood.   She came close to death during and after the surgery.
The Gift Horse ends on Christina's second birthday.

Although not specifically oriented toward women's studies,
the book contains a number of matters of interest.   Knef discusses
her relationship with members of her family: her grandparents, her
mother, step-father, and half-brother, and her feelings about her

father who died when she was six months old. Part of her chilling account of the fall of Berlin involves the wholesale rape of German women by Russian soldiers. She discusses the differences between man-woman relationships in Europe and America. There is an amusing account of the difficulties Palastanga faced trying to be divorced so that he and Knef could marry. There is much emphasis on the feelings of Knef for her daughter. However, without question, the most interesting thing about this book is Knef herself.

The Gift Horse was widely and for the most part favorably reviewed. An occasional reviewer was troubled by her rather surrealistic style, but Arthur Cooper reflects the view of the majority of the reviewers on this point: "This is a bitterly honest book and a very good one. The author's spare, stripped down sentences seem to match perfectly the turbid inner conflicts she portrays" (*Newsweek*, July 5, 1971, p. 73). Nearly all the reviewers praise her description of her war experiences. "Her account of what happened is a phantasmagoric exercise in battle reportage" (Brad Darrach, *Time*, July 5, 1971, p. 72). Many reviewers comment on the fact that this is not just another celebrity book, nor is it particularly gossipy despite Knef's often acerbic comments about the Hollywood and Broadway famous. Many reviewers also note the vividness with which Knef's character and personality come through to the reader. Phoebe Adams observes that "The chip that Miss Knef had always carried on her shoulder in regard to the Nazi authorities soon developed into a sort of international woodpile of grudges and squabbles. Not a comfortable burden, however justified, but readers can be grateful for it. Accumulating rage has finally produced this vivid, often witty, splendidly written roar of protest from an intelligent and talented woman unreasonably beset by lunatics and scoundrels" (*Atlantic Monthly,* July 1971, p. 103).

[167] *The Verdict.* New York: Ballantine Books, 1977. Translated from the German by David Anthony Palastanga. 373 pp.

The Verdict, the second of Hildegard Knef's autobiographical books covers a period beginning on August 10, 1973, and ending on May 16, 1975, with extensive flashbacks to earlier periods of her life. On August 10, 1973, Knef had just been told that she had breast cancer—the *verdict* of the title. The book is mostly a description of her experiences in European and American hospitals, as she underwent a series of operations for conditions dating back to childhood polio, injuries suffered in Berlin during World War II, chronic hepatitis. She concentrates primarily on a number of operations which she believes traceable (although she is careful to say this is unprovable) to the caesarean section birth of her daughter, an operation which left the child afflicted by oxygen deprivation, and Knef herself with a continuing series of abdominal infections. Among the surgeries performed were a hysterectomy, removal of an intestinal obstruction, and a number of treatments of peritonitis. These operations were finally capped by a radical mastectomy. The book also contains three long flashbacks: one deals with a jet-set ski-party weekend; one with the childhood of her husband David Anthony Palastanga; and the third with a "one-woman" nightclub tour she made with her husband. However, the hospital experiences and Knef's attempts to come to grips with cancer are paramount in the book. The book ends on the seventh birthday of her daughter Christina. It concludes with a four-page section of Knef's advice about life to her daughter.

The Verdict would be highly interesting to women's studies. Running throughout the book is the question of unnecessary or incompetent surgery performed on women. Knef is outraged not only at the male doctors who treat female suffering with indifference (she singles out in particular an anesthetist who repeatedly gave her drugs to which she was allergic) but also at female doctors who are crueler than the men. She classifies them as among those so-called feminists who are "intent only on reversing the dictatorship instead of outlawing it altogether" (167). The book also discusses to a certain degree her relationship with her husband whose attitude toward women she finally concludes to be chauvinistic, and it discusses in more depth her relationship with her daughter, a relationship made particularly close, she believes, by their shared illnesses. The book would also be of great interest in Death and Dying courses.

The Verdict, while not as widely noticed as *The Gift Horse*, got generally favorable reviews. One reviewer touches on an aspect of the book that probably caused Knef to begin with a disclaimer stating that while the events of the book are true the characters "are not intended precisely to depict actual persons." Phoebe-Lou Adams, in a brief notice in the *Atlantic Monthly*, wrote "if German

doctors are permitted to sue for defamation of professional character, Miss Knef's troubles with them are not over" (February 1976,
p. 111). Martha Duffy, in a *Time* review typifies the critical opinions. "*The Gift Horse* (1971) revealed that she could have been a
writer as well, perhaps even a novelist. Although that book contains a fine, stringent recollection of Hollywood, it is best about
the war. . . . In *The Verdict* Knef deals just as effectively with
the panic of being sick in a modern hospital. . .the story is told
with a blank lack of self-pity, and there is something inspiring
about Knef's appraisal of her fears, resentments, and rather
gallant hopes" (December 29, 1975, p. 64).

Jean R. Halladay
Old Dominion University

Laird, Carobeth (1895-   )

Author, Linguist, Ethnologist

[168] *Encounter with an Angry God: Recollections of My Life
with John Peabody Harrington.* Morongo Indian Reservation, Banning, California: Malki Museum Press,
1975. 190 pp.

Carobeth Laird is a remarkable woman who only now, in her
eighties, is emerging as a public figure. In the past several years
she has written and seen published two books and many articles
and is awaiting publication of her account of recent experiences in
a nusing home. She was led to write *Encounter with an Angry God*
through inquiries about John Peabody Harrington by his current
biographers, but the story she tells is more about Laird herself and
reveals that she was always a remarkable woman.

In 1915, Carobeth felt an urge to be educated. Having recently
relocated to San Diego with her middle class parents and illegitimate infant daughter and having little formal education, she enrolled for summer courses for diversion and stimulation. Reluctantly teaching linguistics was John Peabody Harrington, who appeared to her like an "angry god" when he first entered the class-

room. Her obvious talent for the subject attracted him and a regular pattern of communication between them developed into a
romance of sorts, during which Carobeth filled in with wishful
thinking and imagination the missing details of a real relationship.
Such fantasizing she continued for the first few years of their
six-year marriage while she served as field assistant, chauffeur,
secretary and general menial which enabled him to pursue his
single-minded driving concern to record disappearing American Indian languages and cultures. Although she deplored his many
bizarre personal characteristics (e.g. his compulsive but self-indul-
gent stinginess; his "perverted" but unspecified sexual practices
after the birth of their daughter designed to prevent further pregnancies; his total disregard and refusal to support this child which
was raised by her parents; his personal unconcern for cleanliness;
his paranoic competition and suspicion of other anthropologists;
and so on), it was his emotional incapacity and general unfeeling-
ness towards her that finally repelled Carobeth and left her ripe
and yearning for a relationship with emotional satisfaction. This
she found with George Laird, a Chemehuevis Indian blacksmith,
twice her age, who served as her informant on the reservation to
which she was sent by Harrington. She divorced Harrington in
1922 and married George Laird with whom she lived in poverty
on a ranch in Poway, California until his death in 1940. The life
she describes was hard and led to a brief period of severe depression for her, but on the whole those are years remembered as filled
with love and with meaning, and the contrast between the two men
and the two marriages is a sharp and telling one. *The Chemehuevis*
(Malki Press, 1976) is her ethnography based on the data supplied
by George Laird; the sensitivity with which the book is written
gives further insight into the profundity of their relationship.

Encounter with an Angry God was surprisingly widely reviewed
for a small press publication and was received with enthusiasm.
T. J. Bazzett writing in *Best Sellers* (November 1975, p. 240) represents the consensus when he writes that "all is conveyed in a
careful precise style that is just intimate enough to make the reader feel privileged to be witness to this varied and eventful life. . .a
very readable memoir of a fascinating and courageous woman."

Two reviews are of special interest. Wilcomb Washburn, the historian, sees the book as specifically about Harrington and says that
"a more devestating or savage expose of a scientist's character has

probably not been written," (*Smithsonian,* April 1976, pp. 126-29). Although the reader must certainly come away feeling that Harrington was a peculiar and indeed, pitiful man, Laird is careful to point out that her own inadequacies in their relationship compounded his problems and that another woman could have helped him in more meaningful ways. On the other hand, Diane Johnson, writing in the New York *Review of Books* (February 3, 1977, pp. 20-21) believes that "Harrington treated her like a man. But that was a condition a woman of her generation could not easily accept until she had made her peace with what society had directed her to believe was woman's destiny." In fact, it is doubtful that Harrington would have treated any man as he believed he could treat his wife or that any man would have endured the role of co-equal worker without status, and general menial without compensation. Although Johnson recognizes Laird's intelligence and energy, she believes that even now a lack of self-awareness makes her unable to explore why she rejected Harrington's world and longed instead for a conventional female life. Her marriage to George Laird certainly did not supply that life, but it provided the respect, concern and emotional attachment which all humans need, and which Johnson evidently assumes must be relinquished for women to engage in "masculine" activities.

Diane Brodatz Rothenberg
Encinitas, California

La Roe, Else Kienle (1900-   )

Plastic Surgeon

[169] *Woman Surgeon: The Autobiography of Else K. La Roe, M.D.* New York: The Dial Press, 1957. 373 pp.

In *Woman Surgeon* La Roe recounts her struggle to become what she knew herself born to be: not only—though significantly—a surgeon uniting "the skills of hand and eye" with "the intuitive sympathies known as womanly," but—most of all—a free, self-actualizing person. Plastic surgery is for her an art, like sculpture. It leads her from Kaiser Wilhelm's Germany (where the provincial schoolmaster's daughter dares dream of a career) to the America of World War II and after (where she finds that a half century of effort has not exhausted her power to heal and to inspire). Her precise yet evocative account interweaves personal, professional, and political—the baby's birth at which the "little doctor" assists her beloved uncle; the gift of her grandmother's life savings for Else's schooling; the strenuously exhilarating hours in class and lab (and the crude jokes of male students who resent her "impudence"); the lover renounced because he vetoes her practicing; the success of her sanatorium, Edenhall—and its loss, together with her first marriage, when she resists the rising Nazis. Pivotal sequences juxtapose sinister festivities where she plays reluctant hostess to Goebbels and Goering with desperate rallies of her pacifist women's opposition, the Deutsche Frauen's Freiheits' Partei. Hitler's take-over brings La Roe's exile and the death of Evelyn Dauber—co-founder of Edenhall and the first woman beheaded by the Nazis. Refuge in France, then Monaco, proves precarious. La Roe is considering Russia, despite her previous medical mission that landed her in Lublianka prison, when she is invited to the United States where a new life awaits her—a life of "fallacies and frustrations but also of triumphs."

In her acute eye for detail, her sense of history, her candid observations of other women and men, her determined optimism, her energetic search for self-definition, La Roe resembles her French contemporary Simone de Beauvoir, but with little of the latter's philosophical probing and existential anxiety: this book is a cornucopia of lively incidents intermingled with reflections on "deep emotions and essential values," all springing from a central commitment to the preservation and enhancement of life. It has much to offer students of women's roles in society; even more, perhaps, to critics interested in the divergence of female forms of sensitivity and creativity from male models. The duality/complementarity of La Roe's life as both woman and surgeon shows in the structure of the text; the heterogeneous openness of the composition, within its overall design, allows her to range from richly-textured descriptions of persons and places to clinical analyses of diseases and treatments, to devote some chapters entirely to her private life, others to her patients (a tragi-comic parade of secretaries, gangsters, showgirls, society matrons and ladies of the Klostergasse, German judges and Caribbean villagers, an infant with a harelip, a famous actress with cancer); still other chapters

are devoted to complex interactions such as the conflicts which
destroy two marriages and the circumstances in which she finally
achieves "a harmonious union" with her third husband, a multi-
talented artist of Choctaw-Scottish descent.

La Roe's thinking and writing, though clearly oriented from a
woman's point of view, is more pre-feminist or proto-feminist than
feminist in the developed sense: she belongs to the "feminine"
branch of the European women's movement, with its liberal
politics, emphasis on social reform, and exaltation of qualities
such as grace, tact, compassion, family devotion. Yet her nightmare vision of women's future under Hitler—"reduction, submission, slavery"—spurs her for a time to radical activism. A self-
made woman, she is ambivalent towards traditional values and the
women who live by them. She shares their concerns about bodily
beauty, love, maternity; she feels simultaneously "moved by their
sincerity and appalled by their triviality." Professionally tolerant
of gay life styles, she is nonetheless disconcerted by tentative
lesbian advances—which she ignores or rebuffs with embarrassed
humor. Her goal is to intervene where nature or civilization de-
fault: she takes special interest in "the creation of perfect breasts"
for women who suffer from ugly lack or excess, and she pays special attention to soldiers mutilated in the wars, whose health and
vigor must be restored. She brings alive even for the nonphysician
the spell of the operating room, a sanctuary, "an ordered world;
not a world to live in, but as a place of work it is flawless." We
see the young assistant practicing hour upon hour the delicate curv-
ing movements of a new surgical technique she will later introduce
in that arena; we understand why a busy surgeon turns to research
into tissue rejuvenation as her most "rewarding leisure-time activity." La Roe's desire and will "to go on working and hoping and
loving" illuminates her story.

Critical response to her book at its publication was mixed,
with several reviewers expressing shock at her frank discussions of
sexual physiology and the blood and guts of medical practice, or
else at her failure to conform to literary standards of the professional biography. B. R. Redman's assessment in the Chicago *Sunday Tribune* (March 24, 1957, p. 4) stresses the entertainment
value of a narrative "spiced with amusing, pathetic, horrifying
anecdotes." More thoughtful commentary comes from Mary Ross
in the New York *Herald Tribune Book Review* (March 31, 1957,

p. 7) and Virginia Peterson in the New York *Times* (March 31, 1957, p. 3): Ross finds that La Roe's "most telling quality. . .is her understanding of the minds and emotions, as well as the bodies, of the people with and for whom she works;" Peterson's largely unfavorable review concedes that La Roe's book will satisfy readers "hungry for the realities of human experience." *Woman Surgeon* was well enough received by the public—despite the critics—that a British edition came out in London the following year (F. Muller, 1958), and interest has persisted. A German translation appeared in 1968, under the title *Mit Skalpell und Nadel. Das abenteuerliche Leban einer Chirurgin* (Muller)—a continuing emphasis on the adventurous side of her story. More recently a paperback version in English by Popular Library has been available. It is clear that La Roe's book has survived and is still attracting new readers.

Kittye Delle Robbins
Mississippi State University

Lee, Gypsy Rose (1914-1970)

Burlesque Dancer, Author

[170] *Gypsy: A Memoir.* New York: Harper & Brothers, 1957. 377 pp.

Gypsy should be compared with the autobiography of Lee's sister, June Havoc's *Early Havoc.* Although the sisters shared a past, their anecdotes, stories and memories sometimes differ. Yet one thing on which they both agree is that their mother, Rose Hovick, "in a feminine way was ruthless. She was, in her own words, a jungle mother, and she knew too well that in a jungle it doesn't pay to be nice" (6).

Gypsy Rose Lee, born Rose Louise Hovick, was four and one half years old, and June just three, when their performing careers began. Gypsy, a plain child, was dressed as a boy and danced with the boys in the act starring "Dainty or Baby June." The sisters' childhood included one night stands, chronic financial crises, shoplifting, working when ill, poor medical care and little education. This information Lee reveals in a chatty, anecdotal style that conveys a residue of bitterness over deprivations. After witnessing her mother's erratic relationships with men and disastrous marriages, Gypsy early made up her mind "that I wouldn't believe any man who told me he loved me" (135).

After June's elopment, Gypsy was groomed to take over the lead, and became at fifteen "Rose Louise and Her Hollywood Blondes." While performing on the vaudeville circuit, the group was mistakenly booked into a burlesque house; and there Rose Louise Hovick, in a last-minute replacement, became "the Strip-Tease Queen—Gypsy Rose Lee."

"I could be a star," she wrote in *Gypsy,* "without any talent at all, and I had just proved it" (231).

Soon a feted celebrity, called "the Gene Tunney of Burlesque," Lee grew increasingly unhappy over the disparity between her public and private life. Her relationship with her mother deteriorated as Rose Hovick squandered her daughter's earnings in wildcat investments. Lee finally left burlesque to join the Ziegfried Follies and in her mid-twenties, traveled for the first time without her mother. While on the road, she was offered a Hollywood contract and, at the book's end, accepts it.

Lee mentions briefly both her mother's disgust with June Havoc's career as a marathon dancer and June's feelings of shame over Lee's burelsque career. Lee, however, reveals nothing of her reactions to the emotions of her mother and sister. At the close of the memoir Lee and June are reconciled; her friendships with Georgia Southern and Fanny Brice are warmly recalled; her love affairs are in order, and her career is in ascendance.

Gypsy was described by William Leonard as "a sketchy recollection of the memorable and amusing" (Chicago *Sun Tribune,* April 28, 1957, p. 2). Allen Churchill thought the story suffered because of the author's "preoccupation with her indomitable mother" (*Saturday Review,* May 25, 1957, p. 31).

T. Gail Adams
Emory University, ILA

Le Gallienne, Eva (1899-   )

Actress, Director-Manager, Translator, Biographer

[171] *At 33.*   New York, Toronto: Longmans, Green, 1934.   *O*
262 pp.

[172] *With a Quiet Heart.*   New York: Viking, 1953.   311 pp.   *B*
LL/96

In the first part of *At 33*, LeGallienne describes her youth in
England and Paris, her debut on the London stage, and her gradual
rise to stardom on Broadway. The second half concentrates on her
experiences as the founder of the Civic Repertory Theater (1926
through 1932) and concludes with her recuperation from a serious
accident in 1931.   *With a Quiet Heart* picks up the narrative
"plus 20" years later, repeating little of the material covered in its
predecessor. This second autobiography is mainly a history of the
author's professional life in the theater and contains her reflections
on its troubled state. Its persistent motifs are LeGallienne's commitment to establishing a national repertory theater and her refusal to compromise her standards for money or other forms of
worldly gain.

By design or not, LeGallienne has been a driving force toward
feminism in the American theater throughout her long career:
she played the leads in *L'Aiglon* and *Hamlet* before androgyny
became a well-known word. Recognizing Ibsen's unique insights
into the feminine psyche, she translated his plays to correct what
she believed to be the inadequacies of the popular versions in use.
Most importantly, although she is lavish with praise and charitable
to all, it is obvious that the mentors and sources of inspiration
and emotional support in her life have mainly been women, beginning with her mother and extending to such stage luminaries
as Eleanora Duse, whose biography she wrote in 1966.

Reviewers were mixed in their reactions to LeGallienne's writing
style and her judgments on the theater. But they were unanimous
in their admiration of the self that she inadvertently reveals.
Edward Wagenknecht (Chicago *Sunday Tribune*, April 26, 1953,
p. 3) said it best: "No sensitive reader will be able to turn the last
page without a new respect not only for her devotion to the best
of human values in the theater but also for her nobility of spirit

as a human being.''

Virginia Cox
University of Wisconsin—Oshkosh

Lehmann, Lotte (1888-1976)

Singer

[173] *Midway in My Song.* Translated by Margaret Ludwig, 1938; reprint. New York: Books for Libraries Press, 1970. 250 pp.

Midway in My Song recounts Miss Lehmann's life from her childhood in Germany (Perlesberg and Berlin) through her successes with leading European opera companies (the Vienna Court Opera, in particular) to international acclaim in the mid 1930's. Concentrating on her professional life, she succeeds largely in her aim "to relate my life from the cool heights of objectivity" (v). Her family and her marriage are discussed primarily as they relate to her career.

Lotte Lehmann came from the Prussian middle class. Her father was a minor bureaucrat, and although he provided the family with a restricted but adequate life, she early became aware of the limited existence possible on a small clerk's salary. Lehmann argues that financial insecurity caused her mother's unhappiness and consequent chronic nervous gastric disorders. Her older brother was unable to attend the university. She, however, insisted on a musical education despite her father's plans for a secure teaching or commercial career. Only her mother's continued support, her own determination, and the proven ability which earned her several scholarships finally won her father's approval. Lehmann apparently accepted her "family-father's" dictates as right and natural; she describes with delight his later pride in her achievements.

Only a few brief sentences mention Lehmann's marriage. She never gives her husband's full name (Otto Krause of the Vienna

Spanish Riding Academy), but she suggests that, at the least, they found mutual understanding and respect for each other. He showed "consideration, understanding and forgiveness" (160), and she took to horses and outdoor activities with gusto.

Two themes run insistently throughout *My Song:* determination and pride. Despite her early financial problems, shyness, and her provincial background, Lotte Lehmann persevered. The resulting achievements justify her pride. And she never lost her determination. In a "Postscript" added after the book was complete, she explains that Germany's actions have made it impossible for her to continue living in Europe. "I cannot paint political boundaries on the measureless ways of the art-world" (vii). Leaving two homes behind, she moves on. "And I who was born a German, and who was bound to Austria with the bounds of deepest love—I stand now at the door of America" (vii).

Critics generally prefer to consider Lehmann not as a writer but as a personable and charming diva. John Erskine pays tribute "first of all to the generous disposition which has omitted from this record all personal animosities and rancors, all professional rivalries and jealousies" (New York *Herald Tribune,* September 18, 1938, p. 4). Although *Midway in My Song* received favorable reviews on the whole, Desmond Shawe-Taylor notes that she gives "regulation opera gossip" when "how fascinating it would have been to learn precisely how she had to vary her performance in *Fidelio* under Schalk and Toscanni" (*New Statesman & Nation,* June 25, 1938, p. 1079).

[174] *My Many Lives.* Translated by Frances Holden, 1948; reprint. Westport, Connecticut: Greenwood Press, Publishers, 1974. 262 pp.

My Many Lives belongs with texts on interpretations of lyric-dramatic operatic roles. Lehmann discusses parts long familiar to her—Elsa, Elisabeth, Sieglinde, the Marchallin, and others. Introductions to chapters and a few chapters in their entirety, however, make this book autobiographical as well as instructive. The discussion of Elisabeth in *Tannhauser* begins with a description of the camaradarie among the younger singers at the Hamburg Opera before World War I. Her characterization of Leonore in *Fidelio* commences with tributes to great conductors she had known. Chapter III ostensibly addresses general problems in preparing for an operatic career, but deals with those problems by citing anecdotes from her own experience: instances of discouraging criticism from teachers, performances given despite personal inconvenience or tragedy, stagefright, and so on. Chapter XII introduces important roles in the operas of Richard Strauss, but allows Lehmann to speak her mind about the Strausses as she knew them—in public and in private. The last chapter becomes a farewell to the world of opera. Much of the material in *My Many Lives* is drawn from the time covered in her previous autobiography. Fortunately, these anecdotes flesh out the accounts given earlier.

My Many Lives was well received by reviewers, but as C. K. Miller points out, it is a book primarily "for *aficionados*" (*Library Journal*, April 14, 1948, p. 653).

Freda F. Stohrer
Old Dominion University

L'Engle, Madeleine (1918-   )

Writer

[175] *A Circle of Quiet.* New York: Farrar, Straus and Giroux, 1972. 245 pp.

Set in Crosswicks, her cherished Connecticut farmhouse, Madeline L'Engle explores in *A Circle of Quiet* the meaning of her life as a "wife, mother, grandmother, public speaker, concerned citizen, practicing Christian and writer." This first autobiographical work chronicles L'Engle's early struggles as she awaited the success which finally arrived when she published *A Wrinkle in Time* and it won the Newberry Medal.

[176] *The Summer of the Great-Grandmother.* New York: Farrar, Straus and Giroux, 1974. 245 pp.

Written ostensibly to commemorate the final summer of L'Engle's mother, the book actually chronicles the author's maternal roots as she traces her ancestral lines in order to come to terms with both her own creativity and mortality. *The Summer of the Great-Grandmother* opens with the arrival of the Grandmother in Connecticut—a traditional yearly journey from her own home in the South—shortly after her 90th birthday. This will be the last such trip as the old lady is losing her grasp on health and on life: rapidly plunging into senility via the effects of atherosclerosis.

The book is divided into four sections. "The Summer's Beginning" sets forth the four-generation household, bound by L'Engle who is daughter, mother, and grandmother in her own right. "The Mother I Knew," the second section, delineates the charm of the dying grandmother, her youth, trials, failures, successes as wife and mother. In the third section, "The Mother I Did Not Know," L'Engle examines the facets of her mother's personality not usually examined by one's own children and then continues by an examination of the mothers who preceeded her—a chain of maternal influences. The final section, "Summer's End," concludes the book with the expected termination of the Grandmother's life and L'Engle, now no longer anybody's child, notes, "I have become the Grandmother. . . . The rhythm of the fugue alters; the themes cross and recross. The melody seems unfamiliar but I will learn it." L'Engle has mastered many unfamiliar melodies, and the reader, sharing her story and her pain, is certain she will master this one, for the book is an affirmation of life in the midst of death and seeming defeat.

A Circle of Quiet was criticized as talking down to the readers, being from a "Reader's Digest point of view, and having a shallow naivete" (*Best Seller*, March 15, 1972, p. 555). *The Summer of the Great-Grandmother* was praised for having "delightful prose" (*Best Seller*, December 1, 1974, p. 395), and being "an honest and courageous account" (*Horn Book*, December 1974).

Beverly Oberfeld Friend
Oakton Community College

BENDER
COLLECTION

LeSueur, Meridel (1900-   )

Journalist, Poet, Diarist, Activist

[177] *Salute to Spring.*   New York: International Publishers, 1940. 191 pp.

The 130 notebooks which make Meridel LeSueur a major writer of life narratives are as yet unpublished, but two short story collections, now difficult to find, have been published which reveal her extraordinary talent. The first collection, *Salute to Spring,* soon to be reissued, includes twelve short stories that were written during the thirties when LeSueur's work in periodicals began to attract favorable attention. LeSueur's stories merge autobiography with fiction and force readers to question the elitist implications of the traditional life narrative forms. Some of her stories are frankly autobiographical; "I Was Marching," for example, relates what Patricia Hempel calls the "central spiritual conversion of her life; her rejection of middle class values for a life of an artist of the working people" (*Ms.,* August 1975, p. 63). In other stories like "Annunciation," LeSueur assumes the persona of a poor, pregnant young woman who is mysteriously sustained by the pear tree outside her window. In "The Girl," LeSueur writes probably her most feminist story describing, without any feminist rhetoric, the problems faced by a young woman driving alone with a male hitchhiker. In all of her stories, even those that contain ostensible marks of fictionalizing, LeSueur describes intimately with "passionate and convincing partisanship" (*The New Yorker,* June 1, 1940, p. 83), the lives of those about whom "nothing is ever said. . .no book is ever written" ("Biography of my Daughter"). The frequent use of third-person rather than first-person narration seems an artistically expedient choice rather than a feature of deliberate fiction-making. In pursuit of her goal, LeSueur often reconstructs the "great warp of myth" ("Corn Village"), describing the common rituals of the communities she knows so well: the farmers in the Midwest, the migrant workers in California and the Southwest, the union organizers in industrial cities of the Northeast.

Alfred Kazin identifies LeSueur's work disparagingly as "proletarian literature," but even he finds that her "characteristic grace and sympathy" redeem her work by displaying her "great gift, that peculiar and rare American intensity" (New York *Herald Tribune*, June 9, 1940, p. 7).

[178] *Corn Village.* Sauk City, Wisconsin: Stanton and Lee, 1970. 74 pp.

In this slim volume, LeSueur collects one poem and four of her best stories which reveal how pervasive is her interest in the "great warp of myth" and how she has anticipated the current feminist interest in redefining traditional myths. Like the work in *Salute to Spring*, these pieces are hard to classify as life narrative or fiction but again the question seems irrelevant. LeSueur obviously writes from her own deeply felt experiences and thinks in mythic terms. About "Persephone," her first published story reprinted here, she writes: "I wrote the notes for it when I was about twenty-one and had this terrible. . .break with Demeter, my mother." The rape of Persephone is symbolic for LeSueur of a woman's painful initiation into the world of the "patriarchy. . .the descent into hell, leaving the mother, becoming a mother, and returning" (this letter and "Persephone" appear in *Lady-Unique-Inclination-of-the-Night*, Fall 1977). By reprinting "Annunication" and "Corn Village" LeSueur shows her continuing interest in depicting the female experience. Patricia Hempel reports that LeSueur is fascinated by discovering "a more communal female identity. She speaks often of the 'river of women,' and feels herself part of it, not isolated or unique" (*Ms.*, August 1975, p. 66). As in her earlier work, this collection shows LeSueur's interest in the working class which remains the basis of "spiritual, creative resources: its fundamental lure for her is the language she finds there" (66). This book is indeed a beautiful display of the luminous art LeSueur has created from such riches. Her work is of importance to women's studies.

Nancy L. Paxton
Rutgers University

Levertov, Denise (1923-   )

Poet, Activist

[179] *The Poet in the World.*   New York: New Directions, 1973. 275 pp.

In no way an autobiography, this collection of the poet's "scattered prose writings" forms a statement of sorts of the writer's views of the world from which a personal portrait emerges. The book is divided into five parts. The first three deal with Levertov's work, her opposition to the Vietnam war, and her experience with teaching. A fourth consists of sketches for fiction and a fifth of reviews of poetry. What impresses most strongly is the generosity of mind and spirit of Levertov, her absolute integrity as a poet, and her life-affirming liberalism as a human being.

A few autobiographical details occur in the essay, "A Sense of Pilgrimage" and occasionally elsewhere. Born and raised in England, Levertov wrote her first poem at the age of five, and in her youth had "a shared sense with her sister of having a definite and peculiar destiny" because of two ancestors, mystics and contemporaries of the late 1700's, early 1800's: Schenour Zalman, founder of Habad Hasidism, and Angel Jones of Mold, a Welsh tailor. Her mother's ancestry was Welsh, and her father was both "learned Jew and fervent Christian." As a child she "did lessons" at home under the tutelage of her mother; on the whole, her experience in the classroom was minimal. Consequently, when she began to teach in 1964, she had "no models of procedure, no memories to draw on." She was married in 1947 to Mitchell Goodwin, came to the United States in 1948. A son was born in 1949. The early 1950's were "transitional, devoted to taking in at each breath the air of American life."

"Glimpses of Vietnam Life," an essay on which the author can be (and has been) faulted for naivete, is the record of a journey to Hanoi that Levertov took with Muriel Rukeyser and Jane Hart in 1973. If all that she saw seemed uncommonly wonderful, her vision reflects her desire to find a people "not only unalienated from their society but enthusiastically identified with it," that is, what she hopes Americans might become. She admits to sighing for "earlier" cultures infused with noble simplicity when, though there was cruelty and grief, there was no ugliness."

Anyone interested in teaching should find Levertov's independent and lively observations of the academic world worthwhile. She taught in various atmospheres (Drew University, CCNY, Vassar, and Berkeley). She attempted to rid her Vassar girls of their "timid perfectionism" and found them "dominated by a desire to please or a fear of committing themselves." She felt all of her students affected by the "tyranny of grades." Many brilliant ones were also "grossly ignorant. . .deprived of a sense of historical continuity, of context."

Several reviews appearing within the first year of publication praised *The Poet in the World*. Although *Choice* condemned its "relentlessly dull prose" and dismissed it, Nathan Scott in *Commonweal* declared that after almost a year of living with the book he had concluded that it is "an important contribution to understanding and appreciating contemporary poetry" and that it "will take its place beside Eliot's *The Sacred Wood* and Pound's *ABC of Reading* as an indispensable guide to modern aesthetics." Hayden Carruth in *Hudson Review*, admitting to being a friend of the poet, asserted that "her title essay should be read by every poet in the country—in the world!" Identifying the source of Levertov's world view as Neoplatonism, Carruth at the same time recognized that the great strength of the book is the "force of the author's good sense and practical wisdom." Linda Wagner in *The Nation* admired Levertov because she "sees life as renewing, joyful, majestic." More guarded in praise because she distrusts "the single-mindedness of a crusader," Josephine Jacobsen in *The New Republic* found "most impressive the vehemence with which Denise Levertov speaks for the reach and dignity of poetry."

James Van Dyck Card
Old Dominion University

Lewis, Faye Cashatt (-   )

Physician

[180] *Nothing to Make a Shadow.* Ames, Iowa: Iowa State
University Press, 1971. 155 pp.

Writing from memory, Faye Lewis Cashatt describes the events
and emotions of her family's homesteading years (1909-1917) near
Dallas, South Dakota. The book is concerned with such things as
her parents, twin sisters of four, two younger brothers, the neighbors (individualized by the way they responded to homestead
conditions), and community projects in church and school. Although Lewis was aware of the harshness of life in a homestead
"claim shack," she recognizes that this was a romantic time, "a
stabilizer between a too idealistic youth and the harshness of
mature understanding" (13-14). The book concludes with her
recognition that a desire for further education removes her family
from the center of her life.

Nothing to Make a Shadow is valuable for women's studies because it records the adolescence and some of the experiences of
the first woman graduate of both the University of South Dakota
College of Medicine and Washington University School of Medicine. She reminisces, for instance, that in recitation in medical
classes: "My girl voice [was] like a black skin in a roomful of
whites" (7). She describes her hardworking parents candidly,
sensing her mother's disappointments and fears, without making
them her own. Of events external to the family, her contact with
educated women and men are the most detailed. Significantly, a
clear picture emerges of an independent woman—one able to cope
and willing to learn. Lewis was one of those women to whom we
now look as a pioneer in the women's movement: she had the
courage to devleop the abilities she knew she had.

Elizabeth Cummins Cogell
University of Missouri—Rolla

Lindbergh, Anne Morrow (1906-   )

Diarist, Essayist, Novelist, Poet

128
L 7429

[181] *Gift from the Sea.*   New York: Random House Inc., 1955. 127 pp.

Originally conceived as a book of reflections on her past life, Lindbergh soon realized that in many respects her life typified modern American womanhood. In eight essays, each symbolized by a different sea shell along the beach, she thus proceeded to analyze the nature of this womanhood. The early essays concentrate on a "life of multiplicity," i.e., a life in which diverse responsibilities demand a woman's attention, the "basic of solitude," and the feminine role of "eternal nourisher." In the main, Lindbergh argues that instinct enforced by training leads a woman to channel her time and energy to family and society often to the point of heroic self-sacrifice. In order to counterbalance this fragmentation, Lindbergh advocates that a woman cultivate a spiritual center, where by means of contemplation and creativity she can establish her self-worth.

In the later chapters Lindbergh meditates on the changing pattern of marriage from the self-contained relationship of man and woman to the larger circle embracing family and society. This subject she develops in greater depth in her novel, *Dearly Beloved* (1962). Throughout the reflections on marriage Lindbergh repeats woman's need for private contemplation and self-development. The final chapter, "The Beach at My Back," celebrates the effects of contemplation on the author herself. Feeling spiritually revitalized by her retreat to the beach, Lindbergh returns to society, where she will more effectively meet her responsibilities as wife, mother, and celebrity.

[182] *Bring Me a Unicorn.* New York: Harcourt, Brace, Jovanovich, 1971. 259 pp.

B106
L7419

This first volume of Lindbergh's letters and diary written between 1922 and 1928 constitutes her juvenilia. Lindbergh records the events of her youth beginning with a letter to her maternal grandmother in which she comments on her travel experiences at age sixteen and ending with a letter to a friend announcing her forthcoming marriage to Charles A. Lindbergh. Most of the letters of this volume are addressed to her mother and sisters, underscoring a strong familial bond as well as a need for feminine companionship and understanding. Matters of mutual domestic interest and her life at Smith, where Lindbergh's interest in writing was stimulated, abound throughout the letters. The diary contains the outpourings of a shy and withdrawn adolescent who finds the lives of others more interesting than her own. Together the letters and diary reveal Lindbergh's upbringing by parents who instilled in their children moral principles and respect for learning.

The personality emerging from this volume is awkward and self-effacing. Lindbergh feels dwarfed by the outgoing personality and success of both her mother and her older sister Elizabeth. The resulting sense of insecurity is accentuated by a lack of faith in her writing talents. Recurring throughout this volume like a leitmotif is Lindbergh's desire for personal recognition, which at this point in her life is dependent upon equaling the achievements of the Morrow women and succeeding as a writer.

[183] *Hour of Gold, Hour of Lead.* New York: Harcourt, Brace, Jovanovich, 1973. 340 pp.

The second volume of Lindbergh's diaries and letters chronicles her experiences as wife and aviatrix from 1929-1932. Assuming the duties of radio operator and navigator, exploring transcontinental air routes with her husband, and flying across the Atlantic while pregannt with her first child increased Lindbergh's self-confidence. The hazardous trip to the Orient undertaken in 1931 was later published in her first book, *North to the Orient* (1935), and the transatlantic flight became the subject of her short novel, *The Steep Ascent* (1944). Travel and the social involvement demanded of Lindbergh as wife of an internationally famous person helped her to overcome some of her former shyness.

The happiness of these years, the "hour of gold," which reached its zenith in the early months of motherhood, was shattered by the kidnapping of Charles Jr. on March 1, 1931, ushering in the "hour of lead." During this period Lindbergh endured frequent nightmares, trauma, and after the discovery of the body a lingering, deep-seated bitterness. As if fate had not been cruel enough, Lindbergh was shocked by her father's sudden death in December of the same year. The emotional strain continued unmitigated until the birth of her second son, Jon, on August 16, 1932, which she poignantly describes in the diary. Lindbergh pours out these bittersweet experiences in letters to her mother and sisters, as if writing about them helped clarify her consuming grief.

[184] *Locked Rooms and Open Doors.* New York: Harcourt, Brace, Jovanovich, 1974. 352 pp.

These letters begin with the Lindberghs' Atlantic survey flight in 1933, part of which Anne described in *Listen! the Wind* (1938), and ends with their sea voyage to England in December 1935. Quoting Thoreau, Lindbergh characterizes this period as "going from—toward." Struggling to escape the problems of publicity and security that besieged them, she together with her husband and child turned to England with hopes of establishing a normal life.

The instability of life at this time brought with it emotional turmoil. Lindbergh's relationship with her husband was unsettled, torn as she was between a sense of inferiority and a feminist drive to equal his distinctions. The inadequacy felt alongside her mother became more acute while the Lindberghs lived with the widowed Mrs. Morrow at the family home, Next Day Hill. Here Lindbergh fell victim to conflicting expectations: her mother's attempts to draw her into an active social life and Charles' desire for their privacy and independence. The letters of 1935 reveal the anxieties wrought from this delicate position. Fortunately, Lindbergh's friendship with Margot Loines provided her with the intellectual stimulus and emotional release necessary to regain her self-assurance. Also at this time Lindbergh's relationship with Elisabeth came of age. Replacing Lindbergh's former envy of her sister was respect and admiration, which culminated in the idealization of Elisabeth after her untimely death in December 1934.

[185] *The Flower and the Nettle.* New York: Harcourt, Brace, Jovanovich, 1976. 605 pp.

This fourth collection from Lindbergh's letters and diaries, spanning the pre-World War II years (1936-1939), depicts her private and public life in a complex European scene. Her private life, divided between two homes, the first in England and the second off the Brittany coast, was consumed by familial devotion, which she perceives to be the chief instrument for a woman's self-fulfillment. In a statement of her feminist views, Lindbergh remarks that most women cannot reconcile marriage and career without sacrificing an essential quality of womanhood, that is, the capacity to be "reservoirs of spiritual, emotional and mental strength." Her preference undoubtedly favors marriage and family, but with the admission that where marriage and career coexist successfully, there is the feminine ideal issuing "pure gold."

During these years Lindbergh moved in the diplomatic circles of Europe, travelling once to Russia and on three occasions to Germany. As World War II approached, she became a pacifist, a position she shared with other European intellectuals and defended in the essay, *The Wave of the Future* (1940). Accepting her husband's opinion of the consequences of German air superiority on the Allies, Lindbergh argued for negotiations with Germany and for the reexamination of democratic principles by free societies. Although Lindbergh's position on the war can be judged naive today, the letters substantiate that she was well-motivated. In general, there emerges from these letters the portrait of a mature woman: self-confident, humane, and sincere.

Although Lindbergh's novels, *The Steep Ascent* and *Dearly Beloved,* and her book of verse, *The Unicorn and Other Poems,* have won at best halfhearted praise, her reviewers including the feminists have consistently acknowledged her articulateness, poetic imagination, and candor. Echoing readers of her early volumes, Alfred Kazin in his review of *Hour of Gold, Hour of Lead,* marvels at Lindbergh's "gift of communication" (New York *Times,* March 4, 1973, p. 1). The self-portrait emerging from the letters and diaries beginning with *Bring Me a Unicorn* has drawn general approval except for the dissenting voice of Jean Stafford, who claims Lindbergh is a better reporter of "fair weather and foul" than of herself (*Vogue,* March 4, 1963, p. 38). Lindbergh's sensitivity to language has established her among the significant contemporary writers. As noted in a review of *Gift from the Sea,* her sensitivity leads her to the perfect symbols for ideas and emotions. Not only is she keenly attuned to nature, but she excels at transmitting her perceptions to the reader (*Saturday Review,* April 2, 1955, 38:22). Without exception the unabashed honesty of the letters and diaries have won kudos. Representing such an opinion is Anne Fremantle, who reviewing *The Flower and the Nettle* praises the volume for its honesty, for its inquisitive spirit, for Lindbergh's humility, and for her frankness about her fear of flying (*America,* February 28, 1976, pp. 162-163).

Understandably the feminist theme in the *Gift from the Sea* has attracted attention since its publication in 1955. Not only is its importance for women of all ages recognized, but the insight into womankind it offers men (Fanny Butcher, Chicago *Sunday Tribune,* March 13, 1955, p. 1) and its universal theme of alienation in a complex civilization have also been praised (J. H. Jackson, San Francisco *Chronicle,* March 22, 1955, p. 22).

Less favorably received has been Lindbergh's method of presenting the letters and diaries in their near original form. In spite of her repeated defense of this method on the grounds that truth might have been obscured had she recast the "raw material" into autobiography (*Bring Me a Unicorn,* xv and *The Flower and the Nettle,* xvi-xvii), reviewers have increasingly objected to stretches of tedium and pedestrian material owing to the prolixity of the letters. As the published volumes of Lindbergh's letters increased, however, there is the growing awareness of her as a remarkably talented woman deserving recognition for her own deeds and not only because of her marriage to the great American hero of the '20's and '30's.

Elsie F. Mayer
Henry Ford Community College

Lone Dog, Louise (-   )

Psychic

[186] *Strange Journey: The Vision Life of a Psychic Indian Woman.* Healdsburg, California: Naturegraph Books, 1964. 68 pp.

Louise Lone Dog's *Strange Journey* is a combination spiritual autobiography, polemic, and prophecy. *Strange Journey* begins with a discussion of Lone Dog's racial background—she is part Mohawk and part Delaware Indian—a background which encouraged the development of her psychic talents. The first half of the book is devoted to that same development, from her childhood encounters with ghosts and spirits to her later revelatory visions. These visions dominate the second half of the book and range from the worldly, visions of President Kennedy's impending assasination, to the cosmic, visions of Indian revival and unity.

Although simply and sometimes poorly written, *Strange Journey* is a valuable testimonial to the preservation of Indian culture and does provide some insight into the psychology of the mystic. And besides, given the recent spate of Indian land suits, her predictions seem to be coming true.

Cynthia L. Walker
University of Alaska—Fairbanks

Loos, Anita (1893-   )

Screenwriter, Novelist, Playwright

[187] *A Girl Like I.* New York: Viking Press, 1966. 275 pp.

[188] *Kiss Hollywood Good-by.* New York: Viking Press, 1974. 213 pp.

A Girl Like I covers the background of the Loos family, the author's California childhood, her early years as a scenarist for D. W. Griffith and Douglas Fairbanks, her move to New York in search of culture, and the writing of the work which made her a worldwide celebrity, *Gentlemen Prefer Blondes*, in 1925. It also includes what proved to be a focal point in Loos' life, her marriage in 1919 to John Emerson, an actor-director 20 years her senior. This relationship provides the keystone of her second volume of memoirs, *Kiss Hollywood Good-by*, in which, through anecdotes about the famous and infamous and accounts of the meaningful events in her personal life, Loos reveals her ambivalence toward the industry to which she devoted much time and energy: she is at once fascinated by and condescending toward Hollywood and all that it represents. Her marriage, though not happy, was the shaping force of her adult years. It crystallized her attitudes about male-female relationships, gave her the impetus to pursue her career, and provided the base necessary to conduct her life the way she wanted.

In this latter book Miss Loos scolds "Women's Lib," which she apparently equates with general, all-around antipathy for men. By her own admission she has always been "a pushover for rogues" and sees nothing amiss in females supporting males, emotionally and financially, because women are happiest when giving and men are naturally "pimps." But beneath this defense of female submissiveness lies the sturdy conviction that men are weaker than women. And although she often expresses her preference for male companionship, she made sure that it remained cerebral and platonic, which is the way she prefers it. She was attracted to older men, particularly dashing scoundrels and intellectuals—H. L. Mencken and Aldous Huxley were among her favorites in the second category. But Loos also demonstrates great compassion for her many women friends, with whom she identifies in their mutual efforts to play the game for which men decide the rules.

Both works were widely reviewed in newspapers and magazines. Opinions ran the gamut from the nasty to the ecstatic. Perhaps one of the more reasonable assessments of Loos's works was *Best Sellers'* observation that *A Girl Like I* "is an intriguing bit of Americana that mirrors the brash confidence, rugged ndependence and changing mores of a rapidly growing, prosperous country" (October 1, 1966, p. 244).

[189] *Twice over Lightly: New York Then and Now.* New York: Harcourt, Brace, Jovanovich, Inc., 1972. 343 pp.

Written with Helen Hayes, *Twice over Lightly* contains some reminiscences and personal opinions of both authors. It is, however, principally a "guide book" of New York City.

Virginia Cox
University of Wisconsin—Oshkosh

Loud, Pat (1926-   )

Television Personality

[190] *A Woman's Story.*   New York: Coward, McCann and
            Geoghegan, Inc., 1974. 223 pp.

In 1971 PBS filmed three hundred hours of the daily life of
the Loud family from which was created the 12-hour television
series broadcast in 1973 as "An American Family." Having received much unexpected criticism both for what she and her family
revealed about themselves and for their willingness to reveal it on
national television, Pat Loud, in *A Woman's Story,* attempts to
justify not only this decision: "wouldn't anybody have done it?"
(92), but the normality of her own and her family's life, the
typicality of their problems and their failings. The title of the
book well indicates her theme, that for all the notoriety, her life
and her experience are in many ways a typical "woman's story."

"Programmed for marriage," as she says of her upbringing, she
describes her early sexual ignorance and timidity, her education at
Stanford which trained her to do nothing in particular, her various
jobs, mainly as file clerks, her efforts to be on her own, but not
very successfully, in San Francisco, her return to her hometown of
Eugene, Oregon, her marriage to a childhood friend, and her acceptance of marriage, heavy domesticity, and motherhood as a
framework for an empty life (187). The five closely-spaced children and the routine kept the marriage going until she could no
longer tolerate her husband's continuous infidelities. She describes
the difficulties of divorcing a husband of twenty years and having,
at age forty-six, to create a new identity, find a job, and take full
responsibility for her family. "Divorce requires you to explain
your life to yourself," she writes (192-3), and what she came to
understand was that she had chosen marriage as a substitute for
personal development. In her acceptance of her new life, she finds
an unexpected freedom and self-respect. At the same time, in
justifying her own and her family's way of life against the judgments pronounced against them by so many television viewers and
critics, she insists that the Louds were neither monsters nor zom-
bies, that their mistakes were everybody's mistakes (161), and
that the pattern of her own life—a lonely adolescence, choosing
to marry a man who confirmed her worst feelings about herself,

continuing in an unhappy marriage for years—is in many ways the pattern of American women's lives and their marriages.

A Woman's Story has not received anywhere near the attention of the television series. Susan Lester reviewed it sympathetically in *Ms.* (July 1974, pp. 87-89), finding in Pat Loud's growth and change a lesson for us all, but most readers have been put off by what Lester herself describes as the book's "oversimplification and slickness" (p. 88). Stephanie Harrington (*Nation*, September 14, 1974, pp. 219-20) criticizes the book and the series for confusing self-exposure with self-realization.

Judith B. Herman
State College at Buffalo

Luhan, Mabel Dodge (1879-1962)

Upper Class Salon Lady, New Mexican Primitivist

[191] *Lorenzo in Taos.* New York: Knopf, 1932. 351 pp.

Addressed to Robinson Jeffers, *Lorenzo in Taos* chronicles the period between 1921—when Luhan first "wills" D. H. Lawrence to New Mexico—and 1930, when he dies. Meshing letters from Lawrence with narration, the book highlights the sexual politics of relations among Luhan, Lawrence, and his wife Frieda. Luhan conceives of human interaction as power struggle; this view is unforgettably exemplified when she describes a lengthy crying fit staged to command Lawrence's attention.

Lorenzo not only records actual events but also mirrors the "permutations of spirit." Overtly tracing Lawrence's growth from aggressive selfishness to passive selflessness, Luhan covertly outlines a parallel metamorphosis in herself which provides the underlying structure for the soon-to-be-commenced *Intimate Memories.* That she and Lawrence have similar personalities—both are conscious manipulators seeking power over others—has more import than their differences in class and sex. She offers an identical image of male and female maturity—passivity and affective being.

Such an ideal perpetuates both sexual stereotypes and fragmented models.

[192] *Background* (Vol. I of *Intimate Memories*). New York: Harcourt Brace, 1933. 317 pp.

Written between 1924 and 1925, *Background* covers the period from 1879-1898. It describes Luhan's childhood experiences in Buffalo, her boarding school activities, a summer in France, and her "coming out." Her milieu is emotionally and aesthetically sterile, morally rigid; her parents and grandparents are ruled by wealth and idleness, propriety and bad taste. Whatever life there is is buried and abnormal. Her father, although trained as a lawyer, has no occupation except raging at her mother, suffering from gout, and (perhaps) secretly writing. Her mother, who spends her time controlling the household, is "obstinate, repressed and unloving." Luhan sees her life as a continuing attempt to escape from "separateness and immobility, [from] the dynamic turned static." To conquer boredom and loneliness, she engages in various inflammatory activities (such as a "breast fixation" on a maid) designed, but failing, to connect her with others. This pattern of alienation continues in her sexual and emotional involvements with schoolgirls, schoolteachers, and finally with men, whom she attemps only to dominate.

Themes appearing in this and later volumes are: boredom and the attempt to find meaningful work, and the need to resolve the conflicts between dominance and submission, intellect and emotion, civilization and nature. Since the first term in each polarity best describes Luhan, she can be seen as an alienated Dostoevskian "underground man." She thus portrays the contemporary female as divided, as exhibiting the same stereotypic qualities as the male, rather than the opposite. Luhan's six autobiographical volumes, including *Winter* and *Lorenzo* ostensibly illustrate growth from the first (negative) term of each polarity to the second; her values, like Dostoevsky's are traditionally Romantic. Finally, neither Luhan nor Dostoevsky offers models of reconciliation; in both the dynamic is "either/or" rather than "both/and," although it might be argued that both aim at integration and wholeness in developing similar opposites.

[193] *European Experiences* (Vol. 2 of *Intimate Memories*).
New York: Harcourt Brace, 1935. 461 pp.

Written in 1925-26, *European Experiences* covers the period
1900-1912. It documents Luhan's early development and search
for reality in European culture. Beginning with her first marriage
to Karl Evans, it details the birth of their son John, the deaths of
husband and father, and Luhan's subsequent breakdown and
therapeutic trip to France, where she meets and marries Edwin
Dodge. She and Dodge, a wealthy Boston architect, buy and re-
model the Villa Curonia in Florence, where they collect people
and art until 1912; boredom then sets in and Luhan returns to
America, having finished with Dodge. The book describes the
Villa; unflatteringly portrays such guests as Eleanora Duse, Gordon
Craig, the Steins and Alice Toklas; and enumerates Luhan's sexual
intrigues with men and women, her depressions and attempted
suicides. It consciously illustrates the life of a social and aesthetic
dillettante, uncommitted and unfulfilled sexually, emotionally,
and intellectually.

Familiar themes are dominance vs. submission, boredom vs.
meaningful work, physical *sturm und drang* vs. emotional and spiritual development, and society vs. nature; all suggest ambivalence
and alienation. The following illustrates the positive values against
which her European experiences are retrospectively measured:
"Never for fifty years, have I left off pursuing, fusing, identifying, devouring, rejecting! People!. . .I built myself a world to
replace the lovely world of nature that I lost. . .for them. . . . But
now, I return to what I always lost. Life is in the natural world."

[194] *Winter in Taos.* New York: Harcourt Brace, 1935. 234
pp.

Winter in Taos consists of Luhan's recollections, on one winter's
day, of nature's annual cycle. Descriptions of the birth and death
of animals, of the sowing and reaping of crops, recreate an Eden
in which she envisions herself as fertility goddess, her husband
Tony as god. As Great Mother, Luhan transforms herself from
complex human being to feminine archetype.

[195] *Movers and Shakers* (Vol. 3 of *Intimate Memories*). New
York: Harcourt Brace, 1936. 536 pp.

Written between 1927-28, *Movers and Shakers* treats the events
of 1913-16. In Manhattan, Luhan creates a salon where "revolu-
tionaries" gather. Neither politically knowledgeable nor committed, she collects figures as varied as Alexander Berkman and
Emma Goldman, Walter Lippmann, and the Sangers; as their hostess she gains a reputation as a radical. Her leftist interest ends
with a year's affair with the activist, John Reed. When her passion
for him dies, she turns to avant garde art and takes up with the
Duncans, Leo Stein and Maurice Sterne. Her relationship with
Sterne starts with her decision to convert him from painter to
sculptor; it finishes with her marrying him and sending him off to
the Southwest since she cannot endure his presence.

Movers manifests Luhan's basic life pattern. Manless she is
vitiated. Such depression is combated by compulsive "busyness"
which terminates as soon as she is emotionally involved again.
Absorbed by affection, she feels powerless which she tries to
counter by controlling her mate. The attraction and repulsion syn-
drome defining her "love," her sense either of being or nothingness—both reveal the romantic dynamic of life experienced only
in extremes.

[196] *Edge of Taos Desert: An Escape to Reality* (Vol. 4 of
Intimate Memories). New York: Harcourt Brace,
1937. 335 pp.

Treating December 1916 to August 1917, *Edge of Taos Desert*
chronicles the start of a shift from the meaninglessness recorded
in the previous three volumes toward a *vita nova*. Paradise is re-
gained in New Mexico; the Navajo, Tony Luhan (who becomes
her fourth husband), is her saviour. Teaching her "how to feel,"
Tony points her toward becoming a "human being, spontaneous,
unconscious, and real." The "new world" Tony introduces her to
is collective not individualistic, instinctual not mechanistic.

Luhan's attempt "to show how life. . .must be lived" is a
typical work of the great Depression. With the bankruptcy of
patriarchal civilization in the thirties, patterns of culture dia-

metrically opposite those of corporate capitalism were highly
touted. Such patterns were ultimately recognized as only apparently different; in fact, they were no more than the flip side of
the same man-made coin. Luhan mirrors the "new" masculine
value system in the Taos trilogy. *Lorenzo* offers male experience
of living "in the blood" as the way to wholeness. The mythic
ideal of female selfhood proffered by *Winter* is centered in the
male: the white goddess exists through the grace of the dark god.
Even *Edge of Taos,* Luhan's final published attempt "to see
Mabel," defines woman's individuation in man's terms.

Representative reviews praise Luhan's writings as supplements
to other topics but deprecate them in their own right. *Lorenzo in
Taos* is an "interesting literary portrait" (Chicago *Daily Tribune,*
20 February 1932, p. 14), a pleasurable "picture of New Mexico"
(Perry Hutchinson, New York *Times,* 28 February 1932, p. 4), but
is "marred by the. . .intrusion of the author" (Geoffrey Hart, *Yale
Review,* Winter 1933, p. 392). *Background* is an "addition to the
history of *moeurs*" (Herbert Gorman, New York *Times,* 26 March
1933, p. 4) yet is flawed by "excessive preoccupation with psychological theories" (*Springfield Republican,* 19 March 1933, p. 7)
and its untiring descriptions of girls and young women (London:
Times Literary Supplement, 12 October 1933, p. 694). Almost
uniform is the dismissal of *European Experiences* as "third rate
writing about third rate people" (New York *Herald Tribune,* 20
September 1935, p. 14). Equally negative is S. J. Roof's pro-
nouncement that *Movers and Shakers* "should enthrall 'confession
addicts' " (*Saturday Review of Literature,* 21 November 1936, p.
7); however, Malcolm Cowley claims the volume is "interesting to
sociologists" (*New Republic,* 25 November 1936, p. 120). Finally,
Edge of Taos Desert is disparaged either as confessional without
"moral or theme" (E. L. Walton, *Nation,* 25 September 1937, p.
326) or as an "ironic [picture] of ruthlessness" (Carrie Cabot,
Saturday Review of Literature, 25 September 1937, p. 6).

Studies focusing on Luhan find her wanting. In her biography
of Lawrence, Emily Hahn implicitly condemns Luhan as manipula-
tive (*Lorenzo: D. H. Lawrence and the Women Who Loved Him.*
New York: Lippincott, 1975, pp. 332-75). This indictment by
innuendo continues in Hahn's *Mable: A Biography of Mabel Dodge
Luhan* (Boston: Houghton Mifflin, 1977, 277 pp.), a work which
does little more than paraphrase, *sans* documentation, Luhan's

published prose, although other views of the heroine are offered from the autobiographies of Maurice Sterne, Hutch Hapgood, and Carl Van Vechten. Patricia Meyer Spacks asserts that Luhan "organizes her sense of identity around other people," is dissatisfied by such an existence, but cannot accept herself as a fully dependent or independent being (*The Female Imagination.* New York: Knopf, 1975, pp. 223-26). In the most detailed analysis, Christopher Lasch argues that Luhan is an "extremely neurotic woman with an irregular emotional history" (*The New Radicalism in America: The Individual as Social Type.* New York: Random House, 1965, pp. 104-40). Concerned with the disintegration of the patriarchal family, his model for female normality is Freudian. While his judgmental criteria are most suspect, Spacks and Hahn measure Luhan against an equally reductive either or concept of what human identity ought to be.

Selma Burkom and Margaret Williams
San Jose State University

Lyons, Ruth (1909-1972)

Radio and Television Personality

[197] *Remember With Me.* Garden City, New York: Doubleday and Company, 1969. 272 pp.

In *Remember With Me,* Ruth Lyons chronicles her life and her career as a phenomenally popular radio and television personality in Cincinnati. Hired first to manage the music library of a radio station, Lyons soon became an accompanist for live musical programs and eventually hostess of her own "Woman's Hour." Her broadcasts were immediately popular, including the "Fifty-Fifty Club" she began after moving to another station. The program moved to television in 1949, and from then until 1967, Ruth Lyons' noon show was standard fare for millions of women in Ohio, Indiana, and Kentucky. Lyons recalls the beginnings of her "Christmas Fund," a fund that continues after her death to raise thousands of dollars each year for children's hospitals. She describes, too, her marriage and her relationship with her daughter, whose death from cancer was a shock from which Lyons never recovered; she left television in 1967 soon after her daughter's death.

The impact of Ruth Lyons on the women who watched her show faithfully and ordered tickets to attend her broadcasts as many as nine years in advance is impossible to measure and difficult to evaluate. She could, as the introduction by her station's owner suggests, sell soap as easily and convincingly as she could promote less commercial and less tangible values to her audience. She maintained, however, a consumerist's skepticism about the products she sold; she did commercials live but never endorsed a product until she or her staff had tested it. Guests on her show sold millions of books, records, and concert tickets as a result of their appearances, but thousands of hospitalized children also benefited from her campaigns in their behalf. And her list of guests included not only sports figures and popular artists but guests of the Cincinnati Symphony and Opera as well as political figures. Lyons was influential enough to attract assassination attempts and to spark a huge controversy when she danced with a black man, Arthur Lee Simpson, on her show in 1952.

A woman with the influence on other women that Ruth Lyons achieved must be taken seriously, and although some readers may view her commercialism with skepticism, one must finally conclude that she projected an important image to her audience: a successful entertainer and businesswoman who never underestimated the intelligence of her audience and gave them a kind of entertainment and information never offered them by any other daytime television show. Her memoirs provide interesting information about the early years of television broadcasting and trace the pattern of an incredible rise to popularity, while recording the personal and often painful side of the life of a complex woman.

Betsy Etheridge Brown
Pennsylvania State University

McCall, Dorothy Lawson (1888-   )

Rancher, Heiress

[198] *Ranch under the Rimrock.*   Portland, Oregon: Binfords
& Mort, 1968. 166 pp.

> Wife of a Harvard graduate, daughter of Massachusetts million-
> aire Tom Lawson (a man who always carried at least $10,000 in
> cash), daughter-in-law of Massachusetts congressman Samuel Mc
> Call and mother of Oregon governor Tom McCall, Dorothy Lawson
> McCall is scarcely a typical ranch wife. Yet *Ranch under the Rim-
> rock* is the personal account of her life in Central Oregon after her
> 1910 marriage. Because husband Hal longed to go into cattle ranch-
> ing, Tom Lawson's wedding present to the young couple was a
> 640-acre ranch on which he built a three-story, five-bathroom man-
> sion, and there "Dote" employed one or two maids, a housekeeper-
> nuse, and occasionally a cook. Each of her five children was born
> at her father's Cape Cod Estate, *Dreamwold.*

> Nevertheless, McCall experienced some of the hardships of prai-
> rie life: a river which could be crossed only by cable seat at high
> water, and later by a swinging bridge which collapsed with Hal on
> it; the difficulties of keeping up mortgage payments during the De-
> pression years; and three disastrous fires. Rodeos, local baseball
> games, communal ice-cutting each winter when the river had frozen
> over, and the grimmer jack rabbit drives (to hunt down and destroy
> these pests) served to draw neighbors together. While McCall avoids
> intimate contact with her reader, preferring to recount anecdotes
> and giving only superficial treatment to her marriage and children,
> she does note, apparently without tongue in cheek, that in 1913 "a
> wife was the most valuable piece of livestock on a ranch."

[199] *The Copper King's Daughter: From Cape Cod to Crooked River.* Portland, Oregon: Binfords & Mort, 1972.
190 pp.

> Although this book outlines Tom Lawson's history ("at the
> turn of the century he controlled all the copper in the United
> States" and was worth thirty million), it is also an account of
> McCall's family life in New England before her marriage. She

recalls how she and her younger brother perched nightly on their father's lap to hear him recite Poe's "Raven." The security of her early childhood was later marred by her mother's failing health.

Girls did not go to college; instead came the "Grand Tour" of Europe. Her first visit cut short by her mother's final illness, Dorothy returned twice more, so enchanted by Paris that she postponed her marriage to Hal McCall for a year in order to stay on. Romanticized "Gibson girl" portraits of the author and descriptions of her elaborate wedding reveal much about the role of such young women in Boston society.

After her marriage, some repetition of the earlier book occurs. But for the first time McCall explains that, after her last childbirth in 1919, she stayed on at *Dreamwold* for nearly two years, first to recuperate, later because "I found myself torn between my father and my husband." Hal came from the Oregon ranch several times, finally delivering an ultimatum, and "Dote" had to make her choice. She returned to Oregon, leaving her father weakened by illness, her children grown and gone. Her own family, the ranch, the achievements of her children she still sees as a testament to her father's strength of character.

Dorothy McCall's books are primarily of regional historical interest and as such have not been widely reviewed. Reviewers generally focus on her husband or her flamboyant father, over-looking the author herself. Only Linda Lampman, writing in the *Oregonian* (January 5, 1969, pp. 12-13), probes beneath the surface of the books to reach the woman. "She admits that she glossed over the hard parts of her life," says Lampman, and quotes McCall: "My husband came from Vermont, the granite state, and I used to say to him bitterly, 'You can endure because you come from Vermont. . . .' Well, you do what you have to do."

Joanne McCarthy
Tacoma Community College

McCarthy, Abigail (1915-   )

Political Wife, Ecumenist

[200] *Private Faces/Public Places.*   Garden City, New York:
Doubleday and Company, 1972. 448 pp.

Written after her husband "left our home," this book is Abigail
McCarthy's attempt to come to terms with thirty years as somebody's wife rather than as a person in her own right.

Her narrative begins when she met Eugene McCarthy. After
they were engaged, he chose to enter a seminary and urged her to
join a convent. She refused. Instead she finished her M.A. and
pursued a career as a college teacher. After Gene left the seminary,
they were married and she gave up her career because she "wanted
nothing more than to be totally part of Gene's life." In her work
in the Catholic Rural Life Movement, as a lay member of the
Benedictine Order, as wife of a college professor, a congressman, a
senator and a presidential hopeful, she confesses that she "spontaneously preferred another existence to my own." The marriage
was subject to emotional strains. She writes of the tension between public and private life, the raising of four children, the difficulty of being both liberal and Catholic, the isolation from the
work of her husband, and the sadness over friendships destroyed
by politics. Throughout these demanding marital years she maintained her interest in ecumenism and the role of women in politics
and in the church.

Private Faces/Public Places is hailed as the "finest example. . .
of its peculiar genre" by Catherine Stimpson (*Nation*, October 9,
1972, pp. 310-12) and is described as a "dispassionate, unself-
pitying" chronicle by Doris Grumbach (*New Republic*, June 17,
1972, pp. 28-30). Edna McCallion (*America*, August 19, 1972,
pp. 98-99 observes that the writing of this autobiography proves
that Abigail McCarthy is no longer the object of someone else's
history, but is a subject worthy in her own right.

Dana Greene
St. Mary's College of Maryland

McCarthy, Mary (1912-   )

Novelist, Essayist

[201] *Memories of a Catholic Girlhood.* New York: Harcourt, Brace, Jovanovich, 1957. 255 pp.

Parts of *Memories of a Catholic Girlhood* began appearing in the mid-forties as independent sketches in various magazines. The first such chapter deals with her indulged childhood, until age six, when her parents lived in Seattle. Other chapters chronicle the immediate aftermath for Mary and her younger brothers when both her parents died of influenza in the epidemic of 1918. The children lived five years in Minneapolis, as she tells us in other chapters, with guardians under the eyes of her McCarthy grandparents. Still other chapters record her formal education in a convent boarding school and later at an Episcopal girls' seminary under the supervision of her Seattle grandparents. One chapter tells of a hilariously disappointing summer vacation when she hoped to elude the watchful eye of her Presbyterian grandfather and taste the sweets of adolescent courtship. The final and most haunting chapter contains a portrait of her enigmatic grandmother, Augusta Morganstern Preston. This moving tribute from the granddaughter has evoked most positive responses from reviewers of the book.

McCarthy remarks in the foreword, which she added to the portions previously published that she is still constantly surprised at the number of readers who mistake her genuine efforts at non-fictional autobiography for more of her "mere story telling." Indeed, her account of her idyllic childhood with her beautiful and romantic parents followed by the Dickensian years with her cruel guardian Uncle Myers does read like melodrama. When she collected these narratives that comprise *Memories,* McCarthy added interlocutory essays that make this issue of veracity versus story telling an organizing theme of the volume. After each of the original sketches (except the last) she adds comments indicating which events can be verified by other sources, which she has admittedly embroidered, and which have been called into question by brothers, aunts, or uncles. This theme of course makes the volume of particular interest to students of autobiography and other efforts to re-create the self. Critical studies of the *Memories,* such as Barbara McKenzie's book, *Mary McCarthy* (New York: Twayne,

1966) do in fact note the effort that McCarthy made to re-create the voices of her various selves: the parentless waif or the twelve year old who fancied herself Byronic or the high schooler who lionized Cataline.

As she explains, because her family included Protestant, Jewish, and Catholic branches, she is necessarily, if only implicitly, concerned with cultural or ethnic definitions of the self, too. Also because she was orphaned at an early age, she is pre-occupied with reconstructing personal and family history. These interests, of course, add another engrossing dimension to the book. Incidentally, because her formal education (except for one unsuccessful year in public school during which she claims, she went "boy crazy") was conducted entirely in female institutions, she provides interesting insight into those schools with their atmosphere, as she records it, of social and intellectual but not sexual competition.

Though its publication excited lively comment from reviewers about the reliability of McCarthy's memoirs (much debated was their varnished or unvarnished quality), the standard dictionaires of biography quote verbatim from the *Memories* without qualification. Doris Grumbach, a biographer whose thesis is that all of McCarthy's fiction is demonstratably autobiographical, quotes liberally from the presumed autobiographical novels to supply details about McCarthy's feeling or state of mind regarding episodes of her life that she has not yet seen fit to record in print.

Although a few detractors insisted that McCarthy's memoir was as acidly heartless as her fiction, on the whole, reviewers responded much more favorably to her *Memories* than to her novels. Victor Lange (*New Republic,* 136:18, June 24, 1957), for example, emphasizes "a quality of gentleness and warmth for which her earlier fiction scarcely prepared us" and praised its "superb gallery of characters." A reviewer like N. W. Logal (*Catholic World,* 186: 157, November, 1957), is almost alone when he accuses her of self-pity, calling the book "the number 1 Cry Baby Book of the year." It is not at all a self-pitying narrative. Indeed, McCarthy utilizes a number of strategies which mitigate that possibility. She calls her Dickensian account of her orphanhood, for example, a political allegory and a speech of deprivation against privilege, clearly making an effort to impersonalize and politicize this most private experience. Likewise, the year with her guardians, Uncle Myers and Aunt Margaret, which years included repeated beatings, under-feeding, and taped mouths at bedtime, she refers to dispassionately as a "study in totalitarianism." Even the lighter years in convent school and girls" seminary are cast as political conflict between romantic individual impulse and Catholic order or Roman law.

Another remarkable quality of her writing is her ability to make even the most intimate and idiosyncratic episodes of her youth seem typical. She casts herself in roles and conveys to the reader the assumption that we are only too familiar with these types: the pitiable waif; the precocious adolescent who deliberately loses her faith to frighten her elders but discovers to her own dismay that she cannot recover it; the would-be siren who is prohibited from dating boys by a too loving grandfather while she is bragging to her peers about her supposed worldliness. McCarthy makes these roles vividly familiar, however remote they may be from the reader's own experience.

Even though she depersonalizes her autobiography through humor, through her political perspective, and through typifying her experience, she humanizes her account by revealing again and again a pattern in her youth of knowing compromise between a private recognition of doing wrong and a public expectation of doing right. This pattern not only forms an underlying and unifying theme of the volume; it also contains McCarthy's message to the reader.

Kathleen Callaway
Florida International University

McCullers, Carson Smith (1917-1967)

Writer

[202] *The Mortgaged Heart.* Boston: Houghton Mifflin Company, 1971. 294 pp.

Edited by Margarita G. Smith, *The Mortgaged Heart* brings together a generous selection of Carson McCullers' previously uncollected work, some never before published. It is comprised of two sections, "Early Stories" and "Essays and Articles;" the latter section gives glimpses of McCullers' childhood in Georgia and later life in New York. She captures the frustration of childhood exquisitely in an essay on Christmas Day: "At twilight I sat on the front steps, jaded by too much pleasure, sick at the stomach and worn out. . . .Christmas was over. I thought of the monotony of Time ahead, unsolaced by the distant glow of paler festivals, the year that stretched before another Christmas—eternity."

The essays on writing trace McCullers' early attempts to put on plays in the sitting-room of her home: "Sometimes, after coaching and drilling half the afternoon, the actors would decide to abandon the whole project just before curtain time and wander out into the yard to play." At fifteen she attempted her first novel: "New York was the happy mise en scene. . . . The details of the book were queer: ticket collectors on the subway, New York front yards—but by that time it did not matter, for already I had begun another journey. That was the year of Dostoevski, Chekhov and Tolstoy—and there were the intimations of an unsuspected region equidistant from New York. Old Russia and our Georgia rooms, the marvelous solitary region of simple stories and the inward mind."

Life and art merged for McCullers as she wrote, "I become the characters I write about and I bless the Latin poet Terence who said, 'Noting human is alien to me.' " *The Mortgaged Heart* gives the reader a concise but rich account of the relationship of McCullers' life to the development of her art.

Phoebe Adams (*The Atlantic Monthly,* November 1971, p. 153) describes the book as "Unpublished stories and previously uncollected magazine pieces, chosen and edited by Margarita Smith, whose introduction provides an understated, touching portrait of her indomitable sister." Thomas A. Gullason (*Saturday Review,* November 13, 1971, pp. 57, 63-64) says, "The essays complement the early stories and Mrs. McCullers' later work by underscoring her movement away from personal reminiscences to larger social commitments."

Anne Rowe
Florida State University

MacDonald, Betty (1908-1958)

Author, Humorist, Children's Author

B
M 1341

[203] *The Egg and I.* Philadelphia: J. B. Lippincott, 1945. 278 pp.

One of the Forties' most popular books, selling well over one million copies, *The Egg and I* chronicles Betty MacDonald's experience as a young bride on an isolated chicken ranch on Washington State's primitive Olympic Peninsula. MacDonald's sense of humor, only slightly exaggerated, enables her to keep her perspective on a backbreaking and lonely farm life where days begin at four a.m. and end at seven p.m., and where social life consists of an occasional discussion of wireworm over coffee. Her trials include Stove, the temperamental wood-burner which dominates her kitchen; wild animals; baby chicks, which tend to drown themselves; and her neighbors—immaculate Birdie Hicks and her senile, tennis-shoed mother; and the slovenly but delightful Kettles (Maw, Paw and fifteen children), who boast a doorless outhouse which companionably faces the back porch, and who set fire to their barn to dispose of the manure pile and nearly burn up most of the county. Between the lines one also reads the story of a marriage in which the partners are slowly drifting apart, so that eventually only their work holds them together.

[204] *The Plague and I.* Philadelphia: J. B. Lippincott, 1948. 254 pp.

B
M134/a

This is MacDonald's account of her struggle with tuberculosis at age thirty, typically (for her) diagnosed during an examination for hemorrhoids. Resisting the urge to become a self-pitying "saddo," MacDonald finds in sanitorium life a variety of unforgettable people: Friendly Organs (who views her internal organs as little companions and reports daily on their behavior), Miss TeaCup Cavities (lungs, not teeth), Gravy Face, The Perfect Day woman, and others. "The cure" consists of good food, open windows, bed rest, and "beautiful thoughts" on each dinner tray (sample: "If you must be blue, be a *bright* blue"). Prevalence of tuberculosis in this country before World War II, its symptoms and treatment, as well as a devastating comment on the occupa-

tional therapy of the times, are some of the factual materials included.

[205] *Anybody Can Do Anything.*   Philadelphia: J. B. Lippincott, 1950. 256 pp.

This book focuses on MacDonald's life as a white-collar worker
in Depression-wracked Seattle, from the time she leaves the
chicken ranch until she begins, at older sister Mary's urging, to
write about it. With her two daughters, MacDonald returns to her
mother's home and her three sisters and brother, to embark on a
series of fly-by-night jobs for which she is totally unprepared,
encouraged by loyal Mary, who insists that "anybody can do anything, especially Betty." Mary, the major breadwinner, continually
finds jobs for any family member who can work—even mother
Sydney authors a successful soap opera—but employment and
survival remain precarious. The necessity of sharing office clothes
("the first one up was the best dressed"), placating bill collectors,
substituting candles when electricity is turned off, and cutting up
logs from a nearby park when there is no money for fuel, does not
dampen this family's spirit or hospitality. Nevertheless, meatloaf,
vegetable soup and humor do not entirely mask the desperation
of life in the thirties.

[206] *Onions in the Stew.* Philadelphia: J. B. Lippincott, 1955.
256 pp.

From Pearl Harbor to date of publication, *Onions in the Stew*
covers MacDonald's second and successful marriage, full-time
raising of her two teenage daughters, and life on Vashon Island in
Puget Sound. MacDonald offers detailed accounts of the daily
dash to the commuter ferry, island vegetation (abundant), weather
(rain), pests (WooWoos and rats that die in walls), social life (sherry
with tuna-marshmallow salad), and adolescents (coke bottles and
shoes on the mantel, and "Marilyn's mother" who always does
everything right). A two-week snowstorm during which the
family subsists on noodles and pet food, a washing machine which
floats out to sea, and a wade on the beach in formal dress (tide's
in) to get to the Junior Prom are some of MacDonald's experiences.
In one chapter she exhibits a keen awareness of the problems

facing the woman writer with a family that regards her work "with the same tolerant amusement they accord my efforts toward making my own Christmas cards."

[207] *Who, Me? The Autobiography of Betty MacDonald.* Philadelphia: J. B. Lippincott, 1959. 352 pp.

Posthumous collection of excerpts from her four previous autobiographies; no new material added.

Four of MacDonald's books were excerpted in popular magazines, and *Egg* was made into the movie which subsequently launched the "Ma and Pa Kettle" series. Still a few readers found her heartiness annoying: Florence Haxton Bullock (New York *Herald Tribune,* August 26, 1950, p. 9) characterizes her as "one of those humorists who enters chuckling, chuckles uninterruptedly throughout the act and exits same. . . . The strain on her audience at times may be considerable." Patricia Spacks, in *The Female Imagination* (Knopf, 1975), views MacDonald in the tradition of the other-directed woman and notes her "tone of self-deprecation . . . . She sees herself, wants others to see her, as a comic figure . . . . Anger is not far beneath the surface. . .but she knows nothing to do with it."

Some critics, like Josephine Lawrence in *Saturday Review* (September 16, 1950, p. 26), question the accuracy of her anecdotes: "It is incredible that the natural impulse to retouch should have been resisted." Many find her stereotypically female: "dialogue. . .thoroughly dipped in feminine venom" (Lisle Bell, New York *Herald Tribune,* October 17, 1948, p. 19); but a few see her rising above those "feminine" limitations: "The wry humor is a woman's, but the language is masculine. . .calling a spade a spade" (*Booklist,* October 15, 1945, p. 54). However, most reviewers enthusiastically praise MacDonald's work. Helen Bard Woodward (*Saturday Review,* May 14, 1955, p. 20) concludes: "Her writing is the projection of a remarkably attractive personality. She manages to sound relaxed, friendly, approachable. . . . Even if Betty MacDonald never writes another book she has earned the right to appear in any anthology of American humor."

Joanne McCarthy
Tacoma Community College

McGinley, Phyllis (1905-   )

Poet, Essayist

B
M 145

[208] *Sixpence in Her Shoe.* New York: Macmillan, 1964. 281 pp.

This is a book about being a housewife, written (according to a profile of the author in *Time* (June 18, 1965) as a rebuttal to Betty Friedan's *The Feminine Mystique.* Poet McGinley does not trace her life chronologically but, as she notes, the book "turned into a kind of autobiography, which is no doubt natural since the experiences I have drawn on are largely my own" (1). The book is a series of essays on the challenges and rewards of housewifery— some comparatively philosophical (for example, Chapter 3, on the value of liberal education) to absolutely practical (for instance, Chapter 14, the basic kit of tools a new cook needs in the kitchen).

Poet McGinley has written two additional books of prose for adults (*Saint Watching* (1969) and *The Province of the Heart* (1959), some seventeen books for children. She is best known, of course, for her books of light verse which number ten (plus one anthology she edited). Her *Love Letters of Phyllis McGinley* (1954) was a best seller (unusual for poetry). But there is little in *Sixpence* about the process of writing. She tells instead how a woman can be a good employer if she is fortunate enough to find a good housekeeper (Chapter 10), how to enjoy a party one gives oneself (Chapter 9), how to smooth the path for houseguests (Chapter 11), how to avoid letting family traditions become burdensome for the woman of the house (Chapter 17). Why write such a book of essays about "wifehood, the house, a family"? Because "they are life's vital elements and no ordered world can endure without them" (255) and, indeed, "As workers in the home we are issued few bulletins."

Sixpence in Her Shoe was warmly received by critics such as Sister Mary Gregory (*Best Seller,* October 1, 1964) as the writing of a real Christian woman. Sidney Callahan (*Critic,* December, 1964) objects, as most feminists would, to McGinley's assertion that "By and large. . .the world runs better when men and women keep to their own spheres," meaning that women are better at housewifery than men. Later, in *Man's World, Woman's Place: A*

Study in Social Mythology (New York: William Morrow, 1971) Elizabeth Janeway devotes the central portion of Chapter 3 to refuting McGinley's assertions about woman's sphere; Janeway also denies McGinley's view that liberationists insist on all women leaving the home.

Some students in Women's Studies will feel sad to read McGinley's defense of the satisfactions of keeping house, knowing as we do that nine out of ten of the young women in school today will work outside of the home at some time during their lives. Many will have no choice about working life-long. Still, she is a champion of women, a serious essayist who must be read on her own terms. As she noted in an interview in *Time* (June 18, 1965), "If you really like being a wife and mother, if that's your basic drive, don't be upset by characters who say you have to get out and do something. Because I think you hold the future in your hand."

Jennie Farley
Cornell University

McGovern, Eleanor (1921-   )

Political Wife, Peace Advocate

[209] *Uphill: A Personal Story.*   Boston: Houghton Mifflin Company, 1974. 234 pp.

A caring woman emerges in this autobiography, one who sees the family as the center of strength in society. Raised in the dust of South Dakota, motherless at eleven, she learned perseverance and confidence from her rugged life. Poverty left its mark in her idealism to create a better America. Bright, popular and articulate, Eleanor and her inseparable twin, Ila, considered themselves fortunate to finish high school. Salutatorian of her class, cheerleader and debater, Eleanor attended college for one year before marrying George McGovern. She raised her five children in difficult financial circumstances and followed her husband's varied career into national politics. She believed in him and his idealism and saw his work as a public servant as "our career." A competent and life-affirming woman, her chronicle contains reminiscences of her melancholy over her early loss of her mother, her inadequacies as a parent, the burden of raising children alone, the endless house-work, the conflict between being one's own person and a political wife, male chauvinism in politics and loss of friends over political disagreements. The conflict between family and political obliga-tions abated, and by the 1972 presidential campaign she portrays herself as an ambitious spokeswoman for important issues.

Although Jane O'Reilly (New York *Times Book Review,* Sep-tember 29, 1974, pp. 6-7) sees McGovern as describing "the bleak-ness of life as an adjunct" she maintains she never resolves the dilemma of the political wife. Gloria Emerson (*Book World,* September 8, 1974, p. 1) and Abigail McCarthy (*New Republic,* October 26, 1974, pp. 30-31) claim this autobiography accurately captures the strength of an issue oriented, family centered woman.

Dana Greene
St. Mary's College of Maryland

McKenney, Ruth (1911-1972)

Journalist, Humorist, Marxist

[210] *My Sister Eileen.* New York: Harcourt, Brace, and Com-pany, 1938. 226 pp.

My Sister Eileen, the first of six autobiographical books by McKenney, was also her greatest popular and financial success. Not only was the collection of short sketches a best seller, but it became the basis for a Broadway play, a movie, and a musical. Like *The McKenneys Carry On; Far, Far From Home;* and *More About Eileen, MSE* is a collection of short, humorous, factual narratives told in the first person and arranged chronologically.

The fourteen stories which comprise *MSE* (all of which had been previously published in *The New Yorker*) describe various adventures of Ruth and her younger, more attractive sister, Eileen, from childhood and adolescence in Misawaka, Indiana, and Cleveland, Ohio, to early adulthood in Greenwich Village. There are chapters about the movies; piano, elocution, and swimming lessons; girls' camp; school; father's inventions; their failure as waitresses; Ruth's being taken for a spy's accomplice in Poland; and, from the New York period, trouble with a slum lord and non-English-speaking Brazilian Navy officers.

Since McKenney's personal sketches usually do not develop any profound theme or exhibit any great creative genius, they do not invite extensive or abstruse criticism; they are meant to be enjoyed, not analyzed. As a reviewer in *Christian Century* observed, "Subtlety is not Miss McKenney's métier. She writes not for smiles but for guffaws" (October 12, 1938, p. 1234). Amy Loveman praised McKenney as a "conversationalist" whose "reminiscences . . .lie within the experience of every one of us" (*Saturday Review of Literature*, July 23, 1938, p. 5).

[211] *The McKenneys Carry On.* New York: Harcourt, Brace, and Company, 1940. 219 pp.

The fourteen stories which constitute *The McKenneys Carry On* (six of which had appeared in *The New Yorker*) cover an even longer period than those of *MSE.* McKenney tells of adventures—with Eileen, alone, and finally with her husband—which span a twenty-five-year period. The book begins with a chapter about the young McKenneys' attraction to the cruel deaths and foreignness of several English kings, described in *The Child's History of England* ("Dickens the Menace"), and ends with a story about a severe winter storm at the Westport, Connecticut, country home of Ruth and her husband, Richard Bransten ("Summer Had Better Be Good"). There are also stories about a large mischievous dog; Valentine's Day card competition at school; religious fanatics; bloomers with broken elastic; ghost-writing college themes; Eileen's debut as advertising model; and foreign fashions. All are humorous, but not, according to most critics, as fine as her earlier stories.

[212] *Loud Red Patrick.* New York: Harcourt, Brace, and Company, 1947. 161 pp.

McKenney again writes about her family in the first person and in a humorous vein. The protagonist is her tall, red-haired maternal grandfather, Patrick Thomas Flannigan of Cleveland, Ohio, called by his family The Loud Red Patrick. McKenney begins with his near-mythic Irish origins, as recounted by Flannigan himself, and ends with the tent wedding of the last of his six daughters, when Ruth and Eileen were young girls. Flannigan's many idiosyncrasies make him a more interesting subject than Eileen. He was a stubborn man with inflexible likes and dislikes: he loved his daughters (though they rarely got along), Ireland, eccentric friends, and long Saturday afternoon baths; he disliked Republicans, undertakers, most politicans, his sons-in-law, and fake shamrocks.

LRP is of interest to women's studies for its depiction of conservative transplanted European attitudes concerning the roles of male and female in family and society. Almost every critic reviewed the book favorably. Thomas Sugrue who wrote that "Ruth McKenney has never been as funny as she is in these hilarious tales of her grandfather" (New York *Herald Tribune,* November 9, 1947, p. 2).

[213] *Love Story.* New York: Harcourt, Brace, and Company, 1950. 303 pp.

Although not lacking an element of humor, *Love Story* is the most serious and profound of McKenney's six autobiographical works; through it, she reveals herself "as a wit as well as a humorist" (W. E. G., *Christian Century,* April 5, 1950, p. 434). *LS* begins in 1937 with McKenney's secret marriage, after only twelve days of "courtship," to Mike Lyman, editor of a left-wing publication, *New Masses.* She humorously describes their troubles as newlyweds in Greenwich Village, she learning the value of money, he learning how to cope with a whimsical wife and an extravagant sister-in-law. The publication of her first book (*MSE,* 1938) is described as a significant milestone on her way to becoming an "Emancipated Female" (118). The *Story* continues in Washington, where Mike's job took them and where she had her first child; in

Hollywood, where husband and wife were successful at script writing, but became unhappy with each other in the process; and finally back East, where Ruth and her daughter, Eileen, suffered serious illnesses.

McKenney satirizes numerous groups: psychoanalysts, Hollywood movie-makers, labor organizers, left-wing politicians, publishers, and avant garde writers. While most of the satire is of the gentle Horatian variety, sometimes it bears the sharpness of Juvenal; one critic in fact dubs the Hollywood satire "bitter" (*Nation*, February 11, 1950, p. 140).

More important than the satiric element is the sociological value of the work. McKenney uses personal experience to elucidate such topics as: the economics of marriage; child-bearing and child-rearing; domination in the home; the role of the working mother; progressive child education; the value of psychiatry; and the artistic merit of cinema. In addition there is an underlying suggestion of rebellion against her former left-wing stance.

Critics did not fail to note the difference between *LS* and McKenney's other autobiographical works. R. L. Blakesley in the Chicago *Sunday Tribune* wrote: "it isn't the subtle, humorous Ruth McKenney of a few years ago who is writing; it is a soberer, more mature woman, one who has been thru a great human experience [marriage]" (March 5, 1950, p. 15). *The New Yorker* found fault with McKenney's "tendency to dwell overlong on family ailments" (February 11, 1950, p. 99), and Phyllis McGinley noted that there were "too many soap-opera flourishes, and an inordinate italicizing of comic speeches" (*Saturday Review of Literature*, February 11, 1950, p. 21).

[214] *All About Eileen.* New York: Harcourt, Brace, and Company, 1952. 283 pp.

With the exception of about sixty pages of new material, the stories which comprise *All About Eileen* appeared earlier in four previously published books. The added material fills in gaps in the lives of the author and her sister-heroine; the resultant collection, arranged chronolgically, covers three decades of their lives.

Themes of earlier works undergo further development. These include the cultural narrowness of middle-class Americans; attitudes toward money; domestic problems; the emancipated woman writer; and the neurotic beauty goddess.

Eileen and her husband, writer Nathaniel West, were killed in an automobile accident in January, 1941; thus this edition serves as a kind of memorial to Eileen's memory. Most reviews were favorable. With this publication, McKenney "incorporated her sister into the American legend (pretty girl division)" (Jane Cobb, New York *Times,* May 18, 1952, p. 12).

[215] *Far, Far From Home.* New York: Harper and Brothers, 1954. 211 pp.

Far, Far From Home consists of eleven short sketches (published first in *Holiday*) based on McKenney's three year stay, along with her husband and three children, in Belgium. After their initial difficulty in passing through customs, they had to learn to adjust to a lifestyle not only foreign, but primitive by American standards. They had difficulties with the comestics and the language (the two boys were for a while enrolled in a school for backward students), as well as with mice and a gigantic rat. While learning themselves, the Branstens managed to introduce the Belgians to birthday parties, pin-the-tale, hot dogs, and Christmas turkey.

McKenney's humor is highly successful in *FFH,* though most critics did not go as far as Nancie Matthews, who called it "her funniest book" (New York *Times,* February 7, 1954, p. 7). Even more significant than her lively, witty comedy is McKenney's insight into human nature; in none of her other works are human foibles portrayed more vividly than in this. Her clever mixture of humor and wisdom "helps a body relax and see what a cockeyed world it is, and. . .to see themselves as others see them" (Ernestine Evans, *Saturday Review of Literature,* February 13, 1954, p. 22).

Justin Paniere
Old Dominion University

MacLaine, Shirley (1934-   )

Actress

[216] *Don't Fall Off the Mountain.*   New York: Norton, 1971.
   270 pp.

Shirley MacLaine's experience has been very different from
that of most American women, yet in a curious way, she is representative. She likes to think of herself as a free spirit who re-
belled against conformity even in childhood. She achieved the
status of stardom in her early twenties, as well as the power and
wealth that go with it. After her early reputation as a "kooky
kid," she came to be identified with a category of folk heroes
favored by American culture, the maverick who breaks the rules
and gets away with it. Being female, she has combined characteristics of the maverick individualist and the girl next door. Being
female in the mid-twentieth century, she has had to confront some
of the questions many Americans have raised about the role of
women and the values of our culture.

Both of MacLaine's books describe her continuing efforts to discover who she is. *Don't Fall Off the Mountain* depicts her life up
to 1970. The title recalls an admonition from her husband before
her trip in the late sixties to Bhutan; it is an apt warning to a girl-
woman who plunges herself into experience, who has moved
through scores of people and places in her quest for self.

In this book she tells her early life briefly. She struggles with
the discipline of ballet as a young girl, rebelling in the usual ways
to her "cliche-loving middle class Virginia family." She works her
way into show business in New York, meets and marries her husband, Steve Parker, and within a short time gives birth to her only
daughter in Hollywood.

There are several noticeable themes in her Hollywood experience. As her career develops, she is faced with the inevitable but
painful conflicts among her roles as star, wife, and mother. She
loves being in the entertainment world, but she hates the artificiali-
ty of it. As she says of the Hollywood Dinner Party, "the feigned
is the accepted code of behavior. Only a fool with bad taste, or
someone extemely naive, would expose his honesty" (87). She

looks for scripts that will conform to her vaguely defined values, but she is often cast in variations of the whore with a heart of gold. (There weren't many scripts around depicting women who broke other kinds of rules.) Rather than free, she is a restless spirit, and one with little sense of direction. Her life includes reactions against middle-class materialism, but seldom movement toward a definite goal. Her political activity is clearly an attempt to define herself, however, as indicated in her campaign work for Adlai Stevenson and John F. Kennedy, her protest against the execution of Caryl Chessman, and in 1968, her representing California as a delegate to the Democratic Convention.

MacLaine's book is well written, conveying the sensibility of a warm and vital woman. There are moments of personal pain, like the Christmas holiday when she puts her two-year-old daughter alone on a jet to join her father in Japan. There are moments of anxiety, like being caught in the middle of a political coup in Bhutan. There are some discoveries, as in her visit with the organizers of the Student Nonviolent Coordinating Committee. There is, however, no coherent pattern in her life. Her uneasy, restless dissatisfaction is transformed into a zest for travel, but in her travels she finds no real answers. She assimilates a lot of information, but she is unable to carry on the kind of introspection and self-criticism that would result in a clearer definition of self.

[217] *You Can Get There From Here.* New York: Norton, 1975. 249 pp.

In her second book, *You Can Get There From Here,* MacLaine is much clearer about what she is doing. This book, which covers four years of her life, focuses on three major events which lead to her decision to return to show business in the Las Vegas arena on July 12, 1974; a disastrous television series, a diastrous presidential campaign, and a confusing trip to China.

The opening chapter stages the reaffirmation of life and laughter that MacLaine is trying to convey to herself and to us. She is back where she started twenty years ago in show business, she says. She is alone at center stage, surrounded by "friends from politics and publishing, from newspapers and magazines, from show business, from foreign countries. Top-drawer, first-rate friends. It was as if all the important phases of my life over the past ten years sat before me" (12). This is a tired rebel, no longer a maverick, but anxious to be accepted, affirmed and applauded by the group.

In describing the failure of her television series, "Shirley," she reveals many of the characteristics we have seen in the first book. She is a woman of great energy, enthusiasm, and vitality; but she is still naive about the effects of power in her personal, professional, and political life. It is surprising to see her so easily taken, or taken over, by the forces of television; it is difficult to believe that someone of her stature in entertainment could be so badly victimized. Still, there is her perception of the experience, and it does have a characteristic ring about it. Whatever her motivation, MacLaine contracted for the series without knowing what the main character or scripts would be like. "Shirley" turned out to be a flighty, superficial, if energetic reporter, who traveled about the world getting into everybody's business. With little substance, and no direction, the character looked both silly and presumptuous. Perhaps the personal parallel, if vague, was too close for MacLaine to be able to admit she had anything to do with developing the series.

Her participation in the McGovern campaign was extensive, and a natural development from her earlier political activity. She was one of the few people still with McGovern on the morning after the election. In this part of the narrative we see again the strength of MacLaine's energy and commitment to causes she believes in; but we also see her inability to deal with power and policy. Her real service to the campaign was the contribution of her emotional support, and the support of voters who identified emotionally with the character of the movie star Shirley MacLaine. In this experience, as in the next, we see a woman who, in spite of her unusual profession, reflects the concerns of many Americans during this time.

Soon after the election, MacLaine was asked to lead a delegation of "typical" American women on an extended visit to the People's Republic of China. Because so many Americans are now allowed to visit China, it is important to remember that MacLaine's group was one of the first, even among politicans. The first-hand account of her own reactions to China, the reaction of the group to China and to each other, is sincere and open, but as in all of her experiences, lacking in self-critical or detached observations. MacLaine was the only experienced traveller in the group, and as might have been expected, the culture shock for most of the women, who had little experience with the diversity of their own country, was difficult to overcome. Some got terribly homesick, hostile within the group, physically ill, and simply bored. What comes through with familiar consistency is MacLaine's zest for travel and diversity of experience, and her apparent belief that these characteristics would affect or be shared by the group. They weren't.

What is most difficult, however, is to understand how MacLaine got there from here, or to know what "there" means to her. Although many of her descriptions of the China tour have the familiar naivete about them, it is clear that the experience offered MacLaine a sense of rebirth, of renewed hope in herself. She says she could never live in China, but she has been encouraged by the progressive changes she saw evidenced in her tour. She talks vaguely about the spirit of hope and friendliness that could not be photographed. What she seems to have done is to absorb that spirit, as she has absorbed others in the past, and used it to generate her own. The process defies logic, but so does her life.

Mary Louise Briscoe
University of Pittsburgh

Maiullo, Minerva (-   )

Singer

[218] *A Tapestry of Memories.* New York: A. S. Barnes and Company, 1972. 335 pp.

Minerva Maiullo warns her readers that she will not provide them with an account of her life, but rather a series of reminiscences about her travels in Europe, especially in Italy, where she studied opera and made a singing debut in 1925. She is true to her word, telling us little about herself outright. Instead, she provides a string of descriptions about tourist sights in Italy, history, architecture she loves, and celebrities she has met, clouded with an aura of nostalgia. We come away knowing more about her admiration for Audrey Hepburn's movies and Perry Como's behavior than we do about the opinion reviewers had of her voice.

One detects that Maiullo feels somewhat guilty about her aversion to the mundane life of child-raising and volunteer work in Detroit and her attraction to the romance of Italy's musical life. She begins her book with an assurance that "I am a wife and mother of four children." But she tells of her hatred of sewing, and her family life is nowhere mentioned in the book, as one might expect from a devoted mother which she feels she ought to be. This work, like her Detroit salons for artists, is an attempt to recapture the glamour she had once and still craves.

In addition to her discomfort with the maternal role and her inability to reconcile a career with marriage, Maiullo reveals other tensions of special interest to those engaged in scholarship on women. One finds a deep admiration for women—her mother, those in the Italian government, those who ran salons in the European past, female journalists in Detroit, and the accompanist who helped her prepare for her debut recital. Coupled with this, but seemingly an incongruent afterthought, is a self-conscious effort to place her husband and her definition of love into the narrative. The autobiography is more useful for what it does not reveal than for all it does tell us. Minerva Maiullo is a woman who wanted to be a performer but felt constrained and tried, unsuccessfully, to fit the traditional mold.

Karen J. Blair
California Institute of Technology

Mannes, Marya (1904-   )

Journalist, Novelist

[219] *Out of My Time.*   Garden City, New York: Doubleday
and Company, 1971. 251 pp.

Mannes has used the story of her life as a frame for her feminist
views. The facts of this life are interesting enough. Her parents
were David and Clara Damrosch Mannes, brilliant musicians and
teachers of music. Her brother Leonard, also a musician, was co-
inventer of the Kodachrome process. Educated at a select New
York private school, she refused college in favor of a year in
England where she studied sculpture and wrote plays. She has
supported herself as a journalist (especially on *Vogue* in the 30's
and on *The Reporter* in the 50's). She has published three novels
and several collections of essays; has worked in television, during
World War II in Intelligence, and as a sculptor. She has been married three times and has raised a son. In her sixties she can look
back on a full life and a measure of achievement.

But she sees herself as "out of her time," as an intelligent,
gifted, and—for the record—beautiful woman wanting the freedom
of a man in a time that begrudged it. She discusses the effects of
this opposition of her education, on marriage and motherhood, on
her life as a single woman accused of promiscuity, above all on her
work in the very lack of pressure to achieve. She sees herself as
"hermaphrodite"—not in any physical sense: sexually she is all
woman and very pleased to be. But there is in her a male alter ego,
whom she has named "Wohleben" (to live well? the good life?)
who refuses the limitations set on women. In a dialogue with this
persona she sees her careers as diminished by the demands society
makes on a woman and by the excuses a woman makes for herself.

Eight reviews are listed for *Out of My Time.* Most criticize it as
being padded with far too many chunks of quotation from her
adolescent writings. Nevertheless most reviewers find it interesting,
not only for its picture of a period but for its evidence, as Elizabeth Janeway says, "that the old roles, even when they are breaking down, make non-conformist behavior and attitudes a liability;
a liability that hurts and limits the non-conformist, not only
publicly but within him-or-herself" (New York *Times,* November

28, 1971, p. 35).

Caroline H. Tunstall
Norfolk, Virginia

Martin, Martha [pseud. for Helen Bolyan] (-1959)

Diarist, Pioneer

[220] *O Rugged Land of Gold.*   New York: The Macmillan
Company, 1953. 223 pp.

O Rugged Land of Gold is the first of two autobiographical
books by Helen Bolyan, who uses the pseudonym, Martha Martin.
The works, written in the first person, cover the years from the
1920's to the mid-1940's, during which Martin and her miner-
prospector husband lived in Alaska.

In *Rugged Land,* Martin describes her solitary experiences on
an uninhabited section of the Alaskan coast during a severe winter.
When her husband goes to meet the mailboat, his open skiff is
shipwrecked, and the arrival of winter prevents his return. Martin,
alone on their gold claim, is caught in a landslide, which results in
severe head injuries and a fractured arm and leg.

Martin, six months pregnant, is forced to care for her wounds,
and to keep herself and her unborn child alive. She delivers her
daughter, Donnas, and is discovered the next spring by Indians.
Her courage and growing sense of self-confidence are evident as
she makes several unsuccessful attempts to leave the claim, hunts
and skins game, and gathers food and fuel.

To preserve her sanity, and to provide a record of her experiences in case she might not survive, Martin begins to write notes
on scraps of paper soon after her accident. One reviewer commented that "there is a general vagueness about the story as it
comes to us" (Ernestine Evans, New York *Herald Tribune,* March
15, 1953, p. 16). The absence of specific dates and precise diary
form can be attributed both to the fact that the diary was not

published until many years after it was written, and to Martin's desire for anonymity.

The general consensus of the reviewers was that Martin's story was accurate. Louise D. Rich, who had experienced similar winters in northern Maine, noted that "how she managed to survive is an almost incredible tale, but the internal evidence convinces me that it is absolutely true" (New York *Times,* March 8, 1953, p. 22). In 1974, Mary Jane Moffat and Charlotte Pointer included excerpts from the book in *Revelations: Diaries of Women* (New York: Random House), and reaffirmed its authenticity in their remarks.

[221] *Home on the Bear's Domain.* New York: The Macmillan Company, 1954. 246 pp.

Martin dedicates this book, which describes her life after the death, in infancy, of Donnas, to "our part-time children" (p. v). After Martin and her husband find a new gold claim on the outer coast of a large island is southeastern Alaska, they adopt a young Yugoslavian girl and boy, and help to raise other children who live in their home for varying lengths of time during the 1930's and 1940's.

Martin describes the family's life on the island, focusing particularly on the education and care of the children. Her ability to meet the challenges of the wilderness increases as she shoots bear, clears land, and participates in construction, mining, and logging operations.

At the encouragement of a woman visitor who finds her burning old letters and diaries in preparation for a final move from the domain, Martin agrees to write about her life, saying only that "perhaps it wasn't too much to hope that someone, somewhere, who was overburdened with work and care might find direction or encouragement from reading of our doings" (246).

Well-received at the time, Martin's story is particularly poignant in an era of women's growing awareness of their own potential. Those who read her works today will find a source of significant inspiration in "the raw elements of courage with which Mrs. Martin

is so wonderfully endowed" (Margaret Parton, New York *Herald
Tribune,* September 26, 1954, p. 8).

Beverley B. Bryant
University of New Hampshire

Maynard, Joyce (1953-   )

Journalist, Radio and Television Commentator

[222] *Looking Back: A Chronicle of Growing Up Old in the
Sixties.* New York: Avon, 1974. 157 pp.

Eighteen-year-olds do not usually write autobiographies, let
alone autobiographies which contain extended arguments. Yet
this is precisely what Joyce Maynard has done. The nature of her
argument helps explain why she produced this seemingly premature confession. Maynard feels that American youth who grew up
in the 1960's were subjected to unique influences which served
not only to set them apart from previous generations but to render
them more disturbed. By presenting her "chronicle," Maynard
hopes to illuminate these influences and reveal the special psychology they shaped.

Her thesis is that she and her contemporaries exhibit a boredom, cynicism and jadedness which one normally finds only in
older, more battered souls. The media are the cause of "old
youth," especially television, which has enabled young people to
experience everything, but always vicariously. Vicarious experiences are not without pain, shock, insult; yet they lack the unmedi-
ated, unscheduled quality of ordinary terrors. Maynard understands that what television showed the children of the 1960's—as-
sassinations, race riots and Viet Nam—was exceptionally disturbing.
But she intimates that the medium by its nature is the overriding
source of the psychic exhaustion she depicts. In her darkly McLu-
hanesque view, television created the "global village"—which no
one wants to inhabit. Television also weakened the springs of individuality: "Having had so many pictures to grow up with, we
share a common visual idiom and have far less room for personal

vision" (52).

Looking Back is of particular interest to the teacher of autobiography because it shows students that one does not have to be
either old or famous to write a personal history. The book's immediacy is particularly appealing to beginning students who usually
find they have much in common with Maynard, since she chronicles their own formative years (1961-72) and focuses on peer group
phenomena (almost to the total exclusion of family). Although
Maynard is no radical feminist, her reminiscences about her school
years in Durham, New Hampshire, provide much raw material for
women's studies courses: the sexist, stereotyped nature of early
sex education; the hero-worship of adolescence (Joan Baez, Jackie
Kennedy, the Beatles); the competitiveness of the peer group,
making sisterhood impossible; the anxious anticipation of physical
development; the tyranny of good looks for popularity and the resulting insecurity that females have about their bodies; the constant diets and mirror-checking; the enslavement to changing
fashions; the consumption of junk food, make-up, jewelry; the
pressures against virginity.

These topics are also of importance as they further strengthen
Maynard's image of lethargy and conformity in her generation.
The degeneration of language, she asserts, can be traced not only
to the "hot" media, but to a drug and music culture with its anti-
intellectualism and emphasis on "non-verbal communication":
"We feel the need for constant sensory stimulation, a bombard-
ment, from all sides, of sounds and tastes and colors, which a-
mounts not to the heightened perceptivity we boast of, but finally
to numbness, anaesthesia" (136).

Looking Back was widely reviewed, but not always favorably.
Annie Gottlieb focuses on the crucial influence of television in her
New York *Times Book Review* (April 22, 1973, p. 26), criticizing
Maynard for confusing the *information* of television with *experience*. She also faults the book for failing to mention the "real"
traumas of Watts or Da Nang, discounting Maynard's claim that her
generation has experienced more traumas than most. Yet, asserts
Gottlieb, Maynard exhibits "a curious courage" in revealing her
own consciousness as both unaware and typical. Jane Larkin
Crain is representative of reviewers who were critical of Maynard's
socially "myopic" view (*Commentary*, July 1973, pp. 72-73). She

chastises Maynard for "mental paralysis in the face of complexity," introspection and world-weariness. She is also critical of Maynard's attempting to speak for her contemporaries without adequate substantiation of the generalizations. Yet the rising suicide rate among affluent teen-agers may tend to confirm many of Maynard's views, despite their overstated character.

Margaret McFadden-Gerber
Appalachian State University

Mead, Margaret (1901-1978)

Anthropologist, Writer, Grandmother

[223] *Blackberry Winter: My Earlier Years.* New York: William Morrow and Company, Inc., 1972. 305 pp.

Reading the autobiography of a brilliant student of human behavior such as Margaret Mead is a unique and stimulating experience. This author of nearly two dozen books of anthropology, who has given us valuable insights on cultures from New Guinea to Nebraska, turns her skills in *Blackberry Winter* to an examination of her own life. She begins with a discussion of her childhood, as the oldest of five, describing the important influence of the academic setting provided by her parents, both of whom held Ph.D. degrees in the social sciences. She also tells of her paternal grandmother, whom she terms "the most decisive influence in my life." These earlier years were the "blackberry winter" of her life, which, "like the winter frost on the blackberry blossoms, is the forerunner of a rich harvest" (Mary Silva Cosgrave, *Hornbook,* February, 1973, p. 76).

She began to reap her harvest in college, first at DePauw, where she was rejected by the sororities, and then at Barnard. She came truly into her element while conducting field work around the world and accomplishing, as she put it, "a lifetime of work by the age of thirty-four." All this she did while experiencing three marriages, the last of which led her into the role of mother. In the final portion of the book, she shares with enthusiasm her thoughts on being a mother and a grandmother.

Although she never refers to herself explicitly as a feminist, her liberation is beyond dispute. She contended with her father for her right to attend college, and with two of her professors, Franz Boas and Edward Sapir, for permission to do overseas field work—they wanted her to study the American Indians so that she would be closer to home. She married three times while maintaining her own surname because "women should keep their own identities and not be submerged." She is, in fact, so liberated that she demonstrates no compulsion to appear liberated, and is willing to state her views without regard to their predictable lack of popularity in certain feminist circles. She is liberated enough to express publicly the sheer delight she experiences in her roles as mother and grandmother, and is a vigorous advocate of the importance of the family unit. Indeed, Jane Howard describes *Blackberry Winter* as "a hymn to her own family and to the idea of families in general," and points out that Mead "argues eloquently for the continuity of generations, and the gift of complete and sustained attention between parents and children" (New York *Times*, November 12, 1972, p. 49). Yet, as Caroline Bird has noted (*Saturday Review*, November 25, 1972, p. 66), "Her sense of family seems to have reinforced, not swamped, her even stronger sense of person."

Mead not only distinguished herself as a liberated woman, but also a liberated behavioral scientist. She respects her values and feelings enough to express them. It is this characteristic for which she is most admired by the general population (see *Choice*, February, 1973, p. 1667 and Anne Fremantle, *Commonweal*, December 15, 1972, p. 255) and for which she is most criticized by other behavioral scientists (see, for example, Sheila K. Johnson, *Commentary*, March 1973, pp. 70-72). In a later review in *Commentary* (August, 1973, p. 23), Johnson insists that Mead's pronouncements are often those of a "deft popularizer and moralizer," rather than a rigorous anthropologist. One must understand that many professionals who study human behavior embrace the value of objectivity in attempts to be value-free, often to the extent that they come close to a denial of their own humanity. They, of course, risk the danger of subconscious bias which accompanies the failure to recognize the influence of their own feelings. Mead, on the other hand, accepts her values, responses, and feelings. She admits to them, and shares them with her readers—not to promote her cause as much as to permit honest evaluation of what she offers. Obviously, this approach, which is widely gaining acceptance among social scientists, lends itself to greater accuracy than does the pretense of complete objectivity.

On the whole, *Blackberry Winter* has been widely and enthusiastically reviewed, praised for its straightforward style and fascinating content. This is, in Caroline Bird's words (*Saturday Review*, November 25, 1972, p. 66), truly "a grandmother's tale for a time that needs grandmothers very badly." More than that, however, *Blackberry Winter* is an important statement—one of the fruits of an examined life.

Laurie Newman Di Padova
East Greenbush, N. Y.

Mehdevi, Anne Sinclair (-   )

Journalist, Novelist

[224] *Persian Adventure.* New York: Alfred A. Knopf, 1953. 271 pp.

Persian Adventure records Anne Sinclair's romance and marriage to Mohammed Mehdevi and their subsequent journey to Iran. Most of the book is concerned with her encounters with her husband's large family, her attempts to see the "real Persia," her futile attempts to understand the Persian temperament, and her frustrations at being an outsider in a culturally and socially alien land.

Mehdevi finds much in Persia to offend both her Western and her feminine sensibility: her husband's suggestion that she temporarily adopt a Persian first name; her isolation among bored, genteel upper-class Persian women; the family's refusal to permit her to go sight-seeing alone. Two major experiences loom in her Persian adventure: her ultimately successful encounter with her father-in-law, the Agajon, a typical irascible, mercurial, tyrannical family patriarch, whose word is law and whose law is based on his own caprice; and her visit to the German doctor's medical post in a tiny, poverty- and disease-stricken village, where she is confronted with the realities of polygamy. Her disdain for oppressed Persian women, rich and poor, is remedied by a trip to the public baths with a servant girl, a polygamous bride-to-be; here she discovers that beneath all the tattered clothes, the girl is more beautiful than she. For the first time she feels inferior to Persian women and realizes that her preconceptions might have prohibited her from appreciating their own quite different culture. The book ends with Mrs. Mehdevi's Moslem marriage, undertaken primarily to please her husband's family, an adventure in joining, rather than judging, an alien way of life.

Virgilia Peterson (New York *Herald Tribune*, August 2, 1953, p. 5) found *Persian Adventure* "skillfully written. . .replete with a peculiarly American blend of charm and candor." The *Times Literary Supplement* observed (December 18, 1953, p. 820) that "if *Persian Adventure* gets the public it deserves, it will be ironic for Englishmen to find the most illuminating book in English on contemporary Persia written by an American; and no less ironic for both Englishmen and Persians to find it written by a woman."

[225] *From Pillar to Post.* New York: Alfred A. Knopf, 1956. 272 pp.

From Pillar to Post traces Anne Sinclair Mehdevi's journeys and adventures through Mexico, the United States, and Europe as her husband's business carries him, and consequently the whole family, from one country to another.

From Pillar to Post is primarily a series of cultural conflicts; in each new place Mrs. Mehdevi must readjust to alien ways of thinking and of coping with reality. In Mexico she is forced to give birth to her first child in what she considers to be the unsanitary conditions of the Sanatorio de San Jose, amidst a group of smiling, non-English speaking nuns. In Vienna she confronts Uncle Abdul, who would rather go hungry than open the "care packages" she sent him; he prefers treasuring the thought of the gift rather than using the merchandise. Her last "home" is in Majorca, where she contends with a shepherd who teaches her sons much nature lore but also instills in them a disregard for life.

Of her autobiographies, *From Pillar to Post* received the least praise. E. P. Monroe (*Saturday Review*, September 1, 1956, p. 16) typifies the critics' attitudes: "one feels as if Mrs. Mehdevi were milking her marriage and her travels for all—and possibly more—than they are worth."

[226] *Persia Revisited.* New York: Alfred A. Knopf, 1964. 271 pp.

Persia Revisited recounts Anne Sinclair Mehdevi's return to Iran, her husband's homeland, after a decade's absence. This account follows the pattern of her first visit, *Persian Adventure*, which detailed a series of cross-cultural conflicts and capped them by stressing a heightened awareness and appreciation of the basic human qualities which cultural differences tend to obscure. In *Persian Adventure* Mehdevi was merely a tourist; in *Persia Revisited* she becomes a resident. Pervading and controlling *Persia Revisited* as well as *Persian Adventure* has been the presence of the father-in-law, the Agajon. At his death, the sons, naturally, inherit most of the property, including the family home; and when they attempt to legalize the mother's possession of it, they are never given the chance. Although the widow has never, since her marriage of over forty years, done anything on her own, she disappears to return a few days later and announce that she has rented and moved into her own apartment. Mrs. Mehdevi the Elder and Mrs. Mehdevi the Younger turn out to be very much alike.

Cynthia L. Walker
University of Alaska—Fairbanks

Meir, Golda (1898-1978)

Stateswoman, Zionist, Socialist

[227] *My Life.* New York: G. P. Putnam's Sons, 1975. 480 pp.

In *My Life* Golda Mabovitch tells the story of her "purposeful, interesting life" (112). After experiencing fear and poverty in Pinsk, Russia, her family moved to Milwaukee, Wisconsin, in 1906, where she gained "an understanding of the meaning of freedom" (70). Seeking her personal freedom, she left home at fourteen to stay with her beloved older sister, Sheyna, in Denver. There she became politically educated, and met the man she was to marry, Morris Meyerson. After two years she left Denver and dedicated her life to building a homeland for Jews. Working first in America with the Labor Zionist Party, and after 1921 in Palestine, she was always regarded by her friends in Kibbutz Merhavia and later by her political colleagues as an "American girl" (88,230), and returned here often to raise money to support her dream. In Palestine Morris, her husband, did not enjoy the pioneer life so she tried to choose "duty" (98) to her marriage by leaving the Kibbutz; but finally she realized their needs were incompatible, and in 1928 she reluctantly left with their son and daughter to work with the Women's Labor Council of the Histadrut in Tel Aviv (112). She modestly traces her political career, so interwoven with the establishment of Israel (1948) and its growth: Ambassador to Moscow, Minister of Labor, Foreign Minister (in 1956 when she took the Hebrew name "Meir," meaning "illuminate," 296), and Prime Minister from 1969 to 1974. She is most proud of her legislation for "social equality and justice" (275), and her foreign assistance program to the emerging African nations (319); she is most regretful that Israel was not mobilized for the October 1973 Yom Kippur War (425).

Golda Meir worked to create a society with "guarantees of full emancipation for women" (131). Moreover, she believes in socialism, which she defines as equality for all (143). But she states that "women's lib" is an "unfortunate term," and that she joined in a struggle for "equal burdens" since she had "equal 'civic' rights" (88). Rather than "the kind of feminism that gives rise to bra burning, hatred of men or a campaign against motherhood," she respects "constructive feminism" that equips women with "knowledge" and "training" to "do their share" (113-114). Contrary to her statement that "being a woman has never hindered me in any way at all" (114), I believe she illustrates how she overcame sexist obstacles. For examples, she ran away to her sister's for an education when her parents would not send her to high school, even though she was elementary school valedictorian—her father told her "men don't like smart girls" (40-41). She also has a consciousness of herself as a woman: she was "enraged" at the "political tactic" of the religious councilman when she lost the Tel Aviv mayorality because he refused to vote for a woman (281-82); and she recognizes the insult in Ben-Gurion's alledged compliment that she is the "only man" in his cabinet (114). With an unpretentious, personal tone, she discusses the difficulties of being a working mother (114-18) and the "perpetually guilty" feeling it instills (130).

This book was widely reviewed, mostly by men, many of whom noted her remarks on women. Dismissing "Women's Lib" as a "meretricious cause," Paul Johnson asserts that "Professional feminists will get little joy from these memoirs, whereas most women will find them both encouraging and moving" (*New Statesman*, September 26, 1975, p. 376). Amos Elon states that a "feminist" would find no "support in these memoirs" (New York *Times*, November 30, 1975, p. 5). I believe these interpretations miss the spirit of the book. By contrast, Paul D. Zimmerman notes that the example of her life and "her experience as an 'American' woman struggling for equality in a pioneer Kibbutz, has much to say about women's liberation" (*Newsweek*, November 3, 1975, pp. 88-89). Zimmerman also appreciates her manner of writing, so "imbued with the rich, humorous style of the great Yiddish writers." In a generally positive review David Brudnoy expresses disappointment at "her annoying tendency at the most crucial points to gloss over the truly fascinating details and rush ahead to yet another homily" (*The Saturday Evening Post*, May/June 1976, pp. 68-69). Her lack of diplomatic details in the final chapters dealing with her Prime Ministership is specifically cited by Elon and Johnson. In one of the few reviews by a woman, Claire Booth Luce, another stateswoman, writes a moving tribute to "this heroic old woman" who is endowed with "vision," "courage," and "the gift of loving" (*New Republic*, April 17, 1976, pp. 25-27).

Patti Renner-Tana
Nassau Community College

Miller, Ann (1923-   )

Movie Actress, Dancer

[228] *Miller's High Life.* New York: Doubleday and Company, 1972. 283 pp.

When Ann Miller was eleven, she and her mother were approached by a shabby gypsy woman in a bus station. "Cross my palm with a coin," the woman said, "and I will foretell the little girl's future." This was her prediction: "I see a Star of Destiny here. This child will have her name in lights and she will be a star for many years. I see music and lights and dancing and money . . . . You will someday remember my words, when you see her name up there in lights."

Four years later, Ann Miller, the former Johnnie Lucille Collier of Houston, Texas, was starring on Broadway in George White's Scandals. This was just one of the many triumphs that came early in the life of a woman who, as a child, was forced to take dancing lessons because she had rickets. Miller began her career at fourteen (she lied about her age) with small parts in forgettable movies like "Radio City Revels" and quickly advanced to more memorable roles in films like "Stage Door" and "You Can't Take It With You."

Her personal life has not been quite so successful. She married three times, each time to a millionaire who turned out to be a cad for one reason or another. But Miller has let none of the negative experiences of her life dampen her boundless energy and optimism. Her story is the kind of fairy tale that all girls, in their childhood dreams, would like to happen to them, she declares.

This autobiography was not reviewed in any of the publications that routinely cover new books. Although Miller's lack of cynicism is refreshing, her story is of limited interest to women's studies.

Virginia Cox
University of Wisconsin—Oshkosh

Millett, Kate (1934-   )

Sculptor, Writer, Artist, Film Maker

[229] *Flying.* New York: Knopf, 1974. 546 pp.

What occasioned Kate Millett to write an autobiography in her early thirties was a combination of circumstances that spelled out identity crisis: first, the success of *Sexual Politics,* which threw her unprepared into the limelight of national publicity and the center of the Women's Movement; and second, the public admission of her lesbianism, reluctantly acknowledged in a confrontation with the gay faction of the Women's Movement. Having become a symbol for everyone else's purposes, Millett needed to recover her self. She also wanted to defend herself, by applying to her own life those theories of bisexuality and multiple love introduced in *Sexual Politics.* Those theories become primarily a celebration of lesbianism, as Millett explores their possibilities with women.   Interestingly, her numerous explicit passages on sex, ranging in style from Masters and Johnson to pulp sentimentality to genuine eroticism, drew very little comment from reviewers. What did draw comment was the form of her autobiography, which Millett refers to as "documentary." This documentary includes over five hundred pages of impressionistic reminiscences of family, friends, lovers, and political happenings—loosely associated within the framework of the year when she made a film, lost the love of Celia, and gained the love of Claire. Response to this somewhat self-conscious soul searching varied in sympathy from "an intelligent, gutsy, loving woman, full of self-hate and a passionate longing for acceptance" (*New Republic,* July 6 and 13, 1974, p. 29) to anger at the "towering, overpowering egotism and destructive narcissism of this book" (*National Review,* August 30, 1974, p. 989). Critics, it appears, tend to speak of Millett personally because personal revelations emerge so strongly in her book.

Flying is an extremely controversial work, both with respect to its form and its content. In order to deal with the book one must distinguish between two critical issues—the merit of the book as autobiography and the merit of the book as lesbian literature. Millett herself feels that *Flying* eludes all literary categories (*Ms.,* January 1975, pp. 26-29). While she is certainly justified in resenting the comparisons between *Sexual Politics* and *Flying,* and while she is probably correct in assuming that the critical analysis of *Sexual Politics* is more palatable to literary critics than the amorphous introspection of *Flying*, still she cannot expect to be exempt from all literary standards. And by most literary standards, the form of the book does not work. Although the inundation of detail is quite effective within a number of specific sections, the book as a whole is unrelieved by either insight or evaluation. With respect to the content, the sexual passages must be seen as a contribution to gay literature; Millett is one of the first to be so explicit. Beyond the sexual, however, I question the value of her contribution to gay literature. Caught up in the nuances of her own sensibility, Millett is unconcerned with reading larger meanings into her experience, meanings which could help others understand their experiences. Recognition in and of itself does not constitute meaning for the reader. Whatever potential there was for Millett's experience to contribute to a greater understanding of problems peculiar to lesbians or women in general, got lost in her documentary form.

Sandra Hunt
Norfolk State University

[230] *Sita.* New York: Farrer, Straus & Giroux, 1977. 322 pp.

Kate Millett describes in excruciating detail the last months of her three-year love affair with a middle-aged mother and university administrator. The book is based on a journal Millett kept during the spring of 1975 when she moved to Berkeley to teach and to resume her place in the house where she and Sita had spent the previous idyllic spring. But Sita, no longer in love with Kate, is absorbed by her job, children, friends, and other (male) lovers.

Kate has recently been divorced and cannot gracefully let go of the woman she had counted on to be her new life partner. Instead she stays to record the minute-by-minute process of love's death: Sita's deceptions, her own helpless anger, their charged silences and false reconciliations, the "little shoots of hope annihilated by the soft closure of a door." Millett ritualistically re-tells the story of their years together, sometimes in memory of a once powerful love, more often in an obsessive hunt for where it went wrong. The author retraces the sequence of events as if to invite readers to participate in the chant-like chorus of a Greek tragedy.

Sita is an important book because it presents realistically a subject that has been neglected, sentimentalized, or deplored in most literature—lesbian relationships. It contains, as does *Flying,* some of the first prose which presents in an author's own voice her experience of lesbian sexuality. In addition, *Sita* explores in unprecedented depth the old themes of power and powerlessness and offers a model for emotional self-revelation of a kind traditionally found only under the cloak of fiction.

Sita received harsh reviews. Many found it repetitious and agreed with Stephen Koch that feminist writers are "mindlessly mired in an undiscriminating autobiographical mode" (*Saturday Review,* May 28, 1977, p. 29). Sara Sanborn, calling *Sita* a "most awful" and "embarrassing" book, faulted Millett for her "New Journalism Rat-A-Tat-Tat" style (New York *Times,* May 29, 1977, p. 13). By contrast, Cynthia Crossen (*Metropolis,* May 31, 1977, p. 9) found "a certain poignancy in Millett's not being able to write in complete sentences, as though half of her words were lost in sobs." Many reviewers seemed more uncomfortable with Millett's sexuality than with her sentences. As Sanborn admitted, when she reads "about women 'taking' each other," she feels as if she has "walked in on a couple of children playing doctor." Valerie Miner commented (San Francisco *Chronicle,* June 26, 1977, p. 48) that most critics, being "scared, threatened, offended or bored by *Sita,* may overlook a brave, if sometimes reckless, experiment in theme and genre."

Nancy Manahan
Napa College

Mitchell, Suzanne (-   )

Social Worker

[231] *My Own Woman: The Diary of an Analysis.* New York: Horizon Press, 1973. 269 pp.

My Own Woman consists of diary entries during the six years while the author consulted an analyst in her attempt to rise out of a depression and find her own identity and self-esteem.

Mitchell's problem of frigidity in her sexual relations with her husband, as well as the difficulties that the couple have with their teenage daughter bring her to analysis. Simultaneously she begins a college career as an attempt at self-improvement. The close inspection of her life in analysis forces the author to understand the sources of her problem, to contemplate her own selfhood, and finally to consider divorce. Her fears, "I suppose I'm afraid of being alone—afraid of other men—afraid of giving up what I have" (75) are accompanied by guilt, "I feel as if this separation is all my fault—I'm the one who changed" (82). Most important, analysis makes her acknowledge her extremely low self-esteem. When asked why she remained married for almost twenty-five years to someone who stifled her personality, she answers, "Because I didn't feel I deserved much better. I thought I should be satisfied with such a 'good man' " (135). This inferior attitude developed in childhood with her highly idealistic impressions of her mother and older sister, complicated by her mother's supposed favoritism for the older sister and Mitchell's self-deprecating feeling about an act of sexual exploration as a child. The sessions with her analyst bolster Mitchell through the divorce, followed by her shocking discovery of her husband's long infidelity. During her extreme loneliness after the divorce, the analyst helps her to accept her anguish as a natural reaction to the marital separation and soul searching she does in analysis. Mitchell gradually learns to know and like herself so that she "can be alone without being so lonesome" (89). After acquiring her Bachelor's Degree in English, she goes on to graduate school to become a social worker, and the book ends when the therapy ends, with Mitchell living and working on her own. So the therapy's goal is achieved. As one reviewer noted, the modern reader can identify "with Mrs. Mitchell's emergence from post-divorce loneliness as a woman capable of giving and receiving love. . .and making her way independently" (*Publisher's Weekly*, May 21, 1973, p. 44).

Betsy Baugess
Old Dominion University

Montgomery, Ruth (1912-   )

Journalist, Psychic

[232] *Hail to the Chiefs: My Life and Times with Six Presidents.* Coward-McCann, Inc., 1970. 320 pp.

Hail to the Chiefs recounts Ruth Montgomery's twenty-five year career (1944-70) as a political journalist in Washington, D.C. Having had previous newspaper experience in Texas, Indiana, and Chicago, Montgomery, after moving to Washington to join her husband, acquired a job as Washington correspondent for the New York *Daily News,* since "thanks to the war. . .newspaper doors in Washington were grudgingly swinging open to feminine scribes." Her Washington career began during the last months of the Roosevelt administration and continued through the first months of the Nixon administration.

If women journalists and journalism students need a role model, Ruth Montgomery could certainly serve as such. Through her ingenuity, intelligence, intuition, and charm, she uncovered government scandals, scooped other reporters, arranged exclusive interviews, won numerous awards for excellence, earned her own syndicated column, was elected president of the Women's National Press Club (women could not join the men's), was awarded honorary doctoral degrees, found time to write six books, covered major political events and traveled extensively. Her problems as a woman journlist are chronicled throughout the book, problems which may have delayed but certainly did not deter her successes. *Hail to the Chiefs* is exclusively an autobiography of Montgomery's career; her husband is mentioned rarely and fleetingly, and her private life is not discussed.

[233] *A Search for the Truth.* New York: William Morrow & Company, Inc., 1966. 237 pp.

A Search for the Truth is one of the first of many books recounting Ruth Montgomery's adventures in the realms of parapsychology. Her purposes in writing this and later books are two: to convince readers of the validity of psychic phenomena and to encourage them to develop their own psychic powers. Through relating her own experiences she becomes, then, both a teacher and a model.

A Search for the Truth is a kind of Cook's tour (for Montgomery and the reader) of the varieties of parapsychological experience. She attends seances, converses with mediums (both in and out of trances), experiments with Ouija boards, automatic writing (later to become automatic typing), and learns of and records countless examples of ESP, precognition, telepathy, and faith healing. Throughout the book she maintains the position of the objective reporter, who observes, records and, whenever possible, verifies facts and observations.

Three relationships in *A Search for the Truth* transform Montgomery from observer to believer. She meets and becomes friends with Arthur Ford, a famous medium; through his spirit control, Fletcher, she is presented (through intimate details of her family's, her friends' and her associates' lives) with "irrefutable proof" of the existence of a realm beyond the obvious. Through her automatic writing and typing she meets Lily, her chief proponent (along with numerous deceased friends and relatives) of first-hand information from the world beyond. Finally she meets Mr. A., a healer of extraordinary ability, who, through tuning in to "the ring," his term for the collective knowledge of the universe, helps to heal her as well as several of her friends.

Montgomery's personal experiences are supplemented with those of others, ranging from the famous to the anonymous.

[234] *Here and Hereafter.* New York: Coward, McCann and Geoghegan, Inc., 1968. 175 pp.

Here and Hereafter is exclusively concerned with reincarnation. Like *A Search for the Truth,* Montgomery wrote *Here and Hereafter* in order to share convictions acquired from personal experience and research. Montgomery argues that an awareness of, if not a belief in, the theories of reincarnation is important "because if this is not our first lifetime it will probably not be our last, and we consequently have it within our power to influence our future circumstances by present conduct." Thus, the book dwells on past lives with the explicit purpose of helping people to understand their present circumstances and improve future ones.

The book begins with a recounting of Montgomery's personal "irrational" affinities for different parts of the globe—primarily Egypt and Palestine. Subsequently her guides, Lily and other entities who communicate with her through automatic typing, begin providing her with information about reincarnation and announce that she is to write her next book on the subject.

The remainder of the book is devoted to accounts of reincarnation, roughly half of which she witnessed herself, the others having been documented or experienced by others. In all probability, claims Montgomery, we have all, at some point, been members of all races, religions, social stations and members of both sexes.

[235] *A World Beyond.* New York: Coward, McCann & Geoghegan, Inc., 1971. 176 pp.

A World Beyond continues Montgomery's adventures with automatic typing and her communications with Lily and the Group of the spirit world. Added to this group is Arthur Ford, the famous medium who died in 1971. From "Lily, Art, and the Group" she is given information about "the world beyond," the life after death. This book is the manuscript of their communications.

[236] *Companions Along the Way.* New York: Coward, McCann & Geoghegan, Inc., 1974. Rpt. Popular Library, 256 pp.

Companions Along the Way is more "autobiographical" than Montgomery's previous book, *A World Beyond.* Yet another installment in her communications with the spirit world, *Companions Along the Way* recounts previous incarnations Montgomery shared with her spirit guides Lily and Arthur Ford.

[237] *The World Before.* New York: Coward, McCann & Geoghegan, Inc., 1976. 208 pp.

Ruth Montgomery's most recent book, *The World Before* is

another collaboration between Montgomery and her spirit guides.

Cynthia L. Walker
University of Alaska—Fairbanks

Moody, Anne (1940-   )

Civil Rights Worker, Writer

B
M8166

[238] *Coming of Age in Mississippi.*   New York: Dial Press, 1968. 348 pp.

Born in 1940 in southern Mississippi, the oldest child of Black sharecroppers, Anne Moody became a worker for Black civil rights in the early sixties. *Coming of Age in Mississippi* is her story of her childhood, education and participation in the civil rights movement.

The first half of the narrative describes her childhood and school days. Able to survive the life of Southern rural poverty, the uncertain harvests, the steady diet of beans, the days alone with her younger brother and sister, tended only by an eight-year-old uncle, her mother's regular pregnancies, the unstable situation between her mother and her "fathers," Anne Moody, from her earliest childhood, was a brave and independent individual. By the age of nine, she held regular after-school jobs as a domestic for white women and so helped to keep herself in shoes. From the beginning she was also a very bright student; outstanding in high school, she won scholarships to a Black junior and senior college in Mississippi.

The second half of *Coming of Age in Mississippi* recounts Anne Moody's years in college when she became an active worker for civil rights, joined SNCC and the NAACP. She participated in the lunch-counter sit-ins at Woolworth's and worked with CORE for voter registration in Madison County, Mississippi. Impressed by her dedication, one of her co-workers in CORE once introduced her in this way: "She has been beaten and kicked all over Jackson.

Remember that bloody sit-in, and the other demonstrations? She was in all of them. She has been in jail four or five times, and as a result, she can't even go home again" (258). Unable to visit or even write to her family for over two years, accepting brutality and terrorizing from white citizens and police, living in fear of being shot at any moment, Anne Moody persisted in her activities. At this time when Negroes were regularly "shot and butchered like hogs" (331) and she herself was on the Klan's blacklist, she gave herself entirely to the cause of voter registration for Blacks. Her narrative ends inconclusively (how could it be otherwise?), anticipating the 1964 Canton Mississippi Freedom Day march, while remembering the burnings, bombings, and murders with which Blacks had had to pay for their freedom.

Coming of Age in Mississippi gives no direct attention to women's issues or the concerns which affect women's daily lives. At the end of the narrative, the author, twenty-four and single, defines herself in terms of the civil rights movement. Yet the book is of interest to women's studies as the story of a strong, self-directed woman whose consciousness of self is as a Black Southerner; if we admire her strength as a woman, growing up in Mississippi made Anne Moody see the issues of her life in racial terms.

Coming of Age in Mississippi was widely reviewed. *The New Republic* called it "a history of our time seen from the bottom up" (March 8, 1969, p. 30). Critics who reviewed the book as autobiography rather than history preferred the section of the narrative dealing with the author's childhood and life in the rural South; Mary Ellmann found the accounts of the civil rights work comparatively uninteresting (*Nation,* January 6, 1969, p. 26) and the *Saturday Review,* on a similar note, complained of "little introspection" in the later sections of the book (January 11, 1969, p. 83).

Judith B. Herman
State College at Buffalo

Morgan, Lucy C. (1889-   )

Educator

[239] *Gift From the Hills: Miss Lucy Morgan's Story of her Unique Penland School.* Chapel Hill, North Carolina: University of North Carolina Press, 1971. 331 pp.

First published in 1958, then reissued in 1971, *Gift from the Hills* is less an autobiography than the history of a remarkable school, established by a woman who spent her life keeping the ancient handicrafts of the Appalachians alive. Lucy Morgan went to Penland, North Carolina, to assist her brother in a school for mountain children, but she found herself more interested in the art of a few remaining local weavers. She had looms built and distributed among area women, reviving interest in weaving and providing them with income above that of their mining husbands. The association of Penland weavers grew gradually into an internationally recognized center, the Penland School of Handicrafts, where all forms of art and handicraft are studied and taught by professional artists. Penland began as a women's cooperative, expanding only as quickly as the profits from its sales allowed, although it eventually attracted the attention of industry, which provided funds for more rapid expansion of its program and facilities. Despite its growth, however, Penland is still run largely on cooperative principles, and its atmosphere is primarily a reflection of the personality of its founder.

Lucy Morgan's history of Penland is itself, as one reviewer noted, "homespun" (*The Booklist,* September 15, 1958, p. 42) and underplays her own achievements and their revolutionary nature. The reader learns little about Lucy Morgan apart from what her school's success says about her, but that very success suggests the dedication, strength and independence of Morgan and other women whose special qualities are reflected in their art.

Betsy Etheridge Brown
Pennsylvania State University

Morgan, Robin (1941-   )

Feminist, Poet, Writer

[240] *Going Too Far: The Personal Chronicle of a Feminist.*
New York: Random House, 1977. 333 pp.

"The personal is political, I know as a feminist. The personal is also the pure ore to be mined for literature, I know as an artist." These words from an introductory passage of her *Chronicle* measure the pulse of Morgan's flow of prose writings of the last fifteen years. Letters, essays, journal entries, parables, and speeches are presented as a record of an evolution from leftist activist to radical feminist, from unmarried woman to wife and mother. Introductions to the various pieces provide the opportunity for a certain dialogue between the writer then (Morgan) with the present editor (Morgan again). The writer of the early sixties was accused of "going too far;" the writer of 1977 concludes that "it is simply not possible to go far enough."

Some of the essays have historical value, such as "Women Disrupt the Miss America Pageant," which records the date of this century's Women's Movement (September 7, 1968). Others have become classics of women's-movement literature: "Barbarous Rituals" (which lists all the trappings—traps?—of womanhood from the first tampon to those troubled efforts at non-sexist child rearing) and "Goodbye to All That" (more lists—her reasons for saying goodbye to the male chauvinistic New Left and hello to radical feminism). Still other pieces have a scholarly value, presenting Morgan's rationale for urging women to study their own history, philosophy, art, literature, and religion. "Metaphysical Feminism" seeks to establish a philosophical definition and watchword for feminism; "The Wretched of the Hearth" chronicles the women's movement of the sixties. Morgan's letters and parables please as fully as the essays and speeches rouse. Her "Letters from a Marriage" are full of anger, love, self-denigration, and pride. Her parables about paranoia are haunting; and "The Amusement" entertains with its gracious wit and teaches the Daughters our feminist lessons.

Morgan's collection is disappointingly reticent about motherhood and bisexuality—two aspects of her life of considerable

interest to the feminist. The collection is also disappointingly
reticent about her creative life. She refers to her poetry as mere
footnotes to her life; the only poem quoted at length is one by her
husband Kenneth Pitchford. Finally, even allowing for the anthology format of *Going Too Far,* it is disappointing to find so
much repetition of idea, expression, and even vocabulary in a
volume by someone devoted to language. We can hope for a made-
from-scratch autobiography from Morgan later on.

Morgan's two volumes of poetry, *Monster,* and *Lady of the
Beasts,* seemingly contain many autobiographical poems, and may
serve as companion books to the prose work, *Going Too Far.*

Margaret Moore Willen
Eastern New Mexico University

Moses, Anna Mary Robertson (1860-1961)

Artist

[241] *Grandma Moses: My Life's History.* New York: Harper
        and Brothers, 1952. 140 pp.

Grandma Moses' autobiography was written from one hundred
thirty-two pages of her own notes in longhand and from dictation,
when questioned by her editor, Otto Kallir. Her sketches of her
"life's history" were put in chronological order, with the spelling
corrected at her request, and the book finished with eight pages of
reproductions of her letters and sixteen pages of full-color reproductions of her paintings. The book is divided into three parts:
Childhood Days, In the South, and Eagle Bridge.

Part one concerns Anna Mary Robertson's ancestry and childhood including her family history dating back to 1740. The third
of ten children of Margaret Shanahan and Russell King Robertson,
she became skilled in sewing, child care, and other household
duties while very young. When she was twelve years old, she
"hired out" and worked for several families. This section contains

some amazingly detailed memories of her "firsts," occasions such events as the carnival, Thanksgiving, and her birthday.

Part two begins with meeting her husband, Thomas, and their trip south to set up housekeeping, and it includes vivid descriptions of farm life, from soap and candlemaking to her business ingenuity (selling homemade butter). The births of her ten children, the deaths of five of them and the hardships her family endured while living in the Shenandoah Valley are interwoven with stories of the family dog, and making apple butter. This section ends in 1905 when the Moses family sold their farm and returned to the North.

Part three begins with the buying of a dairy farm in New York, where her children grew up, and where she remained until after the deaths of her husband and daughter Anna. The last few pages are devoted to her painting: how she painted, her "tip-up" table, her favorite paintings, and her award from President Truman in 1949. This remarkable woman lived through Lincoln's assassination, several wars, inventions such as the radio and the airplane, and the passing of the nineteenth amendment. Both practical and witty, she tells how she bought the frames for her paintings first, then cut the masonite to fit them because she felt it was better "to build the sty before getting the pig." Her perspective about life was that if she had not been an artist she could just as well have raised chickens.

Otto Kallir, Moses' biographer, has also published two volumes about her life and work, extensively illustrated: *Grandma Moses: American Primitive* (New York: Dryden Press, 1946, 136 pp.), and *Grandma Moses* (New York: Abrams, 1973, 360 pp.). Reviewers have generally ignored the autobiography, but have commented enthusiastically on the above-mentioned books.

Linda Hedrick
Old Dominion University

Mountain Wolf Woman (1884-1960)

American Indian

B
M9274

[242] *Mountain Wolf Woman.* Ann Arbor: University of Michigan Press, 1961. 142 pp.

Mountain Wolf Woman was an Indian who grew up in the middle years of Winnebago adjustment to the inundation of whites in Wisconsin. Her childhood was spent as a member of a large network of kinsmen, living by gardening, hunting and gathering. Contacts with white society occurred through visits to town, hiring the family out as cranberry-pickers, and getting government-alloted land and annuities. The family did considerable moving around by white standards.

The occupations of her adolescence were school, which she enjoyed, and seeking a vision through fasting, which she found meaningful. At an early age she was married off according to Indian custom, with the marriage being arranged by her older brother. The marriage was unhappy, and the couple parted after two children had been born. The children were kept and reared by her childless sister. During these years Mountain Wolf Woman joined the traditionalist Medicine Lodge Society.

The second marriage followed hard upon the first, with the encouragement of another older brother, and this time there was a marriage license from the courthouse. The marriage to Bad Soldier was a good one, lasting until his death in 1936. Nine children were born, and Mountain Wolf Woman reared them as well as some of her grandchildren. She and her husband converted to the Peyote church early in their life together, and they soon found themselves members of a beleaguered religious cult among their own people. They later settled permanently near an Evangelical mission at Black River Falls, Wisconsin. During this time, she learned and practiced traditional medical ways among her people, as well as occasionally acting as a liason between her people and white medical and administrative personnel.

Autobiographies of American Indians are not common; autobiographies of Indian women are downright rare. Finding articulate women who have the time and willingness to talk is only part of the problem. Much of the problem is the amount of effort necessary to produce an intelligible autobiography. Modern Indian people on reservations are still living in a milieu that is alien to non-Indian readers, and much explanation is needed beyond the simple facts of an Indian person's life. This is especially true in the case of Indian women, whose work is at home, wrapped up in a kinship network of statuses and obligations which differ from ours and which the women take for granted in their accounts of their lives. Therefore, massive amounts of footnotes and appendices are necessary. In this instance, the editor of *Mountain Wolf Woman*, Nancy O. Lurie, supplies them in clear language, but it inevitably makes for less than smooth reading.

The tone of the book is surprisingly unemotional, to a reader accustomed to hear about the plight of Indians. Mountain Wolf Woman does not speak of bitterness, but of accepting the world as it was, and her survival in it. Her style of speaking is, indeed, very matter-of-fact, stemming in part from a lifelong stability of personality and in part from the serenity of an old lady looking back on a useful life. Her marriages were not matters for great emotion: men's work and women's work were two different things, and close, companionate marriage was not a Winnebago ideal. Instead, her deep, quiet attachments are shown in what she did with her life: she reared children and grandchildren, and she was religious, though her religion took three different forms at various times.

Mountain Wolf Woman is especially interesting because the book can be compared with the classic *Crashing Thunder,* the autobiography of a Winnebago man who also happened to be Mountain Wolf Woman's full brother. Crashing Thunder's story, set in the same matrix of acculturation, shows the greater excitement and drama that was available to Winnebago men. The drama was further intensified by the fact that Crashing Thunder adjusted poorly to the tribe's situation, became a drunk (a "typical" Indian to many readers), and had much farther to go to find salvation. Mountain Wolf Woman, on the other hand adjusted very well, and so her life was much less exciting, though in reality it was more typical of Indian people. Part of her easy adjustment was due to the fact that women's work in both Winnebago and white culture consisted of much the same things: housekeeping and childrearing. Reservation life for her did not mean any great change in occupation, as it did for the menfolk. As a result, her account of her life often sounds downright ordinary. And yet this ordinariness is deceptive since her world of social relations was different from a non-Indian's. It is this different ordinariness that makes the book so valuable for a cross-cultural study of women.

Helen C. Rountree
Old Dominion University

Murray, Pauli (1910-   )

Lawyer, Civil Rights Activist, Educator, Poet, Episcopal Priest

[243] *Proud Shoes: The Story of An American Family.* New York: Harper & Brothers, 1956. 276 pp.

Pauli Murray's *Proud Shoes* is more the story of Murray's family history than it is her personal autobiography. The subtitle, "The Story of An American Family," tells the tale.

Murray details parts of her childhood in North Carolina near Chapel Hill. From age three, following the death of her parents, she was brought up by her maternal grandparents and two adult aunts. She shares some poignant vignettes of being a "soldiers' granddaughter" and thereby being instilled with "courage, honor, and discipline" while living with a cemetery for a backyard and having to cope with "imaginary ghostly legions"at night. But, the overwhelming emphasis of *Proud Shoes* is on the incredible saga of endurance and pride of heritage passed to her through the personal histories of her grandparents. Her grandfather was obviously a central figure in her development and much of the narrative focuses on him. During the Civil War he served in three different branches of the Union armed forces. After the war, he worked as a teacher and in a variety of trades until he finally went blind. But by then he owned his own land and had built the family home on it. Her grandmother, a spirited venerable woman who was a "buffer" to her granddaughter, traced her lineage to the white Smith family closely associated with the University of North

Carolina. Despite the incident of forced miscegenation between her Indian mother and white father, Murray's grandmother was inordinately proud of her indisputable connections to a notable Southern family.

While its principal task is preserving the rich oral history of Murray's family, *Proud Shoes* also offers some interesting portraits of the women who figured prominently in that history. One great-grandmother was a Cherokee Indian; the other a Swedish woman who married a mulatto. Her grandmother, in her seventies, was still capable of a vigorous verbal defense of her rights and property. Both aunts were solid respectable and respected school teachers, one of whom taught from age fifteen until her seventies. In her own right Murray continues the tradition of strong independent and dependable women of the Fitzgerald/Murray clan. She was recently ordained as the first Black woman Episcopal Priest (Sandra G. Boodman, *Virginian-Pilot,* March 3, 1977, p. D2) and has been a lawyer, a civil rights activist, a poet, and an educator. She has also written (an apparently as yet unpublished) sequel to *Proud Shoes* which will cover her later years.

Reviews of *Proud Shoes* were positive and appreciative of Murray's skillful rendering of "history" and "drama" (Saunders Redding, New York *Herald Tribune,* October 28, 1956, p. 3) in her "biography of a family" (Henrietta Buckmaster, New York *Times,* October 21, 1956, p. 26).

Sandra Y. Govan
Emory University

Nevelson, Louise (1900-　　　)

Artist

[244] *Dawns + Dusks.* New York: Charles Scribner's Sons, 1976. 190 pp.

Louise Nevelson's enormous energy and confidence come through quite clearly in *Dawns + Dusks,* her autobiography based on taped conversations with Diane MacKown. Nevelson's story is that of a career woman, an artist who strove for twenty years before achieving recognition. Guiding Nevelson in all those years of courage and despair in her work, in the break-up of her marriage, in her struggle with maternity—was her unshaken belief that she had been born with creative ability. Nevelson's story is a history of her artistic development: from grade school drawing classes where the assignment was to copy to her present methods of intuitive sculpting with found pieces of wood or Cor-ten steel. It is a history, too, of the New York art world; and, unlike O'Keefe's autobiography where no mention is made of the circle of New York artists with whom she associated, Nevelson gives detailed information about Rivera, Mondrian, the De Koonings, and other artists she has known. Nevelson's admirers will appreciate the exposition of her aesthetics as well as the abundance of photographs of the sculptor and her work.

Feminist readers will be interested in descriptions of her mother who suffered an unhappy marriage and later supported the Nevelsons' separation, and in Louise's refusal to acquiesce to the roles of mother and "lady artist." Nevelson also adds her belief that women artists' work is different from that of men artists, but she does not provide specific arguments.

Dawns + Dusks was not widely reviewed, and its few reviewers were not in agreement. Hilton Kramer was both acerbic and rather unjust in his comments, finding the book shapeless, limited, and "in the operatic mode" (New York *Times,* February 6, 1977). Patt Likos more evenly and fairly assessed Nevelson's valuable revelation of her sources of creativity, while praising the lively and open form of the book (*Feminist Art Journal,* Spring 1977).

Margaret Moore Willen
Eastern New Mexico University

Nin, Anais (1903-1977)

Diarist, Novelist

The six published volumes of *The Diary of Anais Nin* cover a third of a century. At the time of her death, in January 1977, Nin was at work on the seventh volume. Begun as a journalistic letter to her estranged father by the 11-year-old Anais, the diary evolved into a monumental lifework of approximately 200 volumes in manuscript. A retrospective distillation of these extensive manuscripts, the six published books exist in the intermediate zone between the lived experience and the formal work of art. Her ever-present companion and confidante, Nin's *Diary* is a chronicle and dramatization of her experiences and relationships. Employed as a source of raw material for her stories and novels, and as an "interior space" where she could be truthful and open while protected from censorship and criticism, the *Diary* is also a forum for her artistic and psychoanalytic theories, and a vehicle for self-analysis and discovery.

Recurring personalities, images and themes, as sifted through Nin's maturing consciousness, give this serial autobiography its unity. Each volume returns to these major motifs: friendship, exile (both geographic and literary), psychoanalysis, the female artist, the supremacy of the unconscious, the confluence of art and life, and the dualities and paradoxes within Nin's own nature. Obsessively introspective, analytical and idealistic—"I speak for all women"—Nin employs staple archetypal imagery as reflective of her mythic quest for self-knowledge: the mirror, the labyrinth, the dream, the voyage, water, death and rebirth. Anais Nin's style is elegant and fluid, capturing the sense of process and transformation; her language is highly sensual and metaphoric. Peopled by larger-than-life personalities, as many famous as representative, Nin's *Diary* is also a vivid portrayal of the cultural and artistic milieu in which she moved. Anais Nin's *Diary* remains the most complete record of the inner life and psyche of the woman artist, and each volume represents a complete period, or stage, in Nin's lifelong struggle to achieve selfhood and creativity.

[245] *The Diary of Anais Nin.* Volume I, 1931-1934. Edited
by Gunther Stuhlmann. New York: Harcourt, Brace &
World, Inc., 1966.

Nin's escape from bourgeois conformity into creativity, from
artistic death to rebirth, is the outstanding theme of the first
volume. Because her father was an artist (pianist-composer Joa-
quin Nin), and her mother, Rosa Culmell Nin, sacrificed her singing
career for marriage and motherhood, Nin deeply believed that only
a man could be an artist; woman's role was to support him, to be
muse to his artistic endeavors. The first beneficiary of this belief
is Henry Miller; their friendship becomes highly symbiotic, and
lasts a lifetime. While Nin supports him, both financially and intellectually, Miller not only encourages her first attempts at fiction
writing, but also introduces her to his bohemian Paris haunts.
This friendship with Miller is the turning-point of Nin's artistic
life. So too is her association with Otto Rank, the psychoanalyst
whose ground-breaking work with the artist greatly influenced
Nin's own understanding of her psyche and imagination. Nin's
mother and foppish father are also introduced, as is Nin's endless
pain and guilt at his early rejection of her. Indeed, Miller, Rank,
and the members of her family are the primary influences Nin returns to—here and in later volumes—for understanding, strength,
solace or direction.

Nin paints complex portraits of her environments and friendships: especially rich are her descriptions of her other-worldly
house at Louveciennes in the Parisian suburbs, and of the genteel
poverty of Miller's Clichy circle. Other personal relationships explored are: Nin's passionate attraction for June Miller, her psychoanalysis with Rene Allendy, and the suffocating madness of the
French surrealist poet and playwright Antonin Artaud.

In August 1934, Nin gave birth to a stillborn child, a girl. She
writes: "Perhaps I was born for other forms of creation. Nature
connived to keep me a man's woman, and not a mother; not a
mother to children but to men" (341). Her elation over this profound acknowledgment of her place in life leads Nin to embrace
experiences with new confidence. Thus, she accepts Rank's proposal that she follow him to New York to assist him in his new
practice. Nin concludes this volume, as she does almost all the
others, with a departure. She strikes out for New York, a self-

assured, forward-looking "adventurous woman."

[246] *The Diary of Anais Nin.* Volume II, 1934-1939. Edited by Gunther Stuhlmann. New York: Harcourt, Brace & World, Inc., 1967. 349 pp.

Volume II opens with Nin's practice as lay-psychoanalyst in New York's "Hotel Chaotica." Her overwhelming involvement and sympathy for her patients leaves Nin no time for her other work, writing. Choosing the latter as her real vocation, she returns to Paris after five months, and remains there until the outbreak of World War II. This period is probably Nin's happiest. She buys a houseboat on the Seine which she renames *La Belle Aurore,* and merges external reality with her inner visions. Her gaze shifts from herself to others, and the diary evolves from a "disease" into a journal of relationships and character delineation. It is during this period that she does her first serious writing (*House of Incest, Ladders to Fire, Winter of Artifice*), but she still considers her work subordinate to that of her friends: Miller, Lawrence Durrell, and Gonzalo More, a Peruvian poet and revolutionary.

The tension between political and artistic commitment is the central motif of this volume. The Spanish Civil War and the rise of Hitler force Nin to confront the destructive nature of hate, anger and prejudice. Against this horror, Nin posits her own belief in the artist's ability to re-create the world by re-creating the self. She thus devotes her energies to the enhancement of life for herself and those close to her, believing that the artist ultimately transcends time and place. By 1937, she has accepted, for woman, this role as artist: "the woman artist has to fuse creation and life in her own way, or in her own womb. . . . Woman has to create within the mystery, storms, the infernos of sex, the battle against abstractions and art" (234).

[247] *The Diary of Anais Nin.* Volume III, 1939-1944. Edited by Gunther Stuhlmann. New York: Harcourt, Brace, Jovanovich, Inc., 1969. 314 pp.

The third volume of the *Diary* concerns "love and pain" (133). As a war refugee in New York's Greenwich Village, Nin suffers from home-sickness for Paris, from poverty, from the indifference of publishers and reviewers, from hard work, from loneliness among Americans who insist on "surface relationships," and from guilt at being a creative woman. However, there are old and new friends that sustain her: Miller, Gonzalo, Caresse Crosby, Robert Duncan, Luise Rainer, Dr. Max Jacobson, Kay Boyle, and a group of Haitians, including Albert Mangones and Josephine Premice.

To alleviate their poverty, Nin and Miller write erotic stories for an anonymous collector. Some of these are reproduced in the *Diary.* To get around the indifferent publishers, Nin and Gonzalo buy a printing press, which they operate by hand. They painstakingly print a collection of Nin's stories, *Under a Glass Bell,* which wins a favorable review by Edmund Wilson in *The New Yorker.* The burden of being an idealized mother-muse to her friends forces Nin to return to psychoanalysis, this time with Dr. Martha Jaeger. With Jaeger's help, Nin resolved the contradictory pulls between her received definition of being female, and that of being an artist: "My concept of love clashed with my desire to create" (256). Freed from that conflict, she learns that love is not synonymous with sacrifice, that she does not have to be the nourisher-protector of men: "In love I played a role to give each man whatever he needed or wanted at the cost of my life" (259).

[248] *The Diary of Anais Nin.* Volume IV, 1944-1947. Edited by Gunther Stuhlmann. New York: Harcourt, Brace, Jovanovich, Inc., 1971. 225 pp.

With the close of the war, Nin's own "alien" life in America draws to an end. She still lives in Greenwich Village, and is still trying to convince publishers of the importance of her writings. In these years she accumulates a devoted, but small, following; she is invited to read from her works and to lecture at colleges, libraries and museums. She cuts her long hair short, "to be free and capable of self-direction."

As refuge from mature (realistic and superficial) relationships, Nin acquires an entourage of young writers and artists, several of them homosexual, whom she calls her "adolescents." She forms the opinion that homosexuals are caught in a "stage of immaturity" (187), insecure, fearful, fragmented. Gore Vidal is a member of this group; a confidante of Nin's, he is instrumental in having Dutton publish her *Children of the Albatross*. Another prominent figure in Volume IV is Edmund Wilson. Although Nin is drawn to him, she resists, because he too closely resembles her tyrannical father.

In 1947, Nin must leave the country in order to re-enter and apply for U. S. citizenship. On her way to Mexico, she travels by car to the West Coast, where she meets Jean Varda and Lloyd Wright. Varda, the collagist who transforms life into myth, renews Nin's own struggle for transcendence through art. But her attempts to renew her friendship with Miller are stunted by her growing strength and self-confidence: "From this day on," she reflects, "I would see Henry from the outside" (220). Nevertheless, this trip relieves her of the "toxic" of New York, and reinforces her decision to become an American citizen.

[249] *The Diary of Anais Nin.* Volume V, 1947-1955. Edited by Gunther Stuhlmann. New York: Harcourt, Brace, Jovanovich, Inc., 1974. 262 pp.

Volume V of the *Diary* opens in Mexico; evoking, as in her journey to Fez (Volume II) Nin's long-standing attraction for the exotic, lush landscape, and warm, soporific climate. She travels extensively in this volume, even revisiting Paris. Ultimately, she re-settles near Los Angeles, an environment she finds more emotionally supportive than that of New York.

Several factors—the continued failure of publishers and reviewers to understand her novels, and particularly the deaths of her parents—lead Nin to turn once again to psychoanalysis. This volume is rich with the process of self-understanding and growth: "Our parents give birth to us twice," she notes, "the second time when they die" (184).

In 1955 Nin agrees, at the request of Dr. Oscar Janiger, to a trial of taking L.S.D. She includes a vivid account of this experience. A reaffirmation of herself as artist, Nin discovers that her consciousness brings up all the images and symbols she has been using in her writing. But drugs operate only as shortcuts to the artist's imagination, she believes, and cannot be employed as substitutes for the difficult labor of creating a work of art itself: "the drug experience does not strengthen the desire to turn the dream, the vision, into reality. It is passive." Her goal is much more ambitious; it involves "integrating the dream with creativity in life, a quest for the development of the senses, the vision, the imagination, as dynamic elements with which to create a new world, a new kind of human being" (262).

[250] *The Diary of Anais Nin.* Volume VI, 1955-1966. Edited by Gunther Stuhlmann, New York: Harcourt, Brace, Jovanovich, 1976. 400 pp.

The sixth volume proclaims an end to "Anais Nin" as the major focus of her diary; henceforth her diary will be called "The Diary of Others." More overtly self-critical, and yet more tolerant of her own shortcomings, Nin develops a stronger defense against adverse criticism. Through conversations with Aldous Huxley and Timothy Leary, she learns that her ability to integrate her unconscious with her conscious life—without the help of drugs—is indeed rare, and finally understands why her fiction has so long been misunderstood. At last Nin finds a publisher: Alan Swallow of The Swallow Press publishes her novels. Not much later, Harcourt, Brace & World agrees to publish the *Diary;* Volume VI ends with the publication of Volume I, and Nin's emergence as an internationally acclaimed writer.

Volume VI celebrates her friendships. She is again in correspondence with Miller and Durrell, with James Leo Herlihy, with Roger Moore (who is in prison), and in personal and telephone communication with Marguerite Young.

In answer to critics who find her world too narrow she writes in 1966: "My span may seem smaller but it is really larger because it covers all the obscure routes of the soul and body seeking truth, seeking the antiserum against hate and war, never receiving medals for its courage. It is my thousand years of womanhood I am recording a thousand women" (400).

Both the number of reviews and the amount of praise for *The Diary of Anais Nin* have increased steadily with the publication of each new volume. Volume I won high praise from a few reviewers

(for example, Karl Shapiro in *Book Week,* May 1, 1966). Volume
II has more reviews, generally very favorable. A few reviews consider the *Diary* to be overly narcissistic, and some are plainly
hostile (see Henrietta Buckmaster's reviews of Volumes I and IV
in *The Christian Science Monitor,* June 16, 1966, and November
11, 1971). Each new volume has brought more serious critical
attention and enthusiasm to the *Diary,* and lengthy studies began
to appear. Of value are: *A Casebook on Anais Nin,* edited by
Robert Zoller, which contains seven essays, of varying quality, on
Nin's *Diary;* and *The Mirror and the Garden,* by Evelyn J. Hinz,
who devotes a chapter to the first four volumes and includes a
bibliography of reviews and articles on the *Diary.* A good overview
of the most widely-accepted ideas on Nin's *Diary* appears in
Valerie Carnes' "Author Tries Distillation of Anais Nin's Volumi-
nous Diary," *Lost Generation Journal,* 4, No. 1 (Winter 1976).
For an excellent generic study of the *Diary* see Robert A. Fother-
gill, *Private Chronicles: A Study of English Diaries.* A compilation
of her lectures and interviews, *Anais Nin: A Woman Speaks,* edited
by Evelyn J. Hinz, contains much information on the *Diary* as well
as on Nin's artistic, feminist and political beliefs. Of course, Gunther Stuhlmann's introductions are fine guides.

Anais Nin was elected to the National Institute of Arts and Letters in 1974. In 1976, a large group of writers and critics sub-
mitted a proposal for a Nobel Prize for her. In 1977, Volume VI
was nominated for a National Book Award for biography.

Ruth L. Mack
Tidewater Community College

Liliane K. Arensberg
Emory University

O'Keeffe, Georgia (c.1893-   )

Painter

[251] *Georgia O'Keeffe.*   New York: Viking Press, 1976.   228 pp.

Georgia O'Keeffe's autobiography is like her painting—it comes from no tradition; people do not figure in it; an event or a feeling may be magnified but not fixed in a framework; and it has a flat realism which gives glimpses of an elusive mysticism. The reader familiar with O'Keeffe might feel disappointed not to learn intimate details of the life of America's greatest living woman painter: her marriage with photographer Alfred Stieglitz, the circle of men painters in which she figured in New York in the twenties, her reaction to fame and honor.

What is learned in O'Keeffe's autobiography are details about youthful encounters with established art and teachers William Merritt Chase and Arthur Dow; and there is an occasional philosophical comment on art, e.g.: "Objective painting is not good painting unless it is good in the abstract sense." But above all, O'Keeffe writes of the genesis of her paintings. The magnificent color reproductions in the autobiography are accompanied by bare-bones explanations of the subject of the painting or the feeling behind it. O'Keeffe provides the explanation in hope of eradicating the "odd things" that have been said about her work. For example, she objects—as she has for forty years—to the sexual imagery critics have seen in her flower paintings. (O'Keeffe refused Judy Chicago an interview when Chicago hoped to include her work in the female imagery theory that forms a major conclusion of Chicago's autobiography, *Through the Flower.*)

Of further interest to feminist readers are infrequent comments by O'Keeffe about her relationship to men painters. She was often the outsider, and was made to feel she was different. At the root of the difference were her independence of style and her ability to do what "the men" hadn't been able to do.

Reviewers stated that O'Keeffe's autobiography was not what many would expect, but found her "natural history of a visual sensibility" to be simple, humorous, and intelligent (New York

Times, December 12, 1976). Katherine Kuh (*Saturday Review,* November 27, 1976) addressed herself to O'Keefe's defense of the flower paintings, stating that they are sensuous and often phallic. She found also that O'Keeffe's silence was eloquent, that what O'Keeffe has excluded from her autobiography is revealing.

Margaret Moore Willen
Eastern New Mexico University

Origo, Iris (1902-   )

Writer, Philantropist

B O69

[252] *Images and Shadows: Part of a Life.* New York: Harcourt, Brace, Jovanovich, 1971. 278 pp.

Iris Cutting Origo is a member of the privileged class; she grew up between the American and Irish estates of her grandparents, travelled through Egypt with her mother and father (who died when she was eight), and lived with her mother in the de Medici villa in Fiesole. Her book is a partial autobiography, as the title informs us—Origo spends much time on her grandparents, and her parents, and tells us about herself only indirectly. We learn about Origo through the stories of other people and places, through childhood experiences with her grandparents, the dim memories of her father, and the eccentricities of her "delicate," somewhat invalid-like mother. Origo went through the required "coming out" balls, considering them a waste of time, and in 1924 married Marchese Antonio Origo. Together they bought 3,500 acres of land in Val D'Orcia in the province of Siena, Italy. They rejuvinated the land which had lain fallow for centureis, employed and helped the farmers who lived there: rebuilt their homes, and constructed a school and hospital. During World War II Origo stayed in Italy and for two years worked in the Prisoners of War office in Rome. Later in the war she built an orphanage, "Casa de Bambini" and with her country people, broke down the "old barriers of tradition and class" working together for survival and aiding partisans. Origo is the author of more than seven books—

essentially a biographer, trying to "bring the dead life," she has written about the Italian poet Leopardi, a 14th century merchant, Francesco Datini, the 15th century saint San Bernardino, and Lord Byron's daughter, Allegra.

Images and Shadows, received warm praise from critics. One article in *Times Literary Supplement* spoke of Origo as the "best writer in English on matters Italian. . .someone who has thought hard and well. . .about the meaning of life" (November 13, 1970, p. 1316). Citing her philanthropic activities, Arthur Marshall in *New Statesman* says that Origo is no "bored cosmopolitan" but a woman with great talent who has worked hard devoting her "life to farming and bringing prosperity back to an uncultivated part of Tuscany." He especially enjoyed her stories of childhood—"the joys of American holidays, the dreary succession of stodgy governesses, the horrors of the Kaiser's war" (December 25, 1970, p. 871). Another critic praises Origo for going beyond the conjuring up of "charming, nostalgic memories," and for succeeding in bringing a "critical, discerning intelligence to bear on her past. Moreover," the review continues, "she is a practiced writer" (*The Economist*, London, November 2, 1970, Vol. 7, p. 237).

Bella Mirabella
Queens College, CUNY

Ovington, Mary White (1865-1951)

Social Worker, Civil Rights Activitist, Author

[253] *The Walls Came Tumbling Down.* New York: Harcourt, 1947. 307 pp.

Completed when she was eighty-two, Mary Ovington's autobiography is a polite and selective portrayal of her role in the civil rights movement, particularly her service for forty years as an officer of the National Association for the Advancement of Colored People.

Born into a comfortable New York merchant's family the day before Lincoln's assassination, Mary Ovington was influenced by her parents abolitionist leanings and their enlightened attitudes about race and sex. She attended Radcliffe College, then known as the Harvard Annex, for two years (1891-1893), and afterwards was employed as a social worker for the Pratt Institute of New York. Finding that the migration of southern Blacks was depressing the level of Black neighborhoods almost to the level of some of the urban ghettos, she enlisted the aid of Mary Simhovitch of Greenwich House and Frances Keller in a study of the problem, the findings of which were published in 1911 under the title *Half a Man*. Based on the findings of the study, Ovington established *Tuskegee*, a Black settlement house, and with Jane Addams, whose progressive principles she esteemed, helped found the NAACP, travelling, writing, speaking and raising money on behalf of the organization.

The Walls Came Tumbling Down tells how Ovington lent her support to groups such as the National Association of Colored Women, founded in 1892, and the League for the Protection of Colored Women, of which she was one of the founders. In the book she asserts that when the story is written of "the work the voterless women of American did for this Republic, the National Association of Colored Women should have a chapter all its own" (124). The autobiography chronicles the full participation of southern Black women and northern White women (into which group Ovington was born) in the campaigns for the NAACP and its kindred organizations. It recounts the use of legal action and, after 1930, political force against lynching, segregation, and discrimination in housing and employment. She reports her role in urging Blacks to shift their support from the Republican party to the Democratic party.

The Walls Came Tumbling Down tells of Mary Ovington's writing for *Charities and the Commons, The Crisis,* and *The Masses.* Her story "The White Brute" appeared in *The Masses* depicting the helplessness of a Black man in the face of the rape of his wife by armed whites. Ovington covered the Scottsboro trial for *The Crisis* and wrote several novels including *Hazel* (1913), one of the first serious attempts to create a literature for Black children.

Ovington's book is important to women's studies because it

shows in the story of a White woman how racism and sexism are entangled and related problems. It shows how those two problems were fought by the outstanding women of Ovington's generation, women who shared her convictions, her courage, her devotion to decency and justice, and worked with her: Jane Addams, Ida Wells Barnett, Annie Besant, Francesa Keller, Florence Kelley, Josephine Shaw Lowell, Viola Roseboro', Mary Simkhovitch, Anne Strunsky Walling and others.

Beatrice Murphy wrote, "there is plenty of excitement, bloodshed, and murder, with the NAACP, under the guiding spirit of such faithful workers as Mary Ovington in the role of hero and emancipator to many who needed, and still need its help." She finds "the one shortcoming. . ." (New York *Times,* November 2, 1947, p. 34) is "the author's tendency to generalize on the subject of racial traits, good and bad." Indeed, in her final effort, *The Walls Came Tumbling Down,* written mostly before 1945 and published in 1947, when the success of the civil rights movement seemed assured, Mary White Ovington is true to her commitment as a protagonist both for civil rights for Blacks and for an enhanced social role for women.

Harold S. Wilson
Old Dominion University

Painter, Charlotte (1926-   )

Writer

[254] *Confession from the Malaga Madhouse: A Christmas Diary.* New York: Dial Press, 1971. 212 pp.

Charlotte Painter's book is about an American widow who has traveled to Spain with her six-year old son, Tommy. After her arrest on a drug charge, a "friend" commits her to the Malaga madhouse for a week, apparently believing it to be a drug clinic. We do not learn of these circumstances, however, until the latter part of the book. We enter a narrative of fragments and splinters, a narrative in which sanity and madness are difficult to distinguish.

In describing her book, Painter writes: "This book is set in a Spain of the mad mind" but it "is not set in Spain at all, except for the gravitational pull of geography upon words. It is groping around someplace in the wasting mind of America, trying to joust with some absolutes: our world is divided; our country is divided; our selves are divided. . .I offer this confession, then, of my own madness, which I believe in." Having entered a narrative of madness, we soon come to the author's questions: "What am I doing here? How do I get out?" The questions are never answered, even when her release from the madhouse is arranged at the end of the book. The splinters and fragments display a world gone mad, in spite of the writer's hope: "We are looking for some way to live in a world gone mad. We have left American the beautiful. But not because we know a better place."

In her expatriate world we get brief glimpses of children from the Why-Yes school (a sharp commentary on the free-school movement), commune hippies, and the "Sub-jet Set." In the madhouse we see characters who suffer more desperately from poverty and alienation. Painter does not try to convince us that they are sane, but that the world outside their experience is insane as well, and that she herself walks on the edge of madness whether she is in or out of the madhouse.

A major theme of the book is the ambivalence of motherhood. The question, "What do you do with a child?" is dramatized by several events and characters, in addition to the author's primary concern about her relationship with her own son. The three voices of her own persons argue:

> Escarlata Pimpernela (political revolutionary): "Nourshing children impedes the nourishing of work. . .Motherhood is a life sentence."

> Gypsy Queen (earth mother): "A baby is a poem."

> Juana Bunion (mystic): "I believe this whole journey of ours must have something to do with sacrifice."

The conflicting statements reflect Painter's confusion about motherhood. In fact, Painter seems immobilized by the confusion on this and many other issues. The book draws us into an unsorted mass of confusion and madness which never explains itself. All we know at the end is that the woman, Painter, has decided to accept the responsibility for her son because there doesn't seem much else for her to do, when she is released from the hospital. She recognizes an experience of release and joy which some reviewers claim is a significant ritual of rebirth. That is surely overstating the case for a book that has so little consistent introspection and coherence.

As a statement in non-fiction about madness in modern women the book may be useful in the classroom, but only after developing a substantial context of the subject with resources like Phyllis Chesler's *Women and Madness.* As an example of autobiographical writing it may raise too many difficult questions to be workable in some courses. What is most troublesome is the fact that we never really see a first person female. We have instead a sense of watching a fictional, if representative experience. We are not left with the sense of having learned something about Charlotte Painter —woman, writer, mother.

Mary Louise Briscoe
University of Pittsburgh

Park, Maud Wood (1871-1955)

Suffragist, Organization Leader, Settlement Worker

[255] *Front Door Lobby.* Boston: Beacon Press, 1960. 278 pp.

Maud Wood Park in her *Front Door Lobby,* edited by Edna Lamprey Stantial, describes her experiences in the suffrage movement during the period 1916-1919. Those were the years when she served as vice-chairman and then chairman of the Congressional Committee of the National American Woman Suffrage Association charged with pushing the Suffrage Amendment through Congress. After two brief chapters in which she gives an impersonal summary of earlier women's rights efforts and a first-hand account of NAWSA's decision in 1916 to adopt Carrie Chapman Catt's "Winning Plan" to secure the Amendment, Park concentrates on the methods and activities of her committee to obtain the necessary votes in Congress. At the same time, she provides illuminating comments about her co-workers, human interest stories about members of Congress, and insight into Congressional maneuverings. She reflects NAWSA's hostile attitude toward the National Woman's Party, and reports the negative reaction of certain Congressmen to the latter's activities. She shares the tensions of the suffragists in the galleries during the House and Senate votes, and their emotions in defeat and victory. In her analysis of the causes of the final success with Congress, she attributes the greatest significance to the long campaign within the states and to Catt's "Winning Plan."

Although it was not Park's intent with this book to give attention to her personal life or to her efforts for women before or after the 1916-1919 period, feminists would be interested at least in reading what caused her to become a champion of women's rights before she graduated from Radcliffe in 1898; they might be interested in learning how her settlement house work affected her attitudes toward women's problems and stirred her to make a two-year world tour to study the conditions of women in other countries; and feminists should find interesting her experiences as a suffrage leader in Massachusetts before she became prominent at the national level. Feminists would also find it worthwhile to know about her activities to promote the interests of women while she served as the first president of the National League of Women Voters and the first chairman of the Women's Joint Congressional Committee.

According to Eleanor Flexner, Park wrote *Front Door Lobby* in 1936-1937 (*Century of Struggle: The Women's Rights Movement in the United States*. Cambridge: the Belknap Press of the Harvard University Press, 1959, p. 367), but it was not published until five years after her death in 1955 at the age of eighty-four. Periodicals that reviewed the volume after it appeared in print were laudatory. *Booklist* (May, 1961, p. 536) considered it to be "a lively account" and noted its descriptions of suffragists, members of Congress, and Congressional tactics. *Christian Century* (June 28, 1961, p. 797) commented that the account would "help correct persistently unfair stereotypes;" and although Thelma E. Smith in the *Library Journal* (October 15, 1960, p. 3657) found the writing style "a bit old-fashioned," she held the book to be worthwhile for its attention to a "neglected aspect of our history," its "intimate picture of the workings of the lobby" and its "entertaining glimpses of Congressmen."

Dorothy E. Johnson
Old Dominion University

Peterson, Virgilia (1904-1966)

Author, Lecturer

[256] *A Matter of Life and Death.*   New York: Atheneum, 1961. 334 pp.

Though well-known as author, lecturer, reviewer, and moderator of a national television series, Virgilia Peterson makes her professional life and literary fame a minor topic in her autobiography. The major subject of *A Matter of Life and Death* is the author's embittered relationship with her mother; she presents herself not as successful author but as rejected child.

Born into wealth and privilege, Virgilia Peterson nevertheless lived a lonely and miserable childhood with a mother whom she describes as unable to respond on any level to the needs of her child. The first section of the book chronicles her mother's relentless indifference.   The second section tells of the author's first marriage and divorce, her second marriage to a Polish prince, and the life in Poland on which she based *A Polish Profile* (1940), the book which established her literary reputation.   Contented with her role as her husband's wife, she was not allowed that pleasure for long; the outbreak of World War II forced her return to the United States, with her two children.   The final section of the book describes her struggles for financial and emotional survival during the war and the intense strain caused by her unavoidable dependence on her mother.   At this time she wrote her novel, *Beyond This Shore*, became moderator of a weekly television program on books and public affairs, and began lecturing nationwide. Yet she gives her literary success second place to the conflicts of her private life in her account.   Guilt-ridden by her love for another man, she attempted suicide. When she recovered, she divorced the husband she no longer cared for, married her lover, and, by her mother's death at this time, found release from that destructive relationship. It is at this point, with the death of her mother and the promise of a rich new life for herself, that the narrative ends.

As an autobiography of a successful literary woman, *A Matter of Life and Death* is of special interest to women's studies precisely because it de-emphasizes the author's literary achievements. Virginia Peterson presents herself first as daughter, second as wife or lover, third as mother, and last as "career woman" or writer. The book is also of interest for its angry, bitter probing of the relationship between mother and daughter; written as a letter to her mother, *A Matter of Life and Death* is in some ways comparable to, and may be thought of as woman writer's version of, Kafka's famous "Letter to His Father."

The numerous reviews of *A Matter of Life and Death* were fascinated by, if not admiring of, its candor. Some linked the book to Philip Wylie's attacks on American momism. While many felt that the book failed to analyze the psychological causes of the maternal rejection it so fully describes, Charles Rolo praised its insights, calling it "one of the outstanding autobiographies written by an American woman" (*Atlantic Monthly,* October 1961, p. 124).

Judith B. Herman
State College at Buffalo

Picon, Molly (1898-   )

Actress

[257] *So Laugh a Little.* New York: Messner, 1962. 175 pp.

These affectionately humorous recollections from Molly Picon's childhood and many years on stage are a tribute to Sarah Ostrow, "my grandmother, who was no one that anyone had ever heard of,

who had made no history,. . .but who had given me as my heritage
her capacity for laughter, for humor, for a joyous appreciation of
life itself." Potentially painful subjects such as poverty, anti-
Semitic prejudice, family difficulties are treated with a light touch,
yet even so the world of "mid-Victorian serenity" which Picon
remembers and lovingly describes has enough hard reality to stimu-
late readers to take a closer look at ethnic inheritances and the
emigrant experience in early twentieth-century America. Her conversational storytelling, though prone to flashbacks and anticipa-
tions, follows for the most part her family's fortunes starting with
the little Russian town of Rexshishtchow, from which Picon's
grandparents and their five children were driven by Cossacks in
1880. With samovar and featherbed they move to Philadelphia,
to begin a never-ending struggle with landlords, boarders, sweat-
shop owners, unthinking schoolteachers, salesmen, and other
hazards. The laughter which enables them to survive with dignity
is sometimes black, often double-edged, thus Grandma's rejoinder
to Miss Apple's pointed question about whether little Molly is
getting green vegetables in her diet: "Pickles ain't green?" The
theatre offers an imaginative escape—and eventually an actual way
out from the tenements. From the age of five when, dressed like
a fairy princess in a red gown her mother made for her, Molly
wins a five-dollar gold piece at amateur night, her career is set.
The various stages of a career that encompasses Yiddish plays,
vaudeville, Broadway musicals, performances abroad—including
an act done entirely in French in Parisian music halls—form the
context for a continual stream of anecdotes about Grandma's
quips and foibles, until at age eighty-five, the indomitable old
woman informs her family that she had to pay the doctor five
dollars to learn that she had an incurable disease—old age itself—
and adds: "I wouldn't give you two cents for it."

Early in the book Picon muses whimsically on her possible
fate had she been the son that her cultivated, leisure-loving father
had wanted. "If I had been Louis Pyekoon's son, I could have had
a classical education." She dreams of perhaps having become a renowned scholar, a professor of languages, an existentialist. There is
no hint, however, of any serious regrets on her part; even if there
had been she would probably not mention them, just as her grandmother, retelling the tale of the Russian wedding in which she sat
in bridal finery and wondered which of the men was the groom
chosen for her, never confided "any pangs of fear or rebellion or

anxiety" she may have felt. These tales of match-making, weddings and funerals, scrubbing and cooking for the Sabbath, wearing finery to the synagogue, gossiping and joking and taking care of the children, give us a good idea of the rewards and limitations of women's roles in a traditional society, and a suggestion of what is lost and gained in adapting to the modern world.

Kittye Delle Robbins
Mississippi State University

Plath, Sylvia (1932-1963)

Poet, Novelist

[258] *Letters Home: Correspondence 1950-1963.* Selected and edited by Aurelia Schober Plath. New York: Harper and Row, 1975. 502 pp.

B
p7/6

Letters Home begins with an autobiographical introduction by Plath's mother who states: "Throughout her prose and poetry, Sylvia fused parts of my life with hers from time to time, and so I feel it is important to lead into an account of her early years by first describing the crucial decisions and ruling forces in my own life" (3). In this brief chronicle about herself, Aurelia Plath points to several major incidents that affected the lives of the mother and daughter, including the death of Sylvia's father.

Aurelia Plath's introduction, described by Maureen Howard as "so lady-like as to be maddening" (New York *Times,* December 14, 1975, p. 1), reveals both "a continuing need for self-justification" and a deep identification with her daughter: "Between Sylvia and me there existed—as between my own mother and me—a sort of psychic osmosis which, at times, was very wonderful and comforting; at other times, an unwelcome invasion of privacy" (472).

Aurelia Plath selects 396 letters from a total of 696 letters written by her daughter and arranges them chronologically, beginning with Sylvia Plath's freshman year at Smith College and continuing until her death in London in 1963. Most reviewers of *Letters Home* found the cutting excessive. J. J. Cain, for instance, wrote that the picture presented in them is "essentially that of a green and vulnerable girl, scarcely recognizable as the poet who wrought the pitiless, controlled rage of the Ariel poems, or even the unmodulated and mannered cynicism of *The Bell Jar*" (*Saturday Review*, November 15, 1975).

Encouraged by her mother to create, Sylvia Plath developed her skills in writing and art during the years when she was lanky and socially inept. Later she developed a "strategy of popularity" which consisted of downplaying her intelligence and creativity. By 1950 she had sold her first short story to *Seventeen* magazine and learned that works with a pathetic twist had better chances for publication. Also included in the introduction is a paean to youth, written when Plath was seventeen and termed herself "a girl who wanted to be God."

The correspondence relates Plath's career as a brilliant student at Smith, holding the scholarship named for Olive Higgins Prouty (her "literary mother"). And these letters reveal "an awareness of her mother's sacrifice" a determination to justify her mother's hopes for her (Margo Jefferson, *Newsweek*, December 22, 1975, p. 83). But as A. S. Byatt notes in an excellent review, her mother's "self-denial, ideals, and expectations were a strain on Sylvia Plath, who probably carried a further strain from her mother's unfulfilled ambitions" ("Mirror, Mirror On the Wall," *New Statesman*, April 23, 1976, pp. 541-52).

Amassing honors and prizes as she continued to publish, Plath won the coveted *Mademoiselle* Guest Editorship in June 1953. She interviewed Marianne Moore and Elizabeth Bowen as part of her assignment. Yet failure to gain acceptance in a desired writing class at Harvard intensified Plath's growing depression, and she attempted suicide. Electric shock, and insulin therapy followed; the poet evidenced "a deep concern that she had not proved herself worthy of the scholarship help given her" (126). Writing about this illness later, Plath said, I remember I was terrified that if I wasn't successful writing, no one would find me valuable or interesting" (133). After six months she reentered college and "following the instructions of Dr. B., she charted each day, checking off as an item was accomplished—a practice she followed the rest of her life" (135). These events are incorporated into her auto-biographical novel *The Bell Jar.*

Plath's senior thesis, termed "brilliant," dealt with the double in literature, a fact noted by many reviewers in attempting to explain the dichotomy between the poet Plath and the correspondent Sivvy. Upon graduation she won a Fulbright scholarship to Cambridge. The women writers she most admired at this time were Sarah-Elizabeth Rogers, Jean Stafford, Hortense Calisher, Phyllis McGinley, and Adrienne Rich, "the girl whose poetry I've followed from her first publication" (339). Aurelia Plath comments that at Cambridge, Sylvia was "seriously searching for an extraordinary male counterpart with whom she could share all the emerging facets of herself; in February 1956 she found him in the poet Ted Hughes" (181). Sylvia Plath wrote of this initial meeting: "he was the only man I've met yet who'd be strong enough to be equal with—" (230). Plath experienced an outpouring of creativity and wrote, "I shall be one of the few women poets in the world who is fully a rejoicing woman, not a bitter or frustrated or warped man-imitator which ruins them in the end" (256).

The two were married in June 1956. The following year Plath accepted a position teaching English at Smith, and after six months in America, she was stifled by the "neat, grey, secondary air of the university" (330). The couple decided to support themselves solely by writing. Her poems written at this time were published in *The Colossus.* Returning to England in 1960, Plath gave birth to a daughter and Hughes' book of poems was accepted for publication. "I am so happy *his* book is accepted first. . .I can rejoice then, much more, knowing that Ted is ahead of me" (297). In an explanatory footnote, Mrs. Plath says, "From the time Sylvia was a very little girl, she catered to the male of any age so as to bolster his sense of superiority. . . . She did not pretend the male was superior; she sought out those who were, and her confidence in her husband's genius was unshakable" (297). In 1961 Plath underwent an appendectomy and suffered a miscarriage, and in 1962 she gave birth to a son Nicholas. This year, in which the marriage began to collapse, the poets moved to the country and busied themselves in restoring an older home, planting a garden, bee-keeping and writing. This section of letters bears a cautionary warning that "only one side of an extremely complex situation" (450) is represented. Hughes was seeing another woman "and

Sylvia's jealousy was very intense'' (458).

Legally separated after Hughes moved back to London, Plath remained in the country and spoke of "the humiliation of being penniless and begging money from deaf ears," a situation which her mother calls exaggerated. Deciding finally to divorce, Plath also decided to remain in England. "If I start running now, I will never stop. I shall hear of Ted all my life, his success, his genius. . .I must make a life all my own as fast as I can" (465). Bitterness at wasted time and a brittle bravado surface in these letters, yet Plath still retained "a love for, and admiration of (Ted's) writing" (467).

After moving to London, Plath heard that *The Bell Jar* was accepted for publication. Although she had written over the years about a novel in progress (to be titled either "Hill of Leopards" or "Falcon Yard") which would have a young American woman in England as its protagonist, and meeting Ted Hughes as its central episode, the subject of the now-accepted novel had not been fully divulged to her family. A rerendering of her *Madmoiselle* summer, subsequent suicide attempt, and breakdown, *The Bell Jar* was initially published under the pseudonym Victoria Lucas (London: Heinemann, 1962), and the writer cautioned both her family and friends against it. "Forget about the novel and tell no one of it. It's a pot-boiler and just practice" (477).

At this time she was also writing the poems that would appear in *Ariel* and said, "I am a writer. . .I am a genius of a writer; I have it in me. I am writing the best poems of my life; they will make my name" (468). Plath assures her mother that she is expanding, now that she no longer "is in his shadow" (470), and gives details of new clothes and hairstyles that help her morale. She even writes that she is able to meet Ted's other woman and "be gracious to her now and kindly" (479). Yet Plath is often ill; the "taking on of the man's responsibilities as well as a woman's" tires her.

In the final letter sent before her death on February 11, 1963 she wrote: "I am seeing the finality of it all, and being catapulted from the cowlike happiness of maternity into loneliness and grim problems is no fun!" (498). Yet, this letter, like all the rest, denies any lasting damage.

The many reviews of *Letters Home* almost all criticized Aurelia Plath's editing; some reviewers found a link between the letters and Plath's poem "The Disquieting Muse," and several indicated the sense of unease generated by the letters. Phoebe-Lou Adams termed the edited work "a gush of girlish glee that is unbelievable, and even revolting" (*Atlantic,* 237, February 1976, p. 111).

Probably the best balanced and most perceptive review is that of Maureen Howard in which she writes: "*Letters Home* is heart-wrenching, but the major tragic effect is not the overpublicized suicide, rather it's the misunderstanding between mother and daughter, set forever, irrevocable" and she indicates that Aurelia Plath's editing was "the mother's need to contain at last her daughter's life." Yet she adds, "On the strength of the good poems, the daughter will always have the last word. They are the laurels at her mother's feet" (New York *Times,* December 14, 1975, p. 2).

[259] *The Bell Jar.* New York: Bantan, 1972. 216 pp. *P7/6b*

The Bell Jar was Plath's "autobiographical apprentice work" (213) and on its first publication was well received. The Bantam edition includes a biographical note by Lois Ames that is useful in supplementing *Letters Home.* Of primary interest in Ames' short piece is a 1970 letter written by Aurelia Plath to Harper and Row prior to the book's appearance in America, in which she states: "Practically every character in *The Bell Jar* represents some-one—often in caricature—whom Sylvia loved; . . .as this book stands by itself, it represents the basest ingratitude. . .Sylvia wrote her brother 'that this must never be published in the United States' " (214-215).

Cameron Northouse and Thomas P. Walsh in *Sylvia Plath and Anne Sexton: A Reference Guide* (Boston: G. K. Hall, 1974) provide a good beginning for Plath researchers, and Charles H. Newman's *The Art of Sylvia Plath: A Symposium* (Bloominton, Indiana: Indiana University Press, 1976) has several perceptive essays. *Sylvia Plath: Method and Madness* by Edward Butscher (New York: Seabury Press, 1975) was faulted for utilizing bio-graphical data to excess in the interpreting of Plath's art (Jo Brans, *Southwest Review,* June 1976, p. 325-330). Brans's review covers both *Letters Home* and Butscher's book. A provocative article, "Sylvia Plath Reconsidered" by John Romana appeared in *Commentary*, April 1974, pp. 47-52, exploring reasons for the popularity of *The Bell Jar*. Letters of discussion which followed in both the July and October 1974 issues of *Commentary* were concerned mainly with Plath's use of holocaust imagery.

T. Gail Adams
Emory University, ILA

Polykoff, Shirley (c.1908-   )

Adveritisng Executive

[260] *Does She. . .Or Doesn't She? And How She Did It.* Garden City, New York: Doubleday and Company, 1975. 131 pp.

The title of Polykoff's book alludes to the Clairol account which brought her fame in the advertising world and brought respectability to hair coloring products for women in the middle 1950's. Polykoff's book, warm, chatty and well written, like her advertising copy, originally was conceived as a book on advertising, but became an autobiography as soon as she discovered that her life and career were enmeshed: "everything that has contributed to me as a person has also contributed to the campaigns I write." She tells of various ad campaigns which she created and of corresponding life experiences. For example, one of the questions asked by her future mother-in-law, an Orthodox rabbi's wife who did not approve of hair as an adornment, was "Does she or doesn't she paint her hair?" This statement twenty-three years later launched the Clairol account from $400,000 to thirty-three million for her employer, Foote, Cone and Belding.

Motivated by a strong desire to be a *fardeener*, a wage-earner, the boy that her Russian immigrant mother wanted, she began her career at age eleven working part-time selling coats in the basement of a Brooklyn department store. Eventually she established her own advertising agency after a successful tenure at Foote,

Cone and Belding, the seventh largest agency in the world. Poly-koff is aware that being female and Jewish were not advantages in the advertising world, but she does not dwell on the problem. She tends to view herself as "lucky" and is genuinely surprised that she was able to make it in the industry. She fails to consider that she has been successful in an area of advertising often relegated to women, that of cosmetics and clothing. She also capitalizes on the belief that a woman's identity was inexorably linked with her appearance and reinforces the image of woman as sex object. "Is it true that blondes have more fun?" and "You can be a rich brunette (the kind men marry)" were some of her slogans for the coffers of Clairol. Letty C. Pogrebin notes (New York *Times,* September 14, 1975, p. 36), "When she makes passing reference to unfair treatment of women in business, she is still overjoyed at being the fortunate token. . . . So do not read this book for feminist enlightenment." Polyoff's book is significant for showing a woman who, during an ebb of female awareness, successfully juggled a career in business, a marriage, and children. Along the way she comes to advocate day care centers for children, careers for her daughters, equal pay for women and maintaining one's maiden name after marriage.

Frances Hassencahl
Old Dominion University

Porter, Katherine Anne (1894-   )

Writer

[261] *The Collected Essays and Occasional Writings of Katherine Anne Porter.* New York: Delacorte Press, 1970. 496 pp.

Once asked by a publisher to write an autobiography, Katherine Anne Porter began the task with delight, but after writing about a hundred pages she soon realized the "hideous booby trap" into which she had fallen. She found that she remembered: "quite a lot of stupid and boring things: there were other times when my life seemed merely an endurance test. . . . There are dozens of things that might be entertaining, but I have no intention of telling them, because they are nobody's business. . . . Then, there are. . . the scalding, the bone-breaking events, the lightnings that shatter the landscape of the soul." The latter, however, should be reserved for a secretly written manuscript, one which your executor will read "with love and attention and gently burn it to ashes for your sake."

What Porter has chosen to give us, instead of an extended autobiography, is a group of essays, included in the "Personal and Particular" section of *The Collected Essays.* Here she writes of her girlhood in Texas, her years in Mexico and Europe. In an essay entitled "A House of my Own" she recounts her inability to settle permanently in one place. The selection of essays is random in nature, including a treatment of the failings of the modern marriage, a defense of Ezra Pound in light of his political persecution, and essays which reveal Porter's love of her country through the difficult years of World War II. Even though readers will not find here anything approaching a complete account of the author's life they will see glimpses of her feelings toward her country, the world and her writing.

Glendy Culligan (*Saturday Review,* March 28, 1970, pp. 29-30) finds that, "To each of these finely honed remarks, unfortunately, the present catch-all collection matches one of shrillness or banality." Culligan concludes, "Surely, Miss Porter deserves better of her editors than the license to publish every ill-considered word, when so many of her passages are among the finest that sensitivity has conceived or art contrived." In contrast, Ed Yoder (*Harper's,* March 1970, p. 112) concludes, "In short, there is no dead wringer of salvation in these essays; there is merely the lifetime's contemplation of one's duty to language, to people and places—by our first lady of letters. A wreath for the secular, sensible Miss Porter." And E. C. Bufkin (*Georgia Review,* Summer 1971, pp. 247-52) finds, "As a record of her thinking and feeling, the selections cover a period of almost half a century, and the book is a virtual cornucopia. . . . Every piece is interesting and, taken together, all of them are important, if for no other reason than their being statements, no matter how occasional, of a great artist who, by virtue of that unique trait and power of genius, reveals to us fresh and hitherto unthought-of ways of seeing."

Anne Rowe
Florida State University

Powdermaker, Hortense (1900-1970)

Anthropologist, Author

[262] *Stranger and Friend: The Way of an Anthropologist.* New York: W. W. Norton & Company, 1966. 315 pp.

Stranger and Friend, The Way of an Anthropologist was written by Hortense Powdermaker as an act of service to her profession, to explicate through first-hand experience the process and procedures of the participant-observer method which is at the heart of the anthropologist's practice. The title refers specifically to the integrated "stranger-observer" and "friend-participant" role which all field workers confront and handle in better or worse ways, but that it also refers to Powdermaker's way of dealing with her own life only becomes subtly apparent. The book's purpose is consciously didactic, and she uses the details of her life only as illustrative of the process of becoming and growing as a field worker through cumulative experience, through personal changes, and through changes in the theoretical orientation of anthropology during her professional life. While we learn much about Hortense Powdermaker in this process, we by no means learn all, only what she believes relevant to her purpose.

Powdermaker came from a family of affluent German-Jews and spent most of her early years in Baltimore. She attended Goucher College, where she majored in history and where her Jewishness, with which she only casually identified, served to isolate her socially and to reinforce that sense of alienation which she had always felt in relation to her family. This background and her interest in social problems led her in the 1920's to an active participation in the labor movement as a union organizer and she worked at this with skill, imagination and a great deal of success. She was unwilling, however, to commit her life to the labor movement and, when boredom set in, she went to London and became a student, at first casually and then seriously, at the London School of Economics where she studied under Bronislaw Malinowski, an important anthropologist and brilliant field worker.

After completing her Ph.D., she undertook her first field trip, to New Ireland, and was the first woman to do field work in Melanesia. The experience, published as *Life in Lesu, The Study of a*

Melanesian Society in New Ireland (1933), was highly satisfactory and was, to Powdermaker, the least difficult of any field work she was to do. Several years later she embarked on a much more difficult project, a community study of Blacks and Whites in rural Mississippi, for which her book, *After Freedom, A Cultural Study in the Deep South* (1939), provided a unique document of southern social dynamics in the 1930's. Her casual observations of the effects of movies on shaping southern attitudes came to dominate her subsequent interests, and her next two major projects were involved with the effects of mass communication in conveying cultural patterns. The first of these, a study of the Hollywood film industry, published as *Hollywood, The Dream Factory: An Anthropologist Studies the Movie Makers* (1950) was an unhappy experience and, in her autobiography, Powdermaker explores in depth her dissatisfactions with this project and the difficulties of being a participant-observer in a situation in which she felt an emotional stake and an inability to acquire objectivity. Her last major project, a study of the effects of media on a Black population in northern Rhodesia, was again a new kind of fieldwork, handicapped by a lack of knowledge of the local language and dealing with a large sample not usually associated with anthropological inquiry. On the whole she was pleased with her results and wrote them up as *Copper Town: Changing Africa, The Human Situation on the Rhodesian Copperbelt* (1965). The autobiography ends with an epilogue in which Powdermaker expresses her feelings about the changes in anthropology and the need to retain humanistic values within the context of a growing scientific rigor.

There is much that Powdermaker does not feel is relevant about her life in relation to the purpose of the book and she leaves that out. The division in the critical response to the book directly relates to these omissions. The reception by the social scientific community, particularly by anthropologists, was uniformly enthusiastic and stressed the novel contribution that Powdermaker was making. A. Irving Hallowell (*The Annals of the American Academy,* March 1967, pp. 188-9) explained that this was "a unique, fascinating book for anthropologists have written very, very little about their experiences as field workers." In an extended review, Margaret Mead (*Holiday,* July 1966, pp. 113-5) enthusiastically endorsed it as "a passionate plea for anthropology as a human discipline as well as a science, as an all-engrossing life experience as well as a profession," and Edmund Leach (New York *Review of*

Books, March 9, 1967, p. 28) remarked that the claim by the publisher that the book is a must for all field workers in the social sciences "does not seem to me excessive." The sociologist, Blanche Greer, writing in the *American Sociological Review* (December 1966, p. 895) commented that "disappointing as autobiography and intellectual history, this is a book which will greatly reward everyone interested in field data and their collection."

The response by the non-social science reviewers was uniformly friendly but, like Greer, modified by a sense of the autobiographical omissions. Muriel Haynes (*Saturday Review,* July 23, 1966, pp. 59-60) complained that "her narrative is neither wholly autobiography nor social science. . .her inner life remains closed to us." Jessie Kitching (*Publishers' Weekly,* June 20, 1966, p. 76) called it a "mellow and thoughtful evaluation of a life's work," and George P. Elliott (*Book Week,* July 31, 1966, p. 13) summed up his feelings by saying, "In plain English, despite her vigorous efforts to depersonalize and case-history herself, she comes through as a woman you'd like for a friend."

Hortense Powdermaker was always a bit of a stranger to her world and the world of American anthropology. That she was also a friend was shown by the tributes to her when she died. Eric Wolf (*American Anthropologist,* Vol. 73, 1971, p. 785) ended his by writing, "To commemorate her passing a cocktail party was held in her living room. She would have liked it that way."

Diane Broadatz Rothenberg
Encinitas, California

Previn, Dory (1929-   )

Composer, Lyricist, Author

[263] *Midnight Baby: An Autobiography.* New York: Macmillan Publishing Company, Inc., 1976. 245 pp.

In the preface to her autobiography, Dory Previn writes, "I

don't think I wrote this book. I think I wrote it down. For someone. . .I used to be. As she demanded it be told." *Midnight Baby*
deals with approximately the first ten years of Dory Previn's life,
and it is told from a child's point of view and with a child's innocence. Her parents were strict Irish Catholics whose dissatisfaction
with each other found its battleground quite frequently in the
manner in which they treated their first born child, Dory. Her
father had been gassed during World War I and had been told by an
army doctor that he might be sterile. As a result of this experience, her father doubted that Dory was his child and alternately
rejected and accepted his daughter. She found she could please
her father by acting out his fantasies that his daughter was a child
star like Shirley Temple. Dory sang and danced; then, in her
father's eyes, she was his daughter. Her mother's passivity kept
her from expressing her anger to her husband. This anger was then
directed to her daughter. Throughout the book, the child does not
take sides, but the confusion and pain of trying to please both
parents make her question herself and develop doubts and fears
about love and God. Her father's manic-depressive states culminate
when, at the birth of his second daughter, he boarded up his wife,
Dory, and infant daughter in the dining room of their home. There
they remained for several months. When Dory went to school, she
was threatened not to tell how her family was living. She begins to
hate her mother for letting herself and her children live imprisoned;
yet, when her father's sister intervenes to end the abuse, the little
girl is afraid to come out of the dining room with her mother and
baby sister, preferring the imprisoned life to freedom. It is ironic
that Dory Previn dedicated this book to her parents.

Clara Delores King
Campbell College School of Law
Buies Creek, N. C.

Priest, Ivy Baker (1905-   )

Former Teasurer of United States

[264] *Green Grows Ivy.* New York: McGraw-Hill, 1958. 270
    pp.

Green Grows Ivy is an account of a woman's life from childhood in a Utah mining town to her second term as Treasurer of the United States. Priest recalls her family's financial problems and their constant threat of disaster due to her father's work in the coal mines. She remembers her gangling adolescence, an unfortunate first marriage, and the problems involved in making a success of her second marriage while engaged in an active political career. She believes in the importance of a close family unit if a woman is to have a successful career, and tells how this allowed both her and her mother to be active in politics. Solutions to the many personal misfortunes while active in her career are also narrated.

Priest discusses the basics of party organization on both a local and a national level. She strongly states that if properly organized, women can be a political force and reach the goals they set out to accomplish.

As a *Kirkus* review states, *Green Grows Ivy* is naively written in a style that does not do justice to the author. The book's main value is to those interested in political organization and political rewards.

Robert Melanson
Old Dominion University

Proxmire, Ellen (-)

Politician's Wife, Mother

[265] *One Foot in Washington: The Perilous Life of a Senator's Wife.* Washington, D.C.: Robert B. Luce, Inc., 1963. 175 pp.

Ellen Proxmire limits her account to the early years of her husband's career as a Senator, which began in 1957. Revealing little of her life before 1957, except to mention two children by a previous marriage which ended in divorce, she stresses her service as a handmaiden to her husband's political career. Quoting and endorsing a statement attributed to Mrs. Warren G. Harding, "I have only one hobby—my husband," she provides us with a description of the taxing life of a Senator, occasionally letting us glimpse the taxing life of his spouse, all with the proper modesty of a hand-maiden.

Proxmire uncomplainingly juggles the multitudinous duties of a mother and a politician's wife. She mentions the difficulties of finding a house in Washington without a husband's help, moving her family, raising four children, bearing two more, one who died shortly after birth—and this is told with a startling stoicism—cooking two sets of suppers, one for the children and one for the unpredictable husband. Only once does she indulge in admission of her talents, suggesting that domestic problems can be as catastrophic as those on the Hill. For the most part, devotion to duty is expressed, with apologies that she doesn't fix her husband's breakfast or that she calls in a girl to wash dishes during dinner parties for political big-wigs.

Most of *One Foot in Washington* emphasizes Proxmire's politically-related duties, which are varied—campaigning, entertaining, answering mail, giving speeches, doing interviews on television and radio (which she shies from), filling in as secretary, and supervising the Senator's Washington office when he is in Wisconsin. Proxmire claims that Washington grew less rigid in social expectations for officials in the early sixties, but her details indicate that any innovation was still viewed with suspicion. For instance, she makes much of her defiance of convention by serving dinner at 7:30 rather than the standard 8 p.m. She also reveals that she is obliged to participate in charity work, as befits the wife of a Senator. If the weekly Red Cross bandage rolling meetings for Senator's wives yields friendships and if the luncheons at the White House are glamorous, these are only incidental bonuses to her unpaid obligations as a Senator's wife.

Proxmire treads cautiously in her autobiography, careful not to brag about her incredible supportive endeavors. One must read between the lines to grasp her strength and achievement at being the strong woman behind a successful man.

Karen J. Blair
California Institute of Technology

Randall, Margaret (1936-   )

Poet, Translator, Journalist

[266] *Part of the Solution: Portrait of a Revolutionary.* New York: New Directions, 1973. 192 pp.

The Margaret Randall who emerges rather reticently from these pages is a fascinating and unusual woman: she is a poet, editor, revolutionary, midwife, mother of four children by three different men, expatriate, sugar cane harvester and valued friend. Daughter of upper-middle class Jewish parents, whose lifestyle was decidedly privileged and bohemian, she and her family early emigrated from Scarsdale to Albuquerque where Margaret became both a Protestant and a Job's Daughter in a desperate attempt to fit in. She married at eighteen a wealthy young man who beat her up if she moved or spoke during love making. In the late fifties she moved to New York, tried to become a writer and knew people like the de Koonings and Robert Creeley.

In 1961 Randall went to Mexico, where, with her second husband (another "hater of women"), she edited and published an increasingly radical bilingual literary magazine. Interested in feminist issues but unable to meet women with whom she could discuss them, she compiled an anthology of documents from the U. S. Women's Liberation movement, wrote the introduction and published it in Spanish. In 1967, after a trip to Cuba, she ended her oppressive marriage and determined to "make Revolution." Afraid she'd be imprisoned or murdered by Mexican authorities, she fled in 1969 to Cuba with her children and third husband, Robert Cohen. There she lives, in a decadent pre-Revolutionary home whose amenities include chandeliers in the bathrooms, and works, mostly as a writer and political leader, but occasionally and enthusiastically as part of a sugar-cane work brigade. Her children are more doctrinaire than she.

This miscellany of poems, prose pieces, and journal entries received some reviews that were critical of Randall's political commitments, particularly of her adulation of Castro. Yet a reviewer who was "disposed to sympathize" said that her vision "frequently comes in strong and true," despite its "familiar paradisal excesses" (*New Republic,* May 12, 1973, p. 31).

One-third of Randall's book is taken over by her husband's prefatory comments, which give the only personal glimpses of her. The bulk of her journal and even some of her one hundred pages of poetry are relentlessly public and political. Some poems, however, are more intimate, less ideological, and hence more faithful to experience, for instance, one haunting poem deals with the shocking suicide of a five-year-old girl, inexplicably determined to hurl herself out a window in green Edenic Cuba. Even though Randall avoids self-revelation, the woman who emerges in the journal and poems seems stronger, more human and complex, than the woman her husband introduces.

Jonna Gormely Semeiks
Queens College, CUNY

Rawlings, Marjorie Kinnan (1896-1953)

Regionalist

[267] *Cross Creek.*   New York: Charles Scribner's Sons, 1942. 368 pp.

Affirming that "we cannot live without the earth or apart from it," Marjorie Kinnan Rawlings' book charts her thirteen-year experience at Cross Creek, Florida, a place with "such beauty and grace that, once entangled with it, no other place seems possible to us, just as when truly in love none other offers the comfort of the beloved." Having bought the Florida orange grove with an inheritance from her father, she and her husband came from New York in 1928 to begin the new venture. (It is noteworthy that she makes no mention of her husband in this volume, although he did accompany her and stayed at the Creek a short while.) Sustained and enriched by the beauty of both the people and the land, she discovers that she and the other residents of "the Creek draw our conclusions about the world from our intimate knowledge of one small portion of it." Her zoological descriptions, pervaded with an aura of beauty, are products of her keen scientific observation. The book progresses through random episodes rich with character and story, treatises on the profusion of flora and fauna, topographical studies, a tract on the seasons, and a regional cookbook, as well. Her friends and neighbors function as folk heroines and heroes: Aunt Martha Mickens with "her face like poured chocolate" who at the Creek was "the shuttle that has woven our knowledge" of local happenings, both present and past; and Marsh Turner, "a man peaceable at heart and definitely a gentleman," whom the sheriff mistakenly shot when Marsh innocently offered him a gift, quietly, stating, "Sheriff, this here gun is for you." All these threads form the design in the tapestry of the Cross Creek that sustained Marjorie Kinnan Rawlings and she emerges a strong, vigorous, independent, and creative woman secure as a part of the continuous chain, the "cycle of life," in which birth and death merge "one into the other in an imperceptible twilight and an insubstantial dawn."

The first literary offering from Marjorie Kinnan Rawlings after winning the Pulitzer Prize for her novel, *The Yearling, Cross Creek* was met in 1942 with critical acclaim, named a Book-of-the-Month Selection, and placed on the Best Seller list; however, for three decades thereafter, literary critics' interest in both the book and in the author seemed to lie fallow. A review by Clifton Fadiman in the *New Yorker* (March 21, 1942, p. 60) summarizes many of the early responses: "The central fact about her is that she is a mystic. Beneath the pawky and tender humor, the sharp, almost New Englandish eye for character, the sturdy common sense, the womanly interest in the baking of a pie, the highly agreeable Rabelaisian vein revealed in *Cross Creek*—beneath all this is a deep-rooted love of the earth, without which her books would be merely little masterpieces of local color and nothing more." Almost no further criticism appeared until 1966, when Gordon Bigelow, in his in-depth literary biography, *Frontier Eden* (Gainesville, Florida: University of Florida Press, 1966), explored various aspects of her personal and professional life; he identifies what she called her "nightmare. . .the masochistic human mind" as the condition "now fashionably called existential despair" which afflicted her contemporaries, Hemingway, Fitzgerald, and Faulkner, who—like Rawlings —"also used alcohol to moderate the pain they felt" (65-66). On a literary level, Bigelow indicts her for producing "no female character of distinction" (157); however, her creations, Martha Mickens, 'Geechee, Dessie, and the Widow Slater stand in direct contradiction to this assessment. Samuel Bellman in *Marjorie Kinnan Rawlings* (New York: Twayne Publishers, Inc., 1974) offers no new insights; his observations closely parallel those previously published.

In a study based upon Rawlings' personal papers, housed in the University of Florida Archives ("Marjorie Kinnan Rawlings: A Study in the Rhetorical Effectiveness of a Novel," Diss. University of Florida, Gainesville, 1977), Edna Saffy finds substantial evidence of Rawlings' skill as an accomplished craftsperson who created the rhetorical effect she intended, in accordance with her personal theory of composition. Thus, *Cross Creek* offers not only broad avenues of exploration, but also provides specific insights into the personal, social, economic, and literary development of a woman.

Edna Saffy
Florida Junior College at Jacksonville

Rich, Adrienne (1929-   )

Poet, Teacher

[268] *Of Woman Born: Motherhood as Experience and Institution.* New York: W. W. Norton and Company, 1976. 318 pp.

In *Of Woman Born* Adrienne Rich weaves her own experience of motherhood and the history of this institution in a single complex story. Since she contends that her life is representative, she treats autobiography and women's history together, alternately drawing upon historical analysis and personal reminiscence, periodically culling from her diary, literature, myth, art and social history. Personal and women's history serve as her politics. Rich argues that the institution of motherhood is the work of a patriarchal conspiracy, and her purpose in nothing less than the transvaluation of values: the destruction of patriarchal power, "the repossession by women of their bodies," and the re-definition and strengthening of relationships between women.

Rich has rejected the conventional form of autobiography, the linear narrative, in favor of a thematic organization. Her design allows her to group personal recollection, political appeal and historical survey under single chapter headings, thus underscoring the conjunction of three subjects: autobiography, feminist politics, and women's history.

First, she investigates mothers' anger and tenderness toward their children, the first emotion prohibited and the second prescribed by patriarchal society, and shows how the home evolved as an isolated unit for mother and child, set off from the work world and from male power. She then defines and traces the idea of patriarchy and women's relationship to it. Once she identifies what has been meant by the feminine principle throughout history, she claims for women's historical awareness of themselves the power to change values, and she attends to a number of themes worthy of historical understanding: for example, various myths of pre-patriarchal goddess-cults, menstrual taboos, and symbolic representations of women in nature; the domestication of motherhood in the Victorian family; the history of obstetrics (a practice usurped from the hands of women by the male medical profession); attitudes toward childbirth; and mother-child bonds.

Rich writes at length about her own life. She sees through and beyond her own experience of labor pains to women's need to participate actively in childbirth, and she envisions a new kind of rapport between mother and son through having raised three sons of her own. But the center of her book is mothers and daughters: "This is the core of my book, and I enter it as a women who, born between her mother's legs, has time after time and in different ways tried to return to her mother, to repossess her and be repossessed by her, to find the mutual confirmation from and with another woman that daughters and mothers alike hunger for, pull away from, make possible or impossible for each other" (218).

Rich taps a well of ambivalent, fierce emotions that she has felt for her mother, emotions raised to the surface when she herself gave birth to her first child and her accompanying feelings of maternal guilt. She identifies the difficulty of writing about her subject: "I struggle to describe what it felt like to be her daughter, but I find myself divided, slipping under her skin; a part of me identifies too much with her" (223-224). And while she angrily addresses a patriarchal society that deems "mother daughter rapture" inconsequential, she calls for a new bond of trust and tenderness between women.

Jill Tweedie (*Saturday Review,* November 13, 1976, pp. 28-31) contends that Rich's discussion of mothers and daughters should make *Of Woman Born* "a vital addition to a feminist library." Francine du Plessix Gray (New York *Times,* October 10, 1976, pp. 3-13) considers the work a mixed success: "When Rich draws from her own life. . .she reaches moments of great poignancy and eloquence. When she writes about 'motherhood as an institution'. . . the intensity of her rage against men" results in "vituperative prose that is not worthy of one of our finest poets."

Janis Forman
Goucher College

Rinehart, Mary Roberts (1876-1958)

Journalist, Playwright, Novelist

[269] *My Story: A New Edition and Seventeen New Years.* New York: Rinehart & Company, Inc., 1948. 570 pp.

Originally published in 1931 as *My Story,* Rinehart's present autobiography is a reprint of the 1931 volume (432 pp.) with twenty chapters added. Rinehart recounts a happy childhood in Pittsburgh, but also notes episodes of violence; for instance, her father committed suicide before a mirror in 1895. At seventeen she entered Pittsburgh Training School for Nurses, where she worked for two years in the Tenderloin, there meeting her husband, Dr. Stanley M. Rinehart, who eventually became her business manager until his death in 1932. Two of their three sons became the "Rinehart" of the New York City publishing world. Beginning writing professionally around 1903 after her husband's finances were destroyed in a stock market panic, Rinehart speaks of herself always as a craftsman rather than as an artist. She details early attempts at playwriting, and association with New York theatrical figures such as David Belasco. With the outbreak of World War I, she went to Europe as a journalist, managing through stubbornness and guile to spend several weeks in the Belgium trenches, scoring many triumphs: She was the first woman to go on a night patrol in No-Man's Land, first journalist to interview the Belgium king in regard to German atrocities, first journalist to interview Queen Mary of England. In the summer of 1915 she made a horse-back trip through Glacier Park, the first of many excursions in the wilderness of North America and other areas of the world. In the period between the wars, she continued her writing—short-stories, plays, articles, novels, mystery stories; worked briefly off and on in Hollywood; made with her husband a home for her invalid mother; and, living in Washington, commented extensively on both the social and political life of the time. She had been a friend of Teddy Roosevelt, and knew personally all the U. S. presidents from Woodrow Wilson to Franklin Roosevelt. She served as "First" or "Only Woman" on various governmental commissions dealing with matters ranging from Conservation and Naval Rearmament during World War I to crime (after publishing an article called "Can Women Stop Crime?"). While not using the term, Rinehart shows an awareness that her presence on most of these commissions was tokenism, since most dealt with matters about which she knew nothing. She describes in great detail a number of family experiences involving apparent psychic phenomena, interesting enough that she was eventually interviewed in 1938 by Dr. J. B. Rhine, the ESP specialist from Duke University. She describes at first hand many of the historical events of this time, emphasizing life in Washington during the Depression. Her comments about the rise of Fascism, Naziism, and Communism are clearly influenced by her own war experiences: she hates wars made by old men for young men to fight (p. 332), yet she believes wars to be inevitable, and believes that isolationists court disaster for the country. In 1937 she underwent a radical mastectomy, and eventually permitted the story of the experience to be published in *Ladies' Home Journal,* in hopes that it would help other women. The book ends with two more incidents in the patterns of violence in her life: the loss of her summer home in Bar Harbor to fire and her narrow escape from being murdered by a trusted family servant gone berserk.

The book is filled with matters of interest to women's studies. In addition to the personal accomplishments, Rinehart discusses: the status and roles of women—comments beginning about 1880's and continuing to mid 20th century—both in U.S. and in countries she visited in Europe, Russia, and the Mid-East; she comments on the liberating influence of the bicycle, adolescent courtship customs of her youth, the problems involved for a woman in having both a successful career and a successful marriage and family; the kind of equal partnership she feels necessary between husband and wife; the problems of a man married to an independently successful woman; the changing relationship between mother and sons as the sons grow to manhood; the relationship between a daughter and an elderly, infirm parent; childbirth, in regard to what male doctors would or would not do to ease the mother's suffering; widowhood. She touches only briefly on the Suffragette Movement (for example, an interview with Alice Paul at a political convention in 1916), in which she played but a minor role. She consistently reiterates the statement, "I'm not a Feminist. I simply believe that men and women should be equal."

The book, particularly the first volume, is effectively written, demonstrating many of the stylistic techniques familiar to readers of Rinehart's mysteries, the teasing use of foreshadowing for suspense, and a wry, self-deprecating humor. The second volume, written in 1948, is somewhat repetitious of the first, and less well organized chronologically, therefore harder to follow. All in all, hers is a fascinating story.

My Story received consistently favorable reviews, with the 1931 volume being more widely noticed than the 1948 edition. The reviews particularly praise Rinehart's honesty and candor and her unwillingness to sensationalize a life story which would easily lend itself to such treatment. Uffington Valentine, in a New York *Times* review (March 15, 1931, p. 5) speaks of her "admirable spontaneity." Writing in the *Saturday Review of Literature* (January 8, 1949, pp. 19-20), Pamela Taylor says *My Story* "brings us up to date on an exceptional woman for whom life is still a pleasure, a challenge, and a privilege."

Jean R. Halladay
Old Dominion University

Rivers, Caryl (1938-   )

Newspaper Reporter, Television Commentator, Teacher

[270] *Aphrodite at Mid-century: Growing up Catholic and Female in Post-war America.* Garden City, New York: Doubleday and Company, 1973. 283 pp.

Aphrodite at Mid-century is a series of light, candid biographical essays. Born in 1938, Rivers' opening chapter relates that her earliest memory "is of Pearl Harbor." She, her father and her mother, "an average American family in 1941" lived in Silver Spring, Maryland, a suburb of Washington, D.C. and at that time quite rural. How "average" the family was is debatable: both her parents were successful lawyers. To Rivers, at four, the war "offered small adventures." Her father volunteered for the Navy and the family followed him to Alabama for the duration of the war. Rivers' brother was born soon after.

Rivers is of the "BEAT-Before Everybody Acquired Television" generation. As a youngster she and her neighborhood pals formed clubs, read Wonder Woman and attended the Saturday afternoon movies. She also attended parochial school from the third grade. Rivers says that "growing up Catholic in mid-century America was both absurd and marvelous. Absurd because as I look back from a distance of some twenty years, I see a world of changeless truth, simple moral choices, and nodding assent that seems as distant from contemporary reality as the age when cross breasted crusaders whacked heathen skulls in the name of Jesus Christ." And it was "marvelous because the theology presented to the Catholic child could have sprung from the gentle brain of Walt Disney." Further chapters in the book describe: Catholic school sports; hitting puberty; the never-never land of 1950's movie stars; attending the convent school; reading "dirty paperbacks;" living according to glamour magazines; attending Trinity College in Washington; and finally, marrying out of the faith.

Most reviewers liked Rivers' style and content. *Christian Century* magazine (September 26, 1973, p. 953) described Rivers' work as a "bittersweet exercise in Catholic Nostalgia." *Library Journal* (September 15, 1973, p. 2543) also advises that "Rivers' commentary, sometimes critical, on Catholic education during (the 1950's) may offend more conservative Catholics;" but that Rivers writes "in an amusing and interesting style." Wilfred Sheed in The New York *Review of Books* (March 7, 1974, p. 19) appears to not like her light treatment of her Catholic upbringing.

John Druska writing in *Commonweal* (January 11, 1974, p. 369-371) is highly critical: "Caryl Rivers' memoirs. . .of a peculiarly female-Catholic girlhood at 'mid-century'. . .doesn't work for me in more than a pedestrian, sometimes faintly amusing fashion" (p. 369). Druska, quite obviously, did not "grow up female" and appears to have missed Rivers' major points. One can not help feeling that he was reacting to Rivers' "uppitty" style and content, that she just didn't know when to stay "in her place." What is so relevant for women's studies here is that despite the mediocrity and stifling atmosphere of mid-century America Caryl Rivers did in fact 'make it'.

Jean B. Palmer
Stoneham Public Library, Stoneham, Mass.

Roberts, Jane (-   )

Medium, Novelist, Poet

[271] *The Coming of Seth.*   Original Title, *How to Develop Your ESP Power.* New York: Frederick Fell, 1966. Rpt. Pocket Books, 252 pp.

The Coming of Seth traces the development of Jane Roberts' interest in parapsychology, which in turn led to her discovery of latent mediumistic abilities. While experimenting with the ouija board Roberts was nagged by her foreknowledge of the board's answers, given by a "personality" who called himself Seth. Eventually she did speak Seth's words, beginning what has become, to date (1977), a fourteen-year collaboration between herself as medium, her husband Rob, as translator, and the energy-essence personality Seth.

The book was originally designed as a "how to" book on parapsychology with Roberts' own expriences serving as models for the readers. Accordingly, she recounts her successful attempts with seances, precognitive and clairvoyant dreams, telepathy, etc. More interestingly, this book relates her discomfort with Seth's claims of being a distinct, "otherworldly" entity, her doubts about her sanity and her attempts to reconcile these bizzare events with her "normal" lifestyle. Thus, *The Coming of Seth* and her next book, *The Seth Material,* become a kind of manifesto of the psychic uncertainty that besets all individuals who have supra-normal talents.

[272] *The Seth Material.* Englewood Cliffs, New Jersey: Prentice-Hall, 1970. 333 pp.

The Seth Material continues what Roberts herself calls the "continuing saga" of her mediumistic relationship with the energy-essence personality, Seth. The first portion of the book summarizes her first encounters with Seth and the establishment of their twice-weekly sessions. The remainder of the book, aside from providing excerpts from the Seth sessions, discusses her attempts to "legitimize" her experiences by contacting psychologists and parapsychologists (few of whom gave her any moral or psychic support) and by subjecting Seth to a battery of psychological tests to determine his telepathic and clairvoyant abilities. Roberts discovers that, during her out-of-trance states, her own parapsychological abilities have grown to include, among other things, astral projection. Through these in-and-out-of trance states evolves Roberts' faith in her own sanity and in Seth as a bona fide separate personality.

[273] *Seth Speaks: The Eternal Validity of the Soul.* Englewood Cliffs, New Jersey: Prentice-Hall, 1972. 486 pp.

[274] *The Nature of Personal Reality: A Seth Book.* Englewood Cliffs, New Jersey: Prentice-Hall, 1974. 516 pp.

Both *Seth Speaks* and *The Nature of Personal Reality* were dictated by Seth through Jane Roberts; her introductions, summarizing and explaining her relationship with Seth are the only strictly "personal" elements in these books. As she herself states in her "Introduction" to *The Nature of Personal Reality:* "I'm proud to publish this book under my own name, though I don't fully understand the mechanics of its production or the nature of the personality I assume in delivering it. I had no conscious work to do on the book at all. I simply went into trance twice a week, spoke in a 'mediumistic' capacity for Seth, or as Seth, and dictated the words to my husband, Robert Butts, who wrote them down."

Cynthia L. Walker
University of Alaska—Fairbanks

Roosevelt, Eleanor (1884-1962)

Stateswoman

[275] *This Is My Story.* New York: Harper, 1937. 365 pp.

[276] *My Days.* New York: Dodge, 1938. 254 pp.

[277] *This I Remember.* New York: Harper, 1949. 387 pp.

[278] *On My Own.* New York: Harper, 1958. 241 pp.

[279] *The Autobiography of Eleanor Roosevelt.* New York: Harper, 1961. 454 pp.

Eleanor Roosevelt is the greatest stateswoman and one of the greatest statespersons this country has ever known. A mere record of her achievements would justify itself in any feminist library. And much of Eleanor Roosevelt's autobiography is just that—a mere record of events. But there is also a recurrent theme that informs these volumes. That theme is the evolution of a "lady" into a liberated woman.

This Is My Story begins the evolution with an account of the training that left Eleanor Roosevelt totally unprepared for living in her own home, let alone the real world. Despite an education abroad and the proper breeding, she entered marriage with no idea how to manage a household or children. Her mother-in-law, Sara Delano Roosevelt, was all too prepared to step in and take over. Because of Eleanor's basic insecurity, Sara Delano was able to dominate the household until the young Roosevelts moved to Albany, after Franklin's election to the state senate.

What Eleanor had been trained for was duty—duty to husband and children. She never questions that her husband should be the center of her life. Franklin's election to the state senate, his appointment as Assistant Secretary of the Navy, and his vice-presidential nomination in 1920 elicit no personal response from her; she simply accepts the fact that her life is not her own: "while I was always a part of the public aspect of our lives, still I felt detached and objective, as though I were looking at someone else's life" (*The Autobiography,* p. 107). But despite the fact that it was her husband's career that defined and determined her life, the very nature of his career (and later the nature of his disability) created opportunities for her to become independent. One of the most important opportunities was the chance to know Louis Howe, FDR's adviser, for he recognized Eleanor's potential for politics and helped her develop that potential—even if he did have the ulterior motive of furthering Franklin's presidential hopes. This first volume ends with her participation in the Democratic Convention of 1924 which nominated Al Smith.

Eleanor Roosevelt very consciously applies the theme of evolution in *This Is My Story;* she continually refers to her lack of confidence and to her gains in independence. Yet she rarely refers to the pain or struggle behind her search for identity. Although she tells us the only emotion she felt at her mother's death was excitement at the chance to see her father, we must turn to Joseph Lash's biography to find out that her mother had rejected her because she was not beautiful. Although she tells us that she grew up in a constant state of fear—fear of displeasing people and of failing—she does not complain of her joyless childhood. Although she resents her mother-in-law's domination (according to her biographers), no resentment seeps into these pages. Although FDR's paralysis must have been a great shock to the marriage and family relations, we see none of the emotional strain and none of the emotional adjustments. This volume was, of course, being written during her husband's presidency, when public images would have to have been taken into account. In fact, James

Roosevelt says in *My Parents: A Differing View* (1976) that his father ruthlessly edited his mother's book (p. 179). Another factor is the sensibility of the times themselves, which is perhaps best reflected in the reviews that praised the book for its openness and good taste.

This I Remember covers FDR's governorship and presidency. Eleanor opens this volume with the self-effacing assumption that the public will surely be more interested in her husband than in herself. Although much of the volume is organized around the presidency, Eleanor Roosevelt the woman is never intimidated by the role of First Lady. Far from being impressed by the new prestige, she is depressed by the prospects of giving up the teaching career that had given her a certain degree of financial and psychological independence, to assume the duties of a glorified hostess. True to her sense of duty, however, it never occurred to her to offer her opinions on the matter to her husband. Yet once again, her husband's career broadened her own experience. In 1935 she began the daily column she would continue until her death. As her husband's good will ambassador (she gives herself no credit for being an adviser), she made many domestic and foreign trips. In her spare time she even managed to write a few books, though she tells us nothing of these independent enterprises. In fact, from her own account of those years in the White House one would never know that Eleanor Roosevelt was as controversial a figure in her own right as FDR. Surprisingly, Eleanor Roosevelt did not see her achievements as her own, as the conclusion of this section of *The Autobiography* (p. 280) makes painfully clear. "On the whole, I think I lived those years very impersonally. It was almost as though I had erected someone outside myself who was the President's wife. I was lost somewhere deep down inside myself. That is the way I felt and worked until I left the White House." One can only wonder at her implacable sense of duty and the compromises it must have demanded—to so alienate her from her own rightful accomplishments, diplomatic and political.

All reviews of *This I Remember* pay tribute to the greatness of Eleanor Roosevelt. This personal greatness, in turn, seems to automatically confer value upon the autobiogarphy itself. Opinion does divide fairly evenly, however, on the issue of how much of the woman is revealed in these pages.

In *On My Own,* Eleanor Roosevelt details her career at the United Nations—first as a U. S. representative to the organization meeting of the U. N., then as delegate to the U. N. and Chairperson of the Human Rights Commission. Her overriding consideration is Communist Russia—how she herself must deal with their disruptive tactics at the U. N., and how U. S. foreign policy must deal with their pervasive influence in the underdeveloped world. The striking difference between Russian and U. S. influence, as she emphasizes it, is that Russia exports Marxist philosophy as well as technology, whereas the U. S. consistently neglects to promote the morality of democracy along with its material achievement. Her diplomatic insights are very persuasive and her moral vision inspiring, yet personal narrative is lost inside the political essay. As was the case with *This I Remember,* the reviews praise the woman, rather than evaluate the autobiography.

There are two other autobiographical volumes: *My Days,* a reprint of Eleanor Roosevelt's daily newspaper column; and *The Autobiography of Eleanor Roosevelt,* an edited version of the three earlier volumes, plus an updated final section, "The Search for Understanding." Reviews of *My Days* were mixed. Some gave token recognition to the coherence of the volume and its positive reflection of the character of Mrs. Roosevelt, though no one found the book contributing anything significant to either history or autobiography. The reviews of the *Autobiography* praised the political achievements and vision of the woman, and noted, some favorably and others not as favorably, the absence of literary achievement and style. The editing eliminated interesting but inessential personal anecdotes, a few political observations that were no longer expedient during the Cold War, and some insights into herself that she obviously felt would not be important to posterity. "The Search for Understanding" continues with the theme of America's responsibility to offer moral leadership to the world by living up to its own principles both at home and abroad. Her seventy-fifth birthday, however, is the occasion for some personal assessments. As she looks over her life, she comments on the sense of duty that inhibited her personal development until middle age. Now in old age, personal objectives have long since blended into public ones—primarily her hope for world peace.

Even readers with the greatest respect for Eleanor Roosevelt's politics must wish that she had spent more time dealing with the private woman behind the public figure. Clearly there is much that was painful in her life: a mother who rejected her; an alcoholic father and brother; a son who died in infancy; a domineering mother-in-law; and a husband whose private and public choices both diminished and developed her potential, but always defined her identity until his death. An understanding of what she had to work through is essential to an understanding of who she became. That is why Joseph Lash's biographies, *Eleanor and Franklin* (1971) and *Eleanor, The Years Alone* (1972) are much more satisfying than the autobiography. However, like many autobiographies, Eleanor Roosevelt's tells much by what it leaves untold. As for what it does tell, her contributions to the causes of world peace and human rights, both at home and abroad, they speak for themselves.

Sandra Hunt
Norfolk State University

Rosenberg, Ethel (1915-1953) and Julius (1918-1953)

Convicted of Spying and Executed

[280] *Death House Letters.* New York: Jero Publishing, 1953. 168 pp.

In an emotional and controversial trial in 1951, Ethel and Julius Rosenberg were convicted of conspiracy to commit espionage on charges of passing atomic secrets to the Russians and later put to death in the electric chair. Their correspondence from their arrest in 1950 until shortly before they were executed in 1953 are contained in *Death House Letters.* (A slightly expanded edition was published in 1954 with the title *Testament of Ethel and Julius Rosenberg.*)

Their young children's immediate problems and future welfare filled most of their letters. On advice of social workers, the Rosenbers did not at first permit their children to visit them in prison fearing permanent emotional damage. Ethel described the separation as a "terrible ache and longing that relentlessly pursues me"

(54). Later, visits were permitted. Custody problems arose; the children were shuffled from a children's shelter, to the Rosenbergs' parents, to a family outside of the New York area, and they did develop emotional problems. Their five year old son, for instance, stopped talking in complete sentences. The letters also expressed the minor joys of parenthood: a birthday card from their son, a second place finish at a swimming meet and a child's birthday party. Their comments show that such parental joys were heightened and yet at the same time the couple's sorrows were intensified by their separation from each other and from their children.

Their separation from each other and from their children provides the dominant topics for the letters. The book contains love letters and expressions of longing for each other. Throughout their imprisonment the couple sustained a warm and supportive wife-husband relationship. And after eighteen months in prison, Julius wrote to Ethel that he "marvelled at the growth of our relationship here in these surroundings" (118).

Very few of their letters contained references to the appeals process, rallies held in their behalf, and petitions for clemency made for them. Even fewer letters expressed anything about the couple's political or social ideas.

Little notice was given to the publication of either of the couple's *Letters.*

Ted Kruse
Annapolis, Md.

Rosenthal, Jean (1912-1969)

Lighting Director

[281] *The Magic of Light.* Boston: Little, Brown and Company, 1972. 256 pp.

The Magic of Light is both an autobiographical and technical book "written" by Jean Rosenthal on a tape recorder while she was in the final stages of her terminal illness, too weak to tend to her professional work. Later edited and collated by Lael Wertenbaker, it describes primarily her professional history in the theatre in the technical area long dominated by men. Complete with a separate photo essay which demonstrates principles of lighting, it also details, with descriptions and lighting charts, her contributions to the development of stage lighting through such major shows as *Plaza Suite* and *Hello Dolly*. Her treatment is primarily chronological but only occasionally personal. What emerges from *The Magic of Light* is the portrait of a professional person profoundly fascinated by the aesthetic medium of light, in which she could see an artistic potential not yet realized on the American or European stage.

Jean Rosenthal's book is important to women's studies because she deals, although only briefly, with her problems as a woman in a "man's domain." She devotes a few revealing paragraphs about her means of coping with the male-dominated technical field: "To overcome rude prejudice, I used courtesy. . . . I also cultivated a careful impersonality, which disregarded sex, in spite of the 'dears' and 'darlings'. . . . My only real weapon, though, in the battle for acceptance was knowledge. I did know my stuff and I knew that the technicians knew theirs" (35-56). She goes on to comment about the even more rigid sexist attitudes of male and female European theatre people. These attitudes, however, distressing as they must have been, are overshadowed by her fascination with the history of illumination, and the varying demands of lighting everything from the house to the stage, from drama to opera and dance.

Rosenthal's book is as much a technical treatise as an autobiography. To some extent, her profession would seem to be her biography: "Light is quite tactile to me. It has shape and dimension. It has an edge. . . . I have always objected to the usual reading of the great line from Genesis. . . . It is read: 'God said, Let there be light, and there was light.' It should be read: 'God said, let there be light, and there was LIGHT'" (39). Such a joyous professional committment speaks as loudly as any direct words of protest about her upward struggle in a masculine field.

Although *The Magic of Light* received no significant critical commentary, it was mentioned in *Best Sellers* and *Library Journal* because of its successful presentation of an aesthetic field which can only be judged successful when it goes unnoticed by audiences.

Jean Klein
Old Dominion University

St. Denis, Ruth (1878-1968)

Dancer, Choreographer, Teacher

[282] *An Unfinished Life: An Autobiography.* Brooklyn, New York: A Dance Horizons Republication, 1969. 391 pp.

An Unfinished Life, dedicated to "the hovering spirit of my mother," is Ruth St. Denis' chronicle of her life as a dancer and the spiritual philosophies that shaped her dance. Using a chronological narrative, St. Denis writes of her childhood as "an exceedingly boyish person" who did not begin dance lessons until age ten. Accompanied by her mother, who played a dominant role in the dancer's life, St. Denis moved to New York at age sixteen in order to further her career. After stints as a stunt dancer in vaudeville, she won fame in Belasco's production of *Zaza.* Her art and technique grew but she remained emotionally immature with "a strange aversion to what I thought sex to be, which drove me back into that dreamland of delicate and vague longings" (51). Her search for release in both dance and self was aided by her conversion to Christian Science and a psychic identification with the Orient. At thirty-five she met Ted Shawn, a dancer many years her junior and they were married against her mother's will. She comments on the difficulty of telling "of this strange marriage so that it will not betray the depths and problems of Ted's life. . .nor unveil my perplexities and sin at the expenses of his" but she adds "it is one of the really great love stories" (156).

An Unfinished Life was written while St. Denis was separated from Shawn in an attempt "to find out where the trouble lies" (152) and she advises that she has "never achieved a reconciliation between my life as an individual artist and my heart as a woman. In this fact lay the seeds of personal sorrow" (209). She writes frankly of the egotism that made her a poor teacher and of her jealousy of the new breed of modern dancers, many of whom she had trained. Past fifty, at the close of the book, St. Denis claims as her greatest dance achievement the work "Istar of the Seven Gates," and is looking forward to a Third Life, one that will be governed by the "gods" of simplicity, joy and peace.

T. Gail Adams
Emory University, ILA

St. Johns, Adele Rogers (1894-   )

Journalist

[283] *Final Verdict.*   Garden City, New York: Doubleday & Company, 1962. 512 pp.

What is ostensibly an account of the courtroom antics of a turn-of-the-century lawyer becomes an introspective study of the teenage daughter who observed and recorded her father's career. As a child Adele Rogers St. Johns, later to become America's premier "Sob Sister," accompanied her father into jails, courtrooms, whore houses and funeral parlors. In electrifying prose she tells of her life with father while he defended everything from the petty pick-pocket to the great Clarence Darrow.

Writing of events a half century in the past St. Johns makes extensive use of old court records and contemporary newspaper accounts. The recollections and perceptions of her childhood, however, constitute the glue and substance, if not the bulk, of this volume. Earl Rogers was an outstanding courtroom lawyer in an age of outstanding courtroom lawyers. The little girl tagging at his heels made him different. The fact that the little girl grew up to become an accomplished writer makes him notable.

St. Johns did not like her mother. She had more affection for the madam at the whore house patronized by her father. The author makes no effort to conceal her feelings about either of her parents. She has an occasional kind word for a female relative, but even as a teenager she lived in a man's world.

Time (November 2, 1962) reviewed the volume as a biography of Rogers and filled a page without saying much. D. C. Rigg in the San Francisco *Chronicle* (August 22, 1962) found the writing excellent but accused the author of trying to rewrite history to make her father greater than Clarence Darrow. Seymour Korman in the Chicago *Sunday Tribune* (September 16, 1962) found her "Sob-Sister" technique "out of style" three decades later.

[284] *The Honeycomb.* Garden City, New York: Doubleday & Company, 1969. 700 pp.

In *Final Verdict* Adele Rogers St. Johns told of the second decade of her life. In *The Honeycomb* she tells of the next five. Her technique is similar. She lines up all the big stories that she did for the Hearst papers, repeats them, and sprinkles her autobiographical data in between. She is no slave to chronology and the reader who is comfortable with order will find these pages discomfiting.

If the earlier volume might be subtitled "Life With Father" the second could be called "Life with William Randolph Hearst." The relationship with Hearst was not like her relationship with her father, but he dominated her life just as thoroughly and paid much better.

St. Johns covers her long and varied career in journalism. She was probably best in covering Hollywood and worst in covering sports. Her father's influence remained with her, however, and she delighted in criminal trials. The Lindbergh kidnapping case was the height of her career.

In spite of its favorable reception this volume was not widely reviewed. Neil Miller in the *Christian Science Monitor* (October 11, 1969) was impressed by the vigor of the writing as was M. D. Harris in *Library Journal* (September 15, 1969). There is no questioning either the author's literary talent or the exciting subjects

about which she wrote. Hearst aimed to sell newspapers, and
Adele Rogers St. Johns helped him. Her abysmal ignorance
about everything other than the story at hand sometimes approach-
es the spectacular, but somehow she managed to preserve that incapacity for a very profitable fifty years.

St. Johns does indeed bare her private life. But there was very
little of it. She loved her father to an excess and hated her mother.
She married Ike St. Johns, a fellow journalist, when she was quite
young. She was more interested in her chilren than her husband,
and the marriage did not last long. Actually Ike did not last much
longer, although they did quit friends. She had another close relationship with a fellow journalist but there was no marriage. She
hated her second husband as much as she did her mother and refused to even mention his name in her book. She even gave his son
the last name of her first husband.

Adele Rogers St. Johns was a woman who made it in a man's
world. She took the rough assignments with the easy. She did
anything Hearst told her to do and was paid well. All of the male
journalists in the Hearst stable did precisely the same thing. She
has been described as a "Sob Sister" and frequently represented
the "Women's Point of View." On the other hand, at the Lindbergh Kidnapping Trial she was hard-nosed while Damon Runyon
was the bleeding heart. She was more interested in the dramatic
than the sentimental. The deaths of her brother and son in World
War II evoked a most dramatic reaction from her, while the hos-
pital-bed passing of Earl Rogers and Ike St. Johns just slipped by
between paragraphs.

In her later years Adele Rogers St. Johns has publicly derided
"women's liberation" and "militant feminism." Her life, however,
reveals a person who remained completely a woman but was willing
to sacrifice liberation for fame and fortune. Besides, she loved her
daddy.

Tom Hamilton
Old Dominion University

Sanger, Margaret (1879-1966)

Reformer, Activist

[285] *My Fight for Birth Control.* New York: Farrar and Rinehart, 1931. 360 pp.

Published in the midst of her struggle to legalize birth control,
My Fight records Margaret Sanger's life through 1931, when the
New York Academy of Medicine approved her Brownsville clinic
and various churches had begun to support the birth control movement. She concludes the book with a plea for legislative action and
appends several documents of support from religious and medical
organizations.

[286] *Margaret Sanger: An Autobiography.* New York: Norton, 1938. 504 pp.

This volume is an expanded version of *My Fight for Birth Control,* including a record of the climax of Sanger's struggle in America to secure for women control over their own bodies: the June
1937 announcement that doctors could legally give contraceptives.

Sanger traces her life from her birth as the sixth of eleven children of a tubercular mother and an improvident father. After her
mother's early death, Sanger trained as a nurse, married architect
Bill Sanger, and went into a period of suburban retreat until her
three children were born. Then she returned to New York and
nursing, and was propelled into a life-long mission when an impoverished patient, who had pleaded with Sanger to reveal the
"secret" of birth control, died from a self-induced abortion. Overpowered by this experience, Sanger determined to find and share
such information, a resolution which led to a life of studying, writing, editing, lecturing, being jailed, and being separated from her
husband and children. In her search for information and attempts
to promote her cause, she travelled to England, France, Germany,
the Netherlands, Japan, China, India, and Russia. Her attention
in the autobiography is focused continually on the plights of the
women she hoped to help, whether overburdened mothers on the
lower East Side or child prostitutes in the Orient. As a result, the
book contains relatively little intimate information, except for a

brief description of her grief over the death of her daughter Peggy and a bare outline of her relationships with her children, Bill Sanger, Havelock Ellis, and Noah Slee, her second husband. Once accused by Heywood Broun of having little sense of humor, Sanger replied, "I'm the protagonist of women who have nothing to laugh at."

Margaret Sanger's reviewers, who admire her courage, steadfastness, and compassion, see her as a "maker rather than a mirror of history" (Mary Beard, *Saturday Review of Literature,* November 21, 1931, p. 312), whose record of her own historical importance is told with "admirable detachment,. . .simplicity and deep sincerity" (Rose Feld, New York *Times,* November 13, 1938, p. 9). The reviews consist primarily of summaries of her suffering and achievements rather than analyses of style or personality. Because Sanger's life is almost completely devoted to the birth control movement, Feld sees Sanger's autobiography as "the biography of a cause rather than the personal story of a woman." Margaret Wallace says it is the record of "twenty-five years of social change . . .described with relentless clarity" (*Saturday Review of Literature,* November 12, 1938, p. 6).

Biographies of Sanger draw heavily on her autobiographical writings but tend not to discuss them at any length. In his extensive bibliographical essay, however, David M. Kennedy maintains that the autobiographies were ghost written (*Birth Control in America: The Career of Margaret Sanger,* New Haven: Yale University Press, 1970, p. 277) and that Sanger occasionally errs in factual detail. Like Lawrence Lader (*The Margaret Sanger Story and the Fight for Birth Control,* 2nd ed. 1955; rpt. Westport Ct.: Greenwood Press, 1975), Kennedy focuses on Sanger's career rather than her private life. Both Emily Taft Douglas (*Margaret Sanger: Pioneer of the Future,* New York: Holt, Rinehart & Winston, 1970) and Joan Dash (*A Life of One's Own: Three Gifted Women and the Men They Married,* New York: Harper & Row, 1973, pp. 1-113) try to explore Sanger's character more closely, and both point out that she omits almost all personal detail in her writings, especially any reference to her daughter Peggy's polio attack which left her lame, a misfortune for which Bill Sanger blamed his wife and about which she felt tremendous guilt. Dash argues that Sanger was obsessed with controlling all facets of her life and asserting her position as the dominant force in the birth control movement, a determination which led her, for example, to minimize the role others played in the cause, especially Emma Goldman. Richard Drinnon made this same point in 1961 in his biography of Goldman, *Rebel in Paradise.* Virginia Coigney has written a biography of Sanger (*Margaret Sanger: Rebel with a Cause,* Garden City, N. Y.: Doubleday, 1969) intended for young people, which presents material from the autobiographies in a condensed and simplified form.

Patricia L. Miller
University of Connecticut, Storrs

Sarton, May (1912-   )

Poet, Novelist, Teacher

[287] *I Knew a Phoenix: Sketches for an Autobiography.* New York: Rinehart & Company, 1959. 222 pp.

I Knew a Phoenix is May Sarton's chronicle of her parents, education and early career. Unlike her novels, it is not a sustained narrative; unlike her poems, it is tranquil, curiously devoid of the tensions of unformed identity and problematic relationships which inform her early verse. Instead of turmoil, she provides evenhanded sketches of her parents' early lives in England and Belgium, their marriage, their Belgian country house, their escape to the United States during the First World War. Neither American nor European in allegiance and acutely aware of her exile, Sarton searches in these details of domestic life and personality for a heritage independent of nationality: from her father, George Sarton, historian of science, she takes dedication and idealism; from her mother, portraitist, clothing designer and interior decorator, the impulse to make self-expressive order. It is only later, in *Journal of a Solitude,* that these persons become demythologized, and Sarton talks candidly about the difficult position of her mother in a bourgeois, male-dominated marriage.

The second half of the book is also written in the form of brief sketches which picture her schooling and apprentice years. These chapters are remarkable not so much for the nature of the experience recounted as for the writer's emphasis on personal influences. At Shady Hill School, the Institut Belge de Culture Grancaise, and later at the Civil Repertory Theatre in New York where Sarton began a brief theatre career, women teachers and artists inspired her. The portraits of Agnes Hocking, Marie Closset, Eva de Gallienne implicitly explain Sarton's own decision to join them by managing her own apprentice theatre group and later by becoming a writer. Taken together, the two parts of the book constitute "the education of a poet;" for Sarton ends this segment of her life story with the image of herself at twenty-six, hesitantly delivering her first book of published verse to S. S. Koteliansky and Virginia Woolf.

[288] *Plant Dreaming Deep.* New York: W. W. Norton & Company, 1967. 189 pp.

Where homage to an earlier, influential generation motivated the writing of *I Knew a Phoenix*, *Plant Dreaming Deep* begins in middle age, at a time when Sarton's self-affirmation must be achieved without family support. The book maintains a remarkable serenity of tone, but its optimism and balance are strained, as the author herself realized when she later wrote, "that book gives a false view. The anguish of my life here—its rages—is hardly mentioned." Instead of rage, *Plant Dreaming Deep* records a life of self-consciously achieved order, a life where pain is explored only as a willed renunciation for art. Sarton writes again through indirections; although she speaks in the first person, her house in Nelson, N. H., dominates the book, as parents and friends had focused her previous autobiography. But familiar personal themes emerge from homemaking details, and it becomes clear that Sarton writes of her New England house as a metaphor for private aspirations: as the hired man clears the garden of weeds, so the autobiographer hopes to clear "the wild disordered past;" as the carpenter combines a sturdy old wood frame house with modern appliances, so Sarton will end her exile by combining past and present, Belgium and America, in an eclectic but harmonious dwelling. A neighbor focuses the view by mowing the grass around the trees in the far field; Sarton will focus her life on an inner landscape. Indirectly but insistently the book explores the preconditions of art and the peculiar situation of a middle aged woman, single and without independent means, who must maintain friendships, manage finances, gardening and self support, without sacrificing the inner clarity and intensity that allow her to create.

[289] *Journal of a Solitude.* New York: W. W. Norton & Company, 1973. 208 pp.

If Sarton's two early autobiographical books are quietly optimistic, *Journal of a Solitude* restores dimension to the author's life by exposing the psychic costs of living and writing alone. The live recorded in these fragmented and brief journal entries is apparently self-contained: Sarton's appreciation of the passing New Hampshire seasons is punctuated by lecture tours, visits from friends, the death of a loved townsman, the deaths of pets. But beneath domestic events are the vulnerabilities of loneliness: resentment, hostility and enervating depressions. Sarton's moods fluctuate with the tensions of an affair: at fifty-eight she experiences the most complete love of her life but admits, with a candor permitted by the death of her parents, that homosexuality imposes "a life where art must become the primary motivation, for love is never going to fulfill in the usual sense." Amid more mundane observations about daily routine, she continues a running commentary on women and creativity: she sees her sex as less whole than men, subject to fragmenting domestic demands and to a general hostility toward "female-oriented art." Her own work is viewed as a way of transposing pain into a more valuable order. "May we agree," Sarton asks in one of her novels, "that private life is irrelevant?"

Although Sarton's journals all reveal anxiety about critical response to her work, these autobiographical books seem to have been well received. A bibliography of reviews of Sarton's poems and novels can be found in her critical biography by Agnes Sibley (*May Sarton.* New York:Twayne, 1972). The New York *Times* called her a person with "the poet's faculty for exorcising troubled emotions;" The Philadelphia *Bulletin* found her "a remarkable woman" and Eugenia Thorton, of The Cleveland *Plain Dealer,* spoke of Sarton's "honorable confession. . .wise and warm within its solitude."

Carol Shloss
Wesleyan University

Schneiderman, Rose (1882/84-1972)

Labor Leader, Suffragist

[290] *All for One.*   New York: Paul S. Eriksson, Inc., 1967.
        264 pp.

Writing late in life, with Lucy Goldthwaite, Rose Schneiderman tells in *All for One* of her experiences from early childhood to retirement. Without bitterness, she recalls the poverty of her first years in Russian Poland, her father's death after the family migrated to the United States, and her mother's difficulties in trying to support four children in New York of the 1890's. These problems, according to Schneiderman's memory, caused her to become the main support of her mother and younger sister when she was thirteen. The major focus of the autobiography is Schneiderman's work with the New York Women's Trade Union League (NYWTUL), which she joined a few years after she entered the factory would and become a trade union member. She tells of her activities as a League organizer (and also briefly as an ILGWU organizer) to get women to join unions and to assist them in strikes; of her many years as president of the NYWTUL; of the numerous persons whom she came to know through her League work, especially Eleanor Roosevelt; and of the honors and responsibilities that came to her as a result of her accomplishments with the League, such as her appointment as secretary of the New York State Department of Labor in 1937, her selection as a delegate of the National Women's Trade Union League (NWTUL) to international conferences in Europe, her election as president of the National League, and her subsequent appointment as the only woman member of the NRA's Labor Advisory Board in 1933. She concludes that the major reasons for the ultimate demise of the National and later the New York League were financial problems and the growth of labor unions' power to the point where they no longer needed the WTUL's assistance.

All for One is of value to feminists especially for its record of one woman-headed family, of Schneiderman's efforts in behalf of female workers, and of her contributions to the suffrage movement, especially in New York. The autobiography is disappointing for its failure to develop Schneiderman's role as president of the National as distinct from the New York Women's Trade Union

League.

Reviewers considered *All for One* a dramatic but modest account of an immigrant family's struggle and of one person's efforts to promote the political rights and improve the economic lot of women. *Publishers' Weekly* (October 16, 1967, p. 56) found Schneiderman's recollections of Eleanor Roosevelt a valuable part of the book. *Booklist* (April 15, 1968, p. 958), however, contended that the labor leader was worthy of "a more eloquent statement" of her record. Audrey Cahill in the *Library Journal* (December 15, 1967, p. 4498) found the autobiography to be "authoritative," but *Choice* (June, 1968, p. 533) came closer to the truth in recommending the book "for its human rather than scholarly interests." None of the reviews pointed out that errors in details mar, to a certain extent, the reliability of the book. Repeatedly, for example, Schneiderman states that the NWTUL disbanded in 1947, although it actually came to an end in 1950. Furthermore, some of the data she gives about her own life are at variance with information she supplied on earlier occasions.

Dorothy E. Johnson
Old Dominion University

Schuyler, Philippa Duke (1932-1967)

Concert pianist, Composer, Linguist, Writer, Newspaper Correspondent

[291] *Adventures in Black and White.* New York: Robert Speller & Sons, Inc., 1960. 300 pp.

Philippa Duke Schuyler, daughter of well-known Pittsburgh *Courier* editor George Schuyler, was a child prodigy who at age twenty months was reading and writing and by age four was a recognized pianist. First as a concert pianist, travelling to over sixty countries, and later, as a foreign correspondent, Schuyler toured the world. In four books, she recounted many of her experiences in foreign nations during the period from the 1940's to the 1960's.

In this first work, *Adventures in Black and White,* the author talked about her musical performances, the well-known musical figures she knew, and the places and the people she met on her concert tours. Included in this work are several passages concerning the treatment of women in a variety of foreign cultures. For instance, in one section she outlined the female circumcision practices of some Congolese ethnic groups and, in another section, she discussed the treatment of women within the Moslem tradition. *Adventures in Black and White* and her other works provide an interesting first-hand account of the experiences and thoughts of a young Black internationally-recognized female artist.

Although not impressed by Schuyler's writing ability, Priscilla L. Buckley's critique of *Adventures in Black and White* is generally favorable. She is impressed with the courage and resourcefulness of Schuyler, but finds some of her book filled with interesting triviality (*National Review* 10, February 11, 1961, p. 90).

[292] *Who Killed the Congo?* New York: The Devin-Adair Company, 1962. 310 pp. Illus.

As a foreign correspondent in the Congo, Philippa Schuyler personally viewed much of the violence surrounding its struggle for independence in 1960. Historian Joel A. Rogers favorably reviewed the book for its detailed and intimate depiction of the Congo crisis as well as for its objectivity (*Crisis* 69, June-July 1962, pp. 364-366). This appraisal of *Who Killed the Congo?* was repeated in the *National Review's* critique (W. F. Rickenbacker, *National Review* 13, October 1962, pp. 281-282). On the other hand, two newspaper reviewers criticize the book for its sensationalism and its inaccuracies (Chicago *Sunday Tribune,* July 29, 1962, p. 5 and New York *Herald Tribune Books,* June 17, 1962, p. 11).

[293] *Jungle Saints: Africa's Heroic Catholic Missionaries.* Rome: Herder, 1963. 223 pp. Illus.

In *Jungle Saints* Schuyler publishes her personal interviews with a number of Catholic missionaries in Africa as well as with African leaders and comments on the presence of Christianity on the African continent.

[294] *Good Men Die.* New York: Twin Circle Publishing Company, Inc., 1969. 256 pp. Paperback.

This posthumously published work is a personal account of Schuyler's Vietnam experience in which her pro-U.S. involvement and anti-communist views are quite apparent.

Sharon Harley
University of the District of Columbia

Scott-Maxwell, Florida (1883-1977)

Writer, Suffrage Activist, Analytical Psychologist

[295] *The Measure of My Days.* New York: Alfred A. Knopf, 1968. 150 pp.

The Measure of My Days in the notes and reflections of eighty-two year old Scott-Maxwell as she reacts: to the daily struggles of being old and alone; to the struggles of human beings as they deal with their differences and their drive toward equality; to the conflict between the good and evil sides of their personality; and to the love and suffering of individuals.

Contrary to our societal expectations that being old is a dreaded condition, Scott-Maxwell experiences her age as time full of passionate, intense feeling and pulsating liveliness. She also describes the delightful pleasures of living alone, noting that she can be true to herself with no need to please others.

Her reactions to the women's movement are mixed. She cares deeply about the quality of women's lives and she perceives how hurt women are by being treated as inferiors and demeaned by men. Yet she is concerned that in their search for equality and identity that they will imitate western white man with his emphasis on achievement and lose their differences; their mysterious, nurturing, life-giving energy, and their undefined qualities. She fears equality will mean sameness while she values uniqueness, thinking each person's most important task is to be true to their inner way and to be differentiated from the crowd. In spite of her fears of the danger involved, she wants women to be honored and thinks they must create their own identity, rather than accepting a male definition of their identity.

E. Fuller praises Scott-Maxwell in the *Wall Street Journal* (June 25, 1968, p. 18) for her insight and ripened wisdom. Katherine Wills (*Library Journal*, April 15, 1968, p. 1622) describes the book as a "notebook of distinction. . .a beautiful book to read."

Pauline Rose Clance
Georgia State University

Sekaquaptewa, Helen (1898-   )

Hopi Woman

[296] *Me and Mine: The Life Story of Helen Sekaquaptewa.* Tucson: University of Arizona Press, 1969. 260 pp.

Me and Mine is an oral autobiography as told to Louise Udall, in which Helen Sekaquaptewa recounts her early life in the villages of Oraibi and Hotevilla. As the daughter of a Hopi family hostile to the federal government, she was forcibly placed by Indian Bureau agents in a government day school at the age of seven. She tells of the daily lives of Hopi women, including matrilineal customs, women's work making mortar and plastering houses, grinding corn, making cooking stones, gathering piñon nuts, and bartering surplus stores with neighbors. The roles of the midwife and the male relative in traditional birth practices are described in detail. Especially vivid are accounts of the arrest and imprisonment of Hopi fathers, including her own, for refusing to allow federal government to take their children away to boarding school in 1906. Like other young Native American girls, at school Sekaquaptewa worked in the kitchen, dining room, laundry, and sewing room under quasi-military discipline. Her account spans the first half of the century, a time in which she attempted to combine what she thought was good in both cultures, the Hopi tradition and what she learned in school. After studying the Book of Mormon and finding many similarities with Hopi tradition, she joined the Mormon church in 1953.

Joan M. Jensen
New Mexico State University

Shaw, Anna Moore (1898-1974)

Pima Woman

[297] *A Pima Past.* Tucson: University of Arizona Press, 1974. 262 pp.

Published when Anna Moore Shaw was seventy-six, *A Pima Past* is a family saga beginning with her grandfather and concluding with her observations about the Salt River Reservation in the 1970's. It contains a detailed description of Pima women's work in gathering and preparing food (including grinding corn), and weaving baskets. Her Christian parents taught her Pima values as well as how to survive in the "white man's" world. They willingly sent her to boarding school in 1906. Later she lived in a multi-racial neighborhood in Phoenix but returned to the reservation in the 1920's for the births of her children.

A Pima Past was seen by reviewers as an account by a Native American who wanted to assimilate the best of the white world while preserving her heritage (*Library Journal,* July 1974) and as an exception to the trend of idealizing the Native American past and condemning white culture (*Choice,* October 1974).

Joan M. Jensen
New Mexico State University

Sills, Beverly (1929-   )

Opera Singer

[298] *Bubbles: A Self Portrait.* New York: Bobbs-Merrill Company, 1976. 240 pp.

Bubbles: A Self Portrait is Beverly Sills's short, conversational and thoroughly enjoyable account of her operatic career. In a straightforward, almost matter-of-fact style, Sills traces her career from its beginning, with her first public aria at the age of three in the "Miss Beautiful Baby of 1932" contest in Brooklyn, through her struggles for acceptance and fame in a European-dominated art to her triumphs at the New York City Opera, at La Scala, and finally at the Metropolitan Opera. Sills is never reluctant to indulge in undoubtedly well-deserved self praise: "If I have ever achieved definitive performances during my career thus far, Baby Doe is one of them. The other three would be Manon, Cleopatra in *Julius Caesar,* and Queen Elizabeth in *Roberto Devereux.* They have been the only times in my career when I have walked out of the theater feeling that I have done everything I wanted to do with a role and that nobody could have done it better." Intertwined with these accounts of Sills's professional successes are the less-well-known accounts of her personal tragedies: the death of her father, the deafness of her daughter, and the mental retardation of her son. The more than two hundred photographs, many in color and picturing Beverly Sills's private life as well as her public career, are a visual delight and often seem to convey more about Sills's intense energy and zest for life than she relates in her text.

Beverly Sills touches briefly on many themes of special concern to women: overcoming her father's objections to an artistic career for his only daughter, balancing a successful career with a happy marriage, and coping with the severe handicaps of her children. Unfortunately, these themes are not developed to the extent that the reader would wish. Haste and brevity appear to be the major weakness of Sills's self portrait. Robert Enequist remarks in his review in *Library Journal* (1 April 1977, p. 814) that "what is needed is a portrait in depth by someone who can be objective. This book is too little, too soon." We must wait for that time when Beverly Sills is no longer "on stage" and will have the leisure and the freedom to relate her life as it "really was"—not as she now believes it should appear to be.

Joan Frederick
James Madison University

Skinner, Cornelia Otis (1901-   )

Actress, Writer, Monologuist

[299] *Family Circle.*   Boston: Houghton Mifflin Company, 1948. 310 pp.

In *Family Circle* Cornelia Otis Skinner traces the very different paths taken by her mother, Maud Durbin, and her father, Otis Skinner, to their careers on the stage, where they met, fell in love, and married. In her account of her parents' life together before her birth, Skinner draws heavily from family legends and her father's letters for her glimpses of two charming people, their associations, travels, joys, and blessedly few travails. The book also covers the author's childhood and adolescence, which she describes with delightful wryness, and her debut as an actress at twenty-one.

Skinner has also published eight collections of humorous essays, most of which are purportedly based on personal experiences. The titles of these volumes are: *Tiny Garments* (1932), *Excuse It, Please!* (1936), *Dithers and Jitters* (1938), *Soap Behind the Ears* (1941), *That's Me All Over* (1948), *Nuts in May* (1950), *Bottoms Up* (1955), and *The Ape in Me* (1959). In collaboration with Emily Kimbrough, she wrote *Our Hearts Were Young and Gay* (1942), the most popular of her works in the vein of humorous reminiscences. It is doubtful, however, that it, like the eight volumes cited above, should be regarded as serious autobiography.

Skinner's writing has attracted considerable critical attention, the preponderance of it favorable to the point of enthusiasm. In one of her humorous pieces, Skinner refers to herself as "a nicely brought up girl. . .with genteel sensibilities." Although she remains true to this image, the person who comes through in her writing is intelligent, perceptive, and self-disciplined. On the night of her

Broadway debut, her father whispered to her, "From now on you're on your own." She hasn't done badly.

Virginia Cox
University of Wisconsin—Oshkosh

Smith, Lillian (1897-   )

Writer, Anti-Segregationalist

[300] *Killers of the Dream.* New York: W. W. Norton, 1949. 253 pp.

In her preface, Lillian Smith says that she wrote *Killers of the Dream* "to find out what life in a segregated culture had done" to her. But though the book is an account of the causes and horrifying manifestations of segregation, Smith never directly speaks of her own life. Smith's book, rich in metaphor and imagery, reads more like a novel than an autobiography, and only tenuously connects her tale of segregation with her personal history.

However, when she speaks of segregation, Smith's writing is intelligent, and, at times, she offers an uncompromising analysis of the political economic, and cultural causes of segregation. She covers the spectrum of this American nightmare from separate drinking fountains and restaurant doors to the fact that 3,148 lynchings of Blacks took place between 1900 and 1946, while only 135 persons were convicted of being "members of the lynch groups." In a vivid setting of the lush South, a South heavy with the smells of jasmine and honeysuckle, the sounds of whippoorwills, tree frogs, and the rustle of the palmettos, she describes the education White children underwent which guaranteed their permanent separation from the Blacks. Smith shows how Southern white children were reared for hatred by the tenets of Southern tradition, the frenzied, hypnotic preachings of Revivalists, and the always gentle yet iron-strong teachings of their parents which said that one was polite to Blacks, but was never to associate with them. Smith obviously defied this conditioning, but never tells us how. Unfortunately, the powerful message of her book is often obscured by vague rhetoric, sensational prose and simplistic explanations.

When *Killers of the Dream* first appeared in 1949, it enjoyed generally favorable reviews. *Booklist* spoke of Smith using the "Freudian method" to lay "bare the weaknesses, errors and anxieties of the South, dwelling on the triangulation of sin, sex, and race segregation." C. J. Rolo in *Atlantic* praised the book as "blunt, fearlessly written. . .couched in swiftly moving prose that is alive with feeling" (December, 1949). However, the New York *Times* found fault with Smith's writing saying that the book is "absorbing and effective when she is in control of her almost religious fervor; when [she] is carried away by fervor, the book deteriorates" (October 23, 1949). *The New Yorker* also praised Smith's topic but criticized its style (November, 1949).

Bella Mirabella
Queens College, CUNY

Smith, Margaret Chase (1898-   )

United States Senator

[301] *Declaration of Conscience.* New York: Doubleday and Company, 1972. 512 pp.

Margaret Chase Smith has chosen several of her significant political statements as a framework for discussing her activities and achievements as a Member of Congress from the Second Congressional District of Maine and later as a Senator from that State.

In her *Declaration of Conscience* she recounts how she succeeded her husband Clyde in the House of Representatives following his death in April 1940. After approximately nine years in the House she was elected to the U. S. Senate and served until 1973. Smith tells how a talk she made on Navy Day 1938 eventually earned her a place in Congress as a member of the Naval Affairs Committee. She reconstructs, of course, the circumstances of her verbal confrontation as a freshman senator with Joseph McCarthy in her now famous "Declaration of Conscience," from which her autobiography takes its title.

Margaret Chase Smith is important to Women's Studies because she belongs with the women of an earlier generation who insisted "I'm no feminist, but. . ." Many of her comments and actions clearly indicate that she was never unaware or unsympathetic about feminist issues. She championed, for instance, the cause of permanent and regular status for women in the Armed Services. Liz Carpenter urges the new political woman to read *Declaration of Conscience* "to remind her that she is not the first, nor will she be the last reformer on the scene" (*Saturday Review*, April 15, 1972, p. 66).

Audrey A. Amerski
Old Dominion University

Stalvey, Lois Mark (c.1929-   )

Housewife, Civil Rights Activist

[302] *The Education of a Wasp.* New York: Willian Morrow & Company, Inc., 1970. 309 pp.

In *The Education of a Wasp*, Lois Mark recounts how she opened her own advertising agency at nineteen and abandoned it, a highly successful business, seven years later to marry Ben Stalvey and become a "typical Midwestern housewife." This was the beginning, not the end, of her education in human awareness—and human deception.

Lois Stalvey exposes both the pain and the beauty in each step in her growth from a sheltered wife to a civil rights activist. Stalvey begins her "education" in Omaha, attempting to find a home for a Negro surgeon. Although she introduces herself as an ignorant and indifferent housewife, Stalvey is never unmoved by the plight of minorities, nor is she without a personal commitment that at times is deeper than her own awareness of the depth of racial bigotry in America. Her education takes her to Philadelphia, to integrated schools, to work in labor and voting discrimination cases, and inevitably draws her into confrontations involving racial hatred. Each chapter is a new lesson, exposing still a more painful wound beneath the open scar of racism.

In *The Saturday Review* (November 14, 1970, p. 77), Zena Southerland noted that Stalvey's "sadness comes through as clearly as her candor." It is the sadness of a frustrated optimist, a believer in the American dream, haunted by American nightmares. G. M. Costello, in *America* (September 5, 1970, p. 130), lamented that "What is most disturbing about this book is the thought that not nearly enough people are going to read it—especially those for whom it could have the greatest impact."

Writing at a time when "consciousness raising," "human awareness," "self-growth," and "assertiveness training" were not yet household phrases in America, Lois Mark Stalvey spoke out with an authentic feminist voice, sensitive to human suffering, and dedicated to interracial understanding, warning America to avert the catastrophe she sees us heading for if we continue racism.

Judith A. Johnson
Old Dominion University

Stern, Elizabeth (1890-1954)

Social Worker, Novelist, Essayist, Biographer

[303] *My Mother and I.* New York: Macmillan, 1917. 169 pp.

Stern's first book has "subsequently expanded under the same name as a fictionalized biography of immigrants in the United States, with an introduction by President Theodore Roosevelt" (New York *Times*, January 10, 1954, p. 86), but even at the time was recognized to be, "in essentials at least, a genuine autobiography rather than a work of fiction." In *My Mother and I,* the eldest daughter of Jewish immigrants newly arrived from Poland describes her early homelife in a single cellar room in the ghetto of an un-named Midwestern town, her first amazed confrontation with

American life, her delighted discovery—in a rag shop—of *Little Women,* her later exploration of the public library, her much-debated desire to attend high school, her working through college and her going alone to New York to study settlement work: all steps in quitting the ghetto and regretfully leaving behind her severe rabbinical father and merry, self-sacrificing "little mother."

Those reviewers who praised the book were impressed with Stern's ability to show the pathos of the older generation of immigrants, and particularly the pathos of the mother-daughter relationship. (For example, see New York *Times,* July 8, 1957, pp. 255, 258.) Yet some reviewers resented the pride in achievement expressed in this narrative. *The Nation's* reviewer, for instance, found unpleasant the daughter's "predominance of pride over tears," and speaking for "impecunious Jews in Poland," called for a more detailed analysis of "the economic and social effort involved in passing from the ghetto to her present position" (August 30, 1917, p. 224).

[304] [Leah Morton]. *I am a Woman—and a Jew.* New York: Sears, 1926; New York: Arno, 1969. 362 pp.

Stern's memories in this book begin with the moment in which, as her father stood chanting in Hebrew on the banks of the Ohio River, she first doubted his authority and disbelieved his religion. They end with her tramping in the Palisades with her adolescent son, attempting to instill in him pride in his Jewish heritage, affirming her own Jewishness. In the years between those two moments, Stern left her family and married a Gentile.

Stern is a woman as well as a Jew, and only part of her book concerns her attempts first to free herself from, then find herself within her religion. In much of this book she portrays herself as a wife, a mother, and a woman fiercely committed to work. She at times was sole support of her family and—in the face of much prejudice against her as both Jew and working mother—was, in turn, a successful social worker, lecturer, saleswoman, personnel director, head of a settlement house, and author. Excerpts from this work have recently been published in *Growing Up Female in America,* edited by Eve Merriam (Garden City, N.Y.: Doubleday, 1971).

Reviews tended to discuss one or the other aspects of the book. For example, The New York *Times* found that the book's chief "importance and value lies in its frank and sincere depiction of Jewish-Gentile relations, a problem that becomes increasingly vital" (March 13, 1927, p. 12). T. L. Masson asserted that "rarely has the psychology of women been disclosed with greater intimacy or with a surer touch" (New York *Evening Post,* October 23, 1926, p. 8). Helen Woodward, who found it "hard to get stirred up over anti-Semitism," roused herself for "moments of sympathy" with the husband, since Stern's "intensely feministic attitude, her demand that he regard her as an equal (the idea of regarding any one in love as an equal) and her heavy sacrifices must at times have been trying" (*Saturday Review of Literature,* December 18, 1926, p. 447).

[305] [Leah Morton]. *When Love Comes to Woman.* New York: Sears, 1929. 313 pp.

Speaking as a grey-haired, fifty-one-year-old career woman and mother of four, Stern continues her life story while focusing on "young people." Stern sympathetically examines the relationships —often alternatives to traditional marriages—of about ten young women, several of whom she encounters in the course of her work with unmarried mothers. Forming a background to these "case histories," as several reviewers would have it, are Stern's accounts of her own marriage, her work, her grief when her daughter dies in childbirth, and her joy in her sons and granddaughter.

Reviewers pronounced themselves bored. Finding it "heavy reading," *Outlook* gave the book lukewarm praise, considering it to be "competently written, humorless, touching, and desperately sincere" (May 8, 1929, p. 70). *The Saturday Review of Literature* felt *When Love Comes* to be "a late and an unnecessary contribution" to the general subject, since "the woman problem has been so thoroughly discussed in recent years that, fascinating as it is, particularly for a woman, one wonders if there is anything sufficiently new left of it to make interesting reading" (September 7, 1929, p. 116).

Jean Tobin
University of Wisconsin—Sheboygan

Stern, Susan Harris (1943-1976)

Weatherperson, Political Activist

[306] *With the Weathermen: The Personal Journal of a Revolutionary Woman.* Garden City, New York: Doubleday
and Company, 1975. 359 pp.

Stern's book opens in 1966 with a cross-country trip with her
husband to get a fresh start on her marriage and to enter the
School of Social Work in Seattle and concludes with her release in
June of 1972 from the Purdy State Prison for Women. By this
time she is divorced, bisexual, an experienced street fighter, and
still "looking for the MAN, the LOVE," but her list of qualifying
characteristics had grown while the type of man that could fill
them was swiftly diminishing. This journal of six years reveals
the intense journey of a shy, insecure woman from a wealthy
family bitterly split by divorce, who sought to find both an identity and acceptance first in marriage, later in the Students for a
Democratic Society, and finally as a violent, confused and angry
Weatherman. Although Stern alienated many by her striving for
leadership, she did not perceive herself as strong, but rather as one
who managed to be present at the major meetings, such as the split
between the SDS and Progressive Labor, the passage of resolutions
toward a Revolutionary Youth Movement, the efforts to ally SDS
with the Panthers, and the takeover of the National Office of the
SDS by the Weatherman. She was tear-gassed, clubbed, and shot
at by the Chicago police in the demonstrations at the Democratic
Convention and after the Days of Rage returned to Chicago to
spend a month in Cook County Jail. As the only female member
of the Seattle 7, she underwent the circus-like trial for conspiracy
for attacks on the Marine Recruiters' Office and the University of
Washington ROTC. For those not familiar with the events of the
student movement, she presents a detailed chronology at the end
of the book.

Stern freely admits that she barely understood the issues discussed in endless debate; she had to seek help from others so she
would know the right lines to repeat in organizing high school
students in Seattle. She has no critique nor any philosophical basis
for her activities. What she does show is the movement from the
standpoint of the led as contrasted with leaders like Mark Rudd,

Bernardine Dohrn, Carl Ogelsby, Cathy Wilkerson, Kathy Boudin, Russ Neufeld, and Mike Klonsky. Working with these people, she can observe their flaws, but her desire for excitement and acceptance from them led her to accept their ideas and tactics, while at the same time articulating a militant feminist position and demanding equality.

With the Weathermen is, to a certain extent, also the story of a woman's attempt to deal with the rampant sexism of the student movement, where women often were viewed as best serving the movement in a "prone" position, that is, flat on their backs. She read and espoused feminist ideas, but found a role as "Macho Mama" cooking, typing and keeping the members in the Seatle Liberation Front supplied with drugs and sex. Ironically, while critical of her topless dancing, the Weathermen accepted her earnings from this activity.

Some reviewers perceptively emphasized how Stern's feminism was suppressed. Wendy Schwarz observed (*Progressive,* November, 1975, p. 54) that Stern's "description of movement life in Seattle is undoubtedly the most damning to be recorded by anyone still sympathetic to left-wing politics. Her accounts of the criticism/self criticism sessions held regularly by members of the Weather collectives are painful to read, particularly because she was being destroyed by them. Instead of leaving, or even trying to defend herself, she meekly internalized the criticism, and continued to struggle into a mold she couldn't possibly fit." Susan Brownmiller (New York *Times,* June 15, 1975, p. 6) compares Stern to "Marjorie Morningstar, free at last from Herman Wouk"; she was more interested in rebelling, drugs, "dressing sexy. . .rapping with high school kids and breaking glass" than the "ins and outs of the Weather political line." While finding the book honest, she criticizes it for "a sensational exploitation of an undeniably authentic experience. . .the vernacular unfaultingly rings true." Peter S. Prescott (*Newsweek,* June 30, 1975, pp. 64-65) finds "it is unique, the only inside glimpse we have of these strangely self-destructive people." In August of 1976 the self-destructive lifestyle of Susan Stern took its toll and she died at the age of thirty-three.

Frances Hassencahl
Old Dominion University

Suckow, Ruth (1892-1960)

Author

[307] *Some Others and Myself.* New York: Rinehart and Company, 1952. 281 pp.

In an autobiographical essay, "A Memoir," in *Some Others and Myself.* Ruth Suckow describes her childhood and the influence her father, a Protestant minister, had on her upbringing. She sees this essay as a "testimony" to dispel certain misconceptions concerning the ways in which minister's children are brought up in a religious environment. Although the memoir covers the period from her childhood through her marriage and career, it is more concerned with her father and his influence upon her.

Despite its elegiac tone, "A Memoir" contains some elements which are of special interest to women's studies. Chief among these is the account of Suckow's conflict to achieve independence in a conventional religious environment. Recognizing that the organized church is geared to keeping women, "especially married women. . .in their place" (254), Suckow describes the intellectual and emotional difficulty of trying to utilize her talents and ambitions in non-religious areas. She describes in detail her alienation from her father's church and her gradual move toward Quakerism.

Although Suckow's work was well received when she was at the height of her career in the 1920's, her later writing, including *Some Others and Myself,* received little attention. Even so, John T. Flanagan describes "A Memoir" as "one of her best pieces of writing" (*American Literature,* January 1953, pp. 568-69). Further discussion of her work as well as a complete bibliography can be found in Leedice McAnelly Kissane's *Ruth Suckow* (New York: Twayne Publishing Co., 1969).

Patrice K. Gray
Emory University

Tarry, Ellen (c.1906-   )

Author, Religious Leader, Reformer

[308] *The Third Door.* New York: Guild Press, 1966. 374 pp.

Ellen Tarry wrote *The Third Door* in the sixties, a period that most will agree marked the turning of the tide of racial inequality in this country. The story of her experiences before and during this period, the story of a young Black woman growing up in the South and later working in the North, makes this book important for Women's Studies.

Through the innocent eyes of the girl, Ellen, we willingly avoid the tragic undertones that marred her early years. We share instead her memories of a generous, warm father, a protective mother, a closely-knit family and teachers who were influential in her decision to become a writer.

Ellen Tarry tells us that she faced three kinds of prejudice: that of White versus Black, Black versus mulatto, Protestant versus Catholic. She balances instances of these forms of prejudice with visits to the North and South. She is candid about her temptation to pass for white, but is emphatic about the urgency for Blacks to unite. She admits her love for the warm rich soil of her birthplace, Birmingham, Alabama, but is unsparing in her exposure of Jim Crow and acts of violence against Blacks. She points to the racism responsible for forcing Blacks into Harlem and directing their energies and talents to serving and entertaining Whites. She describes her frustration of having to settle for a job as a waitress, delaying her plans to study journalism at Columbia University for economic reasons.

The Third Door has value for the information Tarry shares about the intimate lives of such Blacks as Claude McKay, Richard Wright, George Washington Carver, James Weldon Johnson and his wife, Grace, and John H. Johnson of the *Negro Digest*. It has value for Tarry's information about Black history—the efforts of men like Philip Randolph who fought against racism in the military service, for her view of the urban riots of the forties, the struggles to end housing discrimination based on race, and the struggles to integrate southern Black schools.

Throughout her autobiography, Tarry is humble in her accounts of her participation in the fight for civil rights for Blacks, but her courage, faith and generosity of spirit are evident in her involvement with Friendship House and NCCS-USO. In spite of her praise of the Catholic effort to destroy racism in the North and South, the reader deduces that it was Tarry's sensitivity to the dignity of the Black person which was instrumental in changing the policy of some White Catholic leaders from giving "hand-outs" to Blacks to providing them with the opportunity to help themselves.

While Tarry stresses three kinds of prejudice that she faced, implicit in her autobiography is a fourth kind of prejudice—sexism. Gender, she found, was the main obstacle she had to overcome in entering the Black literary circle. Claude McKay's advice that she adopt a "professional air" protected her from social embarrassment but at the expense of some of the typical activities of women of her age. Tarry's story is important for Blacks and for women, especially for Black women, because it offers an alternative to racism and sexism—a third door through which they can walk with dignity and pride.

Elizabeth Nunez-Harrell
Medgar Evers College, CUNY

Terasaki, Gwen (1907-   )

Diplomat's Wife

[309] *Bridge to the Sun.* Chapel Hill: University of North Carolina Press, 1957. 260 pp.

Married to a member of the Japanese embassy staff in 1930, Gwen Terasaki followed her husband to his various diplomatic posts in Japan, Cuba, and China. They were stationed in Washington, D.C. on Pearl Harbor Day and were held in the U. S. for a half year before they were exchanged for American personnel caught in Japan at the beginning of the war. Once again in Japan, her husband's health deteriorated, and the family moved several times to avoid the brunt of the war activities.

Terasaki recounts how her husband had always been an anti-militarist in Japanese politics and had attempted to avert the U. S.-Japanese hostilities and later sought to bring an end to the conflict he regarded as both hopeless and harmful to Japan. She tells of the upheaval in Japan after the surrender, of no government, of civil disorder, military executions, of scarcity of consumer goods, and military occupation. In 1949 when it became apparent that her husband was in the last stages of heart disease, Terasaki and her daughter returned to the U. S.

The lack of critical attention to *Bridge to the Sun* is probably deserved, although several of the incidents Terasaki describes are certainly unusual, such as an audience with the Japanese emperor. Her book lacks focus. She mixes autobiographical bits and pieces with a memorial biography of her husband. The latter might well have been more interesting than she.

Marie R. Oesting
Baraboo, Wisconsin

Terrell, Mary Church (1863-1954)

Educator, Lecturer, Reformer

[310] *A Colored Woman in a White World.* Washington, D. C.: Ransdell, Inc., 1940. 437 pp.

A Colored Woman in a White World details not only Mary Church Terrell's personal life, but also provides a view of the social and political atmosphere of the United States in the seventy-seven years following Emancipation. Born of slave parents, Terrell begins her story with her recollection of an incident when she was four years old in which she notices her father's strong resemblance to his former master. The autobiography then moves from her early childhood in Memphis, Tennessee, to her elementary education at Antioch's "model school," high school and college at Oberlin, two years' study in Europe and to her experiences as educator, wife, mother, lecturer, and political activist. Though her varied experiences are minutely detailed, her concern for the

"emancipation" of black people and for the "universal elevation"
of women emerges as the unifying theme of the book. Terrell
stresses in the introduction that she, unlike a white woman who
had only one handicap to overcome, had two handicaps to overcome, her sex and her race.

A writer of limited talent, she focused her gifted intelligence
and remarkable self-confidence on women's rights—particularly
suffrage, prison reform, anti-lynching laws, and other anti-dis-
crimination laws. Speaking in behalf of these causes, she sought to
persuade her audience as much by example as by rhetoric that the
mind has neither sex nor race.

Among the first five Black women to receive a B.A. degree, she
defied tradition at Oberlin by majoring in the Classical course,
then called the "gentlemen's course." Though chided by friends
and classmates that she would be unable to find a Black man who
had studied Greek, and warned that she could not make a happy
marriage if she knew more than her husband, Terrell persisted.
The only woman in a class of forty men, she was selected by her
professor to read a passage in Greek before Matthew Arnold.

Although deeply devoted to her father, the strong-willed Terrell
insisted upon continuing her intellectual development and professional career as a teacher, to the latter of which he strenuously
objected. Marriage to Robert H. Terrell automatically severed
her teaching career, since married women in Washington, D. C.
were not allowed to teach. But her husband, the nation's first
Black federal judge, not only respected but encouraged her interests beyond the home even though her radical views could
have jeopardized his political future.

Admittedly not domestic by nature, Terrell's strong devotion
to her home and children is evident. She also shows love and
compassion for her invalid mother with whom she had never had a
close relation as a child.

Though vividly depicting her battle to eradicate the double
burden she bore, Terrell, according to *Christian Century* (October
30, 1940, p. 1346), "writes without bitterness, but with keen
awareness of the difficulties to be faced by a Negro in a white
world." H. G. Wells in his preface to the autobiography, concedes

that it is not a "great work of art," but praises it as a subtle account of race conflict in America. Interestingly, neither the reviewers nor Wells comments on Terrell's fight to overcome the obstacle which was to her as great as that of her race—her sex.

Margaret N. Simmons
Hampton Institute

Thompson, Bertha [Box Car Bertha] (c.1903-   )

Hobo, Social Reformer, Statistician

[311] *Sister of the Road: The Autobiography of Box Car Bertha.* New York: Macaulay, 1937. 314 pp. New York: Harper Colophon, 1975. 314 pp.

Unique personal and societal influences led to the development of one of the early twentieth century's most unusual American women. By the time she began hoboing at the age of sixteen, Bertha Thompson had known a series of "fathers" and a variety of homes ranging from railroad labor camps to experiments in communal living, most notably, Home Colony near Tacoma, Washington. Her free-thinking teachers were the I.W.W.'s, anarchists and wanderers who shared in such radical life styles. Her texts were by Oscar Wille, Emile Zola, Whitman, Huxley, Lenin, Emerson, and Darwin.

Bertha's main interest was in being a hobo and she traveled extensively around the country whenever she was restless or wanted to be with the men she admired. These men were generally considered to be labor agitators and anarchists. She makes it clear in her story, as told to Ben Reitman, that she never viewed the men and women she met on the road as social misfits, but as brothers and sisters from whom she could learn.

When not on the road, she was a member of a shoplifting gang, a prostitute, a maid, a lab technician, and a worker in several transient bureaus. So that she might raise her daughter, she eventually settled in Manhattan working for a New York social service bureau which studied the problems of the transient and unemployed. She also did some field research which allowed her to continue traveling and associating with the people in whom she was most interested.

Her account is clear and easily read. Although she speaks primarily of the ideas and philosophies of her companions, Bertha's own beliefs are evident as she describes her travels and her relationships with others. Various statistics are quoted in the text and in the appendix, but Herbert Blumer (*American Journal of Sociology,* 43:679 January 1938) suggests that Dr. Reitman has added from his own knowledge in order to make the story more realistic.

An account of how a non-conformist woman observed the disorganization of life during the 1920's and early 1930's, *Sister of the Road* should appeal to those interested in alternative life styles.

Robert Melanson
Old Dominion University

Toklas, Alice B. (1878-1967)

Friend of Artists and Authors

[312] *Staying on Alone: Letters of Alice B. Toklas.* New York: Liveright, 1973. 426 pp.

In the initial letter of this volume, written on July 27, 1946, Alice B. Toklas announces with great grief the death of her friend, Gertrude Stein. This is an appropriate beginning point; for much of the emotional life of the letters that follow—and of their author —centers around Toklas' memories of Stein. One of the gifts she gives the reader of these letters is a very real and moving portrait of a rich, deep friendship between two women. "I wish to God we had gone together," she writes to a friend. They did not; and Toklas combats Stein's loss in the twenty years she outlived her by constantly recreating her presence, in a myriad of ways: she keeps the famous literary salon open even when she doesn't wish to see visitors; she pours energy into the attempt to publish all of Stein's writing; she fights valiantly to keep the famous picture collection together, even at the cost of financial security for herself ("Security—what a fearfully limiting experience it would be"). In addition to being a fascinating chronicle of friendship, *Staying on Alone* rounds out our image of Gertrude Stein and the creative circle of friends she embraced, from Thorton Wilder to Cocteau, F. Scott Fitzgerald to Picasso. But finally, the central figure who engages us in *Staying on Alone* is Toklas herself. Whether advising a young artist or offering a friend a choice recipe or commenting insightfully on Henry James' influence on Stein, Alice B. Toklas emerges as a woman of wit and courage and style.

Staying on Alone was widely and favorably reviewed. Many reviewers, like Muriel Haynes, commented on Toklas' lively portrayal of "the charmed circle" of artistic friends who frequented the Stein/Toklas apartment: "the names that crowd her letters in witty sketches and sometimes acerbic appraisal are part of the history of music, painting, and literature in the twentieth century" (*Ms*, March 1974, p. 36). Most praise Edward Burns' editing of the book as careful and sensitive, find the notes that decipher private references helpful, and laud the choice and number of photographs that illustrate the people and periods about which Toklas writes. Virgil Thomson is an exception: he comments in a generally astringent review that the book is "editorially not quite first class," argues that "the letters as printed tell no consistent story, however close a portrait they may give of the Toklas daily life," and charges that Toklas' "tastes were peculiar" (The New York *Review of Books*, March 7, 1974, pp. 14-15). (Reading the latter comment one remembers that one of Toklas' "peculiar" judgements was that Thomson was "very wrong about the painters" in his *State of Music*.) But even Thomson concludes that "the book is a joy because Toklas the woman was for real." Reviewer after reviewer stresses the strength and dignity and wit of the central character on this stage. Harriet Zinnes in *Nation* asserts that "her letters reveal her wicked wit, her sharp and agile tongue, and a dignity and independence that occasionally must have shot through the salon like a living fire" (May 18, 1974, pp. 632-633). Francis Wyndham in *New Statesman* gives thanks for "the *real* autobiography of Alice B. Toklas," in a review that is perceptive in its comments on the insights Toklas offers into the nature of her relationship with Stein

(March 1974, pp. 298-299). Finally, the style of the letters in *Staying on Alone* received mostly favorable comment; most view Toklas' writing style as occasionally "coy" and "gushing," but on the whole intelligently articulate. As Margo Jefferson comments in *Newsweek,* her sentences are "as concisely ornamental as her needlepoint. . .and her judgments are gracefully acidic" (January 7, 1974, p. 67).

Sharon Davie
University of Virginia

Truman, Margaret (1924-   )

Writer, Housewife

[313] *Souvenir: Margaret Truman's Own Story,* with Margaret Cousins. New York: McGraw-Hill, 1956. 365 pp.

Published when she was thirty-two, only four years after her father left the White House, *Souvenir* is a breezy, girlish chronicle of Margaret Truman's years as the President's daughter. Although it includes her University years, two European trips, several singing tours, and her father's 1948 whistle stop campaign, much of it is an account of social events. Neither a vindication nor an expose of her family, the book demonstrates the close family relationship and her own sunny disposition. Cliches often mar her serious discussions in this book, which lacks the more mature reflections evident in her 1973 biography of her father (*Harry S. Truman.* New York: Wm. Morrow & Co.).

Living and writing at a time when presswomen were "news hens" to be entertained at tea by the First Lady, Margaret Truman's generalizations about women and herself often depict the stereotype who likes to talk, shop, dance, and look pretty. This self-effacing pose means that the inner thoughts which accompany her disappointments, frustrations, and decisions are never revealed. In spite of this, her strength of character, honesty, and determination (all influenced by female relatives and teachers) is refreshingly dominant. Selected reading is recommended. Chapters 7-8 describe the transition from Vice-President's daughter to President's; Chapter 10 depicts 1940's social whirl. Chapter 25, a remarkable essay in candor, energy, and style, reflectively discusses the aims and limitations of this book, of her parents, of her past life and asserts that her life lies ahead.

Favorably reviewed in the U. S. and Britain, the book is no longer in print. The majority emphasize her accidental rise to national prominence and praise her unaffectedness. They are particularly charmed by her spontaneity, modesty, and honesty.

Elizabeth Cummins Cogell
University of Missouri—Rolla

Turk, Midge (1930-   )

Former Nun, Educator, Author

[314] *The Buried Life: A Nun's Journey.* New York: World Publishing Company, 1971. 196 pp.

Raised in a devout Catholic family, Midge Turk entered a convent at the age of eighteen. Her book chronicles her acceptance and finally her rejection of the religious life.

Entering a teaching mission after her novitiate, she found that the rules and regulations of the nun's life, together with the conservatism, if not hostility, of the diocese hierarchy made it extremely difficult to do the job to which she was totally devoted. She lived and worked for a time in the worst poverty of Los Angeles, came to sympathize with the liberal movements of the early sixties, supported, even marched, with Blacks and farmworkers—and made herself unpopular with her superiors. Despite the indifference of her superiors to the human beings who were supposed to be their charge, Sister Agnes remained with her Order, working for eighteen years "with hope in what the Apostate could accomplish—with the young, with minority groups, and with the poor" (129). After illness, disappointment, and disillusionment, she left the religious

life in 1970; she did not, however, abandon her vocation. Together
with about three hundred of the four hundred sisters of her Order,
she formed a secular community.

While *The Buried Life* is the story of "a nun's journey," it is of
interest to women's studies for the point it quietly makes about
women's struggles in a male-dominated culture. Sister Agnes did
not seriously question the subservience and obedience which were
the discipline of the nun until her confrontation with a superior
who regularly withheld desperately-needed money for her Order's
work in the ghetto. She felt that the male authorities in the
Church treated her as a second-class citizen because she was a
woman: "As a nun I didn't count at all as far as the making of
Church policy went. I was part of the slave labor-force that came
along with the fixtures" (129). Her strategies for dealing with the
complete unresponsiveness of the men who ran the parish resemble
those of other powerless women forced into ingenuity and indirec-
tion to circumvent male authority. She came to realize that the
old "silence, obedience, and dependence" expected from a nun
constituted a sex role, a father-daughter relationship in which the
daughter is never allowed to grow up (172). Her dissatisfaction as
a woman of the Church thus echoes the dissatisfaction of many
women outside the Church as they began to question their assigned roles. She criticizes the Church, as feminists criticize other
patriarchal institutions, for ignoring women, their idealism, and
their potentialities for leadership. Midge Turk left the Church, in
part, because of the role assigned to women within it; she could no
longer be a nun because as she says at the end of her book, she
could no longer bear to be "acquiescent and silent on matters of
importance" (191).

On the whole, *The Buried Life* recieved scant notice. Grumbach
(*New Republic,* June 12, 1971) stresses the religious values the
book affirms and the recent heroes of Catholicism it praises while
denying its relation to the movement for freedom in the sixties
(32).

Judith B. Herman
State College at Buffalo

Untermeyer, Jean Starr (1886-1970)

Poet, Translator, Singer

[315] *Private Collection.* New York: Alfred A. Knopf, 1965. 295 pp.

Jean Starr Untermeyer characterizes her work as a "chronicle. . . written with the express purpose of picturing those people who have been the most meaningful to me" (157).

"Part One: The Family Album" describes her girlhood in Zanesville, Ohio, which was marred by encounters with anti-Semitism, and her parents' incompatibility, but enriched by music and literature. After a brief period at Mrs. Kohut's College Preparatory School in New York, she married Louis Untermeyer. Their friends soon included writers for the *Masses*, members of the Washington Square Players, musicians, and practically everyone associated with the American Renaissance in poetry. She refers to the departure of her husband (1926) and the death of their son (1927), "two events, both catastrophic and immutable, . . .searing my soul" (40).

"Part Two: A Gallery of Portraits"—much longer than "Part One"—focuses on people she knew during and after her marriage, especially American, English, and European writers. Anecdotes often emphasize the relationship of male poets to women and reveal her capacity for meaningful friendships with other women. Individual chapters are devoted to Sara Teasdale, Edna St. Vincent Millay, Amy Lowell, and Ezra Pound, while Sandburg, Lindsay, and Kreymborg share a chapter. Vivid brief portraits emerge of Leonie Adams, Elinor Wylie, H.D., Edith Sitwell, Sylvia Townsend Warner, as well as Alys Bentley, the experimental dance teacher, and Marian MacDowell, benefactor to artists. The longest chapter "Midwife to a Masterpiece" is devoted to "the most educative experiences of Untermeyer's life" (244), her close working relationship with Hermann Broch, whose *Death of Virgil* she translated. This chapter discusses her theory of translation and reveals the complexities of working with an arrogant genius while her "own song was waiting to be sung" (245). Like the innumerable other writers, Broch is presented with both sympathy and honesty.

Although not very widely reviewed, *Private Collection* was praised for its "fine portraits. . .and sometimes penetrating anecdotes" (*Time*, February 26, 1965, p. 104). Dorothy Van Ghent observed that it gave the " 'intellectual physiognomy' to the first decades of the century when American literature made its astonishing resurgence" (*Carleton Miscellany*, Winter, 1966, p. 83). Padriac Colum argued that *Private Collection* "is a life story" as well as a fine rendering of both the literary and musical milieu (*Commonweal*, August 20, 1965, pp. 604-06). *Choice* found "her memoir, taken with Louis Untermeyer's,. . .a useful commentary on the twenties and forties" (December, 1965, p. 686). The work by Louis Untermeyer is the less personally reticent *Bygones: The Recollections of Louis Untermeyer*, Harcourt, Brace & World, 1965.

Although reviewers did not single out for comment the serious and extended attention Jean Starr Untermeyer gives to other artistic women in her memoir, this emphasis makes the book especially valuable for women's studies as well as for a balanced view of literary history.

Agate Nesaule Krouse
University of Wisconsin—Whitewater

Vorse, Mary Heaton (1874-1966)

Author, Journalist, Labor Organizer

[316] *A Footnote to Folly: Reminiscences.* New York: Farrar & Rinehart, 1935. 407 pp.

Termed "one of the notable pieces of autobiographical writing by an American woman" (Beulah Amidon, *Saturday Review of Literature*, December 28, 1935, p. 7). *A Footnote to Folly* is Mary Heaton Vorse's account of her life from 1920 through 1931.

Written in first person the narrative provides an overview of people concerned with women's suffrage, pacifism, labor organization, and birth-control movements prior to the 1930's. Briefly citing her upbringing in a cultured home, her early training in art, her mother's intellectual influence, and her first marriage, Vorse begins her primary story after she is widowed and left the sole support of two children. Writing became a necessity, and as a roving reporter she was in Europe before, during and after World War I; covering talks in Paris, touring Russia to write of the famine, she became involved with, and sympathetic to, radical movements in which she met Elizabeth Gurley Flynn, Mother Jones, and Margaret Sanger.

Married and widowed a second time, Vorse again became the bread-winner, now concentrating on writing for the labor movement. Also active in the women's suffrage movement, Vorse was a representative to the International Women's Conference for Peace in Budapest joining Catt, Eastman, Addams, and others.

Vorse discusses her fiction briefly, describing the autobiographical elements in it. Of particular interest is the work based on her mother's feelings about growing old and the restrictions of age, the fictional *Autobiography of an Elderly Woman* (Boston: Houghton Mifflin Co., 1911). H. E. Stears (*Nation,* January 15, 1936, p. 80) says "Mary Vorse is talking about herself all the time, even if, perhaps without knowing it. For she is really giving us her autobiography. These things are part of her, of her blood and nerves and heart."

Footnote to Folly, her own autobiography, was Vorse's last major work, although a slight reminiscent chronicle containing some autobiographical elements, *Time and the Town* appeared in 1942.

T. Gail Adams
Emory University, ILA

Walker, Margaret (1915-   )

Poet, Novelist

[317] *How I Wrote Jubilee.*   Chicago: Third World Press, 1972.
36 pp.

How I Wrote Jubilee, commissioned by Harper's in 1966 but
never published until 1972, is limited in scope but remarkably
full in the range of information it gives about the genesis of a novel
and the life of an artist. Margaret Walker's *Jubilee* grew out of a
story told by Walker's grandmother about her own parents' experiences during the Civil War and Reconstruction.

How I Wrote Jubilee traces three interrelated strains in the
novel's development: the author's own history, as she teaches and
raises four children, her time constantly taken away from her
writing; her methodical research into the period and the people of
Jubilee, research which gives the novel its compelling and revealing
authenticity; and the writing and revising of the novel itself, as the
author discovers ways of transforming the material of history into
a work of art. The author discusses fictional models and influences, and gives the reader a sense of just how a novel evolves
through years of frustration and delay.

Walker's *How I Wrote Jubilee* is much more than the history of
Jubilee's creation. The author's experience gives us a realistic
picture of what it is like to be a Black female author in America.
She frankly admits the impossibility of being simultaneously a
wife, mother, teacher and writer, and the biographical details of
her work confirm the problems that these conflicting roles often
produce. But Walker's determination, growing out of an identification with her grandmother and her stories, to write a history that,
as her research indicated, had never been told, was finally fulfilled
in *Jubilee.* Although it has received little attention from reviewers
and critics, *How I Wrote Jubilee* is a valuable resource as a companion to Walker's poetry and novel and, more importantly, as
one of a few sources which attempt to document simultaneously
the artistic and personal backgrounds of a novel and its creator.

Betsy Etheridge Brown
Pennsylvania State University

Waters, Ethel (1896-1977)

Singer, Actress

[318] *His Eye is on the Sparrow.* Garden City, New York: Doubleday and Company, 1951. 278 pp.

His Eye is on the Sparrow is the first of two autobiographies by Ethel Waters, both as told to other persons. Developed chronologically, this work begins with her birth in Chester, Pennsylvania, and ends with her finest dramatic triumph in *The Member of the Wedding* which opened on Broadway in 1950.

The book vividly depicts Waters' childhood of sordid poverty, wherein she observed first hand the world of prostitutes, pimps, alcohol, and drugs; it traces her gradual rise to stardom as a singer via Harlem night clubs and the vaudeville circuit; and it charts her successful transition from singer to dramatic actress.

Conceived during the rape of her twelve year old mother, Waters was both unwanted and unloved. She always felt like "an outsider" within her family. Her constant longing to feel loved and to belong emerges as an underlying theme in the book and is reflected in her relationships with her family, her husbands, her lovers, her friends, and her audiences. Feeling keenly her mother's partiality toward her half-sister, a legitimate child, Waters longed for some word of love from her mother, and throughout her life she felt that the absence of such love was the result of the "great pain, sorrow, and humiliation" which her birth had caused. Waters had long wanted to play the role of Hagar in *Maba's Daughters,* feeling that this would provide the chance to tell the story of her mother's life of "shock, bewilderment and insane rage at being hurt, and her fierce, primitive religion." The play which opened on Broadway in 1939, was the first Broadway Drama to star a Black woman, and Waters won critical acclaim for her performance.

Her constant yearning for her mother's acceptance is revealed when Waters poignantly recalls that the greatest thing that happened to her next to "finding God" came when, during a lull in her career, her mother offered some words of priase and encouragement. The book ends with Waters' reaction: "That was the accep-

tance and fulfillment I'd been dreaming of winning all my life. . .
I knew then that she had loved me for many years in her storm-
tossed, buffeted heart. But she had been unable to say it. . .until
. . .she sensed I was down."

His Eye is on the Sparrow received wide and favorable reviews.
Harrison Smith calls it "one of the most moving biographies of the
century" which will "help everyone who reads the book to understand her people's sufferings, their courage, and their claim to respect and admiration" (*Saturday Review of Literature,* March 24,
1951, p. 18). *U. S. Quarterly Book Review* (June, 1951, p. 131)
states that the book has "a sociological value which goes far beyond its show business aspects."

[319] *To Me It's Wonderful.* New York: Harper and Row,
1972. 162 pp.

Waters' second autobiography, *To Me It's Wonderful,* begins in
1957, at a time when both her status as a celebrity and her health
are declining. In this book, whose main theme is religion, Waters
tells how she was "reborn in God" while attending a Billy Graham
Crusade for Christ. Shortly after this rebirth, she joined the
Graham Team as a member of the choir. She explains that she
turned to the Team to escape from loneliness and to experience
the love which neither her family nor the stage had provided.
She recounts that before joining the Graham Team, "I'd been so
hurt. Really hurt and mistreated in my personal life by anyone
I'd ever really loved," she adds that "she was still that overgrown
little girl looking for a lap to sit on—none of that had been changed
by stardom" (pp. 24-25).

While recalling some of the events of her life which she discusses in *His Eye is on the Sparrow,* this second work is primarily
a testimony of Waters' total commitment to Christ and to Graham
and the Crusading Team.

Margaret N. Simmons
Hampton Institute

Webster, Margaret (1905-   )

Director, Actress, Writer

[320] *Don't Put Your Daughter on the Stage.* New York: Alfred A. Knopf, 1972. 379 pp.

Margaret Webster's book is a chronology not so much of her
personal life as it is of her professional life and accomplishments.
In the earlier chapters of the book, she makes frequent references
to her parents (Ben Webster and Dame May Whitty) and their
acting accomplishments both in England and America. Although
she had considerable experience in England as an actress and director, the major portion of her work has been done in the U. S.
After a brief time in California as a film director-in-training, she returned to directing stage productions. During World War II she
directed U.S.O. productions as well as legitimate theatre. Her accounts of her work directing Shakespearean plays contain intepre-
tive data relevant to the works of Shakespeare, the theatre of
Elizabethan England, and the role of the Shakespearean actor.
She writes of her tireless efforts to establish in America a repertory
theatre and of the ardors of traveling by bus, car, and truck across
America. Her accounts of her experiences as the first woman director at the Metropolitan Opera Company in New York provide insights into opera production which are neither widely known nor
frequently discussed. She relates also her experiences as a director
of productions at the New York City Opera Company. One chapter of the book deals with her testimony before the House Un-
American Activities Committee and her opinions of the era of the
Red Scare, which she refers to as "witch hunting." Despite the
fact that she was not blacklisted, she found working in the American professional theatre difficult for a time as a result of being
called to testify. Among her directorial experiences outside the
U. S. were her two trips to South Africa. She is frank about her
dislike of the apartheid policies. The 1960's were a period in
which she spent time as a lecturer, teacher, and artist-in-residence
at universities in America. Her evaluations of the American university system are not favorable. In reviewing her life, she sees herself
as lucky for having been able to enjoy earning her living by being
able to do what she wanted to do.

Don't Put Your Daughter on the Stage does not reflect the

tendency of "name dropping" that one notices so often in the
autobiographies of figures in the entertainment world. Her pro-
fessionalism and dedication are evident. Phoebe Adams (*Atlantic,*
October 1972, p. 90) sees the book as "Altogether, a practical,
justifiably opinionated running history of thirty years of theatre."
Roderick Nordell (*Christian Science Monitor,* November 29, 1972,
p. 22) believes that "some of the material, important to Miss Webster, is not made interesting to the rest of us." The reader is unable
to discern what prejudices, if any, Margaret Webster may have encountered as a woman in an area of the theatre where men are
usually dominant.

Clara Delores King
Campbell College School of Law
Buies Creek, N. C.

West, Jessamyn (1902-   )

Author, Script-Writer

[321] *To See the Dream.*   New York: Harcourt, Brace and
Company, 1957. 314 pp.

To See the Dream is the first of Jessamyn West's autobiographical works. Transcribed from her unpublished journals, it is the account of her experience in Hollywood as a script-writer for her
novel *The Friendly Persuasion* which was to be filmed by William
Wyler. Although the autobiography only covers approximately
one year, it touches upon many themes which West turned to in
more depth in her late works: her special relationship with her
Quaker ancestors (whose lives are directly reflected in *The Friendly Persuasion*), her quest for solitude, her ambiguous relationship
with her mother, her career as a writer, and her love for nature.

While West cannot be considered a feminist writer, many of her
concerns are of interest to women. Among these are her concern
for women writers' special need for solitude, her awareness that
women intellectuals are often perceived as "unfeminine," and her
strong feelings that, as a woman writer in Hollywood, she is working in a man's world. A brief biography of her life and a bibliogra-

phy of primary and secondary sources can be found in A. S. Shivers', *Jessamyn West* (New York: Twayne Publishing Co., 1972).

[322] *Hide and Seek: A Continuing Journey.* New York: Harcourt, Brace, Jovanovich, Inc., 1973. 310 pp.

In *Hide and Seek,* written during a three month vacation period alone on the banks of the Colorado River, West discusses many of the most important aspects of her life: her need for solitude, her love of books, and her special love of nature. The work is a deft intermingling of the past and present—her immediate existence alone on the river and her powerful memories of her past. She describes her childhood as a mixture of pleasure and pain, and describes her relationship with her mother, Grace, for whom she had ambivalent feelings. Although the book is not a chronological treatment of West's life, it provides enough of her past to bring her into focus.

Like *To See the Dream, Hide and Seek* contains discussions of what it means to be a woman writer. Chief among West's concerns is the difficulty women writers face seeking solitude and the guilt they feel once they have found it (8). Throughout the autobiography is an awareness of the sexist pattern which was always a part of her life: piano instead of violin lessons, cooking instead of nature lessons, and the difficulty in presenting herself as a serious writer. Reviews of the book were generally favorable, stressing for the most part its "wise" and "funny" tone (New York *Times,* May 13, 1973, p. 10). One reviewer, however, found fault with West's "deification of nature" and her continual quoting from Thoreau who was the source of her inspiration (*Book World*, April 1, 1973, p. 3).

[323] *The Woman Said Yes: Encounters with Life and Death.* Harcourt, Brace, Jovanovich, Inc., 1976. 180 pp.

This memoir is divided into two sections. The first is devoted to Grace, West's mother, and the second to Carmen, West's sister. It is a tribute to two strong women who said "yes" to life and who were not afraid of death. In the first part West traces her mother's life: her childhood in Indiana, her marraige and subsequent move to Southern California where she spent most of her life, and her growing infirmity and death. Central to this account is West's own story of her fight with tuberculosis, and her mother who literally would not let her die even when the doctors had given up hope. In the memoir West resolves many of the ambiguities she felt about her mother. She also provides much missing information concerning her own life.

The second section is the author's account of her sister's struggle with cancer and eventual death. In it West traces the relationship among the three women of the family and the ties which kept them together. The most striking aspect of the memoir, however, is Jessamyn's and Carmen's plan to ease Carmen's suffering by administering to her a lethal does of sleeping pills. During the last months of her sister's life, the two planned the "suicide," which was finally carried out. It is an eloquent account of sisterly devotion.

Owing to the controversial nature of the memoir, *The Woman Said Yes* received mixed reviews. One review strongly denounced it as "an immoral book" because of its "defense of suicide" (*Critic*, Vol. 35, Winter 1976, p. 80). In general, however, the memoir received favorable reviews because of its sympathetic depiction of death and dying, including one reviewer who called it "a loving book" (*Christian Century*, September 15, 1976, p. 771).

Patrice K. Gray
Emory University

West, Mae (1893-   )

Actress, Playwright

[324] *Goodness Had Nothing to Do With It.* Englewood Cliffs, New Jersey: Prentice-Hall, 1959. 271 pp.

In her autobiography, *Goodness Had Nothing to Do With It,*

Mae West attempts to give the reader an honest chronicle of her life. Born in Brooklyn in 1893, the first of three children of Matilda Doelger and John West, she was of English, Irish, and German descent. She considers personality the most important aspect of an actress' success and recalls with pride that she insisted on her own spotlight even when she was a seven year old child star billed as "Baby Mae—Song and Dance." West's successes in vaudeville, on Broadway, in touring plays, movies, playwrighting, radio, and in dinner theaters are described, and many of her reviews reproduced—all of them complimentary, except when it suits her purposes that they be uncomplimentary.

She tells of the plays that she wrote, and how they relate to her ideas about morality and sex. She recounts the roles in which she starred and enlivens her story with interesting anecdotes about some of her famous co-workers such as W. C. Fields, Cary Grant, and Mike Todd. Interspersed throughout are her versions of romantic encounters with many different men. The names of her lovers are fictitious, for, like many rich, famous people, she has been plagued with lawsuits during her life. She reveals her one secret marriage to Frank Wallace candidly, along with previously undisclosed aspects of her life, including an interest in the occult. When describing the men in her life, she includes information about both their faults and virtues, and sometimes tells of amusing encounters between her jealous suitors that often end violently. There are also some touching scenes, devoid of her classic retorts, when Mae is a grieving daughter or friend. Considering herself a crusader, a symbol, a legend, and an institution, West recounts such diverse experiences as a prison sentence, lion-taming, and a trip to England. Along with sixteen pages of black and white photographs of West at various ages and stages of stardom, she reproduces her famous letters to Dr. Kinsey, and to the boys of the Royal Air Force. The title, *Goodness Had Nothing to Do With It,* is taken from Mae West's response to a checkroom girl's observation, "Goodness, what beautiful diamonds."

West has been described as representative of a type of autobiographer, a kind of "renegade," by William C. Spengemann and L. R. Lundquist in the *American Quarterly* (Fall, 1965, p. 513); they consider her one of the "Outsiders," one of a group that "cares nothing for acknowledged American values," because she rejects "the sexual hypocrisy" of our society. They quote her

assertion from *Goodness* (257): "I have held firmly to my ideas
and my values. . .I have made a peace, or perhaps only an armed
truce, with myself and the universe. I am in key with my world
as I know it and have seen it." Spengemann and Lundquist observe, however, that West, like other "Outsiders," finds it difficult
to maintain a defiant attitude: "Even Mae West felt impelled by
the public nature of the form [autobiography] to intone, irrele-
vantly, 'I have done what I set out to do, which was to review. . .a
life that goes down deep into the human enigma, the problems of
man (and woman) in relation to the godhead and the yet unopened
secrets of the universe,' and to mention the importance of religion
(unspecified) in sexual education" (*American Quarterly,* pp. 513-
14).

Goodness Had Nothing to Do With It received mixed notices.
Saturday Review found it an "immodest book" in which "the
author blows her own trumpet with gusto" and "does not describe
her many love affairs; she lists them" (November 28, 1959, p. 24).
On the other hand the *Library Journal* (September 15, 1959, p.
2636) found *Goodness* a "remarkably incisive account of the
American theatre. . .the amusing story of a talented actress. . .a
warm, likeable human being."

Linda Hedrick
Old Dominion University

Whitney, Eleanor Searle (c.1915-　　　)

Society-Leader, Evangelist

[325] *Invitation to Joy: A Personal Story.* New York: Harper
and Row, 1971. 195 pp.

In *Invitation to Joy,* Eleanor Whitney tells the story of her
seventeen-year marraige to Cornelius Vanderbilt Whitney, her
divorce, and then the new life she found as a "crusader for Christ."

The daughter of a General Practitioner, Eleanor Searle spent a
happy childhood in a small town in Ohio. After a year of college

she went to New York to study singing, and while working at an in-between job as a receptionist for Pan American Airways, met and soon after married one of the executives. Now Mrs. Cornelius Vanderbilt Whitney, a member of a very old and very wealthy New York family, she spent her time in travelling, elaborate entertaining, supervising the Whitney estate, and choosing worthy philanthropic activities. Her life continued in this way until Billy Graham's New York Crusade transformed her from a "pew warmer" to an awakened Christian. In this same year, 1957, her husband divorced her. Her book describes her new found faith, how it changed her life, and how it led her to try to change the lives of others. She organized Bible study groups among her friends in Old Westbury; she began to speak as a "witness" and became increasingly active in a variety of national evangelical organizations such as Campus Crusade for Christ, Athletes for Action, Christian women's and men's clubs, and the Wycliffe Bible Translators, a missionary group which translates the Bible into the languages of local tribes (146). She also travelled abroad: "I visited missions, leprosariums, and retreat centers rather than couturiers, and talked more about faith than about horse races" (147). She continues to be active, travelling, speaking, and, as she puts it, "working for the King."

Eleanor Whitney's "invitation to joy" went unnoticed; not only did newspapers and magazines ignore the book but so did the library journals. *Invitation to Joy* is of interest to women's studies, however, as a combinatioon of the "inspirational" book with the women's "self-help" book. "Abandoned without cause," Eleanor Whitney was able to put her life together after her divorce through her conversion to a newly-awakened religious faith; "crusading for Christ" became the purpose of and chief activity for the rest of her life. Although she affirms that "the most glorious occupation a woman can have is to make a home for a family" (183), she would show by her own example that "a single person can lead an extraordinarily fulfilling life." The fulfillment she found in her life after her divorce was in serving as witness for Jesus and so inviting others to know and share the joy she had found in her new faith.

Judith B. Herman
State College at Buffalo

Wilson, Edith Bolling (1872-1961)

First Lady

[326] *My Memoir.*   Indianapolis and New York: The Bobbs-Merrill Company, 1939. 386 pp.

Edith Bolling Wilson's autobiography was the first volume of memoirs ever written by the wife of an American President. It covered, primarily, the years of her life from the time of her marriage to Woodrow Wilson in 1915 to his death in 1924. In it, Edith Wilson described her courtship and marriage, her relationship with Wilson, the duties of a First Lady, her role at the Paris Peace Conference, her responsibilities during Wilson's illness, and the years she shared with Wilson after the Presidency.

My Memoir was placed in bookstores on March 13, 1939, and by the end of March, it began appearing on the New York *Herald Tribune* and New York *Times* list of best sellers. Marquis James, Pulitzer Prize-winning biographer, who helped Wilson with the book, called it "perhaps the greatest personal and historical memoir to bear the name of an English-speaking woman. Of permanent value and immediate interest, it renders obsolescent much 'history' and provides fresh material for its amendment" (Promotional literature). But, reviews of the book, which appeared immediately in the press of almost every major city, were quite mixed.

Writing for the *New Yorker* (March 18, 1939), Clifton Fadiman found in her memoir "dozens of small sidelights, much amusing White House gossip, glimpses of European greats." Stephen Vincent Benet (New York *Herald Tribune*, March 12, 1939) wrote that "while her story was "full with personal odds and ends," she also had "an eye for great moments and great occasions," and from the book emerged "a portrait not only of a great man but of a human, interesting, highly American woman."

Other reviewers found neither charm nor significance in her work. When Howard Mumford Jones wrote in the Boston *Transcript* (March 12, 1939) that the book was "utterly without literary value," he reflected the view of many critics. Some reviewers were disturbed that she still bore intense animosity toward

Wilson's advisers, specifically Joseph Tumulty, Edward House, and Robert Lansing. Woman writers seemed most critical of the book. Their judgments ranged from mild reproach to caustic reprobation. Maurine Block's article in the *Dallas Times* (March 12, 1939), called the memoirs "bland, conservative and dignified. In style, it is just the sort of book to be expected of a genteel daughter of the South who refers to nightgowns as 'dream robes.' " The Washington *Times-Herald* critic, Betty Hynes, wrote in her column on March 13, 1939, "The tremendous period of history which she shared with one of its greatest figures, she interprets from the trivial things that were once thought to be the 'be and end all' of a woman's world. . .the tragedy of the smallness of her soul makes us wish the silence had never been broken."

Historian Henry Steele Commager presented, perhaps, the most balanced view (New York *Times*, March 12, 1939), when he stated that while it was "not a great historic document nor a profound personal interpretation nor a brilliant literary portrait," it nevertheless was "informative and entertaining; it confirms accepted judgments more than it reveals new truths."

The autobiography is useful for women's studies because it dispels the still-held, popular impression that Edith Wilson became "the first lady president" during the period after Wilson's stroke in 1919. She, herself, used the term "stewardship" to define her position (289). Unpublished documentation contained in the Edith Bolling Wilson Papers, the Woodrow Wilson Papers, Joseph P. Tumulty Papers, State Department records and elsewhere seems to support her claim that she did not make policy decisions on her own. Her biographers, Aldon Hatch and Ishbel Ross, essentially agree with this assessment. Her power was a veto power, for she determined whom Wilson saw and what matters were presented to him, but she used only delegated authority. To give Edith Wilson the label "presidentress" is to disregard her own memorial testimony.

Edith James
Office of the Historian
U. S. Department of State

Wolff, Sister Mary Madeleva (1887-1964)

Educator, Poet

[327] *My First Seventy Years.*   New York: Macmillan Company, 1959. 172 pp.

Sister Madeleva was one of the first women religious in the United States to perceive the necessity of sound, professional preparation for the teaching sister, as well as for women religious seeking other kinds of professional service. She founded the first theological college and graduate school for women at St. Mary's College, Notre Dame, Indiana, where she was president from 1934 virtually until her death. She had herself been educated at St. Mary's College, the University of Notre Dame, and the University of California at Berkeley. Her output of verse and critical essays reveals a minor, but authentic, literary gift. Her autobiography gives an account of a middle-western childhood, an adult life spent at the Indiana college and at St. Mary's of the Wasatch, the second of the Holy Cross colleges operated by Sister Madeleva's religious congregation. Otherwise, her account of her life relies heavily on reminiscences of famous people she met, either during her administration as college president or on her travels, but is valuable chiefly because of the brief glimpse it gives of her determination that religious women should be well equipped to undertake educational or other professional tasks.

Sister Marie Carolyn Klinkhamer
Norfolk State University

Wong, Jade Snow (1922-   )

Artist

[328] *Fifth Chinese Daughter.*   New York: Harper and Brothers, 1950 246 pp.

Fifth Chinese Daughter deals with the first twenty-seven years in the life of Jade Snow Wong, a first generation Chinese-American woman growing up in San Francisco's Chinatown. The author uses the third person voice because "Even written in English an 'I' book by a Chinese would seem outrageously immodest to anyone raised in the spirit of Chinese propriety" (p. vii). As the fifth daughter of Chinese immigrants, Jade Snow Wong straddles her parents' Chinese traditions and the American culture in which she lives. Her father's strong influence on her attitudes and education is emphasized. She ultimately gains the respect of both parents by leaving home, attending Mills College, embarking on a career as a potter, integrating herself completely into the world of the student, artist, American, but retaining her Chinese heritage and attitudes. Aware of the limits of her own sheltered upbringing, Jade Snow resolves to reduce the shock of her youngest brother's entrance into the western world. He calls her his "outside mother" reflecting her influence and her outgoing quality contrasted to their mother's following the traditional stay-at-home role of the Chinese female.

[329] *No Chinese Stranger.* New York: Harper and Row, 1975. 366 pp.

No Chinese Stranger continues in the third person voice until after the death of the author's father when she becomes more comfortable with the first person singular and adopts that voice. In this book Jade Snow Wong deals with her marriage, her children, her career, and her travels. Nearly half of the book is devoted to her "return" to China as she retraces Father Wong's steps to his native village. Her account of the people and attitudes she encounters put China of the seventies in a new perspective. Throughout this book Wong has struck a balance between the creative, public woman and the loving wife and mother; her ability to accept so completely the two roles may be attributable to her Chinese attitudes and background as much as to her independent personality. Although she did not fit into the Chinese female role of her mother, she felt that "public life was never going to matter as much as the tranquil gratification of home and family" (p. 131).

These autobiographies together provide a unique insight into the life of a Chinese-American. Jade Snow Wong's remarkable ambition is epitomized by her writing an autobiography at twenty-seven. Her movement from the sheltered life of Chinatown into the mainstream of America and finally the world is evidence of resourcefulness and growth. She never loses sight of her Chinese upbringing, deriving much strength from her heritage and family. Through the course of the two books the reader watches Jade Snow Wong blend her two cultures, fascinated by the extent to which both fit into her life.

Diane Jefferson
San Luis Obispo, California

Yurka, Blanche (1887-1974)

Actress, Director

[330] *Bohemian Girl: Blanche Yurka's Theatrical Life.* Athens, Ohio: Ohio University Press, 1970. 306 pp.

With great detail as to people and performances, Blanche Yurka describes a theatrical career spanning more than sixty years. The daughter of poor Czech immigrants, she eventually found herself in the company of such notable performers as Katharine Cornell, Mary Pickford, and John Barrymore, to whose Hamlet she played Gertrude. In her teens, she entered the Metropolitan Opera School, but a strained voice cut short her singing career. Without hope of becoming a great opera singer, Yurka turned to acting. The frustrations of looking for work as an unknown and untried actress gave way first to bit parts and finally to a starring role in *Daybreak,* and opportunity provided for her by her friend, the actress and dramatist, Jane Cowl.

Family as well as friends gave her strong emotional support throughout her career. She was very close to two sisters, Rose and Mila, as well as to two brothers, Tony and Charles, who, tragically, both ended their lives by suicide. Marriage, however, did not provide the support she had received from her family. Her marriage to actor Ian Keith lasted for little more than one year. Quoting Millamant in Congreve's *The Way of the World,* she states, "I was never meant to 'dwindle into a wife.' " Untraditional in her independent lifestyle and dedication to her career, she yet had a special insight into the social and psychological realities of women's traditional roles. This knowledge helped her to create a series of successful portrayals in Ibsen's plays, several of which she directed as well. Her Gina in *The Wild Duck* gave the play its first popularity in this country. A strong supporter of government aid to the theater and unionization of actors, she appeared in several productions on behalf of the Actor's Equity Theatre.

Yurka's autobiography was not widely reviewed when it was published, although the several short reviews which appeared are favorable. Mary Bozeman (*Library Journal,* May 1, 1970, p. 1734) called it "a vivid portrait of the theater in America," and *Booklist* (October 15, 1970, p. 165) praises its portrait of a "warm, friendly personality, gallant in adversity and always a thoroughly professional actress."

Naomi Leventhal
State University College—Fredonia

Zaharias, Mildred "Babe" Didrikson (1914-1956)

Track Star, Professional Golfer

[331] *This Life I've Led: My Autobiography.* New York: A. S. Barnes, 1955. 242 pp.

In twenty-five years of competition, Mildred Didrikson Zaharias compiled the greatest sports record of any woman in history—in sports as diverse as basketball, Olympic track and field, and golf. Her autobiography chronicles mainly those years, although the chapter about her early life in a large Norwegian immigrant family are more revealing of her character. The latter part of the book documents her bout with cancer, her determination to recover, her struggle to continue golfing; the work ends as she learns of the recurrence of the disease. While she closes with a defiant, "My autobiography isn't finished yet," within a year cancer was to take her life.

"Babe," whose nickname came from a comparison to Babe Ruth, is not an accomplished writer. The book is "told" to sports-writer Harry Paxton, who makes no attempt to edit out cliches, wordiness or stylistic blunders. Thus, the reader may be appalled by phrases like "stuff like that" or "living high off the hog." The book's main interest lies in two areas: its chronicling of Zaharias's breaking of barriers for women athletes (she helped found the La-dies' PGA in 1949) and its inherent sexism, fifties style. Incessant-ly, Zaharias apologizes for being a successful female sports figure. She assures us that she likes feminine clothes, make-up, cooking; automatically defers to her husband; scorns "girls" playing football and basketball. A comment from Bob Hope, which she quotes ap-provingly, sums up the book's attitude: " 'There's only one thing wrong about Babe and myself. I hit the ball like a girl and she hits it like a man.' "

Still, as friend and colleague Betty Hicks notes in her two-part series on Zaharias in *Women Sports* (November-December 1975), Babe was often accused of being "not all woman;" her manners and style were distinctively not feminine, and she loved to flaunt her penchant for rough language and humor to her fans. She was, however, the first woman golfer to pay any attention to showman-ship. Thus, the attempt in her autobiography to prove that she was "all female" to the satisfaction of a mid-fifties culture is under-standable.

Before she was a teenager, Babe claims that her goal was to "be the greatest athlete that ever lived." Such a dream was extraordinary for a girl in south Texas in the twenties, even a girl with six siblings and parents who encouraged physical training. Babe Didrikson, however, was no ordinary person, and the difficulty with this autobiography is that it probes so shallowly the depths of the personality of this phenomenal woman.

Contemporary reviews of the book were favorable, many noting Zaharias's courageous account of her fight against cancer and the revelations throughout the book of a "warm, vibrant and delightful woman" (Arthur Daley, New York *Times,* December 11, 1955, p. 22). Later commentators, such as Betty Hicks point out perhaps more interesting inaccuracies (such as Zaharias's claim never to have played football), and picture a somewhat different woman from the one the autobiography reveals.

Margaret McFadden-Gerber
Appalachian State University

Zassenhaus, Hiltgunt (-   )

Physician

[332] *Walls: Resisting the Third Reich—One Woman's Story.* Boston: Beacon Press, 1974. 248 pp.

Hiltgunt Zassenhaus' autobiography, *Walls,* tells the inspiring story of her early years in Hamburg, Germany, just prior to Hitler's Germany and of her years quietly and courageously resisting the Third Reich. Before the war, Zassenhaus was a student of Scandinavian languages. When Hitler came into power and the war began, she was given the job of translator between German authorities and Scandinavian political prisoners. Because "she found her personal sense of decency offended by the society she was living in" (*The Nation,* February 15, 1975, p. 184) and with great personal courage, she decided to help the political prisoners in any way that she could, frequently endangering herself in her resistance to Hitler's Gestapo. Zessenhaus is credited with having saved the lives of over 1,200 Danish and Norwegian political prisoners during the war. At the time of her resistance she also pursued her medical studies, all through the terrible bombing of Hamburg. For her wartime resistance work she was nominated for the 1974 Nobel peace prize. She has been a successful physician in the United States for many years.

Zassenhaus' story "is the best possible witness to her faith in the power of the individual. . .the book chronicles her rejection of that soul-deadening caution for a life of courage and commitment" (*Ms. Mazazine,* October, 1974, p. 93). All reviewers of her book recognized the heroism of the writer but some quibbled over the writing style of the story. "Though there have been numerous anti-Nazi autobiographies in the past, *Walls* stands out as a remarkable work that simultaneously manages to be a fine adventure story and a good inspiration tale" (Claudia Dreifus in *The Nation*, February 15, 1975, p. 186). Gordon C. Zahn writing in *America* (April 20, 1974, p. 316) is very critical: "The inspiration one finds in the author's actions is all but smothered by a strange concoction of sentimental gush." Hans Stranska (*Library Journal*, August, 1974, p. 1939) describes many of Zassenhaus' observations as "trite."

Two reviewers recommended the book to younger readers, and in general reviewers agree that the book "succeeds because it rings true" (*Library Journal*, August, 1974, p. 1939). Despite its possible faults, the book is valuable for women's studies: "We need to read more about heroines of this order: women—people—who defy passivity to assert their own humanity" (*The Nation*, February 15, 1975, p. 186).

Jean B. Palmer
Stoneham Public Library, Stoneham, Massachusetts

Ziegfeld, Patricia (1916-   )

Daughter of Theatrical Parents

[333] *The Ziegfelds' Girl: Confessions of an Abnormally Happy Childhood.* New York: Little Brown and Company, 1964. 210 pp.

Patricia Ziegfeld recalls her idyllic youth as the adored child of theatrical entrepreneur Florenz Ziegfeld and actress Billie Burke. After a brief, highly imaginative depiction of her parents' courtship and early married life, she turns to her central theme—her enchanted early years—suggesting its correspondence to her parents' theatrical successes. Scenes shift, but the theme is constant: her parents' lavishing attention and money on their beloved little girl. To emphasize the timeless quality of childhood, Ziegfeld organizes her autobiography through presentations of settings, dialogues and episodes, eschewing chronological sequence (suggestive of a pattern of change). Family settings rivaled Ziegfeld sets in costly extravagance, and the events of the Zeigfelds' private life suggested comparison to full-blown Ziegfeld productions. Patricia Ziegfeld first focuses attention on the family's Hastings-on-the-Hudson mansion complete with an exotic animal kingdom, Mount Vernon playhouse and a gallery of servants and house guests. Then she turns to the family's retreat at their "rustic" Canadian hunting lodge, Palm Springs interludes—sailing, gambling and dinner parties—their first-class European tour and their cross-country jaunt by private railroad car. The New York theatre—especially "Daddy's" New Amsterdam stage for the yearly Follies—is a constant presence in the autobiography, for Flo Ziegfeld and his work fascinated the young Patricia and supported the family in a high style of spending and show. Patricia's charmed life—and so her autobiography—necessarily ends with the Depression's collapse of the Ziegfeld fortune and her father's subsequent death.

Diana Forbes-Robertson (New York *Times Book Review,* November 15, 1964, p. 34) observes that the book "contains a suggestion of fiction, being predominantly written in conversation. . . . She seems to possess total recall of her own and of reported words. Thus the book is the re-creation of a life rather than a biographical study."

Since Ziegfeld is so concerned with the theatrical world of her father, her self-portrait grants a privileged look at a configuration of themes interesting from a feminist perspective: fashion, wealth and beauty in the late nineties and early twentieth century. To a large extent Flo Ziegfeld fashioned trends of female beauty for America by his annual selection of Ziegfeld girls and his public remarks about his choices.

Janis Forman
Goucher College

A List of Topics of Interest to Women's Studies

[Selected by the contributors for the works they annotated. The numbers refer to the entry numbers. Topics one would expect to find in most autobiographical records, for instance, references to "mother," have been omitted.]

Abortion, 2, 37, 55, 94, 101, 110, 125, 139, 143, 154, 163, 203, 285, 286

Adolescence, 13, 20, 24, 29, 31, 36, 39, 41, 46, 47, 58, 60, 63, 70, 82, 91, 93-96, 103, 108, 118, 121-125, 132, 135, 140-143, 153, 154, 156, 168, 169, 182, 192, 199, 201, 202, 205, 206, 210-212, 214, 222, 223, 226, 229, 241, 242, 247, 248, 257, 262, 264, 266, 268, 269, 283, 287, 299, 307, 310, 315, 323, 324, 328

Aesthetics, 244, 251

Alcoholism, 15, 112, 136

Alienation, 2, 12-14, 16, 18, 19, 30, 31, 44, 60, 66, 70, 74, 94, 123, 124, 136, 143, 156, 168, 177, 179, 190-193, 195, 202, 211, 216, 217, 224, 231, 243, 254, 262, 266, 287, 306, 307, 321, 323

Ambition, 112, 113

Anger, Feminist, 1, 5, 48, 54, 74, 94, 101, 135, 142, 154, 169, 184, 216, 219, 224, 226, 230, 232, 240, 247, 258, 259, 266, 268, 289, 306

Appearance, Personal, 14, 21, 36, 39, 45, 63, 65, 90, 91, 104, 115, 139, 147, 153, 154, 169, 192, 193, 195, 206, 230, 243, 260, 266, 270; Beauty, 4, 22, 40, 43, 46, 66, 94, 101, 109, 136, 137, 170, 177, 187, 210, 211, 214, 216, 219, 222, 224, 228, 257, 267, 315, 324, 326, 333; Dress, 1, 4, 21, 22, 35, 118, 119, 132, 136, 182, 187, 188, 219, 222, 224, 228, 231, 241, 244, 250, 257, 265, 315, 326, 333; Ugliness, 1, 12, 13, 40, 46, 70, 94, 99, 101, 140, 148, 170, 210, 211, 224, 248, 249, 267, 299, 315

Artists, Women as, 7-10, 16, 17, 24, 25, 30-32, 36, 45, 50, 54, 58, 65, 67, 69-71, 75, 76, 80, 90-92, 94, 108, 111, 119, 120, 124, 130-132, 135, 139, 140, 166, 167, 172, 179, 188, 202, 213, 218, 219, 230, 239, 240, 241, 244, 246, 249, 250, 251, 257-259, 261, 268, 281, 282, 287-289, 291, 298, 312, 315, 317, 320, 322, 328, 329

Aviation, 61, 183-185

Birth Control, 117, 143, 153, 200, 267, 268, 285, 286, 316

Birth Order, 36, 65, 120, 122, 124, 141, 182, 202, 209-211, 223, 241, 257, 290, 321, 324, 328

Black, 55, 249; Men, 12-14, 60, 62, 66, 93, 108, 117, 131, 132, 141, 143, 144, 243, 253, 262, 267, 291, 302, 308, 317; White Relationships, 12-14, 20, 26, 40, 41, 62, 66, 93, 99, 105, 108, 125, 126, 131, 132, 135, 141, 143, 144, 154, 164, 238, 241, 243, 253, 262, 267, 291, 300, 302, 308, 310; Women, 12-14, 26, 60, 62, 66, 82, 93, 99, 108, 117, 125, 126, 131, 132, 143, 144, 154, 243, 262, 267, 291, 302, 308, 317

Careers for Women, 2, 3, 7-9, 11, 13, 14, 16, 17, 21, 24-29, 31, 35, 36, 40, 41, 49, 50, 52, 54-59, 61, 65, 69-73, 76, 81, 88, 92, 94, 95, 97, 101, 102, 104, 106, 109, 110, 112, 113, 116, 118, 120, 121, 128-131, 135-139, 143, 153, 154, 163, 164, 166, 167, 169, 172-174, 180, 184, 185, 187, 188, 205, 208, 210, 211, 213, 217-219, 223, 243, 244, 256, 257, 260, 262, 269, 275, 279, 282, 285-287, 298, 301, 304, 307, 308, 313, 314, 316, 320, 321, 324, 328-332

Childhood, 5, 10, 12, 16, 18, 20, 24, 25, 31, 40, 41, 46, 51-53, 60, 63, 64, 66, 69, 70, 75, 82, 91, 95-98, 112, 119, 120, 122-125, 130, 132, 135, 140-142, 148, 149, 153, 154, 156, 166, 167, 169-171, 173, 174, 180, 182, 192, 199, 201-205, 210-212, 214, 219, 222, 231, 241, 242, 244-246, 250-252, 257, 263, 264, 269, 270, 282, 287, 290, 291, 296, 297, 299, 300, 307, 308, 315, 316, 318, 321-324, 327, 333

Creativity, 12, 14, 16, 17, 29-32, 39, 41, 45, 47-49, 54, 58, 63, 69, 70, 71, 73, 75, 78-80, 90-92, 94-96, 99, 111, 120-122, 124, 126, 128, 130-134, 138-141, 144, 156, 166-169, 175, 176, 179, 181, 185, 202-204, 206, 211, 213, 219, 230, 241, 244, 245, 247, 248, 251-254, 257, 259, 261, 262, 267-269, 281, 282, 287-289, 291, 298, 312, 315, 317, 320-322, 324, 330

Death, 4, 6, 8, 9, 16, 20, 36, 43, 44, 47, 49, 54, 58, 59, 73, 76, 82, 84, 87, 93, 108, 112, 118, 122, 124-126, 131, 136, 140, 141, 143, 148, 151, 155, 166, 167, 169, 175, 176, 183, 184, 199, 202, 204, 226, 233-236, 241, 246, 250, 252, 266, 267, 269, 271, 272, 275, 277, 279, 284-286, 289, 295-297, 300, 305, 312, 315, 316, 323, 324, 326, 329, 332

Distinctive Voice, 39, 45, 60-62, 78, 108, 142, 166, 168, 169, 177, 179, 186, 230, 257, 262, 315, 328, 329

Divorce, 5, 12, 14-16, 20, 23, 27, 39, 41, 57, 64, 65, 67, 70, 76, 94, 98, 101, 103, 124, 131, 135-137, 143, 156, 166, 168, 169, 190, 200, 205, 213, 228, 231, 258, 259, 261, 264, 265, 306, 325

Drugs, 2, 20, 99, 118, 132, 143, 231, 249, 250, 254, 306, 311, 318

Education for Women, 2, 3, 23, 41, 47, 49, 51, 55, 58, 62, 64, 76, 81, 93, 97, 101, 103, 106, 108, 118, 121, 130, 131, 140, 156, 164, 168, 169, 173, 174, 179, 182, 199, 201, 208, 219, 226, 231, 239, 241, 252, 262, 287, 290, 296, 297, 300, 303, 307, 310, 313, 327, 328

Etiquette, 21, 156, 157

Evasiveness, 43, 95, 96

Exploitation, 2, 5, 16, 41, 60, 66, 74, 101, 117, 123, 132, 135, 143, 154, 164, 168, 170, 177, 190, 191, 195, 205, 230, 231, 266, 290, 300, 302, 314

Fame, Desire for, 2, 14, 16, 17, 24, 47, 61, 70, 71, 94-96, 101, 105, 108, 110, 132, 136, 137, 140, 153, 166, 167, 170, 173, 174, 188, 213, 219, 244, 247, 258, 259, 282, 284, 288, 289, 298, 306, 326, 330, 331; Effects of, 183-185

Family, 4-6, 12-14, 16, 18, 24, 25, 29, 31, 36, 40, 41, 44-48, 51, 53, 59, 60, 63, 65, 68-70, 76, 79, 82, 83, 91, 95, 97, 98, 101, 108, 117-122, 124, 125, 132, 135, 140-143, 147-149, 154-156, 166-169, 173, 174, 177, 181-185, 187, 190, 198-200, 202-206, 210-215, 219, 223-226, 231, 241, 249-, 252, 257, 262-266, 268, 269, 275, 277, 279, 285-287, 295-300, 310, 315, 323, 326, 328-330, 333

Fantasizing and Dreams, 12, 13, 15, 44, 53, 70, 71, 108, 110, 148, 165, 168, 171, 182, 203, 204, 206, 219, 231, 233-236, 243, 245, 246, 250,

257, 270-272, 321-323

Fashion, 4, 21, 22, 45, 153, 156, 199, 211, 215, 250, 312, 315, 333

Father, 3, 5, 6, 12, 16, 18, 31, 46, 51-54, 60, 63, 67, 69, 70, 75, 82, 98, 108, 109, 118-120, 122, 124, 128, 130, 132, 135, 140-142, 148, 155, 164, 169, 182, 187, 192, 198, 199, 203, 210, 211, 223, 228, 229, 231, 245, 246, 249, 252, 257, 263, 266, 268, 269, 275, 283, 287, 290, 296-299, 307, 308, 310, 313, 315, 320, 321, 324, 329

Father Substitutes, 5, 26, 64, 103, 124, 196, 246, 248, 284, 311

Fatherless, 26, 44, 64, 93, 112, 123, 156, 166, 170, 171, 201, 258, 259, 311

Fundamentalism, 211

Foreign Settings, 34, 84-87; African, 118, 292, 293; Asian, 118; Chinese, 217, 309; Congo, 292; Cuban, 309; European, 4, 8, 9, 14, 21-23, 28, 37, 42, 65, 70, 72, 73, 75, 83, 90, 100, 104, 112, 118, 128, 130, 131, 135, 138, 156, 157, 166, 167, 169, 171, 182, 183, 193, 215, 218, 225, 227, 245, 246, 250, 252, 257, 261 287, 290, 310, 312, 326, 332; Israeli, 227; Japanese, 309; Mexican, 76, 225; Middle Eastern, 224, 226; Spanish, 254; Viet-Namese, 294

Grandmother, 12, 269

Happiness, 4, 14, 27, 29, 31, 42, 53, 64, 68, 69, 71, 73, 75, 76, 89, 95, 96, 101, 114, 122, 124, 132-135, 140, 147, 155, 168, 169, 172, 181-185, 205, 206, 208, 213, 231, 241, 246, 298, 310, 315, 320, 322

Homemaking, 14, 20, 22, 27, 29, 31, 42, 48, 69, 71, 74, 76, 93, 97, 101, 117, 124, 128, 143, 148, 157, 181, 183, 185, 193-196, 203, 206, 208, 211, 213, 214, 218-221, 224, 225, 241, 250, 257, 265, 269, 275, 279, 288, 296, 297, 310, 312, 329

Homosexuality (Male), 45, 169, 229, 247, 248

Humor, 4, 31, 58, 76, 108, 122, 130, 133, 134, 141, 145, 146, 149, 154, 166, 169, 203-206, 210-215, 241, 247, 250, 257, 298, 299, 323, 324

Independence, 37, 116, 251

Inferiority Feelings, 4, 30, 36, 39, 46, 54, 63, 64, 93, 112, 114, 137, 142, 148, 182, 184, 203, 204, 211, 224, 230, 231, 245, 254, 256, 266, 275, 279, 306, 318

Infidelity, 20, 31, 39, 42, 128, 136, 168, 187, 188, 190, 230, 231, 256, 282, 289

Isolation, 5, 12, 13, 16, 27, 30, 41, 44, 47, 68, 70, 91, 94, 99, 126, 127, 132, 136, 143, 168, 177, 178, 184, 190-193, 195, 200, 203, 204, 224, 230, 231, 241, 247, 250, 254, 263, 267, 288

Jail, 2, 18, 66, 94, 99, 127, 132, 250, 285, 286

Lesbian Relationships, 5, 7-9, 12, 13, 39, 94, 99, 101, 132, 142, 193, 228, 229, 230, 245, 289, 306, 312

Loneliness, 2, 5, 9, 16, 30, 39, 43, 44, 49, 53, 63, 68, 71, 88, 91, 94, 98, 99, 101, 108, 110, 113, 115 123, 126, 131, 132, 136, 137, 142, 143, 168, 182, 183, 192, 193, 195, 202-204, 219, 224, 230, 231, 244, 247, 267, 280, 287-289, 295, 296, 312, 318, 319, 322

Male Chauvinism, 1, 21, 27, 35, 39, 42, 45, 54, 62, 66, 67, 74, 76, 101, 102, 106, 136, 152-154, 166, 167, 169, 187, 188, 198, 203-206, 212, 213, 219, 224, 232, 240, 246, 250, 266, 281, 301, 306, 315

Marriage, 4-6, 14-16, 19, 20, 22, 25-27, 33, 35, 39, 42, 44, 46, 48, 50, 54, 58-60, 63, 64, 67, 69, 71, 74, 76, 81, 84, 88, 93, 94, 98, 100, 101, 103, 110, 112, 115, 119, 120, 122-124, 128, 131-135, 137, 139, 140, 143, 145-148, 154, 155, 157, 163, 164, 166-169, 175-178, 181-185, 187, 188, 190-200, 203, 206, 208, 211, 213, 216, 218-221, 223-226, 228, 231, 240-242, 244, 257, 260, 261, 263, 265, 267, 269, 282, 296-298, 304, 306, 309, 310, 315, 316, 323-326, 329-331

Menopause, 16, 301

Menstruation, 54, 240, 268

Mental Health, 12, 16, 32, 36, 44, 46, 73, 76, 81, 94, 121, 124, 155, 213, 231, 250, 267, 295, 301

Mental Illness, 46, 81, 90, 94, 143, 155, 171, 184, 193, 195, 203, 231, 246, 258, 259, 263, 298

Middle Age, 16, 17, 20, 43, 44, 59, 101, 121, 131, 133, 134, 137, 154, 172, 206, 219, 241, 288, 289, 315, 321

Mother Substitutes, 30, 46, 49, 75, 82, 93, 103, 104, 108, 126, 177, 178, 199, 200, 283

Motherhood, 6, 16, 25, 29, 41, 45, 46, 57, 62, 64, 65, 67, 76, 79, 88, 97, 113, 120, 123, 139, 148, 157, 164, 168, 175, 176, 218, 220, 221, 223, 227, 242, 245, 249, 256, 257, 268, 280, 284, 295, 298, 304, 315, 316, 317; Married, 4, 5, 27, 48, 60, 69, 74, 83, 93, 101, 103, 117, 124, 135, 143, 145-147, 155, 166, 167, 169, 177, 181, 183-185, 190, 198, 199, 203, 206, 208, 209, 213, 215, 216, 219, 240, 241, 244, 269, 285, 286, 296, 297, 305, 310, 329; Un-Married, 5, 44, 60, 68, 98, 101, 108, 117, 135, 143, 169, 204, 205, 254, 285, 286, 311

Motherless, 24, 26, 141, 144, 178, 200, 201

Mystical Experiences, 78, 103, 141, 177, 178, 186, 191, 193-196, 233-237, 242, 244-246, 269, 271-274, 282, 307, 322

Narcissism, 254

National Background; Belgian, 287; Chinese, 165, 328, 329; Czechoslova-kian, 65; English, 75, 324; German, 75, 140, 167, 169, 324; Irish, 324; Italian, 75; Norwegian, 33, 331; Polish, 290, 303; Russian, 227, 257, 290; Scottish, 241

Nature, 133, 134, 148

Old Age, 6, 8, 9, 30, 36, 41, 60, 65, 69, 76, 99, 108, 115, 121, 126, 167, 177, 178, 219, 227, 241, 257, 269, 278, 279, 295, 297, 312, 315, 328

Pacifism, 15, 18, 19, 33, 41, 68, 93, 106, 164, 169, 179, 185, 202, 245, 250, 253, 307, 316

Parapsychology, 271-274

Parenting, 5, 6, 31-33, 41, 46, 59, 64, 69, 74, 83, 89, 108, 120, 142, 145-148, 157, 166, 167, 183, 184, 190, 200, 203, 206, 213, 219-221, 241, 242, 254, 256, 257, 268, 269, 285, 286, 296, 297, 299

Passivity, 16, 39, 230, 231, 263, 321

Politics, 4, 40, 41, 55, 56, 61, 78, 117, 135, 147, 155, 157, 179, 184, 185, 227, 232, 243, 246, 250, 252, 268, 285, 286, 301, 315; Anti-War, 229; Communist, 66, 278; Conservative, 65, 75, 102, 261, 269, 291, 294; Democrat, 1, 121, 136, 217, 265, 277, 279, 313, 326; Liberal, 1, 18, 19, 90, 95, 96, 101, 136, 137, 164, 169, 200, 217, 261, 277, 279; Radical, 1, 18, 19, 38, 66, 98, 99, 101, 108, 125-127, 154, 177, 195, 213, 240, 253, 266, 277, 279, 290, 306, 310, 311, 316; Republican, 264; Socialist, 150, 213

Poverty, 2, 5, 12, 13, 32, 37, 41, 48, 55, 60, 68, 70, 82, 91, 93, 112, 117, 132, 133, 141-143, 164, 166, 178, 204, 205, 209, 224, 227, 245, 247, 253, 257, 267, 269, 284-286, 290, 302, 303, 311, 318

Pregnancy, 5, 16, 97, 113, 117, 143, 169, 220, 223, 245, 250, 258, 259, 268, 285, 286; Married, 4, 27, 48, 71, 101, 177, 178, 183, 193, 203, 213, 241; Un-Married, 2, 12, 108, 110, 165, 168, 311

Prejudice, 40, 41, 45, 62, 66, 68, 93, 95, 96, 105, 117, 122, 126, 135, 144, 154, 164, 178, 198, 203-205, 224, 243, 257, 260, 261, 297, 298, 300-302, 308, 310, 315, 328

Prison, 19, 50, 66, 99, 127, 132, 250, 266, 280, 284, 306, 311

Prostitution, 2, 13, 74, 117, 143, 153, 154, 166, 269, 283, 311, 318

Racial Background; American Indian, 130, 177, 168, 186, 242, 243, 296, 297; Black, 20, 40, 55, 56, 60, 66, 82, 93, 108, 130, 132, 135, 141, 143, 144, 154, 238, 243, 291, 300, 308, 310, 317, 318; Brown, 18, 130, 177; Irish, 212; Japanese-American, 58

Racism, 5, 10, 26, 41, 48, 60, 62, 66, 105, 117, 118, 122, 130, 132, 135, 140, 143, 144, 153, 154, 164, 185, 197, 204, 205, 243, 247, 253, 300, 301, 310, 320

Radicalism, 7, 54, 65, 68, 98, 99, 101, 125-127, 154, 177, 179, 213, 253, 302, 310, 311, 316

Rape, 2, 57, 82, 94, 117, 166, 178, 230, 243, 253, 318

Regional Setting—USA, Alaskan, 220; Californian, 168; Eastern, 210, 211, 225, 315; Mid-Atlantic, 302; Mid-Western, 95, 96, 108, 118, 130, 131, 133, 134, 140, 178, 180, 197, 200, 209-212, 242, 265, 266, 302, 307,

327; New England, 51, 119, 120, 199, 288; Northern, 6, 44, 47, 55-57, 130, 132, 135, 208, 241, 253, 257, 261, 290, 308; Northeastern, 182, 183, 192, 195, 301, 333; Northwestern, 198, 203-206; Southwestern, 147, 191, 194, 196, 251, 296, 297; Southern, 61, 62, 93, 105, 108, 135, 136, 141, 164, 202, 238, 239, 241, 243, 253, 261, 267, 300, 308, 310, 326; Southern Appalachian, 83, 239; West, 178, 321-323; West Coast, 216, 217

Religion, 15, 41, 62, 78, 84-87, 89, 95, 96, 103, 164, 175, 179, 201, 231, 242, 243, 282, 300, 207, 318, 319, 325; Agnostic, 94; Baptist, 10, 144, 238; Catholic, 16, 68, 94, 100, 101, 138, 143, 155, 158, 167, 200, 229, 249, 250, 263, 270, 293, 308, 314, 327; Christian Scientist, 67, 168; Episcopal, 129; Hopi, 296; Judaism, 1, 29, 45, 140, 166, 257, 290, 303, 304; Mormon, 296; Moslem, 224; Presbyterian, 297; Protestant, 138, 182; Puritanism, 51; Quaker, 33, 321, 322; Swedenborgian, 150

Role Models, 61, 63, 74; Aunt, 36, 165, 243; Brother, 36, 82, 249; Father, 307; Female Relatives, 313; Friend, 68, 126, 245-250; Grandfather, 169; Grandmother, 25, 108, 135, 156, 175, 176, 223, 243, 257, 317; Mother, 39, 42, 49, 59, 75, 95, 96, 98, 106, 108, 120, 156, 165, 175, 176, 182, 184, 218, 223, 228, 231, 246, 247, 249, 250, 296, 297, 321-323; Mother-in-Law, 76; Mother Substitute, 75; Mother Surrogates, 108; Older Women, 171; Sister, 108, 182, 227, 231, 323; Teacher, 49, 59, 80, 130, 131, 169, 179, 201, 275, 287, 313; Uncle, 169

Rural Setting, 27, 51-53, 75, 77, 83, 95-97, 122, 133, 134, 141, 148, 168, 177, 180, 198, 202, 203, 206, 209, 238, 241, 267, 289, 296, 297, 300, 322, 323

Separation from Spouse, 4, 16, 19, 27, 32, 35, 39, 45, 59, 65, 68, 71, 93, 101, 113, 117, 124, 131, 132, 135, 139, 164, 168, 169, 199, 209, 213, 219, 227, 231, 242, 244, 256, 280, 282, 285, 286, 298, 315, 321, 322

Sickness, 1, 8, 9, 16, 35, 44, 60, 73, 122, 124, 143, 154, 156, 157, 167, 169, 199, 204, 231, 241, 243, 250, 267, 277, 279, 315, 331

Single Women, 7-9, 12-14, 16, 21, 22, 24, 28, 39, 44, 46, 49, 68, 70, 73, 79, 90, 95, 96, 102, 106, 108, 113, 121, 122, 124, 126, 131, 138-140, 153, 154, 171, 172, 177, 198, 199, 204, 205, 208, 239, 243, 262, 267, 288-290, 301, 305, 311, 312, 315, 320, 330

Strong Women, 1, 7-9, 12-14, 18, 19, 24, 26, 27, 30, 31, 33, 39, 41, 45, 47,

52, 54, 60, 61, 65, 68, 70, 73, 74, 78, 79, 95-97, 101, 103, 106, 108, 111, 112, 117, 121, 123-127, 131-135, 139, 140, 144, 147, 153, 154, 165, 169-172, 177, 178, 182, 191-193, 195, 203, 205, 220, 221, 227, 241-244, 247, 249, 252, 257, 261, 267, 268, 282, 285, 286, 298, 301, 311, 312, 315, 316, 320, 323, 330, 331

Suffrage, 3, 23, 102, 150, 255, 269, 290

Surgery, 167

Sexuality, 2, 5, 12, 13, 16, 32, 39, 44, 54, 70, 71, 73, 74, 76, 94, 101, 109, 115, 117, 136, 143, 154, 167-169, 187, 188, 191, 193-196, 214, 219, 229-231, 246, 247, 257, 261, 266, 268, 282, 311, 323, 324

Teachers, 45, 52, 63, 88, 106, 122, 126, 131, 138, 148-151, 191, 201, 243, 252, 262, 310, 320

Travel, 10, 21, 34, 83, 157, 182-184, 291

Upper Class, 2, 4, 21, 23, 69, 76, 80, 112, 124, 131, 136, 156, 157, 182-185, 191-196, 198, 199, 208, 224, 252, 266, 325, 326, 333

Urban Setting, 2, 39, 44, 45, 55-57, 68, 101, 105, 106, 117, 122, 135, 153, 154, 166, 179, 184, 189, 199, 204, 218, 219, 244, 247, 253, 260, 269, 297, 302, 306, 310, 314

Vietnam, 1, 18, 19

Violence, 108, 164, 178, 243, 250, 269, 292, 294, 300, 306; Reaction to, 2, 18, 19, 26, 41, 46, 66, 82, 93, 94, 101, 132, 142, 143, 154, 169, 177, 179, 263, 302; Subject to, 2, 41, 82, 94, 117, 142, 143, 154, 169, 188, 197, 198, 238, 263

Women's Liberation, 1, 5, 23, 39, 55, 79, 95, 96, 101, 108, 152, 154, 163, 182, 227, 229, 240, 247, 250, 255, 266, 268, 284, 290, 304, 310, 314, 316

Working Class, 2, 11, 60, 98, 99, 117, 131, 139, 142, 150, 164, 177, 178, 210, 212, 253, 257, 266, 290, 302, 311, 316, 328

Working Women, 2, 11-14, 16, 17, 27, 29, 31, 39, 44, 50, 57, 60-63, 65, 69-71, 79, 82 97, 98, 101, 107, 123, 131, 138, 140, 142, 144, 153, 157,

165, 169, 170, 197, 206, 210, 211, 213, 214, 217, 227, 231, 239, 241, 262, 269, 290, 301, 316, 320, 330

Writing and Being a Writer, 5, 29, 30, 31, 36-41, 45-49, 65, 69, 75, 77, 80, 83, 92, 94-96, 101, 107, 108, 112-114, 116, 122, 125, 126, 128, 131, 133, 134, 138, 140-142, 156, 157, 166, 169, 175, 176, 179, 181-185, 187, 188, 202, 205, 206, 210, 211, 213, 214, 219, 230, 232, 245-250, 256, 258, 259, 261, 262, 266-270, 283-289, 292-294, 308, 315-317, 321-323

American Notes and Queries
Supplement
Volume II

First Person Female American

Composed in IBM Selectric Composer *Journal Roman* and printed offset by McNaughton & Gunn, Incorporated, Ann Arbor, Michigan. The paper on which the book is printed is the International Paper Company's *Bookmark*. The book was sewn and bound by Howard Dekker & Sons, Grand Rapids, Michigan.

First Person Female American is a Trenowyth book, the scholarly publishing division of The Whitston Publishing Company.

This edition consists in 700 casebound copies.